American Business Leaders

Volume II

American Business Leaders

From Colonial Times to the Present

Volume II
M–Z

Neil A. Hamilton

ABC-CLIO

Santa Barbara, California
Denver, Colorado
Oxford, England

Library of Congress Cataloging-in-Publication Data
Hamilton, Neil A., 1949–
    American business leaders : from colonial times to the present /
Neil A. Hamilton.
        p.   cm.
    Includes bibliographical references and index.
    ISBN 1-57607-002-6 (alk. paper)
    1. Businesspeople—United States Biography Dictionaries   I. Title.
HC102.5.A2H36 1999
338.092'272—dc21
[B]   99-27928
                                                                            CIP

05   04   03   02   01   00   99   10   9   8   7   6   5   4   3   2   1   (cloth)

ABC-CLIO, Inc.
130 Cremona Drive, P.O. Box 1911
Santa Barbara, California 93116-1911

This book is printed on acid-free paper ∞.
Manufactured in the United States of America

Contents

List of American Business Leaders

Volume I

American Business Leaders

Volume II

M

Macy, Rowland

(August 30, 1822–March 29, 1877)
Merchant

America has never had an aristocracy, but the nation has its palaces, including the consumers' palaces that appeared in the late 1800s, more commonly called department stores. By founding the first of these, Rowland Hussey Macy propelled changes in retail selling still evident in today's society.

Rowland was born on August 30, 1822, on Nantucket Island, Massachusetts, at a time when whaling ships dominated the local economy and tales of faraway lands gripped every boy's mind. Rowland's father, John Macy, had captained a merchant ship before operating a bookstore, and at age 15 Rowland took to the sea. In December 1837, he boarded the *Emily Morgan*, a three-masted whaler, and sailed first to Brazil, and then around Cape Horn into the Pacific, where he harpooned whales, saw exotic cultures, and met characters he never knew on Nantucket.

He returned home four years later and, for reasons unclear, left the sea and held a variety of jobs. He married Louisa Houghton, daughter of a Boston dry-goods retailer, in 1844 and, two years later, opened his own dry-goods store in Boston. He acquired most of his merchandise from public auction, thus demonstrating an early shrewdness.

Despite his hard work, the store closed in 1848, and the following year Macy joined the California gold rush. When he arrived in the West in 1850, he began a partnership with Charles B. Mitchell and Edward R. Anthony that formed Macy & Company in Maryville, north of Sacramento. The firm sold dry goods to miners, but the partnership dissolved later that year, and Macy headed back east.

Macy ventured into another dry-goods business in April 1851, when he opened a store in Haverhill, Massachusetts. Although like his earlier efforts, this business lasted only a short time, he developed techniques that later brought him success, namely creative advertising, cash sales, and low prices.

After Macy's store closed in 1855, his next prominent venture took shape in New York City. On October 28, 1858, he opened the store that made not only money but also history. Macy's, as he called it, bore little resemblance to its later grand appearance. Only 20 feet wide and 60 feet long, the crowded shop on Sixth Avenue had three long counters, one down each side and another in the middle, that displayed handkerchiefs, feathers, artificial flowers, hosiery, and gloves.

Penurious, hot-tempered, and aggressive, Macy lost little time in pursuing his competition. He took tactics previously used by others (and by himself at Haverhill) and combined them into an effective strategy. In an era when customers still frequently haggled over prices, he sold all his goods at posted low prices, with cash sales only. Macy offered money-back guarantees, and he saturated the newspapers with advertising.

He employed originality in these advertisements. Instead of using the prevailing style of densely packed newsprint, he used unusual letter arrangements, symbols, and display type. One advertisement proclaimed:

STOCK OF GOODS.
COME, COME, TIME, TIME
COME, COME, TIME, TIME
THE TIME HAS COME.
WHAT IS TO BE DONE? IS THE QUESTION
WHAT IS TO BE DONE? IS THE QUESTION
WHAT SHALL BE DONE?
WHAT SHALL BE DONE?
MARK EVERY ARTICLE
MARK EVERY ARTICLE
WAY
WAY
WAY DOWN
WAY DOWN
TO SOME PRICE WHICH WILL MAKE IT
TO SOME PRICE WHICH WILL MAKE IT
SELL AND GO QUICK.
SELL AND GO QUICK.
SELL AND GO QUICK.

Macy used other promotional tactics, too. Beginning in 1863, he attracted customers with an annual clearance sale. In 1867, he kept Macy's open on Christmas Eve until midnight, and broke his daily sales record. As his store grew bigger and expanded into adjoining space, he put up display windows, including one in 1874 for Christmas that featured dolls. Soon Macy's Christmas display gained citywide attention as an annual event.

Gradually, Macy's evolved from a dry-goods store to a department store—the nation's first, where the bountiful output from the modern industrial era spilled forth. Although there is no exact date for Macy's transformation, by 1860 he had several departments, and by 1869, 12 all together including notions and trimmings; flowers and feathers; furs; fancy goods, jewelry and toiletries; white goods, linens, and curtains; house furnishings; and toys and dolls. He bought directly from manufacturers in order to hold down prices, and in some instances manufactured the goods he sold.

After Macy died on March 29, 1877, in Paris, France—where he had traveled in an attempt to restore his health—his partners continued the store. Macy's experienced considerable growth when Isidor and Nathan Straus, admitted as partners in 1888, added new merchandise lines.

Rowland Macy had built a consumer palace that made shopping conspicuous in a nation increasingly beguiled by industry's splendor where consumption meant status.

BIBLIOGRAPHY

Hower, Ralph M., *History of Macy's of New York, 1858–1919: Chapters in the Evolution of the Department Store*, 1943.

Malone, John

(March 7, 1941–)
Communications Executive

Should John C. Malone be hailed as a genius of the new era of high-tech communication or scorned as a ruthless predator? Observers disagree about the leader who built Tele-Communications, Incorporated into a giant cable television company.

Malone came from a comfortable middle-class family. He was born on March 7, 1941, in Milford, Connecticut, where his father worked at General Electric as an engineer. After attending a prep school in New Haven, Malone entered Yale University and majored in electrical engineering. After graduation, he worked at Bell Laboratories as an economic planner, while earning advanced degrees, including a Ph.D. in operations research from Johns Hopkins University in 1967.

He longed for something more than a position at Bell, a company whose bureaucracy he thought stifling, and in 1968 he left to work at McKinsey & Company, a large management consulting firm. He quit that job in 1970 and was hired as a vice president at General Instrument Corporation. The company soon promoted him to president of a subsidiary, Jerrold Electronics, which made equipment for cable television systems.

Malone quickly gained the attention of Bob John Magness, a cattle rancher who had, two decades earlier, started a small cable company, called Tele-Communications, Incorporated (TCI), that served rural residents in the West. Magness offered Malone the position at TCI as president and CEO. Malone accepted and left the East Coast for TCI headquarters in Denver, Colorado.

John Malone (Reuters/Fred Prouser/Archive Photos)

Malone discovered a struggling company, one that under Magness had fallen into heavy debt. But the new president negotiated several deals with bankers and envisioned cable TV as a cutting-edge technology. After Malone refinanced TCI's debt in 1977 based on an improved cash flow, he approached the TV networks. He guaranteed them access to TCI's cable system in exchange for their paying his company in advance for the airing of their shows.

This shrewd move brought in millions of dollars that Malone used to buy other cable companies. By 1987, TCI had taken over 150 smaller cable systems. At the same time, Malone spent billions of dollars to buy shares in United Artists

Communications, Storer Communications, and Heritage Communications. He had, by the end of the 1980s, concluded almost 500 deals, and nearly 8 million people watched TV through systems in which TCI had an interest.

With its annual $1.3 billion dollar cash flow, TCI earned more revenue than the ABC, CBS, and NBC networks combined. The company also acquired investments in Black Entertainment Television (BET), the Discovery Channel, Cable Value Network (CVN), and American Movie Classics (AMC). TCI obtained a 21 percent share in Turner Broadcasting, when it helped to bail out that company, founded by TED TURNER.

Yet as TCI grew, Malone had his critics. They disliked his arrogance and ruthlessness, evident in the way he treated customers. Whenever Malone received complaints about poor reception or unreliable repair people, he showed no concern. He forced several small cities to renew his franchise rights by threatening to end all cable service to their residents. In a much publicized stock manipulation, Malone created a new company, Liberty Media, to handle TCI programming, transferred his investments in TCI to Liberty, and then had TCI buy back Liberty in a move that enriched him by more than $600 million.

So powerful had Malone become that Vice President Al Gore referred to him as head of an evil empire. TCI had 25 percent of the nation's cable subscribers when trouble appeared in 1996. DirecTV,

owned by General Motors' Hughes Electronics and other companies, offered service by satellite. It provided more stations than TCI could and attracted millions of customers. Partly as a result, TCI posted revenue losses totaling hundreds of millions of dollars and laid off thousands of workers.

Malone remained convinced, however, that TCI would continue to grow. He promoted plans that would enable the company to provide not only television broadcasts over its cable systems but also Internet access and telephone service. At the same time, he invested in a satellite system and continued to broaden TCI's investments in telecommunications.

In June 1998, Malone surprised Wall Street by announcing plans to sell TCI to AT&T for $48 billion. Because AT&T was the nation's largest long-distance telephone company, and TCI the second largest cable operator, the merger could transform the telecommunications business. AT&T will be able to use TCI's cable network to provide customers with fast Internet access and dozens of TV channels, along with local and long-distance telephone service, all on one wire.

BIBLIOGRAPHY

Brown, Rich, "The Long Reach of John Malone and TCI," *Broadcasting & Cable*, October 16, 1995; Sloan, Allan, "That Old Malone Magic," *Newsweek*, January 26, 1998; Whitelaw, Kevin, "It's Showtime for the Real Cable Guy," *U.S. News & World Report*, October 28, 1996.

Manigault, Pierre

(ca. 1665–1729)
Merchant

Pierre Manigault, a merchant, was one of the foremost businessmen in South Carolina in the early eighteenth century.

The son of Gabriel and Marie Manigault, Pierre Manigault was born in La Rochelle, France. While his date of birth is not known, it is known that he and his brother Gabriel emigrated from France to London in 1685. After remaining there several years, they sailed to Charleston, South Carolina, arriving early in 1695. They paid for their passage and 100 acres of South Carolina land with earnings from the sale of property in France.

The Manigault brothers began farming their land on the Santee River. After a short time, however, both tired of agriculture and returned to Charleston. Gabriel became a carpenter, and Pierre set up shop as a food merchant. Gabriel, who never married, died after falling from a scaffold, about 10 years after moving to Charleston.

In 1699, Pierre Manigault married Judith Giton Royer, a widow. In 1711, Judith died, leaving behind two children. One of them, Gabriel, eventually became a successful rice planter and merchant in his own right, as well as serving in the South Carolina Commons House of Assembly. Manigault was remarried in 1713 to Ann Reason, the daughter of an Englishman. Though Manigault was proud of his Huguenot background and maintained connections with the French church, he changed his name from Pierre to Peter and began to attend the Anglican Church.

Manigault expanded his food supply store to include brandy, and in 1719 began to offer a variety of dry goods. He traded directly with England and sold his goods to the colonists. His mercantile enterprises prospered, and he became quite wealthy.

Unlike many other French émigrés in South Carolina, his initiative in business enabled him to prosper when others were destitute. Cognizant of his good fortune, Manigault directed in his will that some of his money be left to the French Huguenot church for aiding the poor. Though the exact date of his death is not known, records show that Manigault was buried on December 10, 1729, in the French churchyard of Charleston, South Carolina.

BIBLIOGRAPHY

Crouse, Maurice Alfred, *The Manigault Family of South Carolina, 1685–1783*, 1964; Salley, A. S., ed., *Warrants for Lands in S. C., 1692–1711*, 1913; *St. Phillip's Register*, vol. 1; *Transactions of the Huguenot Society of South Carolina*, vols. 4 and 5, 1897.

Manville, Charles

(December 1, 1834–November 24, 1927)
Manufacturer

Charles Brayton Manville made his Johns-Manville Company the leader in insulation, primarily asbestos. Only after his death was asbestos banned as a health hazard.

Born on December 1, 1834, in Watertown, New York, Manville grew up in Sheboygan, Wisconsin. After attending public schools there, he opened his own grocery store in nearby Neenah, but in 1878 joined the gold rush in South Dakota's Black Hills. After failing at that venture, he settled in Milwaukee, Wisconsin, in 1882 and began manufacturing steam pipe and boiler covering made of kaolin and paper pulp.

By 1886, Manville discovered a superior covering, a mixture of wool felt and blue clay, for which he obtained a patent. Later that year, he founded the Manville Covering Company to manufacture pipe insulation, and his three sons joined him in the enterprise. (Manville was married to Jennie Long, a native of Scotland.) His most prominent—and later controversial—discovery occurred in 1891 when he made a new insulation of carbonate of magnesia mixed with asbestos fiber.

Manville's insulation soon dominated the industry, and his company grew rapidly. He was not alone in using asbestos. Earlier, in 1880, the H. W. Johns Manufacturing Company of Massachusetts had begun making roofing material with asbestos in it, the asbestos acting as a fire retardant. In 1897, Manville bought from H. W. Johns its market west of Ohio, and in 1901 he merged with his competitor, forming the Johns-Manville Company.

Manville had a reputation for building his business without borrowing—a practice he abhorred—and for rejecting laboratories, chemists, and other modern research and development practices. But he and his sons sold his product effectively, increased annual sales to $40 million, and acquired the world's largest asbestos mine in Quebec, Canada.

Manville retired from business in 1902 and moved to Pleasantville, New York, where he died on November 24, 1927. That year, his youngest son, Hiram, sold the family's controlling interest in the company. Johns-Manville encountered enormous problems in the late 1960s, when the first of thousands of lawsuits were filed against it for illnesses related to asbestos. Although an excellent insulator, asbestos when inhaled causes cancer of the lung, abdomen, and intestines. Records suggest that the company suspected the health hazard posed by asbestos as early as the 1930s. One class-action suit against Johns-Manville was settled in the 1970s for $20 million and other suits continued.

BIBLIOGRAPHY

Moskowitz, Milton, et al., eds., *Everybody's Business*, 1980.

Marbury, Elisabeth

(June 19, 1856–January 22, 1933)
Producer

At the forefront of modern theater organization in New York, Elisabeth Marbury helped make that city a cultural rival to London and Paris.

Elisabeth was born on June 19, 1856, in New York City to Francis Ferdinand Marbury and Elizabeth (McCaun) Marbury. Her father was a lawyer who was active in Democratic politics.

Marbury first gained attention in the theatrical world when, in 1885, she organized a benefit performance that raised $5,000. In the late 1880s, she acted as an agent for the author Frances Hodgson Burnett. She also wrote *Manners: A Handbook of Social Customs* and a one-act play, and adapted a French play to the stage.

In 1891, she traveled to France intending to produce a play there and convinced the French writers' organization to make her their representative for the English and American markets. In that capacity over the next 15 years she protected their copyrights, made sure their plays were properly translated and staged, and collected royalties. She also represented other writers, and in addition to her office in New York City, she opened branches in Paris, London, Berlin, and Madrid. The business organization that she and others like her initiated strengthened American theater and elevated New York City to a prominent position in the performing arts.

Prior to World War I, Marbury produced some of the first Broadway musicals written by Jerome Kern and Cole Porter, and in 1914 she joined other agents to form the American Play Company. During the war, she worked as a

Elisabeth Marbury (Corbis/Bettmann-UPI)

volunteer in French hospitals, and, after the United States entered the conflict, she served in New York City on the Mayor's Women's Committee of National Defense and the National Catholic Diocesan War Council.

Her primary interest turned to politics in 1918, and two years later she won election as a delegate to the Democratic National Convention and as a member of that party's national committee. Born a Presbyterian, Marbury converted to Catholicism late in her life, and she never married. Marbury died on January 22, 1933.

BIBLIOGRAPHY

Marbury, Elisabeth, *Manners: A Handbook of Social Customs*, 1888; Marbury, Elisabeth, *My Crystal Ball: Reminiscences*, 1924.

Marcus, Bernard

(1929–)
Merchant

Playing on the American desire for do-it-yourself home improvements, Bernard Marcus and his business partner Arthur Blank founded Home Depot.

Born in 1929 in Newark, New Jersey, the son of Russian immigrants, Marcus obtained a pharmacy degree from Rutgers University but went into retailing instead. In the 1960s, he worked for the Handy Dan home improvement chain where he met Arthur Blank. Marcus eventually became the firm's CEO, and Blank its vice president for finance. They wanted to develop a large discount chain, but in 1978 they had a disagreement with the company's new owner, who fired them both. Marcus later said: "That was a lovely day. It was the best thing that ever happened, no question about it."

That same year, Marcus and Blank founded Home Depot with the goal of building a nationwide discount chain, one that would appeal heavily to home owners who wanted to remodel or repair their own houses. The two entrepreneurs built hangar-size stores with a wide selection of products, and with personnel willing to help customers solve their home improvement problems. They structured the company to encourage creative advice from all levels, personally trained every assistant manager, and offered stock options to even the lowest-level employees. At the same time, they created an aggressive management style.

Although Blank had considerable influence within Home Depot, Marcus assumed the higher public profile and the posts of chairman and CEO. According to one banker, Marcus boldly told Wall Street investors at a meeting that "as long as my team and I are running this company, we'll do just fine. But the minute we get a bunch of Harvard Business School [expletive] in here, things will fall apart."

Home Depot expanded to 4 stores in 1980, 100 in 1988, 400 in 1995, and over 600 in 1997, when net income reached $1.2 billion. Marcus decided to reduce his involvement in 1997, and Blank, 14 years younger than Marcus, took over as CEO. He planned to open the first overseas Home Depot in Chile and to make a greater effort to attract general contractors as customers. Home Depot also started making such acquisitions as the National Blind and Wallpaper Company.

Marcus, married with three children, stated: "Every customer has to be treated like your mother, father, sister, or brother." His formula for success boosted his net worth to about $700 million.

BIBLIOGRAPHY
Steinhauer, Jennifer, "Getting the Chance to Do It Himself," *New York Times*, May 13, 1998.

Marcus, Stanley

(April 20, 1905–)
Merchant

"Doing business by mail really began in February 1908, only five months after the store opened," Stanley Harold Marcus said about his upscale specialty store, Neiman-Marcus. "My father wrote an advertisement saying they would fill all mail orders with the utmost care. Garments will be fitted on models in sizes ordered before sending, assuring satisfactory garments."

Stanley was born on April 20, 1905, in Dallas, Texas, to Herbert Marcus and Minnie (Lichenstein) Marcus. Two years later, Herbert Marcus joined his sister and brother-in-law, Carrie and Al Neiman, to found the Neiman-Marcus Company, a specialty department store in Dallas. Neiman-Marcus distributed its first catalog in 1915, but the next one did not appear until years later. Stanley graduated from Forrest Avenue High School and, in 1925, from Harvard. The following year, he received his master's degree from the Harvard Business School.

Marcus then returned to Dallas and his father's business, where as a boy he had worked during the summers. That same year, Al Neiman retired, and Stanley Marcus assumed more authority in the store. He introduced a fashion show for which Neiman-Marcus became famous—the first weekly shows ever presented in an American department store. That Christmas, Neiman-Marcus issued its second catalog, containing 16 pages listing 78 items, which were expensive and sometimes exotic, and included fur coats and reptile-covered cigarette cases.

Marcus became merchandise manager of all the store's apparel divisions in 1929, just months before the Great Depression began. The worsening national economy barely phased Neiman-Marcus, for oil discoveries in east Texas kept money flowing into the region. Unlike most Americans, Texas' nouveau riche had the "problem" of finding ways to spend their money, and they turned to Marcus for help. "They were willing to be guided," he said, "because they recognized an authority upon which they could depend."

In 1938, Marcus promoted his store through the Neiman-Marcus Awards, nicknamed the "Oscars of Fashion," which were presented to outstanding designers and other notables in the fashion industry. At the same time, the Neiman-Marcus catalog grew in size and circulation by presenting gifts of distinction. The often unusual items gave Marcus the reputation of being able to procure anything and earned sensational publicity for his business. Over the years, he has offered in his catalog such gifts as volcanic craters and a pure-gold omelet pan priced at $30,000.

Upon the death of his father in 1950, Marcus assumed the presidency of the company. By the late 1960s, he had increased the number of Neiman-Marcus stores in Texas from one to four, opening them in affluent suburbs. In 1969, he shocked many of his store's admirers when he sold Neiman-Marcus to Carter, Hawley, Hale, a California chain of department stores under the leadership of EDWARD CARTER and aimed at middle-class shoppers. The new owners expanded Neiman-Marcus by opening nine branches around the nation and appealing to a broader clientele, thus ending the store's uniqueness.

Marcus served as chairman of the board at Neiman-Marcus until 1975, and then as vice president of Carter, Hawley, Hale. He had little of the authority, however, that he enjoyed when he owned Neiman-Marcus. He retired in the mid-1980s. When asked in 1995 about catalogs and retailing, Marcus made several observations:

> Most Expensive Sale: "A chamois bag with assorted sizes of diamonds for $197,850 in 1973."

> Exotic Gifts: "The shahtoosh muffler made from the chin hairs of the Ibex goat from the Himalayan Mountains in Kashmir. The finest fiber in the world. The copy read: 'Its texture is so fine that the whole scarf can be pulled through a man's wedding ring,' and so we called it, 'The Ring Scarf.' Sold for $100 in 1963. Today it would sell for about $3,000."

> Reason for the Growth of Catalogs: "Today's department stores. Most are dull, unattractive, out of date, and no fun."

BIBLIOGRAPHY

Clark, William H., and James H. S. Moynahan, *Famous Leaders of Industry*, 1955; Farmer, David R., *Stanley Marcus: A Life with Books*, 1993; Marcus, Stanley, *Minding the Store: A Memoir*, 1974; Marcus, Stanley, *Quest for the Best*, 1979; Marcus, Stanley, *The Viewpoints of Stanley Marcus: A Ten-Year Perspective*, 1995.

Marriott, J. Willard

(September 17, 1900–August 13, 1985)
Hotel Executive, Restaurant Executive

From a nine-stool A&W Root Beer stand, John Willard Marriott built the multibillion-dollar Marriott Corporation that operated restaurants, hotels, resorts, and an airline catering service.

John was born on September 17, 1900, near Ogden, Utah, to Hyrum Willard Marriott, whose own father numbered among the original Mormon settlers of the state, and Ellen (Morse) Marriott. As a youngster, he helped tend his father's sheep amid the vast stretches of Utah desert. Even though Hyrum Marriott went bankrupt, John managed to save his money from various jobs and, in 1926, graduated from the University of Utah.

Having witnessed the phenomenal business at an A&W Root Beer stand in Salt Lake City, Marriott combined $1,500 of his own money with $3,000 borrowed from a friend and opened an A&W franchise in Washington, D.C., where he thought the warm, humid climate would make root beer attractive to customers. He had robust sales in the summer, but when winter approached, business declined. To offset this, Marriott and his wife, the former Alice Sheets, whom he had married in 1927, decided to add food to their offerings. Alice cooked all the menu items, largely Mexican dishes. "I would make them in our apartment," she recounted, "and take them over to the stand."

Thus emerged Marriott's first restaurant, which he named the Hot Shoppe. By 1932, Marriott had seven Hot Shoppes in the Washington area, each one featuring a family-style environment. When he noticed that customers at one Hot Shoppe near the airport often took their meals with them as food for their flights, he began catering to airlines. This part of Marriott's business grew tremendously when air travel expanded after World War II.

In the meantime, during the 1930s, he had to overcome a personal crisis when he contracted a disease of the lymphatic system. Even though doctors gave him only two years to live, Marriott made a remarkable recovery. He continued his business, but spread responsibility to a management team consisting of his wife, his three brothers, and, eventually, his two sons.

In the mid-1950s, Marriott decided to enter the hotel field, and in 1957 he opened the first Marriott Motor Hotel in Washington, near the Pentagon. The company, which became the Marriott Corporation in the late 1960s, operated 20 hotels by 1972 and founded a franchise chain called Marriott Inns. During that decade and into the 1980s, Marriott obtained a 20 percent annual growth rate with sales in 1985 exceeding $4 billion and net income exceeding $167 million. The firm had 140,000 employees in 26 countries and owned 1,400 restaurants, 143 hotels and resorts, and 90 flight

J. Willard Marriott (UPI/Corbis-Bettmann)

kitchens serving 150 airlines. In addition, Marriott operated Bob's Big Boy Restaurants and Roy Rogers Restaurants. Shortly before Marriott's death on August 13, 1985, the corporation acquired the Howard Johnson Company (founded by HOWARD JOHNSON), whose properties it sold to a third corporation while retaining some of the company's restaurants. In 1997, the Marriott Corporation owned or had interests in more than 300 hotels along with 29 retirement communities.

BIBLIOGRAPHY

Goldwasser, Thomas, *Family Pride: Profiles of Five of America's Best-Run Family Businesses*, 1986.

Mars, Forrest

(1904–)
Manufacturer

A reclusive man with eccentric habits, Forrest Edward Mars took his father's candy business and built it into the national leader in chocolate manufacturers, specializing in candy bars and M&Ms.

Forrest was born in Minnesota in 1904 to Frank Mars and Ethel (Kissack) Mars. His parents divorced in 1910, after which he lived with his mother before enrolling in 1923 at the University of California, Berkeley, and then transferring two years later to Yale. He graduated from Yale in 1928 with a degree in industrial engineering. At that point, Forrest joined his father's business. The elder Mars had begun a candy factory in Minneapolis, Minnesota, and had developed the Milky Way bar, noted for its chocolate coating and malted milk inside.

The Milky Way bar won a large following, and soon after Forrest joined the business, Mars, Incorporated moved to a larger plant near Chicago. He and his father had a falling out during which the elder Mars told his son to take the Milky Way recipe and leave the country. Forrest moved to England, where he opened a candy factory and began making Milky Way bars. The chocolate bar proved just as successful there as it had been in the United States. Forrest then diversified by manufacturing pet food. Britons, who had previously fed their dogs and cats table scraps, embraced the new product.

After World War II began in 1939, Forrest Mars returned to the United States (he left his business in the hands of a trustee), bringing with him the rights to a British candy called Smarties. Mars changed the name of these sugar-coated chocolate tablets to M&M, and began selling the candy in partnership with R. Bruce Murrie, the adopted son of MILTON HERSHEY, founder of Hershey's Chocolate. M&M thus stood for Mars and Murrie.

At the same time, Mars discovered a new way to process rice and started selling it as "Uncle Ben's." With his candy and his rice, both divisions of his company called Food Manufacturers, Mars made a fortune. After the deaths of his father and stepmother, he decided to wrest control of Mars, Incorporated from his half sister and others. The struggle began in 1947 and lasted 15 years, during which time Food Manufacturers far outstripped Mars, Incorporated in sales and profits, largely through the successful marketing of M&Ms. Forrest Mars aimed this candy at children and promoted it through the enormously popular advertising slogan: "The milk chocolate that melts in your mouth—not in your hand."

After finally gaining control of Mars, Incorporated in 1962, and two years later merging it with Food Manufacturers, Mars combined autocracy with a decentralized management system. Under the latter, he forbade any employee from having an office and made executives responsible for their divisions. From company headquarters in Virginia, he maintained a tight hold on quality control. In one memorable incident he reacted to finding a poorly wrapped candy bar by marching his executives into a large room and, in front of them, taking other poorly wrapped bars and smashing them against a wall.

Mars spent about $30 million per year advertising his candy, rice, and Kal Kan, a pet food company he bought in 1968. In the early 1970s, his candy business brought in $200 million a year in the United States and $55 million in Britain. In 1980, he outfoxed his competitors, particularly Hershey, by making his candy bars 10 percent heavier without increasing the price—a move that dramatically boosted sales. The following year, he quietly raised the price of the candy bars without losing his customers. Mars had, in the 1980s, 5 of the 10 top-selling chocolate candies, including Snickers, Three Musketeers, Milky Way, and M&Ms. By this time, he and his two sons, Forrest Jr. and John, controlled a family fortune exceeding $12 billion.

Mars relinquished full control of Mars, Incorporated to his sons in the 1980s. He remained active in business, however, by founding a new company in Las Vegas, Nevada, called Ethel M. The firm produced liqueur-filled chocolates intended as a quality candy and thus expensively priced.

Under the leadership of Mars's two sons, Mars, Incorporated suffered from a bloated bureaucracy and lack of creativity, and its sales dipped, allowing Hershey to gain a larger market share. Meanwhile, Forrest Mars retired from business in the 1990s.

BIBLIOGRAPHY

Moskowitz, Milton, et al., eds., *Everybody's Business*, 1980.

Martin, Glenn

(January 17, 1886–December 4, 1955)
Manufacturer

Stimulated by the flight of the Wright brothers, Glenn Luther Martin began building airplanes. They were awkward at first, but later were among the most innovative and important in the industry.

Glenn was born on January 17, 1886, in Macksburg, Iowa, the son of Clarence Y. Martin and Arminta (De Long) Martin. Two years later, the Martins moved to Liberal, Kansas, where the elder Martin opened a hardware store. Glenn took an interest in kites and designed a box-shaped one that flew without a cumbersome tail. So many other kids liked his kites, he began making them and selling them from his home.

After the family moved to Salinas, Kansas, the youngster attended high school and studied the flight patterns of birds. His interest in flying grew stronger when his mother encouraged him, read him stories about flight, and related how she had dreamed about flying. In 1905, the Martins moved yet again, this time to Santa Ana, California. There Glenn obtained a job repairing cars and a few months later opened his own garage and

Glenn Martin (Library of Congress)

operated an automobile dealership, selling Fords and Maxwells.

His dreams remained with airplanes and were intensified when he learned about the brief, 59-second flight achieved by the Wright brothers in 1903. Martin rented an abandoned church, darkened its windows, locked its doors, and went to work in 1908. At night, while his mother held a coal-oil lamp, he built his dream plane, which was equipped with a Ford Model V engine. He made his first flight in the clumsy airplane—observers said it looked like a box kite—in August 1909, covering 100 feet at a 2-foot altitude, an achievement he later described as the most exciting in his career. Whereas the Wright brothers had used a launching ramp for their early flights, Martin flew from level ground.

That same year, Martin founded an airplane factory—among the nation's first—

and hired three assistants. These activities required money, however, and to help his finances he began barnstorming, flying for audiences at county fairs and other events. Dressed in black helmet, gloves, jacket, gray breeches, and boots, he inspired the nickname, "The Dude." Martin won prizes for his flying and even appeared in a movie, playing the villain who carried Mary Pickford aloft in *The Girl of Yesterday.*

Martin moved his aircraft factory, the Glenn L. Martin Company, from Santa Ana to Los Angeles, and by 1912 he employed 165 workers and sold planes to the army. That same year, Martin gained national attention and set an overwater distance record when he flew 38 miles from Newport Bay (near Los Angeles) to Catalina Island and back in a seaplane he had built.

In 1917, after a brief merger with another firm, Martin founded a new Glenn L. Martin Company in Cleveland, Ohio. Under military contract, he began making the MB-2, a biplane that could carry a bomb load of 1,500 pounds. He moved his factory in 1929 to Middle River, Maryland, near Baltimore, so he could be close to Washington and to the warm water he wanted for testing his seaplanes.

While developing the seaplanes, he continued to improve his bombers, and in 1932 produced the B-10, the first big twin-engine, all-metal monoplane, perhaps his greatest engineering achievement. The B-10 had a range of 1,800 miles, a bomb load of 2,400 pounds, and flew at 200 miles per hour—70 miles per hour faster than previous bombers. In short, the B-10 revolutionized military aircraft. In 1935, while making the B-10, he produced the China Clipper flying boat for Pan American.

Orders form Britain and France in the late 1930s enabled Martin to boost his workforce to 17,000, a number that increased to 70,000 in 1943 after the United States entered World War II and ordered more planes. His B-26 Marauder medium-range bomber with a circular fuselage proved crucial in the war, as did his B-29.

Despite these successes, Martin suffered severe financial reverses after the war when he lost defense contracts. Only a loan from the government kept his company afloat, and in 1952 he was forced out as president, his role reduced to honorary chairman of the board.

Martin, who never married, gave considerable money to the Glenn L. Martin Institute of Technology at the University of Maryland. When he died on December 4, 1955, he left an estate estimated at $14 million.

BIBLIOGRAPHY

Still, Henry, *To Ride the Wind: A Biography of Glenn L. Martin*, 1966; Wagner, Ray, *American Combat Planes: A History of Military Aircraft in the USA*, 1960.

Mayer, Louis

(ca. 1885–October 29, 1957)
Entertainment Executive

Leaving a struggling junk business for the new world of movies, Louis Burt Mayer ran Metro-Goldwyn-Mayer (MGM) studios with an iron hand, making it one of the most prestigious movie studios in the United States.

No records exist as to the exact date or location of Mayer's birth, nor of his family name, which may have been Meyer before it was changed by immigration authorities. Most historians surmise, however, that Mayer was born about 1885 near Minsk, Russia. Not long after his family immigrated to the United States in the late 1880s, economic hardship caused another move to Saint John, New Brunswick, Canada. There his father, Jacob, worked as a junk dealer and his mother, Chaya Sarah, earned extra money selling chickens door-to-door.

Mayer went to school only until age 12 and then entered his father's business—the elder Mayer named it Mayer & Son—which had expanded into salvaging and lifted the family out of poverty.

Wishing to escape what he considered limited opportunities in Saint John, Mayer moved to Boston, Massachusetts, in 1904 and lived in the immigrant South Side where he worked in the junk business. Later that year, he married Margaret Shenberg.

Mayer struggled financially until a new technology attracted him: nickelodeons, the sidewalk machines that showed movie clips. Their expanding appeal convinced him that motion pictures would be a profitable business. As a result, he borrowed money from friends and relatives, and made a down payment of $650 on a vacant vaudeville theater in a run-down part of Haverhill, Massachusetts. The theater complemented the neighborhood—dilapidated and its walls stained with tobacco juice. Mayer renamed his theater the New Orpheum, renovated it, and showed one-reel films. He had figured correctly—the new industry had a great appeal, and his shows earned him a good income. He became an American citizen in 1912 and that same year bought Haverhill's remaining theaters, including the Academy of Music, which offered symphonies and operas.

Mayer used his profits in 1915 to acquire a franchise to distribute the film *Birth of a Nation* in New England. The movie packed theaters throughout the region, and Mayer soon sold his movie houses and consolidated his distribution activities under his firm, the American Feature Film Company. In addition to distribution, he began producing movies—first a serial and then a full-length drama, *Virtuous Wives*, starring Anita Stewart.

With the movie's success, Mayer moved to Hollywood, the emerging center of America's motion picture industry. He produced several movies starring Stewart before signing in 1923 to make four films per year for a distribution company, Metro, operated by theater owner MARCUS LOEW. In 1924, Loew bought the Goldwyn Company and merged it with Metro and Mayer's smaller firm, forming Metro-Goldwyn, to which Mayer's name was added in 1926. To the new MGM studio, Mayer brought with him producer Irving Thalberg, who proved crucial to Mayer's success. In 1925, the studio turned out *The Big Parade* (a project closely guided by Thalberg), *The Merry Widow*, and *Ben Hur*, all of which

proved to be big hits. Although cost overruns resulted in *Ben Hur* failing to make a profit, it won critical acclaim and enhanced the studio's reputation.

Mayer had a knack for discovering talent and hired Greta Garbo, a little-known Swedish actress. After Loew died in 1927, friction developed between Mayer and Loew's successor, Nicholas Schenck, and over the ensuing years, they had an uncomfortable relationship. When Thalberg fell ill, Mayer hired David O. Selznick as a producer, but Selznick soon left to work as an independent.

After a dispute with Thalberg, Mayer undercut him by establishing a system under which several producers were responsible for blocks of pictures. This arrangement led to highly popular films, mainly musicals and light dramas, but Thalberg complained that quality had declined. He called the movies "mediocre pictures possessing a certain ingredient of obvious audience entertainment." He also complained about sagging morale and Mayer's belligerent attitude. Despite the creative loss caused by Thalberg's premature death in 1936, MGM continued to rank among Hollywood's premier studios until the mid-1940s. Mayer, known for his moodiness and fits of anger, ruled the studio unchallenged, earning big profits and, in return, receiving a salary among the highest of any business executive in the nation.

The period after World War II, however, proved tumultuous for Mayer. He left his wife in 1944, and she divorced him in 1948, the year he married Lorena Danker. At the same time, MGM slipped from its peak. The studio released movies that audiences disliked, television emerged as a competitor, and a multimillion-dollar deficit threatened future operations. With these developments, Mayer's long-running disputes with Schenck grew bitter, and in 1951 he was forced out of the company.

Mayer involved himself briefly with Cinerama (an innovative wide-screen concept for showing movies), invested in real estate and racing horses, and fervently supported Senator Joseph McCarthy, who launched a hunt for Communists that smeared many reputations. Mayer tried to take over Loew's in 1957 but failed. A few weeks later, on October 29, he died in Los Angeles. Some condemned him as a ruthless mogul, while others praised him as a creative genius who shaped the emerging business of film into a modern motion picture industry.

BIBLIOGRAPHY

Carey, Gary, *All the Stars in Heaven: Louis B. Mayer's M-G-M*, 1981; Crowther, Bosley, *Hollywood Rajah: The Life and Times of Louis B. Mayer*, 1960.

Mayer, Oscar

(March 10, 1888–March 5, 1965)
Meat Packer

Oscar Gottfried Mayer inherited his father's meatpacking company and converted it from a regional business into a national one. By the 1930s, nearly every American recognized an Oscar Mayer wiener.

Oscar was born on March 10, 1888, in Chicago, Illinois, to Oscar Ferdinand Mayer and Louise Christine (Greiner) Mayer. In 1883, his father had founded a small Chicago meat market, where he sold brockwurst, liverwurst, and other specialties to the largely German neighborhood on the North Side. In the 1890s, Mayer Sr. added a glass-paneled wagon to his business and delivered sausages to consumers and grocery stores. He also began giving his meats brand names in line with the new advertising techniques.

Young Oscar worked in his father's business at age six, learning to link sausages. After graduating from Waller High School in 1905, he enrolled at Harvard, where he studied engineering. He obtained his B.S. degree in 1909 and returned to his father's company as assistant superintendent. In 1913, by which time he had risen to general manager, he married Elsa Stieglitz. They subsequently had four children.

Mayer changed the meatpacking business by introducing such innovations as packaging sausage in cardboard cartons. He also realized that his company had to expand beyond its Great Lakes clientele or else succumb to its competitors, who were developing national markets. In 1919, he bought a farmer's cooperative meatpacking plant in Madison, Wisconsin. This added capacity allowed Mayer to expand his sales.

Mayer became vice president in charge of operations in 1921 and president in 1928, after his father retired from the position. In 1929, he began promoting his products by placing a bright yellow band on every fourth wiener, assuring consumers distrustful of prepackaged meats that the wieners met Oscar Mayer quality. "Look for the yellow band," the company later advertised, for it showed "a wiener with a conscience," meaning a wiener with pure ingredients.

In addition, Mayer advertised with "Little Oscar" (a diminutive chef who attended store openings) and a sausage-shaped vehicle he called a "Wienermobile." Among other new inventions, he introduced a linker that wrapped sausages automatically and twisted them into standard lengths, and in 1950 the Slice-Pak that vacuum-packed sliced meats in plastic.

Although notorious for its low profit margin, meatpacking prospered under Mayer. He retired from the presidency in 1955 but remained chairman of the board until his death on March 5, 1965. By then, the company's yearly sales volume had exceeded $200 million. Long a family-run business, Oscar Mayer was sold to General Foods in the 1970s and is today a division of Kraft Foods.

BIBLIOGRAPHY

Fucini, Joseph J., and Suzy Fucini, *Entrepreneurs: The Men and Women behind Famous Brand Names and How They Made It*, 1965.

Maytag, Frederick

(July 14, 1857–March 2, 1937)
Manufacturer

When Frederick Lewis Maytag sought to offset the seasonal slumps in the sales of his farm implements, he turned to making washing machines. Two decades later he headed the largest appliance company in the world.

The son of Daniel William Maytag and Amelia (Tarebun) Maytag, Frederick was born on July 14, 1857, in Elgin, Illinois. He obtained little formal schooling and spent his boyhood working on his father's farm. In 1880, at age 23, he began selling farm implements for McKinley and Bergman, a dealer in Newton, Iowa. The following year, he bought out McKinley and continued in the business until 1890, when he left to sell lumber. In 1893, he invested in the Parsons Band Cutter and Self Feeder Company that made self-feeders for threshing machines, and one year later he became its general manager.

Because the seasonal nature of selling farm equipment caused cash-flow problems for the company, Maytag decided in 1907 to begin making wooden-tub washing machines. They sold so well that in 1909 he founded the Maytag Company, capitalized at $750,000. In 1911, Maytag introduced an electric clothes washer, and for those rural homes that lacked electricity, his company developed a small gasoline-powered engine.

A major development occurred in 1922 when Howard Snyder, mechanic at the company, perfected the gyrafoam washer that used water currents rather than the traditional rubbing devices for washing clothes. Maytag marketed this machine aggressively, enlarged his factory, and added new production machinery. Annual sales increased from $3 million before Snyder's invention to $53 million in 1926, and with this development, Maytag abandoned making all equipment except washing machines. His factory at Newton, Iowa, became the world's largest washing machine plant and employed 2,000 workers.

Maytag entered politics, too, and served on the Newton city council and as town mayor. He was an Iowa state senator from 1902 to 1912, and the first director of the state budget in 1925. After serving as president of the Maytag Company, Frederick Maytag served as chairman of the board until his death on March 2, 1937. Maytag had married Dena Bergman in 1882, and they had two daughters and two sons, who continued in the company. In the 1990s, Maytag was among the top three major appliance companies in North America, and in addition to the Maytag brand name it made products under the names Hoover, Jenn-Air, Dixie-Narco, Magic Chef, RSD, and Blodgett.

BIBLIOGRAPHY

Funk, A. B., *Fred L. Maytag: A Biography*, 1936; Hoover, Robert, *An American Quality Legend: How Maytag Saved Our Moms, Vexed the Competition, and Presaged America's Quality Revolution*, 1993.

McConnell, David

(July 18, 1858–January 20, 1937)
Manufacturer

David Hall McConnell was a door-to-door book salesman who used complimentary vials of perfume to entice housewives to listen to his sales pitch. Soon discovering that the perfume was more popular than the books he was selling, McConnell started the California Perfume Company, the venture that preceded Avon, his highly successful cosmetics company. Avon became famous for its reliance on door-to-door salespeople and community sales representatives.

Born on July 18, 1858, in Oswego, New York, David was the son of Irish immigrants James and Isabel Hall McConnell. David was raised on his father's farm and educated at the Oswego State Normal School. Though his original inclination was to become a math teacher, he took a job in 1879 as a salesman for a New York bookselling agency. The following year, he moved to Chicago to work for the Union Publishing Company and was assigned after three years the management of the southern sales regions. McConnell made Atlanta, Georgia, his home base.

In 1885, McConnell married Lucy Emma Hays of La Porte, Indiana, with whom he later had two daughters and a son. During the early 1880s, McConnell, eager to increase sales, had taken to using free vials of perfume to win him an audience pitching his books at people's doors. With his new family to think about, McConnell sought further avenues to success. He shortly realized that his perfume gambit inspired more interest in the perfume itself than in his employer's books. In 1886, McConnell began making his own perfume under the name California Perfume Company, though he continued to sell it alongside the books of Union Publishing.

As popularity of the perfume increased, McConnell abandoned the bookselling and opened a factory in Suffern, New York. He expanded the product line, added toiletries such as talcum powder and lotions, and later created a line of household articles. From the beginning, McConnell distributed his products based on the concept that customers would respond better to friends and neighbors than strangers or salesmen. To this end, he adopted the practice of hiring housewives and other women to work part-time distributing products. The first "Avon Lady," as the agents came to became popularly known, was P. F. E. Albee, a woman who also recruited for McConnell his initial network of salespeople.

McConnell incorporated the California Perfume Company in 1916. The trade name of Avon Allied Products, Inc. was not adopted until 1929. McConnell chose the name based on his perception of the similarity between the Suffern landscape and the pastoral beauty of Avon, England. Over the next few decades, the company spun off a number of subsidiaries, including Avon Products (which focused on cosmetics), Perfection Household Products, Hinz Ambrosia, Inc., and Technical Laboratories, Inc.

The years of the Great Depression were surprisingly strong years for McConnell's company, due largely to the decision to have agents canvas the selling territory every three weeks rather than once per month. Though much of corporate America suffered during these years, Avon experienced an increase in sales revenue of 70 percent.

In addition to his work with Avon, McConnell served at various times as treasurer of G. W. Carnick and Company (a pharmaceutical supply company) and Holly Hill Fruit Products, Inc. (an orange grove and canning business). McConnell was the founder of Suffern National Bank, and he served as the Suffern superintendent of schools and treasurer of the Rockland County Republican Committee.

After McConnell's death on January 20, 1937, control of Avon Allied Products, Inc. was assumed by his son, David Hall McConnell Jr.

BIBLIOGRAPHY

Ingham, John N., ed., *Biographical Dictionary of American Business Leaders*, 1983; Morris, Betsy, "If Women Ran the World It Would Look a Lot Like Avon," *Fortune*, July 21, 1997; Moskowitz, Milton, et al., eds., *Everybody's Business*, 1980.

McCormick, Cyrus

(February 15, 1809–May 13, 1884)
Manufacturer

Cyrus Hall McCormick revolutionized American agriculture through his invention and manufacture of the reaper. This machine opened vast new lands to farming, and provided the food that fed Union soldiers during the Civil War and the urban dwellers in America's burgeoning cities.

Born on February 15, 1809, in Rockbridge County, Virginia, to Robert McCormick and Mary Ann (Hall) McCormick, Cyrus grew up on his family's farm and obtained little formal education. Inventive in mind, however, in 1831 he patented a hillside plow that he had developed. Later that year, he tackled the problem of making a reaper, an invention his father had tried and failed to perfect.

After some success on his father's farm with a crude model, McCormick added parts, refined the mechanisms, and in late July 1831 gave a public demonstration at a nearby farm. In one continuous motion, a revolving drum on the horse-drawn reaper positioned stalks in front of a blade that cut them and sent the grain falling onto a platform.

The following year, McCormick made additional improvements to his machine and used it on several farms near Lexington, Virginia. At the same time, he patented a self-sharpening horizontal plow. Between 1832 and 1833, he largely abandoned his reaper and produced iron. Financial problems during the latter year, however, caused him to forego iron manufacturing and return to the reaper. He began promoting it, and in 1847 opened a factory in Chicago, at that time a small town close to the farm belt.

Cyrus McCormick (Library of Congress)

McCormick had many rivals, some of whom infringed on his patent, others of whom waited until his patent expired in 1848 to exploit his technology. In the 1850s, more than 30 other companies made reapers. But McCormick met the challenge—he kept making improvements and added a mowing attachment. In order to penetrate the European market, he traveled to the 1851 World's Fair in London. At first, Britons ridiculed him. The *London Times* described his reaper as "a cross between a flying machine, a wheelbarrow, and an Astly chariot." But in competitive tests the reaper's performance silenced the critics. McCormick won major prizes at several European fairs and made progress, albeit slow, in getting his reaper accepted there.

In the United States, the reaper boosted agricultural production. Now a single farmer could plant and harvest much larger acreage. The machine allowed European immigrants settling in the Midwest to farm lands previously considered marginal, and to farm them efficiently. The bigger grain harvests fed an urbanizing nation, and during the Civil War not only fed Union troops but also helped the federal coffers when the bountiful harvests were traded overseas for much-needed revenues.

McCormick contributed in other ways to a modernizing American business world. His use of field trials were innovative, as were the testimonials he used in advertising, the installment plan he allowed customers to use in purchases, and the mass production he organized in his factory.

McCormick opposed the breakup of the Union prior to the Civil War and became very active in Democratic Party politics. In 1864, he ran for Congress in Illinois, but lost. He endowed professorships at the Presbyterian Theological Seminary of the Northwest, edited a Presbyterian newspaper, and invested in many enterprises. McCormick died on May 13, 1884.

BIBLIOGRAPHY

Heikkonen, Esko, *Reaping the Bounty: McCormick Harvesting Machine Company Turns Abroad, 1878–1902*, 1995; Hutchinson, W. T., *Cyrus Hall McCormick: Seed Time, 1809–1856*, 1930; McCormick, Cyrus, *The Century of the Reaper*, 1931; Thwaites, R. G., *Cyrus Hall McCormick and the Reaper*, 1909.

McCormick, Robert

(July 30, 1880–April 1, 1955)
Publisher

Robert Rutherford McCormick, known as the "Colonel of Chicago," was an opinionated, isolationist editor who made the *Chicago Tribune* the principal newspaper of the Midwest. He was the last of the flamboyant, wealthy editors to use his paper as a vehicle to trumpet his beliefs and lambast opposing views. He was fiercely devoted to his hometown, giving generously to its institutions and working relentlessly to better its civic, cultural, political, athletic, and environmental landscape.

Robert was born in Chicago, Illinois, on July 30, 1880, the son of Robert Sanderson and Katharine Van Etta Medill McCormick. He was the second son, both in age and status, as his parents clearly favored his brother Medill. His father was a diplomat, and his mother was the daughter of Joseph Medill, the longtime editor and publisher of the *Chicago Tribune*. Robert was educated in England, an experience that made him a dedicated Anglophile in terms of mannerisms and dress, yet instilled in him an intense American patriotism and disdain for foreigners.

From 1894 until 1899, McCormick attended Groton, an elite Massachusetts preparatory school. He later attended

Yale University, graduating in 1903. In deference to his father's wishes, McCormick returned to Chicago to attend law school at Northwestern University. He never graduated from the program, but did pass the bar exam in 1908. At this juncture, he became involved in local politics, becoming a moderate reformer on the city council. In 1905, he was elected to the Chicago Sanitary District, where the impeccably dressed young man employed engineers to expand the city's drainage systems. In 1910, after failing to be reelected, McCormick went to work for a law firm.

In 1911, McCormick's uncle Robert Patterson died. Patterson had become editor of the *Tribune* in 1899 upon Medill's death. In 1911, McCormick and his cousin Joseph Medill Patterson persuaded the stockholders of the *Chicago Tribune* not to sell it. Though McCormick became president of the *Tribune* that year, it was not until 1914 that he and his cousin actively took charge of the paper, which they did enthusiastically by emblazoning the slogan "World's Greatest Newspaper" across the masthead.

During the next five years, the cousins were a formidable team, differing in political outlook but dividing the labor, with Patterson devising hugely popular comic strips and advice columns and McCormick improving the financial bottom line. Over time, McCormick vastly increased the newspaper's revenue. One reason for its high profit margins was McCormick's decision to acquire cutting rights to a vast tract of Canadian timberland and establish a paper mill to supply the *Tribune* with cheap newsprint.

The onset of World War I in 1914 launched an era of isolationist editorializing from the *Tribune*. The tone adopted by the paper largely reflected the conservatism of Midwest residents. During this phase of his life, McCormick began to exhibit some of his contradictory ideas. He had always been fascinated by warfare and despite his isolationist politics decided to travel to Europe in 1915 to explore England and the territories along the western front. After his marriage to Amy Irwin later that same year, he traveled to Russia where he stayed with his father, the ambassador at St. Petersburg.

Despite McCormick's insistence that mainstream America was not, and should not be, in favor of the European war, he advocated aggressive action in the Western Hemisphere. He volunteered for duty when the United States and Mexico became antagonists during this period. Regarding the situation in the Panama Canal, McCormick stated that "great nations cannot have their existence threatened by little nations that will not allow them to occupy the places indispensable to them." McCormick would eventually be blasted for his grandiose claim that his purchase of machine guns for his troops in Mexico amounted to the beginning of the mechanization of the American military.

McCormick also served during World War I on the western front, rising to the rank of colonel. When he returned to the United States, he was promptly designated the "Colonel of Chicago," a nickname he encouraged and was known by the rest of his life. In 1925, Patterson left the *Tribune* to head the *New York Daily News*. By that time, the *Tribune* had a remarkable circulation. Over the next few decades, the newspaper became McCormick's personal soapbox for hammering home his views with little concession to objectivity.

Though vilified by liberals, his strident voice carried tremendous weight. A politician with opposing views was invariably either ignored or lambasted. McCormick abhorred the New Deal policies of his former Yale classmate, President Franklin D. Roosevelt. It was only after the bombing of Pearl Harbor that *Tribune* editorials advocated U.S. participation in World War II. Though his views on World War II caused readership to drop dramatically, McCormick was a man of tenacious principles.

McCormick's tenacity was apparent in his dedication to "Chicagoland," the nickname of the city and all its environs. He gave millions of dollars to charities, hospitals, the Northwestern Medical School, and the Medill School of Journalism. Through the force of his personality and the vehicle of his newspaper, he strove constantly to improve every aspect of life in Chicago, from promoting civic and cultural activities to instigating city beautification campaigns.

The aggressive grandstanding and blatant subjectivity of the newspaper's reporting led to many lawsuits. McCormick used each opportunity to vigorously champion freedom of the press. One of the paper's greatest assets was a highly loyal staff, which McCormick was able to retain because he paid the highest salaries and pensions in the profession, gave liberal bonuses, and established a personal acquaintance with all of his employees.

After the death of his wife in 1939, McCormick was remarried in 1944 to Maryland Mathison Hooper. He had no children and died of a heart condition on April 1, 1955.

BIBLIOGRAPHY

Edwards, Jerome E., *The Foreign Policy of Col. McCormick's Tribune*, 1971; Gies, Joseph Smith, *The Colonel of Chicago*, 1979; Norton, Richard, *The Colonel: The Life and Legend of Robert R. McCormick, 1880–1955*, 1997; Tebbel, John, *An American Dynasty*, 1947; Waldrop, Frank C., *McCormick of Chicago*, 1966.

McCoy, Joseph

(December 21, 1837–October 19, 1915)
Cattle Rancher

Joseph Geating McCoy pioneered the American cattle trade by turning Abilene, Kansas, into a shipping point for cattle from Texas. He strong-armed the railroads into starting the successful practice of shipping cattle as freight on trains. By improving access to Texan cattle, he dramatically increased the demand and availability of beef nationwide. Considered to be generous, creative, and powerful in character, McCoy was one of the most famous men in Kansas during his time.

Born in Sangamon County, Illinois, on December 21, 1837, Joseph was the son of a Virginian, David McCoy, and Mary Kirkpatrick McCoy, a native of Kentucky. After attending local schools, Joseph attended Knox College from 1857 to 1858. On October 22, 1861, the year he decided to enter the cattle trade, Joseph married Sarah Epler. The couple, who had one son and two daughters, moved west.

McCoy believed that the scarcity of beef in the eastern states indicated that there was a niche available for transporting cattle from the West to the rest of the country. The situation he found in Texas confirmed his suspicions. The number of cattle in Texas was on the increase, yet Texan cattlemen had access to few markets. The cattle could be driven to Louisiana for shipping from the Gulf Coast, but the steamship operators resold the animals at a higher price, thus reaping the profits and infuriating the ranchers. Some ranchers drove the cattle to Missouri, but the route there was difficult, filled with perils for crossing Native American lands and the threat of bandits that stampeded and rerouted the cattle.

McCoy believed that the problem could be remedied by creating a central point to serve as a depot for the shipping of cattle. He selected Abilene, Kansas, a small town along the Kansas Pacific Railway (soon known as the Union Pacific Railway, Eastern Division) between Texas and the Missouri border. He purchased the entire town site for about $2,400 and immediately began construction on a shipping yard with a capacity for 3,000 cattle, a barn, an office building, a hotel, and a bank. Meanwhile, his negotiations with the railroads for shipping arrangements were proving complicated. McCoy's plan was ridiculed, but the lack of cooperation did not prevent McCoy from completing work on a trail from Abilene to Corpus Christi, Texas. By the end of 1867, almost 35,000 cattle were driven to Abilene on the Chisholm Trail.

Kansas Pacific Railroad executives, having little faith in the endeavor, reluctantly agreed to ship the cattle and pay McCoy one-eighth of the freight on each car of cattle shipped. By 1868, the trade was moving rapidly, and McCoy was earning a lot of money. He bought and sold cattle, charged the buyers for the use of the cattle pens, and earned a profit from buying and selling land, which had increased in value as the cattle trade invigorated the small town of Abilene. Though McCoy was owed $200,000 from the Kansas Pacific by 1869, the railroad reneged on their original deal, claiming that the contract was invalid as they had had no idea that such large shipments would be made. McCoy eventually had to sue in order to recover the money owed him.

During his years in Abilene, McCoy served as mayor and held a number of federal appointments, including director of the livestock branch of the eleventh U.S. census. In 1871, more than 800,000 head of cattle arrived in Kansas. This was the year that the largest number of cattle moved through Abilene, but it was also the last year that Abilene ruled the cattle trade. The same railroads shipping the animals east had, in the meantime, brought a number of settlers west, many of whom had acquired land around Abilene and had begun working at year-round industries more stable than the cattle trade. Texan cattle was also a concern to many because the longhorns brought ticks that carried "Texas Fever," an ailment that was fatal to other breeds of cattle. Over time, it was estimated that 10 million head of cattle were exported via the Abilene-Corpus Christi trail.

In 1872, McCoy settled in Wichita, where he worked as a revenue collector for the Cherokee Nation Indian tribe. Over the next few years, the entrepreneurial McCoy pursued a number of ventures, as a salesman of everything from iron fences to groceries, as a speculator, as a cattle inspector, and as a narcotics agent for the U.S. Treasury Department.

McCoy was a dedicated Democrat. Over the years, he took part in several Democratic conventions and was nominated (though defeated) in 1890 in a bid for Congress. A man of diverse talents and strong character, McCoy also authored a book, *Historic Sketches of the Cattle Trade*, which was published in 1874. He died in Kansas City, Missouri, on October 19, 1915.

BIBLIOGRAPHY

Dary, David, *Entrepreneurs of the Old West*, 1986; *Kansas City Journal, Historic Sketches of the Cattle Trade*, 1874; McCoy, Joseph, October 20, 1915.

McDonnell, James

(April 9, 1899–August 22, 1980)
Manufacturer

For a man interested in aviation, James Smith McDonnell had a troubling start. When he test-flew a plane he had built, it crashed. So did several others later in his life. In between, however, he built McDonnell-Douglas into a major government contractor.

Born on April 9, 1899, in Denver, Colorado, to James Smith McDonnell and Susan Belle (Hunter) McDonnell, James earned a B.S. degree with honors in physics from Princeton University in 1921. He continued his studies at the Massachusetts Institute of Technology, from which he graduated in 1925 with a degree in aeronautical engineering. During those years, he learned to fly by joining the army air service.

McDonnell formed a company in 1928 to make the small airplane that he entered in the 1929 Guggenheim Safe Aircraft Competition, but his plane crashed. McDonnell refused to bail out and sustained injuries, but he went back to flying the next year. During the Great Depression of the 1930s, he worked for various aircraft plants, including the GLENN MARTIN Company, where he learned the industry inside out.

In 1934, McDonnell married Mary Elizabeth Finney and they had two children. Seven years after his wife died in 1949, McDonnell married Priscilla Brush Forney, and they had three children.

With money borrowed from friends and from Laurence Rockefeller, McDonnell founded the McDonnell Company in 1939, explicitly linking it to the national government when he said he would design and manufacture planes for the military's use. Within three years, his company became a major industry based in St. Louis, Missouri, and was the first to make jets to fly from aircraft carriers. For the Korean War in the early 1950s, McDonnell made the Banshee F2H-2, immortalized in James Michener's novel *The Bridges of Toko-Ri.*

McDonnell made other fighter jets, too: the F3H Demon (the first swept-wing jet), the Voodoo, and the Phantom. Then, in 1959, he landed a contract with the government to make America's first orbital spacecraft, a project that produced the Mercury space capsule in which a single astronaut could ride, shoehorned in among the instruments. He followed this with the larger Gemini capsule that held two astronauts. During the Vietnam War, he made the F-4 Phantom II jet fighter.

Although McDonnell and his company made considerable money from these contracts—often generous and often, critics said, padded with waste—he saw his role as going beyond financial gain to support the United States in its fight against communism. Thus, during the cold war he fervently endorsed American foreign policy and rejected isolationism in favor of internationalism. He praised the United Nations and chaired an organization of business leaders who backed the goals of the North Atlantic Treaty Organization, the multilateral military alliance formed by the United States, Canada, and several Western European nations.

In 1967, McDonnell acquired the ailing Douglas Aircraft Company, thus forming

James McDonnell (Archive Photos)

McDonnell-Douglas. To counteract Boeing's 747 commercial jumbo jet, he manufactured the DC-10, a wide-bodied jet airliner. The DC-10s suffered from design flaws and were blamed for several crashes.

Adding to McDonnell's problems, a government investigating committee found in July 1980 that, in order to sell its DC-10, McDonnell-Douglas had bribed foreign governments. McDonnell claimed that the U.S. government knew all along about the payments.

McDonnell retained a tight hold on his company right up until his death on August 22, 1980. He had made his nephew, Sanford McDonnell, president in 1971 and CEO the following year. But McDonnell remained as chairman of the board, and in wielding his power prompted Sanford to complain about being a mere figurehead. McDonnell replied to Sanford: "That's right. You're the CEO and I'm the boss."

BIBLIOGRAPHY

Moskowitz, Milton, et al., eds., *Everybody's Business*, 1980.

McGovern, Pat

(1936–)
Publisher

As computers appeared in greater numbers during the 1960s, Patrick J. McGovern recognized a problem. The manufacturers of the machines and their buyers knew little about each other. He responded by beginning a computer marketing survey and by establishing a newspaper, *Computerworld*, the first of dozens of other magazines and weekly newspapers published through his company, International Data Group (IDG).

McGovern was born in 1936, the son of a construction manager. At age 15, he developed an interest in computers and made a machine that played tic-tac-toe and never lost. The machine and his academic record earned him a scholarship to the Massachusetts Institute of Technology (MIT). At MIT, he earned money by editing a small Boston-based computer magazine. In 1964, several years after graduating, and while working as associate editor of *Computers and Automation*, he pursued an idea to provide computer manufacturers with information about their customers. At that time, computers were just entering a wider consumer market, and the manufacturers knew little about the type of people buying them.

McGovern first approached Univac and offered to do a market census. To his surprise, the computer company not only agreed to the proposal but also paid him more than he had originally asked. He sold his idea to several other companies as well, and all told obtained $70,000 in prepayments. With that money, he founded IDG in 1967.

Building on his surveys, he decided to bring manufacturers and consumers together with a newspaper, and shortly before a trade show in Boston he put together a 16-page tabloid. He was so rushed to meet his deadline that he failed to discover until the last minute that the full name of his publication, *Computer World News*, took too much space on the cover. He hurriedly changed its title to *Computerworld.*

McGovern attracted subscribers at the trade show and used the money to expand *Computerworld.* From there, IDG grew rapidly, gathering and selling market research on the computer industry and publishing its magazines and newspapers. In 1972, he exported the *Computerworld* concept to Japan and founded *Shukan Computer.*

McGovern established a decentralized organization at IDG, and by 1984 his company had 41 corporate units with yearly profits of about $20 million. His own wealth reached $250 million, yet he lived frugally, offered shares in the company to his employees, and maintained what many considered a friendly, even enlightened, work environment.

By the 1990s, the number of corporate units in IDG increased to over 70, and the company had more than 60 publications. McGovern had taken IDG into the global market, with magazines in Europe, China, and elsewhere. "People are very cautious in their own country about talking to the press," said McGovern. "But then they fly off to Stockholm and have a couple of drinks. They're amazed that what they thought was a quiet little Swedish story appears round the world the next day."

Despite its success, rivals sometimes outdid IDG in the 1990s. *PC Magazine* and *PC Week*, both owned by Zig Communications, outsold IDG's most popular publication, *InfoWorld*. McGovern, however, diversified IDG and bought a chain of PC-training schools in the United States. In 1990, he launched IDG Books Worldwide, and it sold more than 40 million copies of its *For Dummies* series, such as *Internet for Dummies* and *Finance for Dummies*. IDG sponsored more than 100 conferences and expositions around the world, and with McGovern as chief executive officer, its 1997 revenues exceeded $2 billion. IDG called itself the world's leading computer publishing, research, and exposition management company.

McGovern, who after a divorce from his first wife had remarried and had two children, was described by *Inc. Magazine* as follows, "Knows start ups cold—grows them by launching them constantly within his own company. Craves customer contact, responsiveness, speed. More than any other CEO around, McGovern gets it: preach the mission, provide information, give folks plenty of rope—then get out of the way."

BIBLIOGRAPHY

Behar, Richard, "As You Give," *Fortune*, April 29, 1985; "Rich and Titled," *The Economist*, March 30, 1991; Silver, A. David, *Entrepreneurial Megabucks: The 100 Greatest Entrepreneurs of the Last Twenty-Five Years*, 1985.

McGowan, Bill

(December 10, 1927–1992)
Communications Executive

When William George McGowan founded MCI Communications, he did so with a crusading zeal, for he wanted to do more than make money; he wanted to humble the American Telephone & Telegraph Company (AT&T) and revolutionize telecommunications.

The son of a railroad union organizer, McGowan was born on December 10, 1927, in Ashley, Pennsylvania, in the heart of coal-mining country. He earned money in high school by working summers for the Central Railroad of New Jersey, a line that carried anthracite coal. McGowan later claimed that since the

Central was so poorly run, his experience with it provided an invaluable lesson in what not to do.

After serving in the army from 1945 to 1947, McGowan entered King's College in Wilkes-Barre, where he earned a bachelor's degree in chemical engineering. He decided, however, that he wanted to pursue a different career and so he enrolled in the Graduate School of Business at Harvard where he earned recognition as a Baker Scholar, ranked among the top 5 percent of his class. With that accomplishment, McGowan could have obtained a job at practically any big New York firm. Instead, he opted for Hollywood, where he thought he could be more creative. In 1954, M.B.A. in hand, he joined the Magna Theater Corporation, owned by show business leader Mike Todd.

The job failed to fulfill his expectations, however, and in any event he wanted to build a business on his own. Leaving Hollywood, McGowan worked in New York City as a management consultant and investor. His most notable endeavor, and the one that enabled him to amass great wealth, involved the Ultrasonic Corporation. For just $25,000 he took over the struggling electronics company in 1959, rebuilt it, and then sold it three years later for $3 million. With the profit he made from Ultrasonic and other investments, he retired at age 39, a wealthy man.

Contentment nevertheless eluded him. Energetic and adventurous—some people called him overbearing—McGowan searched for another challenge. He found it in 1968, when he learned about Microwave Communications, Incorporated, a small company then seeking approval from the Federal Communications Com-

mission (FCC) to provide private-line phone service over microwave towers between St. Louis and Chicago. The company had been founded by John D. Goeken, a radio-equipment salesman. But Goeken needed capital and struck a deal with McGowan whereby for $50,000 the financier got half the company's shares and became its chairman and CEO. McGowan envisioned applying Goeken's idea on a larger scale and creating a microwave-based national telephone network.

McGowan renamed the firm MCI Communications and aimed at ending the telephone monopoly held by AT&T. As a corporate giant, AT&T controlled nearly all local and long-distance telephone service, and even forbade consumers from attaching to its lines any phones made by companies other than its own Western Electric. McGowan obviously had a tough fight ahead, one that required building MCI's infrastructure and hiring lawyers to take on AT&T in Congress, the courts, and before the FCC. This would require enormous sums of money.

Thanks to Goeken's work, shortly before McGowan took over MCI, the FCC approved the company's request to operate its St. Louis–Chicago service. With this victory in hand, McGowan used his contacts on Wall Street to raise $110 million, followed by a public stock offering in 1972 that raised an additional $30 million. Meanwhile, MCI built its microwave relay towers and started its midwestern service.

McGowan decided to use the antitrust laws to bring down AT&T. In 1974, he asked the FCC to permit MCI to offer long-distance service, at first intended only for businesses, using its own computers and microwave relays, thus bypassing AT&T. The FCC approved McGowan's request, and then changed its mind. Fortunately for McGowan, a federal court ruled in July 1977 that MCI and other companies could provide whatever long-distance service they desired—a ruling that ended AT&T's monopoly and opened telecommunications to competition.

With his battery of lawyers, McGowan went to court again in 1980 and convinced a jury that AT&T was guilty of antitrust violations. The judge gave MCI $1.8 billion in damages, which was the largest antitrust settlement ever. Although a second trial lowered the amount, McGowan's victory further unraveled AT&T, and in 1982 the corporation signed a consent decree with the Justice Department under which it divested itself of its 22 regional Bell companies while retaining its long-distance division, along with Western Electric and Bell Laboratories.

A truly open market remained elusive, however, for the arrangement allowed each Bell company to wield monopolistic power in its region. A court decision late in 1997, however, posed another challenge to AT&T when it allowed the regional Bells to offer long-distance service. By then, MCI was offering national service to residential customers at rates as much as 50 percent lower than AT&T's, and its annual revenues surpassed $1 billion.

In the late 1980s, McGowan led MCI into new technologies, among them cellular radio, electronic mail, and nationwide paging. At the same time, he ran a strict antiunion business known for providing few benefits to its workers. In 1987, McGowan suffered a massive heart attack and underwent a heart transplant operation that caused him to limit his role in the company.

While on the surface McGowan's triumph over AT&T seemed like a victory for consumers, analysts cautioned that while the end of AT&T's monopoly had brought lower long-distance rates, offered by MCI and other companies, the development had resulted in higher charges for local phone service. They pointed out that over the years AT&T had been using its inflated long-distance fees to subsidize local service and make it possible for nearly everyone to own a phone. As a result, when local service charges increased, so did the number of homes without phones as poorer families had to discontinue their service.

Before his death in 1992, however, McGowan had reached his goals. He had humbled AT&T, ended the corporate giant's national monopoly, and revolutionized telecommunications. He had also built a company attractive to other businesses, and in 1997 MCI announced its takeover by Worldcom, Incorporated. By that year, MCI was earning most of its $18.6 billion annual revenue as a provider of wholesale Internet communications and fiber-optic networks, rather than through long-distance phone service.

BIBLIOGRAPHY

Coll, Steve, *The Deal of the Century: The Breakup of AT&T*, 1986; Henck, Paul W., and Bernard Strassburg, *A Slippery Slope: The Long Road to the Breakup of AT&T*, 1987.

McKnight, William

(November 11, 1887–March 4, 1978)
Manufacturer

When William Lester McKnight first stepped through the front door of the Minnesota Mining and Manufacturing Company (3M), he thought he had entered the headquarters of the world's largest sandpaper-making business. He found out otherwise—3M tottered near collapse and soon owed its survival to the unsuspecting McKnight.

William McKnight came from a midwestern farm family. He was born on November 11, 1887, in Brookings County, South Dakota, near the Minnesota border, to Joseph McKnight and his wife Cordelia. All of William's brothers became farmers, but he got no pleasure in raising wheat or slopping hogs. He decided, instead, to enter business, and at age 18 enrolled in Duluth Business University.

He dropped out of school in May 1907, however, when he accepted a job as assistant bookkeeper at 3M. The company had been founded in 1902 and had begun to make sandpaper in 1905. Up to 1855, workers using sandpaper had made their own sheets of abrasive, but after that year, sandpaper machines appeared, able to manufacture the product in large quantities, and this had stimulated 3M's entry into the field.

As America industrialized, the demand for sandpaper grew. Despite such demand, 3M struggled with expenses that far exceeded its sales, a fact McKnight discovered only after joining the firm. His loyalty and application led to his promotion in 1909 to cost accountant, and in 1910 to sales manager, even though he had no experience in sales. McKnight flourished, as he convinced 3M, by then

based in St. Paul, Minnesota, to improve its quality control and communication between the factory and its sales force. McKnight's determination that 3M would sell only superior products, and that it would avoid highly competitive markets, turned the company around and led to its prosperity. In 1914, a new product, Three-M-ite, greatly helped. An abrasive cloth made with aluminum oxide, Three-M-ite proved superior to natural mineral emery, then widely used.

After McKnight gained appointment as general manager in 1916, he directed the company's daily operation. World War I eased the marketing challenge facing him when it increased the demand for abrasives, but McKnight's goal was to greatly diversify 3M's product line. As a result, in the 1920s, the company began making waterproof sandpaper, and in a move that took it beyond abrasives, Scotch-brand masking tape. With an adhesive made from cabinetmaker's glue and glycerin, it sold well in the automobile industry where it was used in painting two-tone cars.

In 1930, 3M marketed a cellophane tape invented by Richard Drew, one of the company's laboratory assistants. Scotch Tape, as it was named, came on a roll and fitted a dispenser that 3M invented. During the Great Depression, the tape seemed a miracle, a way to cheaply mend broken items and make them last.

By that time, McKnight had ascended to the company presidency, and in the 1930s he pushed strenuously for yet more diversification. 3M produced resin, rubber, and synthetic adhesives. It also developed a reflective sheeting, called Scotchlite, that when applied to school buses improved safety on dark highways, and when applied to advertising signs enhanced their visibility.

McKnight pumped even more money into research and development beginning in 1937, and although some products failed, many others succeeded, including Safety-Walk, a lining that made decks and airplane wings less slippery during World War II. By 1949, with McKnight serving as board chairman, 3M had nearly 9,000 employees, annual sales over $100 million, and numerous plants.

McKnight pushed his workers to search everywhere for new ideas. He pursued his own in the 1950s when, as a horse racing fan, he noticed that even a light rain made racetracks muddy. As a result, he got the 3M laboratory to develop an all-weather track, first used in 1963.

The soft-spoken McKnight held a management philosophy that stressed faith in individual initiative. He said:

> As our business grows, it becomes increasingly necessary for those in managerial positions to delegate responsibility and to encourage men to whom responsibility is delegated to exercise their own initiative.

> Mistakes will be made, but if the man is essentially right himself, I think the mistakes he makes are not so serious in the long run as the mistakes management makes if it is dictatorial and undertakes to tell men . . . exactly how they must do their job.

McKnight retired in 1966, but remained on the board of directors until 1973 and engaged in other enterprises. He financed several Broadway shows, including *Hello Dolly*, *The Music Man*, and *Auntie Mame*, and owned four theaters. He remained active in the McKnight Foundation, which he and his wife had founded in 1953 to fund social programs.

After McKnight's death on March 4, 1978, 3M continued to grow until the mid-1980s, when increased competition in videocassettes and computer diskettes, along with poor management decisions, caused a crisis. But another profitable product appeared when Arthur Fry, a 3M chemical engineer, invented an adhesive with low sticking power and applied it to paper, thus creating Post-it Notes. Sales for Post-it quickly reached into the millions, and with other product developments, 3M recovered in the 1990s to achieve annual sales topping $15 billion.

BIBLIOGRAPHY

Huck, Virginia, *Brand of the Tartan: The 3M Story*, 1955; Moskowitz, Milton, et al., eds., *Everybody's Business*, 1980.

McNamara, Robert

(June 9, 1916–)
Manufacturer

Known primarily for his role in the Vietnam War, Robert Strange McNamara first gained the attention of political leaders when he made the struggling Ford Motor Company a financial success.

Robert McNamara (Yoichi R. Okamoto/LBJ Library Collection)

Robert McNamara was born on June 9, 1916, in San Francisco, California, to Robert James McNamara and Claranel (Strange) McNamara. His father was the sales manager for a wholesale shoe company and provided young Robert with a middle-class upbringing. In high school,

Robert excelled at his studies, and when he enrolled at the University of California, Berkeley, he pursued mathematics, economics, and philosophy. After graduating with a B.A. degree in 1937, he entered the Harvard Graduate School of Business and received his master's degree in 1939. He then briefly worked at an accounting firm before returning to the Harvard business school as an assistant professor. In 1940, he married Margaret McKinstry; the couple had three children.

During World War II, the air force sent McNamara to England to establish a statistical control system for its B-17 bombers. Commissioned as a captain and then promoted to lieutenant colonel, McNamara coordinated the planes and their crews, making sure they were ready for their missions. He became known as a "whiz kid" and in 1946 joined the troubled Ford Motor Company, where he applied his managerial expertise.

From 1946 to 1949, McNamara served as manager of Ford's planning and financial analysis offices. He then won promotion to comptroller, followed by assistant general manager of the automotive division, vice president, and, in 1957, group executive of the car and truck division. The changes he implemented in administrative structure and in cost accounting boosted Ford's productivity and profits.

In 1960, he was made president of the Ford Motor Company, the first person to hold that position who was not a member of the Ford family. He continued his earlier reforms and used consumer surveys that led to Ford producing popular new-model cars, among them a family version of the sporty Thunderbird and the Falcon compact.

McNamara's success at Ford caused political leaders to take note, and in 1961 President John F. Kennedy appointed him secretary of defense. McNamara quickly made it clear he would radically change the defense budget to reduce waste. He established an entirely new budget system that coordinated the purchases of the army, navy, and air force. In addition, he convinced Kennedy to employ what he called a "flexible response," which combined nuclear weapons with conventional troops and antiguerrilla forces.

McNamara helped plan the blockade of Cuba during the Cuban missile crisis of 1962, and then made a momentous decision for himself and the United States when he urged Kennedy to increase the American military commitment to South Vietnam. McNamara believed that American troops and technology would win in Vietnam. His statistical analyses supported him, and he thought them infallible. His critics said that McNamara failed to understand anything that could not be measured quantitatively. In any event, his analyses proved wrong, and although he eventually pushed for peace negotiations with North Vietnam, his decisions, and his deceit—for he sometimes lied to Congress and the public—deepened the American involvement and increased civilian and combat deaths.

McNamara decided to leave the Defense Department in 1967, and later that year convinced President Lyndon B. Johnson to nominate him as the director of the World Bank. He assumed the presidency of that institution in April 1968 and won reelection by the executive board in 1972 and again in 1977. As an international lending agency, the World Bank made loans to underdeveloped countries. McNamara directed the bank to fund local projects to help poor villages and to support oil, gas, and coal exploration. During his presidency, World Bank loans increased from about $1 billion to over $11 billion annually.

McNamara retired from the World Bank in 1981, and since that time has worked for nonprofit organizations. He raised a storm of controversy in 1995 with his autobiography, *In Retrospect.* He wrote that American assumptions leading to the nation's involvement in Vietnam had been misguided, and the entire American involvement there was wrong. In reaction, some Vietnam War veterans complained he had besmirched their sacrifice, and other critics said he was less than forthcoming about his own culpability. One said "Robert McNamara . . . was a poor guide to judgment while he was secretary of defense, and he remains a poor guide today."

BIBLIOGRAPHY

Hendrickson, Paul, *The Living and the Dead: Robert McNamara and Five Lives of Lost War,* 1996; McNamara, Robert S., *In Retrospect: The Tragedy and Lessons of Vietnam,* 1995; Shapley, Deborah, *Promise and Power: The Life and Times of Robert McNamara,* 1993.

Mead, George

(November 5, 1877–January 1, 1963)
Manufacturer

George Houk Mead took over his family's failing paper business, the Mead Paper Company, and made it the world's largest producer of cardboard containers.

George was born on November 5, 1877, in Dayton, Ohio, to Harry Eldridge Mead and Marianna (Houk) Mead. After graduating from Wyland's private school in Dayton, he received degrees from Dayton College in 1897 and the Massachusetts Institute of Technology in 1900. He began working for the Mead Paper Company in 1902, when he founded a chemical laboratory at its pulp mill in Chillicothe. The company had been started in 1846 by Daniel E. Mead, George's grandfather, when he bought into Chafflin & Company, a small paper mill. In 1882, it was renamed Mead Paper.

George Mead continued working at the pulp mill as foreman, superintendent, and then manager, until 1904, when he left to help build a factory for the General Artificial Silk Company in Philadelphia. He returned to Mead Paper the following year, however, as the business went into receivership. With his father-in-law, Harry E. Talbott, he reorganized it, forming the Mead Pulp and Paper Company that acquired the assets of the Mead Paper Company. He served as vice president and general manager of Mead Pulp and Paper until 1912—guiding it through a great slump in the paper market in 1908—and thereafter as its president. In 1914, he married Elsie Louise Talbott; they had six children.

By 1915, Mead had placed the company on a firm footing, and during the 1920s his researchers discovered a way to convert wood chips into cardboard. During the next decade, this discovery enabled Mead Pulp and Paper to establish several plants for making cardboard containers. In 1930, Mead reorganized the company again and incorporated it under its present name, The Mead Corporation.

At the same time, he entered the Canadian paper business when he organized the Lake Superior Paper Company at Sault Ste. Marie, Ontario. He later merged the firm with the Spanish River Pulp and Paper Mills and served as its president from 1915 to 1928.

To expand The Mead Corporation, George Mead acquired other companies in the 1930s: Dill and Collins Mill in Philadelphia; the Tennessee Extract Company in Nashville; the United Paperboard Company in Rockport, Indiana; the Menasha (Wisconsin) Paper Corporation; the George W. Wheelwright Paper Company in Leominister, Massachusetts; and the Waverly Paperboard Company in Newark, New Jersey. In 1936, he incorporated Mead Board Sales as a separate organization to sell paperboard.

George Mead continued as president until 1942 and then as chairman of the board until 1948. He died on January 1, 1963, by which time his company ran 41 plants in 17 states making paper, paperboard, wood pulp, folding boxes, and shipping containers. In 1972, The Mead Corporation defeated a takeover attempt by ARMAND HAMMER, chairman at Occidental Petroleum. In 1994, the company acquired Hilroy, a major manufacturer of home, school, and office supplies.

BIBLIOGRAPHY

Moskowitz, Milton, et al., eds., *Everybody's Business*, 1980.

Mellen, Charles

(August 16, 1851–November 17, 1927)
Railroad Executive

Charles Sanger Mellen made a number of innovative changes while president of the New York, New Haven, and Hartford Railroad and became a controversial figure for his fervent efforts to eliminate competition.

Mellen was born on August 16, 1851, in Lowell, Massachusetts. His parents, George and Hannah Mellen, were the descendants of Scottish immigrants. Charles attended school in Concord, New Hampshire. After graduating from high school in 1867, Charles obtained work as a clerk in the cashier's office of the Northern New Hampshire Railroad. He was married on September 23, 1875, to Marion Beardsley, with whom he had two children, Graham Kingsbury and Marion Foster. Over the next few years, he attained increasingly more responsible positions, working for the Central Vermont, followed by another stint at the Northern New Hampshire, and finally the Boston and Lowell. In 1888, he became the general purchasing agent of the Union Pacific Railroad, and this was followed by promotion to general traffic manager.

Mellen's next career advancement, to general manager of the New York, New Haven, and Hartford Railroad in 1892, enabled him to become acquainted with J. P. MORGAN SR., who had been appointed to the board of directors. During that same year, Mellen's wife died. On November 15, 1893, he married Katherine Lloyd, with whom he eventually had five children—Kathryn, Amory, Raymond, Candace, and Priscilla.

During this time, Morgan became a mentor to Mellen, who owed much of his future advancements to Morgan's influence. Mellen was proud throughout his career to be a "Morgan man." In 1897, Morgan interceded on Mellen's behalf to gain him the presidency of the Northern Pacific Railroad.

Mellen's initiatives as president were overshadowed by the fierce financial struggles then under way as JAMES J. HILL of the Great Northern Railroad attempted to gain a significant financial interest in the Northern Pacific Railroad. Mellen was little involved in the financial power struggles of the railroad. Instead, he focused on improving the infrastructure and maintaining efficient operations. As Hill's power over the Northern Pacific increased, Mellen became increasingly uncomfortable with his own role. In 1903, Mellen, once again advancing through the clout of his friend Morgan, returned to the New York, New Haven, and Hartford as president.

It is this period of Mellen's career that is marked simultaneously by energetic advances and controversial decisions that left blots upon his legacy in the story of American railroads. On the positive side, Mellen shouldered an ambitious expansion plan that involved making long-overdue repairs to the line's operating facilities, augmenting the amount of tracks and number of new stations, and placing new emphasis on installing safety features. For the most part, however, Mellen focused on creating a transportation monopoly in New England. Any mode of transport that took business away from his railroad was added to the holdings of the railroad. The railroad bought trolley lines, steamships, and intercity trolley lines. When steamship lines that traversed Long Island Sound offered lower rates than the New Haven Shore Line run by the railroad, Mellen purchased them and put them out of business. He also purchased and became president of the Boston and Maine Railroad, the Maine Central, and other railway lines.

Though Mellen's acquisitions expanded the influence of the New York, New Haven, and Hartford, they also drained it financially. Morgan paid for the expansion by repeatedly moving bond issues. The use of the bond issues, in addition to the railroad's obvious expansionism, created a resentful political climate among New Englanders, who were fearful of losing control over their states' assets to outsiders. The Interstate Commerce Commission, which had been called upon to investigate the railroad's practices, declared Mellen's management "one of the most glaring instances of misadministration revealed in all the history of American railroading." In 1913, as charges of poor financial management and operational neglect continued to mount, Mellen was forced to resign.

Mellen returned to his home in Stockbridge, Massachusetts, where he remained involved with the activities of the Republican Party. A lifelong conservative, Mellen had been a delegate to the Republican National Convention in 1904. He was also called upon to advise President Theodore Roosevelt on railroad matters. Mellen died on November 17, 1927, in Concord, New Hampshire.

BIBLIOGRAPHY

Allen, Frederick Lewis, *The Great Pierpont Morgan*, 1948; Allen, Frederick Lewis, *The Lords of Creation*, 1935; Barron, Clarence, *The More They Told Barron*, 1931; Staples, Henry Lee, and Alpheus Thomas Mason, *The Fall of the Railroad Empire*, 1947.

Mellon, Andrew

(March 24, 1855–August 26, 1937)
Banker, Investor

Aloof, reserved, and strongly committed to business, banker Andrew Mellon provided the financing that stimulated America's corporate development. As a political leader, he promoted tax policies that favored the wealthy.

Andrew Mellon was born on March 24, 1855, in Pittsburgh, Pennsylvania, to Thomas Mellon and Sarah Jane (Negley) Mellon. His father earned money and influence as a lawyer before turning to finance in 1869 and establishing a private banking house, T. Mellon & Sons. After graduating from public schools in Pittsburgh, young Andrew attended the Western University of Pennsylvania (later the University of Pittsburgh). He left before receiving a degree, however, in order to start a lumber business in the nearby town of Mansfield. In 1874, he joined his father's bank and showed such talent for finance that in 1882 the elder Mellon turned the business over to him.

By that time, Pittsburgh and America as a whole had entered a period of intense industrialization. Mellon involved his bank in this development and showed a genius for identifying young inventors and businessmen who had great potential. For example, he provided financing for Charles Hall and his electrolytic manufacture of aluminum. Hall's process led to the formation of the Aluminum Company of America (Alcoa), in which Mellon acquired many shares.

Mellon's bank helped fund the Gulf Oil Corporation and the Union Steel Company, which later became part of United States Steel. His involvement helped

Andrew Mellon (Library of Congress)

make Heinrich Koppers a leading company in the gas, sulfur, and coal-tar industries; and a partnership he formed created a firm that built the Panama Canal locks, the George Washington Bridge, and the Waldorf-Astoria Hotel.

Mellon dominated several banks. He served as the first president of the Union Trust Company of Pittsburgh, which he had organized with industrialist HENRY C. FRICK. In 1902, he incorporated T. Mellon & Sons as the Mellon National Bank that soon gathered other Pittsburgh banks under its control. In short, he created a national center for banking.

More intent on business than anything else, Mellon did not marry until 1900, when he wed Nora Mary McMullen. They had two children, but the marriage faltered since Mellon remained preoccupied with business, and the couple divorced in 1912.

Meanwhile, Mellon emerged as a powerful figure in Pennsylvania politics, supporting conservative Republican Party causes. When Warren Harding won the presidency in 1920, he named Mellon his secretary of the treasury. The appointment surprised many people, as few had heard of the reticent Mellon and his vast fortune.

Mellon quickly emerged as the power in Harding's Republican administration, and as a Social Darwinist who considered life to be a struggle for the survival of the fittest, he helped direct the national government away from reform programs. Mellon's financial policies raised opposition from many Democrats, but they were representative of the materialistic 1920s. In general, he favored heavy tax cuts for the wealthy and for corporations, believing that any savings they received would result in greater investments and in prosperity trickling down to the masses. He cut federal spending, too, in order to reduce the national debt.

After Harding's death in 1923, Mellon continued as secretary of the treasury under Calvin Coolidge. Critics attacked Mellon for granting huge tax refunds to corporations, including $15 million to United States Steel in 1929 and to several companies in which he held a direct interest. Despite these controversies, when Republican Herbert Hoover succeeded Coolidge as president in 1929, he retained Mellon as secretary of the treasury.

As the Great Depression deepened, however—a depression perhaps sparked in part by Mellon's earlier treasury policies—Hoover persuaded Mellon to step down and accept appointment as ambassador to Britain. Mellon did so in 1932 and served one undistinguished year in the post.

Mellon collected great works of art, especially in his later years. These included Rembrandts, Vermeers, and Titians, which were valued at more than $35 million. In 1937, he gave his collection to the federal government, along with several million dollars to erect a museum. Congress accepted the gift and approved building the National Gallery. Mellon died on August 26, 1937, shortly after construction had begun.

BIBLIOGRAPHY

Murray, Lawrence Leo, *Andrew W. Mellon, Secretary of the Treasury, 1921–1932: A Study in Policy*, 1970.

Milken, Michael

(1946–)
Financier

In the mid-1980s, Michael Milken created a junk bond empire that earned him more than $1 billion. It also financed hundreds of corporations and corporate acquisitions, and led to his arrest and conviction on civil and criminal charges.

Born in 1946 in Van Nuys, California, Milken grew up in an upper-middle-class family and after graduating from Birmingham High School received a bachelor's degree in 1968 from the University of California, Berkeley. He then married and continued his studies at the Wharton School of Business in Pennsylvania. It took him 10 years to earn his M.B.A., mainly because he spent considerable time dealing in junk bonds. Many investors avoided junk bonds because they were issued by companies with shaky financial standing, had a low investment quality, and were deemed risky. Milken, however, researched companies with the low-rated bonds and found they had a default rate no greater than other corporations.

Thus, while at Wharton in the 1970s, he began working for Drexel, Burnham & Company, a brokerage house. Milken built a junk bond network with other investors and by 1976 had become an independent power within Drexel and received a $5 million bonus. The profit Milken made for Drexel came mainly from large fees he received for selling previously undesirable bonds. His sales raised billions of dollars for corporate expansions and takeovers that often resulted in predatory practices by investors. This caused some companies to spend millions in fighting takeovers, and cost thousands of jobs. In 1987 alone, however, Milken earned $550 million.

Milken's empire tottered in 1988 when the Securities and Exchange Commission filed civil charges against him and Drexel for devising and carrying out "a fraudulent scheme involving insider trading, stock manipulation, fraud . . . failure to disclose beneficial ownership of securities as required, and numerous other violations of securities laws." The following year, a federal grand jury indicted Milken on criminal charges, based in large part on information provided by another investor, IVAN BOESKY, who was then serving a prison term.

"The three-year investigation has uncovered substantial fraud in a very significant segment of the American financial community," said the U.S. attorney. "A serious criminal problem has infected Wall Street." Milken faced 98 felony counts for securities and mail fraud, insider trading, racketeering, and making false statements to the government.

In a settlement, Milken pleaded guilty to six felony counts, paid more than $1 billion in fines, was banned from securities trading for life, and sentenced to 10 years in prison. He served 22 months before receiving parole in 1993. Still wealthy, after his release he remained active in business and in 1997 formed Knowledge Universe to make educational software. He had, however, been diagnosed with cancer and was fighting to contain the disease.

BIBLIOGRAPHY

Bruck, Connie, *The Predators' Ball: The Junk-Bond Raiders and the Man Who Staked Them*, 1988; Labaton, Stephen, "'Junk Bond' Leader Is Indicted by U.S. in Criminal Action," *New York Times*, March 30, 1989; McNatt, Robert, "Mike Milken's Vision Thing," *Business Week*, February 9, 1998; Teicholz, Tom, "Fighting a Hostile Takeover," *New York Times*, June 5, 1994.

Monaghan, Thomas

(March 25, 1937–)
Merchant

Happiness for millions of Americans is a hot pizza, and Thomas S. Monaghan delivered—so well that he made Domino's Pizza a leader among fast-food businesses.

Monaghan experienced considerable hardship as a child. He was born on March 25, 1937, in Ann Arbor, Michigan, but at age four his father died, and because his mother had difficulty raising him and his brother, she sent them to a Roman Catholic orphanage. Monaghan remained there until 1947, when his mother again tried to keep him at home, only to decide she could not make it financially. As a result, she sent him to a work farm in northern Michigan, where he did chores but also earned extra money as a soda jerk.

After graduating from high school, Monaghan joined the Marine Corps. He wanted, however, to be an architect, and returned to Ann Arbor in 1959 and entered the University of Michigan. Finances forced him to quit college, but in 1960 he and his brother James borrowed $900 and purchased a small, struggling pizzeria called DomiNick's. Within a year, Thomas Monaghan bought his brother's share of the business, and in 1965, after the former owner of DomiNick's threatened to sue over the use of his name, Monaghan called the shop Domino's.

Monaghan soon discovered a way to boost sales. He decided to deliver pizzas, to deliver them hot, and to promise delivery within 30 minutes. He fulfilled the hot obligation by installing warming ovens in his delivery vans and by using insulated bags. In fact, over the years Monaghan developed several innovations in the pizza trade, including corrugated pizza boxes.

By 1969, Monaghan had 12 stores, and undertook a plan to open dozens more, but while doing so he ran into problems. For one, the Domino Sugar Company sued him in 1975 for infringement on its name. (This case dragged on until 1980, when the U.S. Supreme Court ruled in Monaghan's favor.) For another, Domino's fell deeply into debt, with some 1,500 creditors. Finally, Monaghan lost control of the company while the creditors filed lawsuits.

Monaghan struggled to right the situation, and when he regained control, he forged ahead by expanding in college and military towns where young people ordered plenty of pizzas. By the early 1980s, he had 750 Domino's stores, and in the mid-1980s about 2,800. More than 1 store per day opened somewhere in the nation, boosted by a policy that enabled managers to become franchisees. At the same time, Monaghan broke ground for a new headquarters in Ann Arbor, Michigan, called Domino's Farms. The 300-acre complex included a Frank Lloyd Wright home, dismantled from elsewhere and brought to the site at the behest of Monaghan, who greatly admired the architect.

About that time, Monaghan wrote his autobiography in which he expressed his philosophy:

> I view money much the same way as P. T. Barnum did: it's important only for the things it can allow you to do.

> Our system is simple. Each step is clearly defined and logical.

> My talent for making pizza was always my ace in the hole in the process of building Domino's.

With his newly earned wealth, Monaghan pursued his lifelong love for baseball by purchasing the Detroit Tigers in 1983. The club won the World Series in 1984, an event that brought Monaghan national attention.

Domino's—which always stressed a simple menu—introduced its first new

Thomas Monaghan (UPI/Corbis-Bettmann)

product, pan pizza, in 1989, the same year it opened its five thousandth store. Buffalo wings followed in 1994, as did the firm's first East European store, in Warsaw, Poland. Domino's had its best year ever in 1997 when gross sales topped $3.1 billion, and in 1998 it planned to open store number 6,000.

BIBLIOGRAPHY

Monaghan, Tom, and Robert Anderson, *Pizza Tiger*, 1986.

Moody, Paul

(May 21, 1779–July 8, 1831)
Engineer, Manufacturer

Paul Moody made a series of significant developments to mill machinery that allowed cotton to be processed into textile more efficiently. These developments were crucial to the expansion of the emerging cotton industry, the backbone of America's industrial revolution.

Moody, the sixth son of Capt. Paul and Mary Moody, was born on May 21, 1779, in Byfield Parish, Newbury, Massachusetts. His father was a commander of a unit in the American Revolution. Moody, who demonstrated mechanical aptitude at a very young age, began working at age 12 in a wool factory in Waltham, Massachusetts.

Soon Moody moved on to a nail-making plant, but shortly thereafter left to do a series of other jobs in quick succession. His goal, with an eye toward a future as a mechanic, was to learn as much as possible about the operation and manufacture of machinery.

On July 18, 1800, Moody was married to Susannah Morrill, with whom he would have three sons. They lived in Amesbury, where Moody entered into a partnership in a cotton mill. With his associate, Ezra Worthen, Moody managed the mill for 14 years. He secured contracts primarily with people eager to support the development of local industry and thus replace the need for importing foreign goods.

In 1814, FRANCIS LOWELL and Moody formed the Boston Manufacturing Company. Located in Waltham, the plant manufactured cotton mills and other machinery. In addition to his management role, Moody was directly involved in the repair and manufacture process. The time was well spent, as he learned enough about the equipment to invent improvements for the machinery.

On March 9, 1816, Moody was awarded a patent for his invention of a device that wound yarn from bobbins or spools. Two years later, he secured another patent for improving the operation and efficiency of the Horrocks' dressing machine. In 1819, he secured a patent for his improvements to the "double-speeder" used for roping cotton. Finally, in 1819, two patents were issued for Moody's inventions for making cotton roping and for roping and spinning cotton. All of these devices were significant contributions to elevating the system of cotton manufacture to its highest efficiency.

In 1823, Moody moved to the mill town of Lowell, Massachusetts, to obtain work as the superintendent of a cotton-mill factory. In 1825, Moody became the manager of the Lowell Machine Works, where he continued his work to improve the design and performance of cotton machinery. Soon the Machine Works was turning out every type of equipment needed for cotton-mill operation. It gained national acclaim and business, as well as a reputation for quality workmanship.

Moody was active in community welfare and education. He was also an advocate of the temperance movement. His main interest, however, was inventing. Moody died suddenly at the age of 52 on July 8, 1831, after a three-day illness.

BIBLIOGRAPHY

Appleton, Nathan, *Introduction of the Power Loom, and Origin of Lowell*, 1858; Coburn, F. W., *History of Lowell and Its People*, 1920; Moody, C. C. P., *Biographical Sketches of the Moody Family*, 1847; Van Slyck, J. D., *Representatives of New England Manufacturers*, 1879; *Vital Records of Amesbury, Mass.*, 1913; *Vital Records of Newbury, Mass.*, 1911.

Moore, Gordon

(January 3, 1929–)
Manufacturer

Often referred to as the "accidental entrepreneur," Gordon Moore helped invent the silicon chips that made personal computers possible. He founded Fairchild Semiconductor, and then the multibillion-dollar corporation, Intel.

Born on January 3, 1929, in Pescadero, California, Moore received a B.S. degree in chemistry from the University of California, Berkeley, in 1950, and a Ph.D. in chemistry from the California Institute of Technology in 1954. He then worked in the Applied Physics Lab at Johns Hopkins University in Baltimore, Maryland, but tired of research that, he later said, "had no practical application" and longed to return to California.

In 1956, he accepted an offer from William Shockley, the coinventor of the transistor, to become a research chemist at Shockley Semiconductor. He and several other engineers, however, soon had a falling out with Shockley. In the summer of 1957, Moore, ROBERT NOYCE, and six colleagues obtained financial backing from the Fairchild Camera and Instrument Company of New York and founded Fairchild Semiconductor. Noyce headed the new company in California's emerging Silicon Valley, south of San Francisco.

Working from a two-story warehouse built on concrete slabs, they produced semiconductors at just the right time, for in 1957 the Soviet Union launched the first space satellite, *Sputnik I*, and the demand for computer technology in the United States boomed. In 1958, International Business Machines (IBM) ordered 100 mesa silicon transistors from Fairchild, setting the company on its way. The following year, Intel obtained a contract to provide the transistors for America's Minute Man I missile program.

Noyce and Moore dominated the company, with Noyce the visionary and Moore the reserved engineer. In 1959, the visionary invented an integrated circuit, the same year Jack St. Clair Kilby invented one at Texas Instruments. Integrated circuits combined several electronic components onto a single silicon chip, rather than devoting a separate chip to each function. The invention was extremely important, because integrated circuits filled with transistors launched the computer revolution by making it possible to manufacture much smaller computers.

In 1965, Moore formulated Moore's Law, in which he said that the power and complexity of the silicon chip would double every 18 months, with proportionate decreases in cost. He proved right—in 1995, a four-megabit chip was 4 million times more powerful that its predecessor, the transistor.

Noyce and Moore built Fairchild into a $150 million business, but in the mid-1960s sales flattened, and the two engineers disagreed with the ever-larger Fairchild bureaucracy. As a result, Noyce, Moore, and ANDREW GROVE, a development expert, left Fairchild in 1968, and with the backing of venture capitalist Arthur Rock founded Intel. Noyce served as CEO and Moore as executive vice president. In 1969, Intel produced its first product, a bipolar memory chip, and two years later the firm showed a profit.

That year, they marketed their 1103 memory chip; smaller than a fingertip, it contained 4,000 transistors and became the industry standard for computers. In 1971, Noyce and Moore introduced their revolutionary microprocessor, basically a small computer on a collection of four chips programmed to work in calculators. Between 1971 and 1973, the microprocessor tripled the value of Intel stock. In 1972, Intel's sales reached $23.4 million, and the number of employees exceeded 1,000. A year later, sales topped $66 million.

Increased competition and a bad decision to market a digital watch hurt Intel's profits in the mid-1970s, but by 1979 the company's revenues reached $650 million and the number of employees 14,000. After that year, Noyce played a smaller role in the company, while Moore's role expanded as did that of Grove, who in 1979 took over as president. (Noyce died in 1990 from a heart attack.) In 1983, Moore engineered IBM's payment of $250 million for a 12 percent

interest in Intel. Moore said: "The idea came along at a time when we were going to have to raise a significant amount of money, and we were careful to assure ourselves that IBM has no intention of interfering with our independence."

Another challenge appeared in the mid-1980s, however, when Japanese companies introduced their computer chips into the American market, causing Intel to lose money in 1986 and lay off 2,000 workers. That year, Intel decided to stop making memory chips and instead concentrate on microprocessors. Moore announced that Intel had developed a new microprocessor that had the power of a medium-sized computer. "The one thing I've learned over the years in this business," said Moore, "is that you never get well on the old products. You've got to keep your development work going full bore even through recessions."

Moore retired from the post of CEO in 1987, turning that position over to Grove. He was named chairman emeritus in 1997. That year, Intel released its Pentium II microprocessor, which was packed with 7.5 million transistors.

Moore, who was married and the father of two children, always insisted he was the reluctant entrepreneur, never intending to head a company, let alone build a large corporation. Events, he said, simply propelled him in that direction.

BIBLIOGRAPHY

Hanson, Dirk, *The New Alchemists*, 1982; Kaye, Glynnis Thompson, ed., *A Revolution in Progress: A History of Intel to Date*, 1984; "Let's Make a Deal," *Fortune*, June 24, 1983; Reid, T. T., *The Chip: How Two Americans Invented the Microchip and Launched a Revolution*, 1984.

Moore, William

(October 25, 1848–January 11, 1923)
Financier

William Henry Moore and his brother James formed one of the most aggressive venture capital teams at the beginning of the era of corporate consolidations and mergers. Moore realized that the success of a merger lay in its monopolistic control by a small group of investors, reorganization of production and marketing to take advantage of economies of scale, and legal shelters to avoid antitrust prosecution. After losing a huge stock market gamble in his first corporate endeavor with the Diamond Match Company, Moore began corporate consolidations on a grand scale, organizing conglomerates in the biscuit, steel, and railroad industries.

William was born in Utica, New York, on October 25, 1848, to Nathaniel and Rachel Beckwith Moore. His father was a banker, and his mother was the daughter of a banker, so it seemed that William was destined for a career in finance. He first attended a seminary school at Oneida, New York, and then went on to Cortland Academy in Homer, New York. He enrolled at Amherst College in 1867 but left without graduating three years later because of a persistent illness.

After being admitted to the bar, he moved to Chicago and joined the law firm of Edward A. Small, an attorney specializing in corporate law. William worked for a year and a half as a managing clerk before becoming a partner in the firm. In 1878, he married Small's daughter, Ada W. Small. She eventually bore him three sons—Hobart, Paul, and Edward, all of whom would eventually join their father's financial empire.

William invited his brother James Herbert Moore to join with him in taking control of the law firm after Edward Small's death in 1882. The pair made the firm one of the most prominent in Chicago, serving clients such as American Express, Vanderbilt Fast Freight Lines, and other large corporations. James handled most of the paperwork and research while William performed duties as a trial lawyer and established his reputation for the skillful application of corporate law. Around 1887, the brothers began to turn their attention away from their legal practice and toward the field of corporate organization and promotion. They were among the first to recognize the potential for merging smaller, competing corporations into conglomerates.

The first corporate venture undertaken by William was the reorganization of the Diamond Match Company, which was comprised of the four leading match manufacturers. The company dominated the domestic market, but in the late 1880s Moore was called upon to increase the firm's capitalization for expansion into the international market.

One year later, William helped organize the New York Biscuit Company, which was composed of seven leading cracker manufacturers. At a time when the nation's stock market lacked sufficient regulation, William saw great opportunities beyond the fees paid to him for organizing and promoting the companies. The Moore brothers formed an investing pool with other Chicago financiers to artificially inflate the prices of Diamond Match Company and the New

York Biscuit Company by gradually buying large amounts of each stock with the hopes of then unloading it all on an unsuspecting public at the peak price. Each stock's price nearly doubled in the first four months of 1896, but the scheme started to unravel when members of the pool began selling out early. The Moore brothers tried desperately to cover their margins as the price began falling, but they were unable to do so when the officials of the Chicago Exchange closed the market for three months to prevent further wild selling. William lost about $4 million in the process.

As a result of this disaster, William was forced out of the Diamond Match Company and turned to his interest in the New York Biscuit Company in order to restore his damaged career. He launched a price war against the company's major remaining competitor, the American Biscuit Company. The pressure left American Biscuit with little choice but to accept a merger agreement, and in 1898 the National Biscuit Company was born and William's reputation was restored.

William was subsequently inundated with requests to organize other large corporations throughout the country. In rapid succession, he organized the American Tin Plate Company, the National Steel Company, and the American Steel and Hoop Company. With William's promotion, the stock issues for each company were eagerly purchased.

The companies that William had established in the steel industry were primarily makers of finished steel products and relied heavily on their main supplier, Carnegie Steel, for providing semifinished steel. Fearful that competition from the Federal Steel Company, owned by J. P. MORGAN SR., would drive Carnegie Steel to start making its own line of finished steel products, William assembled a group of investors in an attempt to buy out Carnegie Steel. The deal ultimately fell through because of ANDREW CARNEGIE'S personal dislike for William and William's inability to secure enough financial backing from banks to finance what they considered a reckless idea. Carnegie did begin manufacturing his own finished steel products, but both Carnegie and the Moore brothers were bought out by J. P. Morgan's new United States Steel Company in late 1900.

In that same year, the Moore brothers turned their interest to railroads and began a nine-month campaign of buying stock in the Rock Island and Pacific Railroad. By 1901, William had forced his way into control and enacted an elaborate plan of expansion for the railroad to compete with other rail lines. The expansion was successful, and William announced a deceptive reorganization of the company in which three new companies would be created in a double-holding arrangement. With this dangerous scheme to raise capital in place, he began acquiring additional railroads over the next few years. In time, the companies began to fail one by one, and William was charged with reckless business practices and was issued a stern warning by the Interstate Commerce Commission in 1916. One year later, William was ousted from the Rock Island Railroad and retired from his business career altogether. He died six years later on January 11, 1923.

BIBLIOGRAPHY

Dewing, Arthur S., *Corporate Promotions and Reorganizations*, 1914; Josephson, Matthew, *The Robber Barons*, 1934; Manchester, Herbert, *The Diamond Match Company*, 1935.

Morgan, J. P., Jr.

(September 7, 1867–March 13, 1943)
Banker

Son of a wealthy financier, John Pierpont Morgan Jr. continued his family's prominence in investment and arranged loans that were important to Britain and France during World War I.

Morgan, usually referred to by his family as "Jack" to differentiate him from his father, was born to J. P. MORGAN SR. and Frances Louisa (Tracy) Morgan on September 7, 1867, in Irvington, New York. He grew up, however, in New York City, where he lived in exclusive town houses. The elder Morgan had founded J. P. Morgan & Company, a banking firm, and made a fortune trading stocks and bonds.

Jack graduated from St. Paul's School in Concord, New Hampshire, and continued his education at Harvard, from which he received a bachelor's degree in 1889. The following year, he married Jane Norton Grew of Boston. The couple subsequently had four children.

In 1892, Jack joined his father's bank as a partner, and from 1893 to 1901 he worked in the company's London office. When World War I began, the elder Morgan—an Anglophile who once entertained the archbishop of Canterbury on his yacht—arranged for J. P. Morgan & Company to serve as the purchasing agent in the United States for Britain and France. The bank obtained orders for war supplies exceeding $3 billion, for which it received commissions. Without compensation, however, Morgan arranged a syndicate of banks that provided Britain and France with war loans. Critics later said these loans gave the United States a financial stake in an Allied victory and thus pulled the nation into the war.

During the booming 1920s, when, after his father's death in 1913, Jack headed J. P. Morgan & Company as senior partner, the firm sold billions of dollars in stocks and bonds for American companies. In 1933, a Senate investigation into banking irregularities cleared Jack of any wrongdoing but found that he had used legal loopholes in 1931 and 1932 to avoid paying any income taxes.

Jack donated considerable sums to the Episcopal Church and the Red Cross, and endowed the Morgan Library in New York. He died on March 13, 1943, while on a vacation in Boca Grande, Florida.

BIBLIOGRAPHY
Forbes, John Douglas, *J. P. Morgan, Jr., 1867–1943*, 1981.

J. P. Morgan Jr. (Library of Congress)

Morgan, J. P., Sr.

(April 17, 1837–March 31, 1913)
Banker

As the United States industrialized during the late nineteenth century, the rise of big corporations brought about economic consolidation. No other person did more to finance these developments than John Pierpont Morgan, who attracted the domestic and foreign money needed to make it happen.

J. P. Morgan obtained his financial training from his father, a prominent international banker. He was born on April 17, 1837, in Hartford, Connecticut, to Junius Spencer Morgan and Juliet (Pierpont) Morgan. At age 14, J. P. moved with his family to Boston and entered English High, a prestigious school. After graduating in 1854, he went to Germany, where he studied math for two years at the University of Göttingen. In 1856, he began working for his father, who had moved to London to accept a partnership in the banking house of George Peabody & Company.

The following year, J. P. relocated to New York City where he worked for several firms and represented his father's business. In 1861, he married Amelia Sturges, but she died the next year. He then married Frances Louisa Tracy, the daughter of a prominent New York lawyer, in 1865. They would have four children, including J. P. MORGAN JR., who later continued his father's banking house.

Morgan joined financier ANTHONY DREXEL in 1871 to form Drexel, Morgan & Company and gained public notice when, in 1879, he sold a large amount of stock in CORNELIUS VANDERBILT's New York Central Railroad to English investors. He went on to arrange financial deals that consolidated several railroads at a time when the entire process of industrialization relied on them for transportation. Morgan strove to promote wise investment and temper the injurious speculation then rampant among the railroads.

At the same time, his tactics increased his power. He often used voting trusts, whereby the voting power of stock was placed in the hands of trustees selected by him, and held numerous directorships. As a result, he had more influence over the nation's railroads than any other man. In 1895, soon after Anthony Drexel's death, Morgan's firm changed its name to J. P. Morgan & Company. Morgan stirred enormous controversy when, during a financial panic in 1895, he helped the national government by forming a syndicate that acquired gold for the treasury in exchange for federal bonds. When he and his fellow bankers resold the bonds to the public, they made excessive profits.

Morgan's greatest attention, and perhaps his greatest achievement, came when he formed United States Steel. In 1901, competition among several financially shaky steel companies threatened to hurt the industry. At the same time, ANDREW CARNEGIE wanted to sell his mammoth Carnegie Steel. Morgan stepped in and bought out the companies, combining them into United States Steel, the world's largest corporation.

In 1912, the Pujo Committee of the U.S. House of Representatives investigated Morgan. The committee uncovered no illegalities, but its hearings revealed the extensive "Money Trust" that dominated

J. P. Morgan Sr. (Library of Congress)

Whatever the criticisms, Morgan had been crucial in attracting and organizing the foreign financing that spurred America's emergence as an industrial power. Through his British contacts, he obtained money from England and other European countries. He instilled confidence in foreign and domestic investors alike with his determination, acumen, and straight talk.

Morgan disliked social reform and condemned President Theodore Roosevelt's antitrust measures, but he gave considerably to churches, hospitals, and art museums. When he died on March 31, 1913, a few months after his appearance before the Pujo Committee, he had an estate valued at over $100 million. The Metropolitan Museum of Art in New York City received a large part of his art collection, which was valued at some $50 million. In 1924, Morgan's extensive private library was made public and named the Pierpont Morgan Library.

the nation. Morgan and his 11 partners held 72 directorships in 47 large corporations. J. P. Morgan & Company had investments and interests in U. S. Steel, International Harvester, American Telephone & Telegraph, and International Mercantile Marine, among others. Morgan and other investment bankers directed banks, trusts, and life insurance companies—the power of the new American economy was founded on bigness.

BIBLIOGRAPHY

Chernow, Ron, *The Death of the Banker: The Decline and the Fall of the Great Financial Dynasties and the Triumph of the Small Investor,* 1997; Chernow, Ron, *The House of Morgan,* 1990; Corey, Lewis, *The House of Morgan,* 1930; Hoyt, Palmer Edwin, *The House of Morgan,* 1966; Jackson, Stanley, *J. P. Morgan: A Biography,* 1983; Wheeler, George, *Pierpont Morgan and Friends: The Anatomy of a Myth,* 1973.

Morris, Edward

(October 1, 1866–November 3, 1913)
Packer

After assuming control of the well-known packinghouse started by his father, Edward Morris continued its rapid expansion to make himself one of the major business leaders in his hometown of Chicago. He acquired large stock holdings and sat as a director on the boards of several banks and other companies. He was also a member of numerous trade clubs and the Chicago Board of Trade. At the end of his career, Morris became a generous supporter of various charities.

On October 1, 1866, Edward was born in Chicago, Illinois, the son of Nelson and Sarah Vogel Morris. Edward's father had emigrated from Hechingen, Prussia, and had founded the prestigious packinghouse of Morris and Company in Chicago. During the late 1800s and early 1900s, Chicago had become the national center for packinghouses, plants that processed and canned meats or fruits and vegetables for future sale and distribution. The business prospered while Edward was attending the Chicago public schools, and at age 16 he joined his father in the company.

Soon afterward, Edward began to assume many of his father's duties in the business as a result of his father's failing health. On October 1, 1890, Morris married Helen Swift, a writer who was the daughter of GUSTAVUS SWIFT, the colorful founder of the influential Swift & Company meat packinghouse. Their union produced four children—two boys and two girls.

After the death of his father, Morris assumed total control of the company by buying up a large portion of the shares held by his brother and two sisters. Morris carried out the wishes of his father by continuing the rapid expansion of the packing company. During the first decade of the twentieth century, the firm's development was remarkable under Morris's leadership. In appreciation of his employees' hard work in building up the company, Morris established a generous pension plan in 1909 for employees and their families. At a time when labor's demands were largely unmet, this pension plan was progressive and unusual.

Having accumulated much wealth in the packing industry, which included real estate in Mexico, Morris began investing his fortune in the stocks of several large banks. He acquired substantial holdings in and was a director of the First National Bank, Live Stock National Exchange Bank, Savings Bank of Chicago, Mid-City Trust Company, Security Bank, West Side Trust Company, and Rothschild and Company. He was elected president of the Fairbanks Canning Company and the St. Louis National Stock Yards Company and a director of the National Packing Company. He was also a member of numerous trade clubs as well as the Chicago Board of Trade.

As a philanthropist later in his career, Morris gave more than $250,000 to diverse charities. In 1905, he purchased the home of the ancestors of John Harvard at Stratford-on-Avon and donated it to Harvard University. In his spare time, Morris became a collector of fine art and was a world traveler. He died in Chicago on November 3, 1913.

BIBLIOGRAPHY

Barrett, James, *Work and Community in the Jungle: Chicago's Packinghouse Workers,* *1894–1922,* 1990; *National Cyclopedia of American Biography,* 1922; Neyhart, Louise, *Giant of the Yards,* 1952.

Morris, Robert

(January 31, 1734–May 8, 1806)
Merchant, Financier

To look at the destitute, spiritually broken Robert Morris in his last years would have given no indication of what he had once been: a wealthy and powerful man who funded the American Revolution and helped to make its success possible.

Robert Morris, born on January 31, 1734, in Liverpool, England, immigrated to America with his family about 1747 and settled in Maryland. While his father, also named Robert Morris, handled tobacco exports, young Robert attended school in Philadelphia, but only briefly. He soon began work in that city's prominent merchant house owned by Thomas Willing, and by 1754 had risen to a partnership in the firm, renamed Willing, Morris & Company. He remained with the business for 39 years.

In that age, merchants did more than import and export goods. They owned ships and, importantly, engaged in banking, handling notes of exchange and currency. Successful merchants often wielded considerable power in their communities by engaging themselves in politics. Morris entered politics at a time when crisis gripped America in its relationship with Britain.

With his wealth and financial expertise, Morris assumed a leadership position early in the Revolution, although he moved cautiously. When the colonists protested Parliament's passage of the Stamp Act in 1765, he signed the nonimportation agreement, pledging to boycott British goods, and served on a committee appointed to force the stamp tax official at Philadelphia from his job and thus prevent collection of the levy.

After the first revolutionary shots were fired at Lexington and Concord in 1775, the Pennsylvania Assembly appointed Morris to its Council of Safety, and he immediately put to use his merchant background, procuring supplies and acting as a banker. Beginning in November, he was appointed to several secret committees charged with acquiring munitions for the army and navy.

An energetic and outgoing man, known for his elaborate social gatherings, and considered by most people to be essentially honest, Morris had no qualms about mixing his political and business interests. While Morris helped the emerging American government out of a sense of patriotic duty, he intended to make a profit, too. Thus, he handled business for the government through his merchant house and received handsome commissions. Whatever Morris's personal gains, with the prestige of his signature he obtained much-needed funds and supplies for the Revolution.

Despite his early revolutionary activity, as a delegate to the Second Continental Congress in 1776 Morris voted against the Declaration of Independence, calling it premature. He signed it, however, and continued his work to secure money and supplies. Ineligible for reelection to Congress under the Pennsylvania constitution, Morris won election in November 1778 to the state assembly.

Morris had his critics, among them the revolutionary propagandist Thomas Paine, who attacked him for conflict of interest in handling government affairs while maintaining his connection to Willing & Morris. Committees appointed to investigate Morris found no wrongdoing, but the public thought otherwise, and in November 1779 he lost his bid for reelection to the assembly. He ran again, however, the following year and won.

Meanwhile, financial chaos enveloped the American government—the states were failing to provide moneys to Congress, the paper currency was nearly worthless, and additional loans from Europe appeared remote at best. Congress turned to Morris for help, and in February 1781 appointed him superintendent of finance. In that capacity, he insisted on funding the outstanding debt so creditors would have faith in the government's ability to pay them their interest.

Morris abolished waste in several government departments and used notes backed by his signature to obtain loans. He arranged financing that helped George Washington to defeat the British at Yorktown. In 1782, he also secured a $200,000 loan from France that enabled him to form the Bank of North America, the first national bank intended to attract investments and stabilize the currency.

Robert Morris (Library of Congress)

Yet in the end, the government under the Articles of Confederation defied Morris's best efforts, and in 1783 he resigned. Morris subsequently won reelection to the state assembly, and served as a delegate to the Annapolis Convention that led to the meeting of the Constitutional Convention, at which he also served as a delegate, albeit one who participated little in its debates. At the same time, he pursued his commercial business and secured a contract with France that gave him a monopoly of the tobacco trade between that country and the United States.

Morris declined President Washington's offer to appoint him secretary of the treasury, and instead, in 1789, won election to the U. S. Senate, where he served until 1795. Before leaving the Senate, his finances unraveled, as a result of unsound business practices. Morris speculated in land, buying vast tracts in western

New York and elsewhere, and acquiring tax bills and loans he could not pay.

As his fortune dwindled, Morris retired to his country estate, but in 1798 a creditor had him arrested. Morris was thrown into debtor's prison in Philadelphia and confined there for three and a half years. Released in August 1801, he lived his remaining days in poor health in a small house in Philadelphia, forgotten by most people. He died on May 8, 1806.

BIBLIOGRAPHY

Morris, Robert, *The Paper of Robert Morris, 1781–1784*, 1973; Ver Steeg, Clarence, *Robert Morris: Revolutionary Financier*, 1972; Young, Eleanor May, *Forgotten Patriot: Robert Morris*, 1950.

Morton, Joy

(September 27, 1855–1934)
Manufacturer

From an advertising campaign begun during World War I, Americans got to know the little girl with her umbrella and the slogan "When It Rains It Pours." Together they were used to promote Morton Salt, a small business transformed into a major corporation by Joy Morton.

Joy was born on September 27, 1855, in Detroit, Michigan, one of three sons born to Julius Sterling Morton and Caroline (Joy) Morton. He grew up in Nebraska City, Nebraska, where his father worked as a newspaperman and a Democratic Party leader. At age 16, Joy Morton joined the Merchant National Bank in Nebraska City and by 1876 served as one of its directors.

The railroad industry, then propelling America's economic modernization, attracted Morton, and in 1877 he began working as a clerk in the treasurer's office of the Burlington and Missouri in Omaha. Two years later, he moved to Aurora, Illinois, and worked as supply agent for the Chicago, Burlington, and Quincy.

Morton entered the salt industry when he joined E. I. Wheeler & Company, a salt firm that had been founded in 1848 as an agent for lumber businesses that made the commodity as a by-product. When Wheeler died in 1885, Morton reorganized the business as Joy Morton & Company. In an era of consolidation, he joined his business with others in 1902 to form the International Salt Company. In 1910, he and his brother Mark Morton bought some of International Salt's properties to form the Morton Salt Company, with Joy as president.

Joy oversaw factories in Kansas and Michigan as well as salt mines in those states and elsewhere. The company obtained salt by two methods. In one, it pumped brine from wells into vats, where the salt settled to the bottom before being separated from the water. In another, it mined rock salt in huge underground operations.

Morton began adding an anticaking agent to its salt in 1911, allowing it to flow freely even in humid weather. From this feature came the "When It Rains It Pours" campaign, introduced in 1914 and adopted from an old proverb, "It never rains but it pours." The advertisements, which first appeared in *Good Housekeeping* magazine, made Morton Salt a household favorite.

By 1927, Morton Salt produced 600,000 tons of evaporated salt per year, and distributed 400,000 tons of rock salt. The company owned large storage houses on the waterfronts in Chicago, Illinois, and in two Wisconsin cities, Milwaukee and Superior. At each dock it operated cooperage shops where workers made wooden barrels that held the salt.

Beginning in 1931, Morton Salt extracted from the brine and sold such inorganic chemicals as ammonium, potassium, sodium bromides, and magnesium. Meanwhile, Joy Morton held directorates in several companies, including the Chicago & Alton Railroad, Western Cold Storage, American Hominy Company, Equitable Life Assurance Society of New York, and Continental and Commercial National Bank, the largest financial institution in Chicago.

Morton, who had married Carrie Lake in 1880 and, following her death, Margaret Gray in 1917, died in 1934 and was survived by his second wife and two children by his first wife.

BIBLIOGRAPHY

Olson, James C., *J. Sterling Morton*, 1942.

Mott, Charles

(June 2, 1875–February 18, 1973)
Manufacturer

Charles Stewart Mott once ranked among the 10 richest people in America, a fortune he amassed by linking his family business to a new invention, the automobile.

Born on June 2, 1875, in Newark, New Jersey, to John Coan Mott and Isabell Turnbell (Stewart) Mott, Charles moved with his family to New York City in 1880. There the elder Mott managed the family's Mott Cider and Vinegar business. In 1892, Charles graduated from Stevens High School in Hoboken, New Jersey, and entered the Stevens Institute of Technology. After two years at college, he traveled to Europe, where he studied fermentation. He then returned to Stevens, receiving his degree in mechanical engineering in 1897.

Although Mott considered operating the family's cider business, after serving in the U.S. Navy during the Spanish-American War, he decided to join another family enterprise, the Weston-Mott Company, based in Utica, New York, which manufactured bicycle wheels. He eventually sold the Mott Cider and Vinegar business, although the Mott name remained on its products.

After becoming president of Weston-Mott in 1903, Mott tied the firm's fortunes to the emerging automobile industry when he began making car axles and wheels. Two years later, WILLIAM DURANT, head of the Buick Motor Company, convinced Mott to move the Weston-Mott Company to Flint, Michigan, where automobile production was under way. Mott did so, and by 1908 his annual sales exceeded $2 million.

In 1909, the General Motors Corporation (GM) bought 49 percent of Weston-Mott and sales increased again. Four years later, Mott exchanged his shares in Weston-Mott for stock in GM, the deal that eventually made him one of the 10 richest people in America, with a fortune exceeding $500 million. Mott served as a director at GM from 1913 to 1916, and as a vice president from 1916 to 1937, but he exerted little power in the corporation's management.

By that time, he was more interested in politics, having won election in 1912 as mayor of Flint, where he opposed attempts to implement socialist policies.

He won reelection in 1913, lost the following year in trying for a third term, but returned to office in 1918. Later that year, he entered the military and served during World War I as chief of production of the motors branch in the U.S. Army Quartermaster Corps. He ran for governor of Michigan in 1920 as a Republican but lost.

Mott established the Mott Foundation in 1926 to help develop community projects in Flint, and by the 1970s it had provided millions of dollars to the city's schools. In the 1950s, he donated land to start a community college and a branch of the University of Michigan. Mott died on February 18, 1973, survived by his fourth wife, Ruth Mott Rawlings, and six children.

BIBLIOGRAPHY

Gustin, Lawrence R., *Billy Durant: Creator of General Motors*, 1973.

N

Nash, Charles

(January 28, 1864–June 6, 1948)
Manufacturer

Charles Williams Nash was a leader in the early automobile industry. With his organizational skill and business acumen, he shepherded the Buick Motor Company out of difficult times, restored the success of General Motors, and positioned his own business, the Nash Motors Company, as one of the primary independent automobile producers.

Charles, the only son of David L. and Anna Caldwell Nash, was born on January 28, 1864, in De Kalb County, Illinois. The separation of his parents in 1870 compelled Charles to take on work for a farmer in Genesee City, Michigan. Unable to stand the situation, Charles ran away at the age of 12, obtaining work as a laborer on a farm. After some time, he became the operator of a steam hay press. Charles married Jessie Halleck, the daughter of a farmer, on April 23, 1884. The couple had three children—Mae, Lena, and Ruth.

In 1891, the illness of Nash's wife caused him to move to Flint, Michigan, to have access to greater medical facilities as well as to gain access to higher-paying jobs. In Flint, he found work as an upholstery trimmer for the Durant-Dort Carriage Company. Soon Nash began to realize his innate managerial skills. He quickly rose through the ranks of the company, becoming plant superintendent within a few years.

In 1904, Dort's partner, WILLIAM DURANT, left the company to head up the Buick Motor Car Company. Nash was selected by Dort to replace Durant as general manager. During his six years in this role,

Charles Nash (Baldwin H. Ward/Corbis-Bettmann)

Nash streamlined the carriage-making process, increasing plant efficiency by adopting the straight-line belt conveyor in the assembly procedure.

Nash continued to find his fortunes tied to those of William Durant. By 1908, Durant had founded the General Motors Company, but was still acting as president of Buick. In addition to stretching himself thin managing the organization of the two companies, Durant realized that both companies were becoming strapped financially. The economic trouble also affected the Durant-Dort Carriage Company, as it was, by this time, one of the principal builders of the automobile bodies used by Buick. Nash, sensing an opportunity that would benefit all concerned, offered to take over the management of the Buick Motor Car Company.

Nash was immediately successful in putting Buick's affairs in order. After two years, Durant stepped down as head of the General Motors Company, and Nash succeeded him as president. Nash's tenure at General Motors sparked mixed reactions. On the one hand, it was widely acknowledged that Nash was instrumental in restoring financial stability and introducing organizational methods to keep the company on track. But one of his policies did not sit well with stockholders: he felt that the goal of stability would be best served by lowering expenditures and withholding the dividends that had been paid out to stockholders.

Largely as a result of stockholder sentiment, Durant successfully regained the presidency of General Motors in 1916. At this juncture, Nash decided he was ready to strike out for himself. He purchased the Thomas B. Jeffrey Company, the maker of the popular Rambler automobile, and renamed it the Nash Motors Company. Nash took a hiatus from direct management of the Nash Motors Company during War World I, when patriotism compelled him to do his part in the war effort by running the military's aircraft production program.

The 1920s were an intensely competitive time in the automobile industry. Nash, who harbored no aspirations to compete in the same mass market of the "Big Three" automakers (General Motors, Ford, and Chrysler), emerged by 1929 as a very profitable independent manufacturer. Nash's preference was to focus on creating a well-built car in the upper-medium price range. Eventually, however, he recognized that the Nash Motors Company would need to diversify its product line. After purchasing the Lafayette Motor Company, he attempted to manufacture a luxury automobile. The venture was not a success, but Nash's next attempt at diversification, the production of the medium-priced Ajax, yielded greater results.

Nash's management style was generally cautious, and while he passed up some opportunities with great promise, he also built up a record of steady growth that enabled his company to survive the Great Depression.

In 1932, Nash stepped down as president of the company and assumed the role of chairman of the board. During this time, he facilitated the merger of the Nash Motors Company with the Kelvinator Company, an appliance manufacturer.

Nash conducted his personal finances with the same caution evidenced in his business transactions. His childhood poverty had a lasting effect on his life. His need for security was evident in that while he eventually amassed a fortune of over $43 million, he kept the majority of it tied up in bonds.

In addition to his financial dealings, Nash was an active participant in civic activities in Kenosha. After his retirement, Nash and his wife moved to Beverly Hills, California. On June 6, 1948, a year after his wife had passed away, Nash died of a heart ailment.

BIBLIOGRAPHY

Dictionary of American Biography, supplement IV, 1974; Lewis, Eugene W., *Motor Memories*, 1947; *New York Times*, Obituary, June 7, 1948; Rae, John B., *Automobile Manufacturers: The First Forty Years*, 1959; *Time*, June 14, 1948.

Nast, Condé

(March 26, 1873–September 19, 1942)
Publisher

Guests glided across the parquet-floored ballroom at the parties of Condé Montrose Nast. They displayed the style their host had advocated through his magazines geared to elite attitudes, and payed tribute to the "class concept" in publications that he had pioneered.

Condé Nast was born on March 26, 1873, in New York City to William Frederick Nast and Esther Ariadne (Benoist) Nast. Although his father failed at several investments, due to his mother's wealth Nast grew up in comfortable surroundings in St. Louis, Missouri. He received a B.A. degree from Georgetown University in Washington, D.C., in 1894, and an M.A. degree the following year. Nast received a degree in 1897 from the St. Louis Law School at Washington University.

In 1898, he pursued a different career from law when a friend who was editor of *Collier's Weekly* convinced him to join the struggling magazine as its advertising manager. Nast worked a miracle. In less than a decade he boosted advertising revenue from $5,500 per year to over $1 million. At the same time, circulation jumped from about 19,000 to over 568,000. Under Nast's guidance, *Collier's* changed from a dull publication to a pioneering venture in color pages, double-page spreads, and special issues.

While working at *Collier's*, Nast served as vice president of the Home Pattern Company that distributed women's dress patterns. In this position he learned how to shape publications to women's tastes. In 1909, two years after leaving *Collier's*, Nast bought a 17-year-old magazine, *Vogue*.

With the help of staff member Edna Woolman Chase, whom he made editor in 1914, *Vogue* emerged as a prestigious women's fashion publication that freed its readers from their Victorian corsets. Although other women's magazines existed, *Vogue's* appeal to wealthy women—and to those who wanted to be or feel wealthy—established a new "class concept" niche.

A driven perfectionist, Nast wanted to create beautiful magazines steeped in art and style. He insisted on the best-quality paper and printing, and according to one biographer "his publications proved that a connection between fashion and art was not only plausible but also promotable."

Soon after acquiring *Vogue*, Nast bought Dress and *Vanity Fair* and appointed Frank Crowninshield its editor. Crowninshield shortened the magazine's name to *Vanity Fair*, and, under Nast's direction, targeted high society as its audience with entertainment and literary topics.

Over the next few years, Nast expanded his holdings. He established the Vogue Pattern Company in 1914, and in 1915 became sole owner of *House and Garden* magazine. The following year, he founded a *Vogue* edition in Britain, and in 1917 one in France. In 1921, he began another magazine in France, *Jardin des Modes*, and bought a printing plant in Connecticut that he developed into Condé Nast Press. Nast consolidated his holdings in 1922 as Condé Nast Publications, Incorporated.

By 1928, *Vogue's* circulation climbed to over 138,000 from its initial 16,853 subscribers, and Nast's income allowed him to invest heavily in the stock market. In 1929, however, the Great Depression shattered Nast's empire. As his company's revenue plummeted and his stock investments soured, he went heavily into debt. Salvation came only when Lord Camrose, chair of Allied Newspapers and Amalgamated Press Ltd. in England, bought into Condé Nast Publications.

Lord Camrose left Nast in charge of the company, and the shaken entrepreneur worked relentlessly to recover. In 1936, Nast merged *Vanity Fair*, a money loser, into *Vogue*, and in 1939 he bought another magazine, *Glamour*.

To many Nast seemed less confident and more tentative than he had been before the Great Depression. He retained his taste for the elaborate parties he had begun in 1925, however, and these would continue until his death. Nast's 30-room penthouse at 1040 Park Avenue had 10 rooms for entertaining on the second floor and a suite of rooms on the floor below. Chinese eighteenth-century wallpaper bedecked Nast's ballroom, and the windows were covered by salmon pink draperies edged in blue-green fringe and undercurtains made from silver gauze. Every notable appeared at his twice-monthly soirées including politicians, actors, writers, artists, and models. Author F. Scott Fitzgerald claimed, "The parties of Condé Nast rivaled in their way the fabled balls of the Nineties." The shy Nast seldom drank, and usually remained in the background.

Despite (or perhaps because of) such ostentation, Nast had severe financial problems. At his death on September 19, 1942, he owned stock worth millions, but his debts exceeded $5 million. His magazines continued, however, and today Condé Nast Publications, based in England, publishes, among others, *Vogue*, *GQ*, and *Traveller*. Looking back on his life, Nast once said: "Think of it. Here I was just a boy from St. Louis, and Edna Chase a Quaker from New Jersey. Between us we set the standards of the time. We showed America the meaning of style."

BIBLIOGRAPHY
Seebohm, Caroline, *The Man Who Was* Vogue: *The Life and Times of Condé Nast*, 1982.

Neuharth, Al

(March 24, 1924–)
Newspaper Owner

Allen Harold Neuharth's life reads like a Horatio Alger story. He rose from newsboy to operator of Gannett, one of the nation's most important newspaper and communications businesses.

Allen Neuharth was born on March 24, 1924, in Eureka, South Dakota, to Daniel J. Neuharth, a farmer, and Christina Neuharth. Neuharth Sr. died when Allen was only two years old, causing financial problems and forcing the youngster to deliver newspapers at age 11 in order to earn money for his family.

After graduating from Alpena High School, Neuharth joined the army and during World War II fought overseas as a combat infantryman, winning the Bronze Star for valor. Upon his return home in 1946, Neuharth enrolled at the University of South Dakota, where he majored in journalism and served as editor of the campus newspaper. He worked, too, as a summer intern at several different newspapers, an experience that helped him land a job after graduation in 1950 as a general assignment reporter with the Associated Press (AP) in Sioux Falls.

Neuharth was ambitious, and "wanted to leapfrog the normal, dull career ladder." He quit his AP job in 1952 and with a partner founded *SoDak Sports*, a weekly, statewide paper. Although at one point *SoDak* reached a circulation of 18,000, it eventually flopped. Now in debt, Neuharth moved to Miami, Florida, to get far away from his failure and start anew. He began working at the *Miami Herald*, where he formed a strong relationship with the newspaper's managing editor, George Beebe, and its publisher, James Knight. Neuharth rose quickly. After winning acclaim for his investigative reporting, he worked at various times as copy editor, Latin American correspondent, Washington bureau reporter, executive city editor, and assistant managing editor before Knight made him assistant executive editor of the *Detroit Free Press*, another Knight newspaper, in 1960.

In 1963, the Gannett Company, which owned newspapers in small to medium-sized towns, lured Neuharth away from Detroit to manage the *Times-Union* and the *Democrat and Chronicle* in Rochester, New York. "Most of my friends thought I was loony to leave Detroit for the boonies of Rochester," Neuharth later said. "I figured it differently. I was ready for a new adventure. . . . Too many people pass up good career opportunities because they're afraid of what other people will think." He proved so adept at improving profits that in a short time Gannett promoted him to executive vice president of its newspaper chain, and president of its newspapers in Florida.

True to character, Neuharth made a bold move when he founded *Today* in Cocoa, near Cape Canaveral. He took a chance that this newspaper would succeed because the Cocoa region would undergo tremendous population growth—and it did. "Coworkers were betting that I'd either be the next president of the company or a copy boy, depending on the success or failure of the new newspaper," Neuharth recounted.

Gannett made Neuharth its president in 1970 and three years later, its CEO. Between 1970 and 1975, Neuharth increased profits by adding 20 papers to the chain. His efficiency and cost-cutting moves, with such innovations as establishing a central purchasing subsidiary, placed Gannett among the most profitable newspaper companies.

Neuharth became chairman of Gannett in 1978, and led the company into diversified mass media when, in 1979, he bought the Combined Communications Corporation that owned, along with two newspapers, several radio and television stations, and a national billboard company.

Working against critics who predicted failure, he launched a national newspaper in 1982, *USA Today*, and it quickly gained an audience. Readers liked its color photographs and bold graphics, although newspaper purists criticized it for shallow reportage, which they derisively called "fast-food journalism." Neuharth said he wanted to "reinvent the newspaper" and pull the newspaper industry "into the twenty-first century, albeit kicking and screaming."

Although Neuharth made additional acquisitions, he remained most noted for founding *USA Today*. He retired as Gannett chairman in 1989 and wrote a weekly column for that paper. In the 1990s, he made several speeches criticizing assaults on the First Amendment, and in 1997 lashed out at a Supreme Court ruling that allowed high school administrators to censor public school newspapers.

BIBLIOGRAPHY

Neuharth, Al, *Confessions of an S.O.B.*, 1989; Wolper, Allan, "Neuharth to Academics: Butt Out," *Editor and Publisher*, January 11, 1997.

Newhouse, S. I.

(May 24, 1895–August 29, 1979)
Publisher

Samuel Irving Newhouse built a multimillion-dollar communications empire that controlled newspapers, magazines, and television and radio stations.

Born on May 24, 1895, in New York City the son of Russian immigrants, Newhouse quit school after the sixth grade in order to earn money for his family. He worked for Judge Herman Lazarus doing odd jobs, and when the judge came into possession of the small and financially troubled *Bayonne* (New Jersey) *Times*, he asked Newhouse, then 16 years old, to run the newspaper. Thus began Newhouse's career in publishing. While operating the *Times*, Newhouse completed his Regents exam to make up for his lack of a high school diploma and began studying law at night. He passed his bar exam in 1916 but quit the legal profession after he lost his first case.

Newhouse then turned his full attention to publishing, and in 1921, in partnership with his friend Judge Lazarus, bought the *Staten Island Advance* for $98,000. In the 1930s, he bought the *Newark Star-Ledger*, the *Long Island Press*, the *Long Island Star-Journal*, and the *Syracuse Herald-American*, creating the Newhouse newspaper chain.

Other acquisitions followed, with Newhouse buying newspapers that were losing money and turning them around through cost cutting and an antiunion strategy. Newhouse did allow each newspaper to maintain its own editorial policy. In 1950, for the first time, he bought a newspaper that was profitable, the *Portland Oregonian*, for $5.5 million.

When he purchased two newspapers in Alabama in 1955, as part of the deal he obtained a television station and three radio stations. Four years later, he entered the magazine industry when he acquired controlling interest in CONDÉ NAST Publications. The magazines included *Vogue*, *Glamour*, and *House & Garden*.

Later in 1959, he bought Street & Smith Magazines, including *Mademoiselle.*

In 1960, Newhouse gave $2 million to Syracuse University for use in establishing a mass media center, and he announced the formation of the Newhouse Foundation to further fund the center after his death and to engage in other philanthropic projects.

Newhouse died on August 29, 1979, leaving an estate valued at more than $100 million. He had married Mitzi Epstein in 1924, and their two sons took over his business. In the mid-1990s, through Condé Nast and Advance Publications, they owned 29 newspapers, 15 magazines, and several cable television systems.

BIBLIOGRAPHY

Maier, Thomas, *Newhouse: All the Glitter, Power, and Glory of America's Richest Media Empire and the Secretive Man Behind It,* 1994; Meeker, Richard H., *Newspapermen: S. I. Newhouse and the Business of News,* 1983.

S. I. Newhouse (UPI/Corbis-Bettmann)

Nielsen, A. C.

(September 5, 1897–June 1, 1980)
Market Surveyor

When most Americans hear the name A. C. Nielsen they immediately think "television ratings," and rightly so, for Nielsen developed an evaluation system that could make or break shows. *Newsweek* magazine once mentioned his "literal life-and-death power over network programming," but Nielsen's company made most of its money from other market surveys.

Arthur Charles Nielsen was born on September 5, 1897, in Chicago, Illinois, to Rasmus Nielsen and Harriet Burr (Gunn) Nielsen. After graduating from Morton High School in nearby Cicero, he entered the University of Wisconsin. In 1918,

Charles received his B.S. degree in electrical engineering with the highest grades ever achieved in the college's engineering school.

After serving in the navy during World War I, Nielsen returned to Chicago, married Gertrude Smith, worked as an engineer at a refrigerator machinery company, and then at a publishing firm. In 1923, he organized the A. C. Nielsen Company to make performance surveys of industrial equipment. The business unraveled, however, when the Great Depression hit, and companies trying to reduce their budgets dropped Nielsen's service.

In 1933, he launched the Nielsen Food and Drug Index, the nation's first research service that measured the flow of retail goods. Nielsen gathered the necessary statistics by sending surveyors to carefully selected grocery and drug stores—sample stores chosen to accurately reflect a bigger market—and recording all sales, together with the sales price of each product. Once analyzed, the data let a manufacturing company know how its sales compared to competing products, the rapidity of stock turnover, the average order size, and the like.

Nielsen—who worked 70-hour weeks and sent streams of memos to his employees—claimed that his index helped the economy by showing companies how they could better sell their products, thus stimulating sales, revenues, profits, and employment. He soon expanded his service and replaced the Food and Drug Index with the Retail Index that measured a greater variety of products. In 1939, he established a subsidiary in England, and over the next decade additional subsidiaries in Canada and Australia.

During the late 1930s, Nielsen secured a patent from the inventors of a machine that could measure the number of people tuned to a radio program. The Nielsen Audimeter, as he called it, was plugged into a radio's electric wire and received a signal every time someone changed the dial. In that way Nielsen determined which programs people were hearing. He began offering the results of his measurements, the Nielsen Radio Index, to subscribers in 1942. By 1950, he had attached the Audimeters to radios in 1,500 homes, again using a representative sample to reflect a much larger market. For income, however, Nielsen still relied on his Retail Index and other services that brought in 90 percent of his company's revenue.

Nielsen applied his ratings service to television in 1950, and advertisers studied the ratings results to determine when to buy airtime, and thus decide which shows would survive. So much depended on Nielsen's ratings that, in 1963, Congress investigated his service. Despite Nielsen's denials, the committee hearings showed that the households in which Nielsen had placed measuring devices could be manipulated by advertisers or anyone else who wanted to influence results.

Although the revelation damaged Nielsen, the company in quick order improved its system and maintained command of the ratings business. Nielsen died on June 1, 1980, and one son, Arthur C. Nielsen Jr., served as director of the A. C. Nielsen Company, while another, Phillip Robert Nielsen, served as its vice president.

BIBLIOGRAPHY

Moskowitz, Milton, et al., eds., *Everybody's Business*, 1980.

Noble, Edward

(August 8, 1882–December 28, 1958)
Manufacturer

As a young advertising agent in the early 1900s, Edward John Noble saw potential in a poorly selling hard candy mint marketed by the Mary Garden Chocolate Company. Sensing the business potential for a well-advertised, tasty product, he bought the trademark and remaining inventory of Life Savers. From an initial investment of $2,900, Noble built a multimillion-dollar company. Noble subsequently invested heavily in the radio industry, purchasing the Blue Network, which would later become the American Broadcasting Company (ABC).

The son of Harvey H. and Edna L. Wood Noble, Edward was born in Gouverneur, New York, on August 8, 1882. As a youth, Edward and his friend Roy Allen dreamed of riches to be made in the advertising industry. Noble attended Syracuse University, but transferred to Yale, from whence he graduated in 1905. He quickly gained employment with Ward & Gow, an advertising agency in New York City.

As Noble gained experience in the advertising trade, he kept a vigilant lookout for the product that would earn him the lucrative profits he witnessed others making on a regular basis. In 1913, Noble identified a sideline product of the Mary Garden Chocolate Company. Believing that their Life Savers breath mint could yield stronger revenues, Noble urged Crane, the company's owner, to advertise on a larger scale. Crane's lack of faith in the product was such that he instead offered to sell Noble the trademark as well as his remaining inventory of the mints for a mere $5,000.

Excited by what he characterized as a "$50-a-day repeat business," Noble pitched the prospect to his boyhood friend Allen. As the pair had difficulty coming up with the purchase price, it was decided that Allen would run the new company, while Noble would keep his advertising job and contribute cash each week. Though they were unable to raise the whole sum, Crane lowered the price to $2,900.

Though Noble's intuition would soon prove correct, Life Savers were initially a flop. Noble quickly found that very few of Crane's sales led to repeat business, largely due to the product's lack of freshness. Noble created new packaging with cardboard cartons and foil wrap that was resealable, thus retaining the mint's freshness. Allen aggressively researched new markets, successfully making Life Savers a fixture in area saloons. Noble then hit upon the idea of the miniature display case to set up next to cash registers in local stores. Requiring no effort from the retailer, the idea proved to be a component for acquiring that precious commodity—the repeat customer.

During these first tough months, Noble's paycheck from the advertising firm went directly to pay the Life Savers employees. Over the next two years, however, revenues steadily increased. Noble's business career was interrupted briefly when he served as a major in World War I. During his absence, Life Savers continued to grow, showing a net profit of $280,000 in 1918. A new Australian subsidiary, Life Savers, Inc., was earning $1 million annual profit by 1920. On November 6 of that same year, Noble married

Ethel Louise Tinkam. Of the Nobles' two daughters, only one survived to adulthood.

In 1925, Noble and Allen took the company public. Allen retired $3.3 million richer than he had been 12 years before. The company was worth over $11 million and continued to grow over the next decade. By 1938, the firm that Noble considered "a happy, whimsical little business" was worth $22 million. Noble's positive attitude was largely the result of his wise decision in 1925 to turn over the firm's daily management to an executive. Though he remained involved, he spent much of his time on his 80-foot fishing boat in Florida, the Thousand Islands, and a summer home in Canada.

In 1938, Noble was appointed as chairman of the Civil Aeronautics Society, an appointment based on his business acumen, his understanding of the industry gained through years of investing in aviation, and his longtime hobby of flying. In 1941, Noble began to show an interest in radio, purchasing New York's WMCA radio station for $850,000. Noble's major foray into the arena of radio was his purchase in 1943 of the Blue Network, which had originally been owned by the National Broadcasting Company (NBC) before the Federal Communications Commission (FCC) made an antimonopoly ruling that caused NBC to sell it to the Radio Corporation of America. The network, which Noble bought for $8 million, was a profitable enterprise that in 1944 earned gross sales of over $16 million. That year, it was also the only major network to experience improved ratings. By the end of 1944, the FCC authorized Noble to change the name to the American Broadcasting Company. ABC remains today one of the major communications networks of the entertainment industry.

In addition to his business concerns, Noble was a director of a number of banks, the trustee and founder of the Edward John Noble Foundation (a charitable organization), and served on the board of trustees of St. Lawrence University until his death on December 28, 1958.

BIBLIOGRAPHY

Business Week, August 7, 1943; *Fortune*, February and September 1938; *Time*, July 18, 1938, and August 9, 1943.

Norris, William

(July 14, 1911–)
Manufacturer

In building the Control Data Corporation, William Charles Norris raised a storm of controversy with his social reform programs, which critics claimed drained millions of dollars from the company.

Born on July 14, 1911, in Inavale, Nebraska, Norris grew up on his family's farm. As a boy in the era of radio, he liked electronics, and after he graduated from high school he enrolled at the University of Nebraska to study electrical engineering. When his father died of a heart attack in 1932, Norris quickly finished his college studies and, degree in hand, returned home to help his mother save the family farm. With the farm once again operating at a profit in 1934, he took a job with Westinghouse, selling X-ray equipment. In 1941, he joined the navy and encountered computers for the first time when he worked as a cryptologist, breaking enemy codes.

After World War II, Norris and a friend, Howard Engstrom, decided to establish a company to design and develop computers. With financial support from an investment banker, John Parker, they founded Engineering Research Associates. The company's computers earned a reputa-

William Norris (R), with Robert M. Price (Corbis/Bettmann-UPI)

tion for reliability, but in 1951 Parker sold the firm to Remington Rand, makers of electric shavers and typewriters. Norris disliked the corporate environment, and he further disliked a second sale of the company in 1955 to the Sperry Corporation, creating Sperry-Rand. Although Sperry-Rand put Norris in charge of the computer division, the corporation had little interest in developing computers, and he soon saw his budget cut.

As a result, Norris quit Sperry-Rand in 1957 and founded the Control Data Corporation (CDC). He acquired capital through the unusual and risky method of selling stock directly to the public without the backing of an underwriter before any product, employees, or facilities had materialized. Yet the stock sold well, and with his new corporation Norris decided he would develop computers for scientific uses and sell them to the government and universities, markets largely bypassed by International Business Machines (IBM). He hired Seymour Cray, a genius in computer design, to make the most powerful computers yet built.

Cray built the 1604, a compact computer that could sell at less than the comparable machine produced by IBM. Unlike earlier computers that relied on bulky vacuum tubes, the 1604 ran on transistors and contained advanced printed circuit cards. The 1604 sold well, and CDC won a $1.5 million contract from the navy to supply its Bureau of Ships.

Cray designed a desk-sized computer in 1959, the Model 160, that sold for $90,000 and also boosted company profits, which in 1964 reached $121.4 million. Norris rapidly diversified and acquired 21 companies. This expansion may have been too rapid, for in 1966 Norris was forced to obtain a $120 million credit loan from a bank consortium.

Norris recovered, however, after IBM abandoned its work on supercomputers in 1967, leaving the market open to CDC. In 1968, Norris decided to challenge IBM directly by selling computers to businesses. At the same time, he sued IBM for monopolistic practices. The legal battle promised to be a long one, but in 1973 IBM settled out of court. At a bargain price IBM sold Norris its Service Bureau Corporation, a lucrative data processing business, and at the same time provided CDC with subsidies exceeding $100 million.

Norris returned to acquiring companies and in 1969 bought out the Commercial Credit Corporation, a finance company. In the early 1970s, Norris directed CDC away from supercomputer production and toward joint ventures in making such computer peripherals as high-speed printers, magnetic tape systems, and punch-card equipment. In 1973, he bought Ticketron, a computerized ticket service, and Auditron, a television and radio audience rating service.

At the same time, Norris decided that CDC would undertake several projects combining business with social reform. Among these, he opened a large factory in a riot-torn ghetto in Minneapolis. In 1980, he began the Rural Venture, a consortium with several other corporations to promote small-scale agriculture, bucking the trend toward larger and larger farms. He established, too, the City Venture Corporation to rehabilitate slum buildings in several cities.

Meanwhile, earnings at CDC fell (although sales increased). Competition from other companies had cut deeply into CDC, and pressure mounted for

Norris to resign. After the company lost $270 million in the first nine months of 1985 and defaulted on bank loans, Norris quit. He was replaced by Robert M. Price, who promptly sold some troubled divisions, laid off workers, and ended nearly all of Norris's social programs. Under Price, CDC's financial picture failed to improve, but in the early 1990s the company reorganized and profits returned, and between 1992 and 1997 it nearly tripled its value.

BIBLIOGRAPHY

Fishman, Katherine Davis, *The Computer Establishment*, 1981; Nader, Ralph, and William Taylor, *The Big Boys: Power & Position in American Business*, 1986; Worthy, James C., *William C. Norris: Portrait of a Maverick*, 1987.

Northrop, John

(November 10, 1895–February 18, 1981)
Manufacturer

John Knudsen Northrop failed to reach his goal of mass producing a Flying Wing bomber, but he made airplanes that ranged from the Lockheed Vega flown by Amelia Earhart to the Black Widow, the first plane built specifically for night flying.

Born in Newark, New Jersey, on November 10, 1895, to Charles Northrop and Helen (Knudsen) Northrop, John moved with his family to California in 1904 and graduated from Santa Barbara High School in 1913. Technologically oriented, he held jobs after high school as an architectural draftsman and a garage mechanic before joining Loughhead Brothers in 1916 as a draftsman-engineer in building a twin-engine flying boat.

After serving in the army during World War I, Northrop married Inez M. Harmon (they had three children), returned to Loughhead, and then, in 1923, began working for Douglas Aircraft as draftsman, designer, and engineer. In 1927, he and W. K. Joy, Anthony Stadleman, and Allan Loughhead, formed the Lockheed Aircraft Company. Northrop designed and built the advanced Vega airplane, which set several speed and endurance records and was used by Amelia Earhart on her 1932 transatlantic flight.

Northrop left Lockheed in 1928 and founded the Avion Corporation to build a Flying Wing airplane. High costs forced him to scrap the project, however, and in 1930 the United Aircraft and Transport Corporation bought out Avion. Two years later, Northrop founded the Northrop Corporation, and under his leadership the firm designed and built commercial aircraft and, more prominently, planes for the military. Northrop made the A-17 and A-17A attack planes for the army, as well as the BT-1 dive bomber for the navy.

In 1937, he merged his firm with the Douglas Company, but later that year he formed yet another business, Northrop

Aircraft, Incorporated, and served as its president and head of engineering and research. Northrop developed the N3-PB, at that time the world's fastest military seaplane. He tried again, unsuccessfully, to build a boomerang shaped Flying Wing, but produced the Black Widow P-61, rated the world's largest and most powerful fighter.

Based on the Black Widow, he manufactured the Northrop F-15 photo reconnaissance plane, which had a range exceeding 4,000 miles. In 1946, Northrop produced the XB-35, a 104-ton tailless bomber that cost $13 million to build, but had a range of 10,000 miles and a speed 20 percent faster than conventional bombers. It was a state-of-the-art aircraft.

Northrop retired from the presidency in 1959, and died on February 18, 1981. In 1994, the Northrop Corporation acquired the Grumman Corporation to form Northrop Grumman. Three years later, the company, prime contractor for the air force's B-2 stealth bomber, announced it would merge with the Lockheed Martin Corporation to create a business with annual revenues of about $37 billion and with employees numbering nearly 230,000.

BIBLIOGRAPHY

Allen, Richard Sanders, *The Northrop Story, 1929–1939*, 1990.

Noyce, Robert

(December 12, 1927–June 3, 1990)
Manufacturer

A pioneer in semiconductor development, Robert Noyce cofounded the Intel Corporation.

Born on December 12, 1927, in Denmark, Iowa, the son of a Congregational minister, Noyce obtained a bachelor's degree in physics and mathematics in 1949 from Grinnell College in Grinnell, Iowa. He then continued his studies at the Massachusetts Institute of Technology, and in 1953 earned a Ph.D. in physical electronics. Upon graduation, he joined the Philco Corporation as research engineer.

In 1956, Noyce left Philco to work for William B. Shockley at the Shockley Semiconductor Laboratory in Mountain View, California. The following year, he and several other friends founded the Fairchild Semiconductor Corporation. As research director, Noyce worked at improving digital electronics. He invented an integrated circuit in 1959, the same year that Jack St. Clair Kilby invented one at Texas Instruments. Noyce used silicon chips to make entire networks of components. The invention was extremely important, for integrated circuits launched the computer revolution by making it possible to manufacture much smaller machines, like personal computers.

Fairchild Semiconductor took out its patent in 1959, as did Texas Instruments, and the two companies engaged in a legal battle that lasted through the 1960s, until they decided to cross-license their technologies. In the meantime, Noyce became vice president and general manager at Fairchild and then, in 1968, cofounded the Intel Corporation with GORDON MOORE and ANDREW GROVE. Intel developed into a multibillion-dollar corporation, manufacturing semiconductors and the first microprocessor.

Noyce served as president of Intel until 1974, and as chairman of the board from then until 1979. He was awarded the National Medal of Science in 1980, by which time he was a legendary figure in the computer industry and in the business world. In 1988, he was appointed chief executive officer of Sematech, a consortium created by semiconductor businesses to make the United States more competitive with Japan. He called the appointment an honor.

Noyce died on June 3, 1990, in Texas due to heart failure. He had over the years obtained 16 patents for his inventions involving semiconductor devices. A writer who interviewed Noyce in the 1980s said of him: "[He] projected what people call the halo effect. People with the halo effect seem to know exactly what they're doing and, moreover, make you want to admire them for it. They make you see the halo over their heads."

BIBLIOGRAPHY

Jackson, Tim, *Inside Intel: Andy Grove and the Rise of the World's Most Powerful Chip Company*, 1997.

O

Ochs, Adolph

(March 12, 1858–April 8, 1935)
Publisher

"All The News That's Fit to Print" was the motto of the *New York Times*. Adolph Simon Ochs lived up to that boast, creating a newspaper whose prestige to this day exceeds all others in the nation.

Born on March 12, 1858, in Cincinnati, Ohio, to Bavarian-Jewish immigrants, Julius Ochs and Bertha (Levy) Ochs, Adolph had a poor childhood. Soon after his family moved to Knoxville, Tennessee, he was forced to quit school at age 11 and earn money by working as a copy boy at a local newspaper, the *Knoxville Chronicle*. After a brief departure, in 1871, Ochs returned to Knoxville and the *Chronicle* as an apprentice. He swept the office floor and cleaned the press rollers. In 1875, he went to Louisville, Kentucky, and worked in the job-printing department of that city's *Courier-Journal*. Once again he returned to Knoxville and obtained work in the composing room of a new daily, the *Tribune*. In short order, he earned promotion to reporter, and then to assistant business manager.

Ochs worked at the *Chattanooga* (Tennessee) *Dispatch* in 1877, but after it folded in just six months, he had to scramble to make money. When he noticed that the city lacked a directory, he published one. With the profits he earned he purchased a controlling interest in a failing newspaper, the *Chattanooga Times*. As publisher, Ochs had just $37.50 in working capital, but he quickly turned the publication around, eventually making it one of the South's leading Democratic newspapers. In 1880, Ochs bought out his partners.

Adolph Ochs (Museum of the City of New York/ Archive Photos)

Three years later, Ochs married Effie Miriam Wise, and she joined the paper as a book reviewer and drama critic. In 1891, he formed the Southern Associated Press as a wire service and acted as its general manager until it folded in 1894.

Enthused with the newspaper life, Ochs wanted to expand his business and in 1896 stumbled across an opportunity. On a visit to New York City, he learned that the *New York Times*, founded by Henry J. Raymond, was nearing collapse. The paper's circulation stood at only 9,000, and its debts were mounting at the rate of $1,000 per day. Ochs believed he could again achieve success, and this time in the nation's largest city. So he bought the *Times* for $75,000, coined his slogan, and wrote the paper's credo: "It will be my earnest aim that the . . . *Times* give the news, all the news . . . in language that is parliamentary in good society . . . to give the news impartially, without fear of favor, regardless of any party, sect, or interest involved. . . ."

Ochs modernized the paper's appearance, and added a Saturday book review and a pictorial Sunday magazine supplement. Circulation increased to 25,000 in just two years, but he faced tremendous competition from JOSEPH PULITZER's *New York World* and WILLIAM RANDOLPH HEARST's *Journal*, which were sensational "yellow journalist" newspapers that sold for just one penny. Ochs reacted in 1898 by lowering the price of the *Times* from three cents to one—a risky move given that readers might have interpreted it as Ochs's surrender to sensationalism. The tactic worked, however, and *Times* circulation surged to 80,000 while Ochs maintained his commitment to quality.

Under Ochs and his managing editor, Carr V. Van Anda, the *Times* developed worldwide news coverage that included stories about the sinking of the *Titanic;* the battles of World War I and the full official statements of the European governments involved in that war; and Admiral Byrd's expedition to the South Pole. The *Times* developed a reputation for conservative but independent political views and an editorial policy that welcomed balanced discussions of leading issues. In 1918, the *Times* received the first Pulitzer Gold Medal in journalism for its "disinterested and meritorious service." The newspaper's circulation reached 325,000 in 1920, and, 10 years later, 430,000.

Ochs established several subsidiaries to the *New York Times:* the *Analyst,* a weekly financial review; *Current History Magazine,* a monthly; and the *Mid-Week Pictorial,* an illustrated review of the week's news. He also helped begin the *Dictionary of American Biography* in the late 1920s.

After Ochs died on April 8, 1935, his son-in-law Arthur Hays Sulzberger, took over as publisher of the *Times* and further advanced its reputation.

BIBLIOGRAPHY

Johnson, Gerald W., *An Honorable Titan: A Biographical Study of Adolph S. Ochs,* 1946.

Oliver, Henry

(February 25, 1840–February 8, 1904)
Manufacturer

Henry William Oliver, one of the foremost iron and steel manufacturers of the late nineteenth century, pioneered the prospecting and distribution of the vast iron-ore resources of Minnesota. He was also active in the construction of railroads and financed copper and coal interests.

Oliver, born in Dungannon, Ireland, on February 25, 1840, was one of six children born to Henry William and Margaret Brown Oliver. In 1842, the family immigrated to Pittsburgh. Oliver became a student at a public school and then the private Newall's Academy. At age 13, he got an early start on his business career, leaving school to become a messenger boy for the National Telegraph Company with fellow budding entrepreneur ANDREW CARNEGIE. Oliver subsequently spent several years with Gaff, Bennett & Company, an iron manufacturing company.

When the Civil War broke out in 1861, Oliver responded to President Abraham Lincoln's first call for troops, enlisting in the 12th Pennsylvania Volunteers Corps. In 1862, after a three-month term of service, he married Edith A. Cassidy of Pittsburgh, with whom he had one daughter. In 1863, Oliver reenlisted, participating in the Battle of Gettysburg.

In late 1863, Oliver organized the company of Lewis, Oliver & Phillips to manufacture nuts and bolts. Two years later, he was joined by his brothers David and James. In 1880, upon the retirement of W. J. Lewis, the firm adopted the name Oliver Brothers and Phillips. By 1888, Oliver was the chairman of the board of the newly incorporated Oliver Iron & Steel Company.

The post–Civil War years were a tremendously prosperous time for the company, which had diversified to include a number of ferrous industries, including sheet and tinplate, steel wire, and pressed-steel cars. Oliver had also become interested in the construction of railroads, recognizing the advantage of a strong rail system to a growing industrial city such as Pittsburgh. Oliver was one of the original owners of the Pittsburgh and Lake Erie Railroad. From 1890 to 1893, he served as president of the Pittsburgh and Western Railway Company. Hoping to secure better freight arrangements for shipments to the West, Oliver was a supporter of the Akron & Chicago Junction Railroad. He was a pioneer in the use of steel railcars to increase safety.

In 1892, Oliver heard of the discovery by the Merritt brothers of an expansive region of iron-ore deposits in Minnesota. Learning that the high-quality ore lay close to the surface and could be gathered and loaded for shipment at minimal cost, Oliver quickly formed the Oliver Iron Mining Company. He immediately began construction of a railroad from the site he purchased to Lake Superior, establishing a system to transport the ore by way of the docks to mills in Pittsburgh.

At this time, Oliver's old crony, Andrew Carnegie, thought that ore prospecting was a harebrained idea. But the manager of Carnegie Steel Company, HENRY C. FRICK, put his trust and active support into Oliver's venture. In eight years, the ore company Oliver had started with an original investment of $600,000 was bought out by the United States Steel Corporation for $17 million.

Though "Oliver luck" became an often-voiced phrase in Pittsburgh, Oliver's good fortune was largely due to his immense drive to succeed and solid knowledge of business. In addition to steel interests, Oliver directed his energy to real estate investments in Pittsburgh, and to Arizona copper mines, and was the largest stockholder of his time in the Pittsburgh Coal Company.

Oliver's energy also found outlets outside of business. He was politically active, serving from 1879 to 1882 as president of the Common Council of Pittsburgh. An ardent Republican, Oliver was a delegate to four Republican national conventions, was a presidential elector-at-large in 1880, and was nominated in 1881 by caucus for U.S. senator. He also represented steel and iron interests on a commission established in 1882 by President Chester A. Arthur to determine metal tariffs. Oliver remained influential in industry and politics until his death on February 8, 1904.

BIBLIOGRAPHY

Boucher, J. N., *A Century and a Half of Pittsburgh and Her People*, 1908; DeKruif, Paul, *Seven Iron Men*, 1929; Evans, Henry Oliver, *Iron Pioneer: Henry W. Oliver, 1840–1904*, 1942; Fleming, G. T., ed., *History of Pittsburgh and Its Environs*, 1922; *Pittsburgh Dispatch*, February 8, 1904; *Pittsburgh Gazette*, February 8, 1904.

Olsen, Kenneth

(February 20, 1926–)
Manufacturer

A talented engineer and a puritanical moralist, Kenneth Harry Olsen used his experience at the Massachusetts Institute of Technology (MIT) to found the Digital Equipment Corporation that challenged International Business Machines (IBM) for leadership in the computer industry.

Born to Oswald Olsen and Svea (Nordling) Olsen in Bridgeport, Connecticut, on February 20, 1926, Kenneth grew up in Stratford and may have picked up his liking for engineering from his father, who worked as a machine tool designer. As a child, Kenneth read technical manuals and repaired radios. After graduating from Stratford High School, he joined the navy in 1944 and served for two years. Kenneth enrolled at MIT in 1947 and, just three years later, received his B.S. degree in electrical engineering. He then continued his education and received his master's degree in 1950.

While at MIT, Olsen learned about interactive computing, a concept that he later developed in his business. He worked on a government project to build an early-warning system (Semi-Automatic Ground Environment, or SAGE), and did so well with it that IBM hired him to oversee its manufacturing of the computer equipment. This experience convinced Olsen that he could do better than IBM, which he considered to be a sloppily run company. He also believed that he could design a small interactive computer able to perform 80 percent of the functions of a large mainframe computer. While selling at a fraction of the mainframe's cost, the machine would be able to handle everyday tasks without requiring an expert operator.

Olsen founded the Digital Equipment Corporation (DEC) in 1956, and with his colleague Harlan Anderson, secured $70,000 from venture capitalist General Georges Doriot's American Research and Development Company (ARD) in 1957. Olsen opened DEC in the corner of a vacant woolen mill in Lincoln, Massachusetts. At first he made printed-circuit logic modules used by engineers to test equipment, but after the company made a profit and received an infusion of $1 million from ARD, he used the modules to make Digital's first minicomputer, the PDP-1, which appeared in 1960. The International Telephone and Telegraph Company, among other corporations, adopted the PDP-1. Olsen followed this machine with the PDP-4, bought by original equipment manufacturers who added their software to it.

A breakthrough occurred in 1965, when Olsen developed the PDP-8 that used integrated circuits, which were cheaper and faster than transistors. The PDP-8 approximated a personal computer (PC) in size, for it could easily fit into the trunk of a car. In fact, DEC could have started making a PC at that time, well ahead of a later pioneer, Apple Computers, but Olsen viewed computers as industrial products intended for businesses, and was convinced that no one would ever want one in their home.

Olsen's management plan proved as important as his computers. He devised a decentralized system whereby each senior manager took responsibility for developing and marketing a product and making money with it.

In time, Olsen's refusal to make PCs came back to haunt him. His decision did not at first damage DEC, and in the 1970s the company experienced a 30 percent annual revenue and profit growth and developed a VAX technology that allowed computer networks to link to one another. But as the PC market expanded, DEC suffered. Olsen eventually decided to make PCs, but his late entry proved damaging. DEC's personal computers sold poorly and in 1983 caused a serious drop in the company's net earnings. Olsen reacted by centralizing DEC's operations, and by introducing the Venus mainframe and the MicroVAX II workstation—popular with businesses that wanted powerful computing.

In 1986, company profits headed upward toward revenues that approached $8 billion, and *Fortune* magazine said, "DEC today is bigger, even adjusting for inflation, than Ford Motor Co., when death claimed HENRY FORD, than U.S. Steel when ANDREW CARNEGIE sold out, than Standard Oil when JOHN D. ROCKEFELLER stepped aside."

Olsen infused his life with puritanical religious beliefs and told his workers that they should follow the virtues of humility, gentleness, neatness, and temperance. He ruled his company autocratically, which took its toll on individuals and the company itself, and raised questions in the 1990s as to whether Olsen should continue as president and CEO. Finally, a declining profit margin accompanied by layoffs and losses exceeding $150 million caused the board of directors to accept Olsen's resignation. Olsen then founded a small computer company, Advance Modular Solutions. In January 1998, the Compaq Computer Corporation, the nation's leading company in making personal computers, announced its purchase of Digital, a move that represented the largest takeover in the history of the computer industry.

BIBLIOGRAPHY

Freiberger, Paul, and Michael Swaine, *Fire in the Valley: The Making of the Personal Computer*, 1984.

Otis, Elisha

(August 3, 1811–April 8, 1861)
Manufacturer

In 1854, the *New York Daily Tribune* noted "an elevator, or machine for hoisting goods . . . which attracts attention both by its prominent position and the apparent daring of the inventor, who, as he rides up and down the platform occasionally cuts the rope by which it is supported." The inventor was Elisha Graves Otis, whose safety mechanism made possible the building of passenger elevators, which in turn made the construction of skyscrapers practical.

Born on August 3, 1811, in Halifax, Vermont, to Stephen Otis and Phoebe (Glynn) Otis, at the age of 19 Elisha Otis moved to Troy, New York, where he worked in construction. He liked to tinker, and after moving to Albany, New York, in the 1840s, he invented a railway safety brake and devices to improve the operation of turbine wheels.

Then, in 1852, while employed as a master mechanic at the Yonkers Bedstead Company in Yonkers, New York, he built an unusual elevator that included a safety device of his own invention. The device consisted of a wagon spring that attached to the top of the elevator platform and the overhead lifting cable. A break in the cable would cause the spring to snap open and grip the saw-toothed ratchet bars that Otis had installed on either side of the elevator shaft. As a result, the elevator would stop, its passengers and cargo safe from harm.

At first, Otis did little more with his invention. But soon nearby businesses asked him to install his elevators in their buildings. After the initial flurry of requests, however, business stagnated. Many refused to believe his assurances about the safety device, and feared that if they installed elevators for passengers to use, an accident would hurt or kill those aboard.

To soothe these fears and gain publicity, Otis displayed his elevator at the 1854 New York World's Fair and Crystal Palace Exposition. As described in the *New York Daily Tribune*, he rode his elevator skyward while a crowd gathered below. On his signal, an assistant cut the cable, and the startled spectators watched as the elevator abruptly stopped after a short drop.

Despite his successful, attention-getting feat, orders for his elevators only trickled in, all of them for factories or warehouses, none for use primarily by passengers. Then, in 1857, he sold the world's first passenger elevator, an enclosed hoist installed at the five-story E. V. Haughwout store at Broadway and Broome Street in New York City.

Otis realized that the stores, hotels, and office buildings that might use his elevator lacked the power to run the lifts. To solve this problem, he invented a small steam engine. But widespread use of passenger elevators awaited the changes in building construction that occurred after his death on April 8, 1861. His sons, Charles and Norton, continued the Otis Elevator Company, and in the late 1860s developed and installed the first practical electric elevator.

Finally, in 1885, the passenger elevator became a necessity when William LeBaron Jenney perfected a method for constructing buildings using an iron frame that made tall structures possible. By 1900, buildings 20 and more stories tall necessitated a way to transport their occupants, and Otis elevators came into their own.

BIBLIOGRAPHY

Fucini, Joseph J., and Suzy Fucini, *Entrepreneurs: The Men and Women behind Famous Brand Names and How They Made It*, 1965; Peterson, Leroy A., *Elisha Graves Otis, 1811–1861, and His Influence upon Vertical Transportation*, 1945.

Otis, Harrison Gray

(February 10, 1837–July 30, 1917)
Publisher

Forceful and dominating, Harrison Gray Otis expanded the *Los Angeles Times* by using a fierce anti-union policy.

Harrison Otis was born on February 10, 1837, in Marietta, Ohio, the son of Stephen Otis and Sarah (Dyer) Otis. After limited formal schooling, at age 14 he became a printer's apprentice. Five years later, he briefly attended Wetherby's Academy at Lowell, Ohio, and after that took a commercial course at Granger's College in Columbus. A supporter of Abraham Lincoln, he campaigned for the Republican Party in 1860, and after the Civil War erupted, enlisted in the Union army and served with the 12th and 23rd Ohio Infantry. Twice wounded, he attained the rank of captain, and after the war he returned to Marietta and published a small newspaper.

In 1868, Otis moved to Washington, D.C., and worked as foreman in the government printing office for a year. Later he ran the *Grand Army Journal*, a paper for Civil War veterans. Otis moved to California in 1876 and operated the *Santa Barbara Press*. He went to Alaska after

Harrison Gray Otis (UPI/Corbis-Bettmann)

that, where he worked as a treasury agent before returning to California in 1882 and settling in Los Angeles. Over the next few years, he bought shares in the *Los Angeles Times* and in 1886 took full control of the newspaper.

As editor, manager, and president, Otis boosted the newspaper's circulation and promoted Los Angeles' economic development. With this goal in mind, in 1888, he organized the Los Angeles Chamber of Commerce.

Otis hated labor unions, inveighed against them in his editorials, and kept them from organizing at the *Times*. In 1910, a group of union men retaliated by dynamiting the *Times* plant, destroying the building and killing 21 workers. In a sensational trial, the accused McNamara brothers drew national attention, and before the jury deliberated they confessed to their guilt.

Unlike ADOLPH OCHS at the *New York Times*, Otis received few favorable reviews for his newspaper; many observers considered it to be of poor quality. But he kept the paper alive, and it would improve in later eras. Otis also did much to develop Los Angeles into a major city. He returned to military service in the Spanish-American War and served in the Philippines during the uprising there against American occupation. He died in Los Angeles on July 30, 1917.

BIBLIOGRAPHY:

Halberstam, David, *The Powers That Be*, 1979.

Ovitz, Michael

(December 4, 1946–)
Entertainment Executive

After founding Creative Artists Agency and representing some of the most prominent entertainers in Hollywood, Michael Ovitz stunned the industry when he agreed to head Disney Studios, a move that turned out to be ill fated.

Born on December 14, 1946, in Chicago, Illinois, to Leon and Molly Ovitz, Michael moved with his family in 1952 to

Encino, California, a suburb of Los Angeles. His father distributed liquor for Seagram's and provided Michael with a comfortable, middle-class environment. While growing up, the youngster had thoughts about becoming a doctor, but changed them soon after he graduated from Birmingham High School in 1965, when he obtained a job as a tour guide at Universal Studios.

The entertainment industry excited him, and he continued guiding tours while enrolled at the University of California, Los Angeles (UCLA). Ovitz majored in psychology and received his bachelor's degree in 1968, whereupon he enrolled in law school. The lure of entertainment remained strong, however, and in 1969, the same year he married Judy Reich, he quit law school and joined the William Morris Agency in Beverly Hills as a trainee. Ovitz later explained: "When I was at UCLA, I worked my way through school as a tour guide . . . and I came in contact with a lot of people in the agency business. I realized that there were a lot of areas in the entertainment business that I was interested in, and the career that offered me the widest exposure . . . was the agency business. Agents can allow creative people to achieve their visions, and that's why I did it."

Ovitz, however, started not as an agent but as a mail-room worker. He used his position as a classroom to learn all he could about the agency. What he saw thrilled him—the constant movement, the meetings with authors, actors, and producers. He later said: "I loved the business. It was incredible. A deal a second. It was constant, perpetual motion. . . . I realized I could be anything I wanted to be, I could make myself over. . . ."

A quick study in a firm that liked to put its trainees through a long program, Ovitz advanced to the position of assistant to the president in little more than three months. He thought a law degree might still help him in future agency dealings, however, and after a year at William Morris he returned to law school. Yet once again, law soon bored him, and within a short time he went back to the agency.

Among his clients, Ovitz counted television stars Bob Barker, Chuck Barris, and Merv Griffin. This was not enough to prevent his disenchantment with William Morris, its clashing egos, and the unwillingness of senior agents to share a greater portion of the wealth with the younger ones. Consequently, in 1974, Ovitz and four other William Morris agents began meeting to discuss starting their own business. When the agency heard about the meetings in January 1995, they fired the entire group.

Ovitz and his colleagues then founded Creative Artists Agency (CAA), with a $100,000 credit line, a $21,000 bank loan, and an office furnished with folding chairs. The Spartan conditions lasted only a short while as Ovitz began bringing in $30,000 worth of business each week. By 1980, CAA had bookings of over $90 million a year, making it the third largest agency in Hollywood.

CAA made its money in television and handled few movie deals. Ovitz changed that when he titled CAA a "literary and talent agency," and started representing screenwriters. Movie stars realized that by having CAA represent them, they could have access to the scripts they wanted. From that development, Ovitz started "packaging" for studios. He presented the studios not just an actor or a writer, but both. He soon added directors to his list of clients. Through the Ovitz agency, studios avoided having to deal with many different agents. This development eroded the power of studios and enhanced that of agents, to the point that they became central to doing business in Hollywood.

Critics claimed Ovitz was more concerned with image than anything else, and that he reveled in his picture appearing on the cover of the *New York Times Magazine* in 1989. The real power, they said, was not with Ovitz but with the stars he represented. Furthermore, he relied heavily on others at CAA who always had to bail him out for overreaching.

Ovitz also exerted influence in corporate boardrooms. In 1989, he assisted in Sony Corporation's acquisition of Columbia Picture Entertainment and the Matsushita Corporation's acquisition of Music Corporation of America (MCA) the following year. In 1993, the French banking corporation Credit Lyonnais retained him to help manage its loans in entertainment and the media.

CAA employed more than 100 agents, executives, and assistants in the early 1990s. Ovitz boosted the careers of such actors as Sean Connery, Tom Cruise, and Dustin Hoffman, and such directors as Richard Donner and Sydney Pollack. In 1994, CAA represented 10 of the 50 top-grossing music acts. Of the prime-time television series that premiered in the fall of 1995, 16 were packaged by the agency. To many, CAA seemed the most dominant force in show business since the era of LEW WASSERMAN and MCA in the 1950s.

In spite of this success, Ovitz had grown bored with the business and searched for a new outlet. In October 1995, he left CAA when MICHAEL EISNER, chairman of the Walt Disney Company, lured him away to become Disney's president. Ovitz was given responsibility for all three Disney divisions—theme parks, filmed entertainment, and consumer products—along with its new acquisition, Capital Cities/ABC.

Problems appeared immediately. Disney insiders disliked having an outsider as president. More important, Eisner kept a tight reign on Ovitz. In December 1996, Ovitz quit Disney, receiving a severance package worth over $100 million. He later said he should never have joined the company: "I made the biggest mistake of my business career. It was a stupid idea that I could come in and change this culture." With his departure, he did little in Hollywood, and many speculated that his days as an entertainment power were over.

A comeback may have begun, however, in April 1998 when Ovitz announced he was taking over Livent, a struggling company known for its production of the Broadway shows *Ragtime* and *Show Boat.* "Everyone has an opinion of my life, and I don't really have one at this point," said Ovitz. "Twenty-five years of building CAA—it's as if I was never there. One year at Disney, and the rest of it, I guess, was an accident."

BIBLIOGRAPHY

"Former Disney President Takes on Broadway," *Miami Herald,* April 15, 1998; Slater, Robert, *Ovitz: The Inside Story of Hollywood's Most Controversial Power Broker,* 1997.

Packard, David

(September 7, 1912–March 26, 1996)
Manufacturer

Said Apple cofounder STEVEN JOBS about David Packard and his business partner Bill Hewlett: "These guys started Silicon Valley. Hewlett-Packard was the first company I ever worked at, and when we started Apple, we modeled it after HP." Apple chairman John Sculley added: "Packard is one of the truly great business leaders of this century."

Born on September 7, 1912, in Pueblo, Colorado, to Sperry Sidney Packard, a lawyer, and Ella Lorna (Graber) Packard, a high school teacher, David decided in grade school that he wanted to be an engineer. When he entered college at Stanford University, he studied electrical engineering and made two important friendships, one with Fred Terman, a professor who encouraged his students to start their own businesses, and another with Bill Hewlett.

Packard graduated from Stanford with a B.A. in 1934 and joined General Electric, while Hewlett enrolled at the Massachusetts Institute of Technology as a graduate student in engineering. A few years later, Terman reunited the pair by encouraging Hewlett to begin a venture with Packard. In 1939, the two former classmates scraped together $538 and in Packard's Palo Alto garage they started Hewlett-Packard, with Hewlett the inventor and Packard the promoter.

They achieved success with their first invention, an audio oscillator used by WALT DISNEY in making the animated film *Fantasia.* After that, the company grew quickly, making mainly electronic devices that measured and tested audio signals.

When the company went public in 1964, Packard became chairman, and held that position into the 1980s, except for the period from 1969 to 1971, when he served as deputy secretary of defense under President Richard Nixon.

By the end of the 1960s, company sales reached $500 million, and Packard had installed his infamous "HP Way." He never clearly defined it, but it emphasized lowering the barriers between workers and management, and emphasizing teamwork. As Packard ran the day-to-day business, he roamed the halls of the company's headquarters, exchanging ideas. "I believe people want to do a good job," Packard said. "They enjoy doing things right and they enjoy making a contribution and they will further respond both in terms of compensation and other nonmonetary rewards."

Hewlett and Packard took the company in a new direction in 1972 when they ordered production of a hand calculator. The HP-35 sold so well that by 1978 the company's overall sales had tripled to $1.8 billion. HP also began manufacturing minicomputers and personal computers. In the microcomputer field, the HP-3000 proved popular, and the company made laptop personal computers rather than desktop models. (HP entered the desktop field in the 1990s.)

In the late 1980s, HP dominated the laser printer market, while David Packard was semiretired. When the company plunged into a financial slump in 1991, Packard returned as chairman and boosted sales. He retired completely in 1993 and died on March 26, 1996, from pneumonia. Packard, whose wife Lucile had died in 1987, was survived by four children.

Over the years, Packard's business reputation was exceeded only by his reputation for philanthropy. He established the David and Lucile Packard Foundation, which in the mid-1990s had assets of $2.3 billion. In 1995, the foundation distributed $116 million to more than 700 recipients. He gave generously to Stanford University—in all, more than $300 million, including the largest single gift in the school's history, $77.5 million for a new science and engineering complex.

BIBLIOGRAPHY

Packard, David, *The HP Way: How Bill Hewlett and I Built Our Company*, 1995; Pitta, Julie, "Silicon Valley Icon Dies," *Los Angeles Times*, March 27, 1996; Silver, A. David, *Entrepreneurial Megabucks: The 100 Greatest Entrepreneurs of the Last Twenty-Five Years*, 1985; Workman, Bill, "Memorial Pays Tribute to Packard," *San Francisco Chronicle*, March 30, 1996.

Paley, William

(September 28, 1901–October 26, 1990)
Entertainment Executive

An impeccable dresser who loved the good life, an autocrat in business, and a genius at programming, William Samuel Paley bought a struggling collection of radio stations and built the most profitable of all broadcasting networks, the Columbia Broadcasting System (CBS). Paley later said his entry into radio began in 1925 when he first heard the sounds of the new medium through earphones attached to a friend's crude crystal set. He could not believe that music was actually being transmitted without wires. "I was very dubious," he said. "I thought my friend was playing a trick on me."

William Paley had no worry about money while growing up. He was born on September 28, 1901, in Chicago, Illinois, to Samuel Paley and Gold (Drell) Paley. His father was an immigrant from Russia who had established the thriving Congress Cigar Company. In 1918, William graduated from the Western Military Academy in Alton, Illinois, and enrolled the following year at the University of Chicago. He left school, however, a few months later when his father opened a branch factory in Philadelphia, Pennsylvania, and moved the family there. Paley worked in the cigar business, and then resumed his education at the University of Pennsylvania's Wharton School of Business, where he received his B.S. degree in 1922, and returned to Congress Cigar.

Everything indicated that Paley would continue in the cigar business, and while he served as vice president and secretary between 1922 and 1926, sales jumped from $75,000 to $1.7 million. Paley was fascinated by the radio, however, along with many other Americans. By that time, more than 2 million radios had been sold, and the Department of Commerce had granted more than 1,400 broadcasting licenses.

In addition, Paley's father bought commercial time on a radio station to advertise his La Palina cigars (though William later took credit for this decision), and followed up the advertisements by presenting a half-hour radio program of music and jokes called *The La Palina Smoker.* William Paley supervised the show and, according to one of his biographers, when it became popular, "Paley was hooked on radio."

While *The La Palina Smoker* attracted listeners, the network on which it was broadcast, United Independent, struggled. When its owners decided to sell, William Paley agreed to buy. He paid about $500,000 for its 16 stations, with his father investing about $80,000 of the total. "My friends were amazed," he recalled, "that I would go for anything so gimmicky, that they thought would be short-lived."

Paley moved into the United Independent office in Manhattan in October 1928 and immediately went to work building his network. He had the talent to quickly absorb developments around him and in that way learned the business while fighting fears of failure.

Early in 1929, Paley changed the name of the company to CBS, and over the next few months expanded the number of affiliates from 49 to 70. He initiated an innovative system with which he supplied network programming to affiliates free of charge but retained the right to schedule shows. This allowed him to sell national commercial time without having to negotiate with the affiliates.

In the 1930s, he broadcast several acclaimed programs, including an educational show, *Columbia School of the Air;* a religious show, *Church of the Air;* a dramatic series, *The Columbia Workshop;* and performances of the New York Philharmonic Symphony Society. Most notably, he built a prestigious news organization with correspondents Larry Lesueur, Howard K. Smith, Charles Collingwood, and Edward R. Murrow. Yet over the years, Paley lost several journalists who were rankled by his autocratic style.

Paley temporarily turned over the administration of CBS to Paul Kesten in 1943 so that he could go overseas and work for the Office of War Information. During World War II, he reconstructed the Italian radio network, and after being commissioned a colonel in April 1945, he served as deputy chief of the Psychological Warfare Division under General Dwight D. Eisenhower.

Paley returned to CBS in November 1945 and soon appointed Frank Stanton president, while he held the position of chairman of the board. Although Stanton had leeway in running the network, Paley exerted considerable authority and determined its programming. In the late 1940s, he raided talent from his main competitor, the National Broadcasting Company, then headed by DAVID SARNOFF. Through raids and other deals, he acquired stars such as Jack Benny, Red Skelton, and Bing Crosby.

He later introduced these performers to television. CBS had entered television in 1941 with only limited broadcasts because Paley failed to see it as a cutting-edge medium, but broadcasting expanded in 1947 as consumers bought TV sets. Paley displayed consummate programming ability. Stanton said about him,

"Call it skill, inspiration, or luck, it takes all of them, and he had all of them in abundance. Moreover, he had the resources and courage to implement his ideas." Paley said, "You have to develop a kind of inner feeling about something and you're not sure what brings that on. You get a sense . . . a gut reaction. And if it's strong enough, you have enough conviction, you go with it. . . . Some of the biggest successes have come through going against every rule that we used to live by. That's a thing you call showmanship."

For decades, CBS achieved the highest network ratings and earned a reputation for quality (it was known as the "Tiffany Network"), although like his competitors, Paley stressed profits above all else. The company's news division exceeded the other networks in coverage, especially in the 1960s with news reporter and anchorman Walter Cronkite.

Meanwhile, Paley's marriage to Dorothy Heart Hearst (they had married in 1932) ended in divorce in 1947. Several days later he married Barbara (Cushing) Mortimer. Paley had two children by his first marriage and two by his second.

Over the years, Paley established a successful laboratories division and a record division (Columbia Records). But he also had his failures. He lost considerable money in acquiring the Hytron Radio and Electronics Corporation, a tube manufacturer; poured $40 million into a video recording technology that lost out to videocassettes; and took a $30 million drubbing in a failed cable TV venture.

In 1966, Paley promised to retire and promote Stanton to CEO. But at the last minute he reneged, saying there was nothing more he would rather do than continue at the network. He remained CEO until 1977, and chairman of the board until 1983, when he temporarily retired. In 1987, the board reinstalled Paley as its chairman, but also appointed LARRY TISCH as president and CEO. (Tisch had previously been the acting president.) As the company's largest shareholder, Tisch limited Paley's power.

Paley died on October 26, 1990, of a heart attack. He had said of his tenure at CBS: "I sort of fell into it accidentally. . . . I did it as well as I could and every time I did something, I liked it, and I'd go another step in that direction. I was always going upward, but it wasn't really a path I laid out for myself to follow. It just happened."

BIBLIOGRAPHY

Dillon, Susan J., and Donald V. West, "Farewell to the Man in the CBS Eye," *Broadcasting*, November 5, 1990; Paley, William S., *As It Happened: A Memoir*, 1979; Paper, Lewis J., *Empire: William S. Paley and the Making of CBS*, 1987; Smith, Sally Bedell, *In All His Glory: The Life of William S. Paley*, 1990.

Palmer, Potter

(May 20, 1826–May 4, 1902)
Merchant, Real Estate Developer

In the United States in the late twentieth century, the ability to exchange or re-turn merchandise is viewed as an almost inalienable right, and the practice of emphasizing presentation to sell goods is standard operating procedure. These concepts of merchandising are part of the "Palmer System," a method of retailing originated by the innovative Chicago merchant, Potter Palmer. He is also notable for the scope of his Chicago real estate holdings, including the internationally renowned hotel, the Palmer House.

Potter, the son of Benjamin and Rebecca Potter Palmer, was born on May 20, 1826, in Albany County, New York. Potter was raised a Quaker and received no formal schooling beyond the elementary level. From 1844 until 1847, Potter worked at a general store in Durham, New York, as a clerk. He eventually purchased his own dry-goods business, which he first established in the neighboring town of Oneida and later moved to Lockport.

The stagnant small-town pace eventually inspired Palmer to search for new business opportunities. With his father's support, he opened a dry-goods store in Chicago, Illinois, in 1852. The store was located on Lake Street, then the main commercial area of the city.

Palmer's notions of merchandising were peculiar, but encouraged strong customer loyalty. He allowed customers to take goods to their house for inspection prior to purchasing them. He also permitted the return or exchange of sold merchandise, a practice unheard of at

Potter Palmer (Library of Congress)

that time. This concept proved to be worth the risk; the method, now dubbed the "Palmer System," was subsequently adopted by the largest retailers in Chicago. Palmer also emphasized advertising and the importance of creating attractive displays of merchandise in store windows and on the sales floor.

His retail sales methods paid off, and after 15 years, Palmer became quite wealthy. By this time, both MARSHALL FIELD and Levi Z. Leiter had become partners in the store. Palmer's health was suffering, and he turned over the management of the store to Field and Leiter in 1867.

Palmer spent the next three years traveling abroad and recuperating. By 1870, he had regained his energy, and he turned to the pursuit of real estate development. Palmer was responsible for the transformation of a country road called State Street into a major commercial avenue. He built a hotel, the original Palmer House, and approximately 32 other buildings, bringing commerce and activity to the area.

In 1871, the great Chicago fire blazed through the city, sweeping away much of what he had built. Palmer vowed to recoup his losses and began new construction, with an emphasis on larger and more permanent structures. The second Palmer House was erected at the corner of State and Monroe. It would become a world-renowned hostelry.

Palmer was joined in this frenzy of activity by his wife, Bertha Honoré Palmer, whom he had married in 1871 before the fire. Potter and Bertha, the daughter of a prominent real estate owner, subsequently had two sons together. Palmer spent vast sums of money to transform the lakeside region north of the Chicago River, and he and his wife chose this location to build a huge and ornate mansion.

Chicago, Palmer's adopted home, was also the recipient of Palmer's time and energy in community affairs. He served on the board of directors of the World's Columbian Exposition, was president of the Chicago Baseball Club and commissioner of the South Side parks, and was a supporter of the Chicago Young Men's Christian Association.

Palmer died in his Chicago home on May 4, 1902.

BIBLIOGRAPHY

Bateman, Newton, Paul Selby, and J. S. Currey, *Historical Encyclopedia of Illinois*, 1925; *Chicago Daily Tribune*, Obituary, May 5 and May 7, 1902; Currey, J. S., *Chicago*, vols. I and III, 1912; Wood, D. W., *Chicago and Its Distinguished Citizens*, 1881.

Park, James

(January 11, 1820–April 21, 1883)
Manufacturer

Unlike ANDREW CARNEGIE, James Park received little public attention. High-quality steel made by Park lacked the glamour of larger, more massive production. Yet through his business Park, Brother & Company, his Black Diamond Steel Works, and his politics, he contributed greatly to America's steel industry.

James Park was born on January 11, 1820, in Pittsburgh, Pennsylvania, to James Park and Margaret (McCurdy) Park. He obtained only limited formal schooling before working in his father's china and metal store in 1837 and becoming a full partner in 1840. Three years later, after his father died, he and a younger brother, David, took over the business, dropped the china line, and sold only metal goods.

Park prospered and invested in a cotton mill, and in the Lake Superior Copper Works, manufacturer of copper sheathing. His most prominent role as a business leader, however, began in the early 1860s, when he entered the iron industry. Two developments at the time encouraged his activities. First, the federal government passed protective tariffs that limited foreign competition. Second, another company, Hussey, Wells, showed it was practicable to manufacture a high-quality steel called crucible cast steel to be used in tools. In 1862, Park, Brother & Company opened its Black Diamond Steel Works in Pittsburgh, and after some failures, produced its own crucible cast steel.

The development epitomized Park's character. Neither an inventor nor an original thinker, he nonetheless understood new ideas and pursued technological improvements. Thus, in 1864, he opened a mill at Wyandotte, Michigan, and produced the first steel in America made from the complete Bessemer process, which used air blasted at great force against molten pig iron to remove impurities. At about the same time, Park pioneered in using the Siemens gas furnace for metal conversion at his copper works. In 1867, he used the furnace to make crucible cast steel.

Park influenced the steel industry through his politics, too, when he fought to increase tariff rates. Critics called the tariff damaging to consumers since it limited competition by making foreign steel expensive. As a Republican member of the United States Tariff Commission, Park blunted the criticism and convinced Congress to use a clever ploy that boosted tariffs but hid the increases behind a complex classification system.

Park died on April 21, 1883, at his home in Allegheny, Pennsylvania. He was survived by his wife, Sarah Gray Park, and five sons and two daughters.

BIBLIOGRAPHY

Gilmer, Harrison, "Birth of the American Crucible Steel Industry," *Western Pennsylvania Historical Magazine*, March 1953; James, Henry K., "James Park, Jr.," *Magazine of Western History*, 1886; McHugh, Jeanne, *Alexander Holley and the Makers of Steel*, 1980.

Parker, George

(December 12, 1866–September 26, 1952)
Manufacturer

America's love of games is largely due to the creative energy of George Swinnerton Parker. An avid fan of parlor games from childhood through adulthood, Parker used his company, Parker Brothers, to develop games still popular today, including the board game "Monopoly," mass-produced jigsaw puzzles, and "Ping-Pong" (or table tennis).

The son of George Augustus and Sarah Hegeman Parker, George was born on December 12, 1866, in Salem, Massachusetts. His father was a wealthy merchant sea captain of English descent. Fond of games like many children, George devised a game while still in high school similar to chess that he called the "Battle of Brannockburn" in 1882.

A prime reason that Parker eventually became successful, and his own impetus for creating games, was that the American-made board games of the early 1800s were moralistic and far from playful. Dice and cards were considered the devil's pastime, and not until the 1860s did companies like MILTON BRADLEY emerge with games intended for amusement.

At age 16, Parker created "Banking," a game whose goal (to see who could make the most money) created a stir with its contrast to the educational and spiritual offerings from traditional game manufacturers. Parker borrowed money from his high school principal, took a leave of absence, produced 500 copies of the game, and took to the road to sell it. With his profit from the sales, he began George S. Parker and Company. Over the next few years, Parker continued to market "Banking," devised new games, and even bought the W. and S. B. Ives Company, the oldest and most straitlaced games manufacturer in the United States. The money from the moralistic but reliable sellers made by Ives enabled Parker to finance some of his more playful offerings.

In 1888, George was joined by his brother Charles. In 1896, he married Grace Eliza Mann, with whom he had two sons and a daughter. Two years later, George and Charles were joined by their other brother, Edward. By 1901, the company had incorporated under the name Parker Brothers, with George retaining the role of president. The following year, branch offices were established in New York City and London.

The company enjoyed a number of successes, but George occasionally introduced products that failed. As it turned out, he revealed a flexibility and resilience that, over time, taught his company how to deal with the many failures that preceded every winner. One invention of Parker's early days that has remained incredibly popular is "Child's Tennis," the game played with two bats and a ball over a net stretched across a table that became known as table tennis. After a company in England improved upon the game's design, George gained the rights for the newly named "Ping-Pong," a game that quickly became an international hit. In 1906, George invented the popular card game "Rook," followed by the astoundingly well-received "Pastime Picture Puzzles," a product so popular that it eventually merited its own factory.

Over the decades, George developed a knack for devising games that charmed Americans, appealing to their sense of adventure by honoring historical feats and individual achievement. He commemorated the California gold rush in a game, memorialized the flights of Charles Lindbergh, and developed games based on travel themes. He also proved to be an aggressive, hands-on salesman, capable of selling a crate of games for one price, and then turning around and selling the same thing to another retailer for more.

Of the more than 300 games sold by Parker Brothers at the time of George's death, over 100 of them had been invented and developed by George himself. The greatest and most famous of all their products, however, was invented by an unemployed laborer, Charles Darrow, and initially rejected by Parker Brothers. "Monopoly, " which remains one of the best-selling games of all time, was developed during the Great Depression. The real estate speculation and potential for high-stakes riches provided a wonderful escape from the economic woes of the decade. George, however, whose standard for excellence was high, maintained that not only did the game contain 52 errors, it could not be completed within the 45-minute time period that George believed to be the attention span of the game-playing public. But after the inventory that Darrow sold to the toy store FAO Schwartz sold rapidly, George changed his mind and bought up the rest of the games. Though the inventory quickly sold out, Parker Brothers, assuming "Monopoly" to be a fad, did not resume production until orders began to pile up so much they had to be stored in laundry bags. Soon Parker Brothers was selling 20,000 copies of "Monopoly" weekly.

Though George was a great idea man and aggressive salesman, his financial management was poor. Prior to the depression, revenues had fallen from $900,000 to $450,000 per year. Within one year, the success of "Monopoly" pushed the company over the $1 million mark. Over the next few years, Parker Brothers continued to develop a number of new games, though nothing sparked the public's enjoyment as much as "Monopoly," which continued to sell strongly.

When George Parker died on September 26, 1952, Barton and other family members took over to lead Parker Brothers into the next era of toy making.

BIBLIOGRAPHY

Parker Brothers, *Ninety Years of Fun, 1883–1973: The History of Parker Brothers*, 1973; "Where Monopoly Is Not a Dirty Word," *Business Week*, March 26, 1967; Wojahn, Ellen, *Playing by Different Rules*, 1989.

Patterson, John

(December 13, 1844–May 7, 1922)
Manufacturer

An energetic, temperamental leader, John Henry Patterson took a small manufacturer and converted it into the National Cash Register Company. In doing so he revolutionized salesmanship and developed an "industrial welfare" program.

John Patterson was born on December 13, 1844, on a farm near Dayton, Ohio. His parents, Jefferson Patterson and Julia (Johnston) Patterson, had prospered, and they provided John and his 10 siblings with a comfortable upbringing. After graduating from Central High School in Dayton, John entered Miami University in 1862. He stayed there only a year, however, and in 1864 enlisted in the Union army. Stationed in Baltimore, he saw no combat in the Civil War. Patterson continued his college education at

John Patterson (North Wind Picture Archives)

Dartmouth, in New Hampshire, and in 1867 graduated with a B.A. degree.

After returning to the family farm, Patterson went to Dayton in 1868 and worked as a canal tollgate keeper. Presently, he joined with his brothers in a coal business, but he wanted something more profitable. In 1884, he obtained a controlling interest in a financially troubled Dayton firm, the National Manufacturing Company—producer of Ritty's Incorruptible Cash Register.

Those who doubted that Patterson would succeed did not foresee the enormous expansion in retail stores that would occur in the late 1800s, an expansion bound to stimulate a demand for cash registers. Patterson changed the firm's name to the National Cash Register Company—often called The Cash—and set to work improving his product. He studied the cash register mechanism and simplified it, and then let his engineers make additional changes while he turned his attention to sales.

Patterson believed that people responded best to the fear of punishment and the reward of money. He wanted only those employees who wholeheartedly agreed with this view, especially when it came to salesmen. Patterson pushed them hard, sometimes mercilessly berating them, at other times encouraging them with motivational rallies. His bold innovations in salesmanship included a continuing training program, a quota system, and guaranteed sales territories.

Patterson initiated an industrial welfare program whereby he provided employees with attractive working conditions. He built factories that had glass walls, flowers, lunchrooms, swimming pools, and other health facilities. Benefits included free hot meals, medical care, and family counseling. As to why he did this, he said, "It pays. Hungry people, people with bad diets or in poor health, are not good producers." He expected complete obedience, however, and ruled his company with an iron hand. In one instance, he required executives to take up horseback riding for their health, and local wags called them "the National Cash Rough Riders."

Patterson believed that only The Cash should sell cash registers, and he decided to eliminate his competition through illegal methods. In his most infamous scheme, he employed THOMAS WATSON and others to open dummy shops, supposedly independent from The Cash, but actually financed by it, where they sold cash registers at prices low enough to put competitors out of business. At the same time, he made machines that looked like those of his competitors, and that he represented as genuine. Once disclosed, these activities resulted in Patterson and 29 others being convicted for criminal conspiracy in restraint of trade in 1912.

The Cash, however, had already captured 90 percent of the cash register market. Patterson retired from the presidency in 1921, but served as chairman of the board of directors until his death on May 7, 1922. Patterson's wife had died in 1894, but two children survived him.

BIBLIOGRAPHY

Crowther, Samuel, *John H. Patterson: Pioneer in Industrial Welfare*, 1923; Johnson, Roy Wilder, *The Sales Strategy of John H. Patterson: Founder of the National Cash Register Company*, 1932; Marcosson, Isaac Frederick, *Wherever Men Trade: The Romance of the Cash Register*, 1945.

Paulucci, Jeno

(July 7, 1918–)
Manufacturer

Frenetic, highstrung, and pugnacious, Jeno Francisco Paulucci once emphasized a point to his vice presidents by jumping atop a table, staring down at them, and striking fear in their hearts. With such antics, along with his zeal and determination, Paulucci built two successful food companies, Chun King and Jeno's Pizza.

The son of an Italian immigrant iron miner, Jeno, born on July 7, 1918, in Aurora, Minnesota, to Ettore Paulucci and Michelina (Buratti) Paulucci, had a poor childhood and lived in a four-room, cockroach-infested flat. His father's frequent unemployment forced the youngster to roam neighborhood railroad tracks to collect lumps of coal that could be used for fuel. At age 12, after the family moved to nearby Hibbing, he sold iron-ore samples in glass vials to tourists.

During the Great Depression, when Jeno's father deserted the family, Jeno's mother bought an abandoned house from a mining company, moved it to a lot in the south part of town, and opened a grocery store in the living room. Jeno helped out and then, at age 14, obtained a job at the Downtown Daylight Market. Paulucci impressed the store owner, David Persha, with his energy and labor. In 1934, Paulucci worked as a sales representative for Minnesota Markets, a food wholesaler, and two years later, for the Hancock-Nelson Grocery Company of St. Paul. He turned out to be such a good salesman that he earned more money than the company president.

Paulucci wanted his own business, however. Having observed Asian families growing bean sprouts hydroponically during World War II, Paulucci began a soybean business in partnership with Persha. At first the firm struggled, but with $2,500 borrowed from a local bank, he began mixing the sprouts with celery and pimentos to make chop suey that he canned and sold under the Foo Young brand name. By obtaining the celery, an essential ingredient, at reduced cost, and using discounted scratched cans, Paulucci produced Foo Young at a price that allowed him to invest in advertising and give retailers a higher markup than they received for other canned foods. This, in turn, got him more shelf space. While his business grew, in 1948 he married Lois Trepanier.

In 1951, Paulucci opened a new factory in Duluth, Minnesota, and renamed Foo Young the Chun King Corporation, using the first Chinese-sounding name that came to his mind. His mother improved the taste of his food by adding Italian seasonings, creating a Chinese-Italian mix. Paulucci launched a national advertising campaign featuring comedian Stan Freberg in 1960, and the clever advertisements boosted Chun King's sales, as did the American desire for quick food.

In 1966, Paulucci sold Chun King to the R. J. Reynolds Tobacco Company for $63 million. The deal made him chairman of the board of R. J. Reynolds Foods, but he bristled at corporate behavior and soon quit. "These people came to work at nine in the morning," he said. "I thought I was late walking in at six!"

The following year, Paulucci took the money from his sale of Chun King and founded Jeno's Pizza, which he created from another company he owned, Northland Foods. Again he understood the market and demand. At that time, the only frozen pizzas in stores were those sold regionally, and America's population, with its large number of young people, wanted easy-to-prepare foods. By 1972, Jeno's emerged as the national leader in frozen pizza, but intense competition came from Pillsbury, Quaker Oats, and other giant corporations. Paulucci reacted by closing his Duluth plant and relocating to Ohio, where he had access to cheaper transportation. The move cost Duluth 1,500 jobs and angered the city's residents.

Paulucci sold Jeno's Pizza to his main competitor, Pillsbury, in 1986 for $150 million. His subsequent business ventures failed to equal his earlier success. *Attenzione*, a magazine he founded for Italian Americans, lost $4 million; a 3,000-acre residential and office development in Orlando, Florida, struggled; and Pizza Kwik and China Kwik, home food-delivery services, both folded shortly after he founded them in 1986. Paulucci, however, remained a multimillionaire despite these setbacks.

BIBLIOGRAPHY

Pine, Carol, and Susan Mundale, *Self-Made: The Stories of 12 Minnesota Entrepreneurs*, 1982; Silver, A. David, *Entrepreneurial Megabucks: The 100 Greatest Entrepreneurs of the Last Twenty-Five Years*, 1985.

Peabody, Joseph

(December 12, 1757–January 5, 1844)
Shipping Executive, Merchant

Joseph Peabody, a merchant ship-owner, commanded a large and highly profitable fleet of ships in the nineteenth century. He amassed an impressive fortune for that era and was a strong contributor to the economy of Salem, Massachusetts. Though he dabbled in the manufacture of iron, he was principally known for his prowess in privateering and trade. Peabody's business presaged a period of flourishing maritime activity in Salem that decreased significantly after his death.

Joseph, the ninth of the 10 children of Francis and Margaret Knight Peabody, was born on December 12, 1757, in Middleton, Massachusetts. When the American Revolution erupted in April 1775, Peabody marched to Lexington intending to fight with the minutemen. Arriving after the battle was over, Peabody continued on to Salem, where he found work aboard a ship. Initially, he served on the *Bunker Hill* and then on the *Pilgrim.*

Though Peabody was fascinated by the sea, he astutely realized that he could benefit by a fuller education. To this end, he studied for a year in Middleton with the Reverend Elias Smith, although his studies were interrupted by a brief stint in the militia. After completing his education, Peabody took a job aboard the *Fishhawk,* but was imprisoned in Newfoundland when the privateer was captured by the British.

Eventually, Peabody was released in a prisoner exchange and became the second officer aboard the *Ranger.* Once again, he found himself on the defensive when a band of British Loyalists attacked

Joseph Peabody (North Wind Picture Archives)

the ship. This time, Peabody was able to rally and fight them off. By the end of the war, he had secured the post of captain on a Salem merchant ship. With his savings, he purchased the schooner *Three Friends* and spent several years traveling around the West Indies and Europe engaged in trade.

By 1791, Peabody established his own merchant ship business and set up shop in Salem. On August 28 of that same year, he married Catherine Smith, the daughter of the reverend who had been his tutor. The marriage was cut short with her death in 1793. Two years later, Peabody married Catherine's sister, Elizabeth, with whom he shared a long, happy marriage that yielded six sons and a daughter.

Always a thorough and hardworking individual, Peabody's instinct for business enabled him to build a thriving operation over which he retained sole control. He maintained a large fleet of ships that conducted trade in the Baltic, with the Mediterranean countries, and in the West Indies. His most lucrative connections, however, were in India, China, and the East Indies. His goods from these locales included opium, indigo, tea, and pepper.

While records are unclear about the extent of Peabody's fortune, much can be determined from the official records of the duties he paid on his goods. Over a period of years, Peabody paid out over $1 million in government duties, and it is estimated that his profit was at least equivalent to that amount. His annual tax burden was in the neighborhood of $200,000. Undoubtedly, he commanded a considerable fortune for the time.

Notable ships in Peabody's fleet included *Sumatra*, *Friendship*, and his favorite ship, a swift privateer bought for just over $5,000 named *George*. *Friendship* became known for its unfortunate fate: the only one of Peabody's ships to fare badly, it was attacked by the natives of Quallah Battoo in the East Indies, and her crew was massacred.

During the course of his career, Peabody employed over 6,500 crewmen. Over 35 of these had entered service as boys and remained to become masters of ships. Peabody was an influential figure in the economy of Salem, employing sailors, shipbuilders, and all manner of clerks and assistants to help him manage his enormous business. Though costs may have been lower elsewhere, Peabody consistently built his ships in Salem boatyards. He also distributed goods from Salem and along the coast rather than using larger cities like New York or Boston as his base of operations. In addition, he owned and operated the Salem Iron Works.

Peabody was known to be an altruistic man, who extended credit readily and could be counted on to give generously to charity. He was short-tempered but fair, and most conflicts in which he was engaged were settled equitably. He was generally apolitical and was a devout member of the Unitarian Church.

Peabody died in Salem on January 5, 1844, at the age of 87.

BIBLIOGRAPHY

Endicott, William Crowninshield, *Captain Joseph Peabody, East India Merchant of Salem (1757–1844): A Record of His Ships and of His Family*, 1962; Hunt, Freeman, *Lives of American Merchants*, 1858; Maclay, E. S., *A History of American Privateers*, 1899; Payne, R. D., *The Ships and Sailors of Old Salem*, 1909.

Penney, James Cash

(September 16, 1875–February 12, 1971)
Merchant

From a small, cluttered dry-goods shop in Kemmerer, Wyoming, James Cash Penney developed a department store chain that reshaped American retailing.

Born September 16, 1875, on a farm near Hamilton, Missouri, James was the seventh of 12 children in a family headed by James Cash Penney and his wife, Mary Frances (Paxton) Penney. The elder Penney preached at a local church and worked his farm. He encouraged his children to get an education, and as a result James completed high school. Soon after, he began working at a general store in Hamilton, where he swept the floors, kept the shelves stocked, and sold goods.

In 1897, Penney moved to Colorado, where he worked briefly at two stores in Denver before relocating to Longmont, a farming town. There, with the help of partners, he opened a meat market and bakery. While running his business, he observed how the city's Golden Rule Store, part of a dry-goods chain, almost always had customers. After Penney's meat market and bakery failed, he jumped at the chance to work at a Golden Rule Store in Evanston, Wyoming. He learned that Golden Rule's success depended on attractive advertising for its shoes, hats, shirts, petticoats, corsets, and other clothes, and on a cash-only policy that allowed the stores to sell goods at low prices.

In 1902, three years after marrying Berta Hess, by whom he had several children, Penney moved to the small town of Kemmerer, where he operated a Golden Rule Store with two partners. Many predicted his failure, for the townspeople, largely miners, purchased their goods on credit from stores owned by the mining companies. Penney crammed goods into the small store, stayed open long hours, and advertised low prices, often 50 percent below the prices elsewhere.

During his first year in business, he sold nearly $29,000 worth of merchandise, and earned a profit of over $8,500. In 1904, he and his partners moved to a more spacious location and opened other stores in Cumberland and Rock Springs that also prospered. In 1907, Penney's partners decided they wanted out, leaving Penney the sole owner of the stores.

He searched for another partner who would provide the loyalty and leadership to allow further expansion, and found one in Earl Coder Sams. In time, Sams became second only to Penney in running the business. By 1910, Penney owned 14 Golden Rule Stores, and had several more partners. He still avoided fancy fixtures, and kept his merchandise piled on tables where customers could touch the items they wanted. He envisioned owning 50 stores.

In 1911, after his wife's death, Penney plunged into more expansion and incorporated his interests as the J. C. Penney Company, although his stores continued to carry the Golden Rule name until 1917. "We cater to the masses," said Penney, "and we do it in a simple way."

Penney married Mary Hortense Kimball in 1919, settled down on a 50-acre estate in White Plains, New York, and oversaw his company's continued expansion after World War I. By the end of 1929,

Penney had 1,395 stores, and the company reported record sales of $209 million, with more than $12 million in profits. After World War II, Penney's new stores grew into true "department stores" that in the mid-1960s averaged more than 86,000 square feet and were located in shopping centers and malls. At the same time, the company changed its policy and for the first time offered credit sales.

Penney remained chairman of the board until 1958, after which as a board member he helped transform the company into its modern form (although he never did like credit sales). He attended numerous store openings and served as a real-life figure many customers could relate to in an increasingly impersonal corporate world. When Penney died on February 12, 1971, at age 95 from a heart attack, he left an estate worth more than $25 million and a company that, today, remains prominent in the department store business.

BIBLIOGRAPHY

Curry, Mary Elizabeth, *Creating an American Institution: The Merchandising Genius of J. C. Penney*, 1993.

Pepperell, William

(June 27, 1696–July 6, 1759)
Merchant

William Pepperell earned a fortune as a merchant and a historical reputation as the military leader in command of the siege of Louisbourg during King George's War.

William was born on June 27, 1696, in Kittery Point, Maine, the son of William Pepperell, a prosperous merchant, and Margery (Bray) Pepperell. After assisting his father in the merchant business, he became a full partner in 1717. He then expanded the trade considerably, pursued new markets in Europe and the West Indies, and engaged in shipbuilding. In 1723, he married Mary Hirst with whom he would have four children.

Beginning in 1726 and continuing for 20 years, Pepperell was chosen by his fellow townsmen to represent them in the colonial legislature at Boston (Maine then being a part of Massachusetts). He also served on the colonial council, as a justice of the court of common pleas for York County, and was a junior officer before becoming commander of the Maine regiment. In short, he held a prominent position in the colony, as did most any successful merchant in that era. By the early 1740s, Pepperell was one of New England's wealthiest men.

Thus, when war erupted between Britain and France in 1744, the British authorities considered Pepperell's support to be important. When Massachusetts Governor William Shirley called for an assault against Louisbourg, the formidable French fortress on Cape Breton Island, Pepperell promoted the idea in the colonial legislature, winning approval for what many believed was an impossible mission.

Under Lt. Gen. Pepperell, 4,000 volunteers, accompanied by three ships of the Royal Navy and several small colonial ships, laid siege to Louisbourg for six weeks, beginning April 30, 1745. After the French surrendered, Pepperell led his troops into Louisbourg. The British government rewarded him for his services by making him a baronet.

Much debate continues as to whether Pepperell contributed significantly to the victory at Louisbourg. During the siege, he hesitated in launching a direct attack on the French, and his junior officers were probably more aggressive than he in placing artillery in crucial positions. Indeed, Pepperell's greatest contribution may have been in promoting the assault to begin with, and in maintaining unity among the officers and between the colonials and the British navy.

Pepperell retired from business soon after returning from Boston in 1746, although he remained active in politics. He died at his Kittery Point estate on July 6, 1759.

William Pepperell (Library of Congress)

BIBLIOGRAPHY

Fairchild, Byron, *Messrs. William Pepperell: Merchants at Piscataqua*, 1954; Pepperell, Sir William, *The Pepperell Papers*, 1899; Rawlyk, G. A., *Yankees at Louisbourg*, 1967.

Perdue, Frank

(1920–)
Manufacturer

Frank Perdue did not invent the devices that signaled the automation of the chicken industry, but he adopted them to his family business and made Perdue Farms a lucrative company.

Born in Salisbury, Maryland, in 1920, Frank grew up around chickens. His father, Arthur Perdue, owned a small coop in the 1920s and shipped eggs to markets in New York City. The business expanded to the point that it prospered even during the Great Depression. In 1939, Frank quit Salisbury State College and joined his father's business. Tragedy struck the following year, however, when an infectious disease killed nearly all their chickens. The Perdues then decided to buy hardier New Hampshire Reds and switch from egg sales to the production of chickens to eat, known in the business as broilers. They began hatching their own chickens, raising them on a special feed mix, and selling the live birds at auction.

By 1953, Perdue Farms had annual revenues of $8 million on sales of 2.6 million broilers. That year, Frank Perdue took over from his father and as president introduced mechanization and shifted from selling mainly live chickens to selling mainly dressed chicken meat. The mechanized broiler industry promoted by Perdue and others began changing American diets. Chickens, formerly a luxury item, became commonplace.

Perdue built a large, new complex at Salisbury, Maryland, in 1958 that included a feed mill and machinery to make meal from soybeans. He used the meal for his chickens and sold surpluses to other companies. The following year, he equipped a plant with more modern machinery and processed tens of thousands of chickens an hour. Perdue invested $7 million on a larger poultry processing plant in Accomoc, Virginia, in 1971, and launched an aggressive advertising campaign. Never before had chickens been so heavily promoted.

Perdue advertised the yellow color of his chickens—a cosmetic yellow that came from the feed and had nothing to do with quality—as indicating a superior bird. He appeared in television commercials where his chickenlike face left an impression. In fact, shoppers began remembering Perdue chickens as much for the image of Frank Perdue as for his product. They remembered, too, Perdue's catchy statements: "My chickens even get cookies for dessert" and "It takes a tough man to make a tender chicken."

Perdue chickens appeared mainly in New York City and elsewhere in the Northeast, where they sold well. Perdue opened a hatchery and yet another processing plant in Lewiston, North Carolina, in 1976, by which time he had a total of 3,000 employees. They worked for abysmally low wages as Perdue defeated unionizing attempts and hired mainly African-American women who had few other employment options.

By the late 1980s, Perdue's annual sales topped $1 billion. But the company's growth generated controversy when a federal crime commission revealed dealings between Perdue Farms and Mafia-run distributing companies. Perdue later said he should never have dealt with the companies, while the government exonerated him. In fact, other poultry firms did business with the Mafia-run companies, a rather common practice where distributors had the power to determine which chickens appeared in supermarkets.

Perdue retired as CEO of Perdue Farms in 1988 after having accumulated a fortune of at least $350 million. His son, Jim Perdue, took control, and in 1994 Perdue Farms, the nation's third largest poultry producer, had sales of $1.5 billion.

BIBLIOGRAPHY

"Chatting Up a Mob Boss," *U.S. News & World Report*, March 17, 1986; Farnham, Alan, "Skewering Perdue," *Fortune*, February 24, 1992; Sheraton, Mimi, "They're Fencing Beak to Beak: A Celebrity Duel Is Joined for Fatter Chicken Profits," *Time*, September 28, 1987.

Perelman, Ronald

(1943–)
Financier

Often likened to corporate raiders T. BOONE PICKENS and CARL ICAHN, Ronald O. Perelman earned his greatest notoriety in his takeover of Revlon, the giant cosmetics manufacturer.

Born in 1943 in Greensboro, North Carolina, to Raymond Perelman and Ruth (Caplan) Perelman, Ronald grew up in a wealthy family. His father owned Belmont Industries, a holding company for several businesses whose assets totaled $300 million. As a boy, Ronald attended Belmont's board meetings, and he and his father discussed possible acquisitions. After attending the exclusive Haverford School in Philadelphia, Perelman graduated from the University of Pennsylvania in 1964 with a B.A. degree in economics, and from the Wharton School of Business with an M.B.A. in 1966.

He then rejoined his father at Belmont and together they bought companies, disposed of unwanted operations, and borrowed against their assets to buy yet more companies. Perelman used this strategy throughout his business career.

By 1978, however, he wanted to be independent, and thus left Belmont and began investing on his own. In April of that year, he bought a 34 percent interest in Cohen-Hatfield Industries, a jewelry retailer, for $2 million. He then sold most of the company's holdings except its wholesale watch distribution, and improved its cash flow. In the process, he accumulated $15 million for further acquisitions.

He next targeted MacAndrews & Forbes, a manufacturer of licorice extract and bulk chocolate. Perelman bought the company in 1980 for $45 million. Unlike many other corporate raiders, Perelman involved himself extensively in company operations, and at MacAndrews & Forbes he entered the European market and expanded the product line to include spices.

After buying Technicolor, a film-processing company, in 1983, Perelman's next big deal was his acquisition of

Pantry Pride, a Florida-based supermarket chain. In gaining control of Pantry Pride he acquired several tax benefits, and thus accumulated enough capital to pursue Revlon, the cosmetics manufacturer founded by CHARLES REVSON. Revlon had annual sales exceeding $2 billion and marketed its cosmetics and health-care products in 130 countries. Perelman bought Revlon in 1985 for $2.7 billion, a deal that placed him among the ranks of the wealthiest and shrewdest of the corporate raiders.

Perelman sold most of Revlon's health-care subsidiaries in order to concentrate on cosmetics. He then boosted its image by introducing new products, such as a one-coat nail enamel and Bill Blass fragrances, and by hiring Susan Lucci, star of the TV soap opera *All My Children*, as the company's spokesperson. In 1987, Revlon's sales increased 41 percent over the previous year, and Perelman bought Max Factor, another cosmetics company, to merge it with Revlon.

While leading Revlon, Perelman's personal life changed when he married Claudia Cohen, a television entertainment reporter. (His first marriage to Faith Golding had ended in divorce.) On the business front, he continued investing in other companies in the late 1980s. For example, he bought a 15 percent interest in the Transworld Corporation, operator of hotels and food-service businesses. Although he failed to gain control of Gillette, the giant manufacturer of razors and razor blades, in his takeover bid he forced the company to buy back his own shares and reaped a $43 million profit. In another venture, with government help, he bought the San Antonio Savings Association.

In 1991, trouble with debt payments from his deals forced Perelman to sell Max Factor, but he remained in control at Revlon. In 1994, his marriage to Claudia Cohen, with whom he had a daughter, ended in divorce, and he married Patricia Duff. They had one child.

About Perelman's investments, *Forbes* magazine observed: "Charles Revson made his fortune figuring out how to persuade women to buy his products. Ron Perelman has made a bigger fortune at Revlon figuring out how to buy and sell businesses. It's the story of our time."

BIBLIOGRAPHY

Hack, Richard, *When Money Is King: How Revlon's Ron Perelman Mastered the World of Finance to Create One of America's Greatest Business Empires, and Found Glamour, Beauty and the High Life in the Bargain,* 1996; Sloan, Allan, and Lauara Jereski, "A Tale of Our Times," *Forbes,* May 18, 1987.

Perkins, George

(January 31, 1862–June 18, 1920)
Insurance Executive, Banker

Americans faced a new economy in the early 1900s, one that was increasingly directed by big corporations. In the ensuing debate as to whether that development was harmful or beneficial, George Walbridge Perkins was a strong advocate of corporate power. As vice president of the New York Life Insurance Company (NYLIC), as a banker with J. P. Morgan Sr., and finally as a political activist, he promoted his views.

George was born on January 31, 1862, in Chicago, Illinois, the son of George Walbridge Perkins Sr. and Sarah Louise (Mills) Perkins. The elder Perkins, superintendent of the Chicago Reform School when his son was born, eventually left that position and became assistant superintendent of the New York Life Insurance Company's agencies in the Chicago region. Young George had only limited formal education, and quit school at age 15 to clerk for his father. After Perkins Sr. died in 1886, the young man began selling insurance in Indiana for NYLIC.

He quickly outsold his colleagues, and the company appointed him district supervisor. Perkins subsequently advanced rapidly within the firm, and while serving as third vice president in 1892, he initiated a reform that changed the insurance industry. He replaced the practice of selling policies through general agents who received commissions, and over whom the company had little control, with a branch office system in which bonuses and a pension plan fostered loyalty to the corporation. A few years later, he successfully applied his innovation to the European insurance market.

George Perkins (Library of Congress)

By the early 1900s, Perkins was first vice president of NYLIC and had begun underwriting securities and buying railroad bonds overseas. Financier J. P. Morgan Sr. cast a wary eye on this activity, fearing it would infringe on his investments. He then offered Perkins a partnership in the House of Morgan, which he accepted while retaining his vice presidency at NYLIC.

Over the following decade, Perkins negotiated some of the most momentous mergers in American economic history. For example, in a deal between Morgan and EDWARD HARRIMAN he helped create the Northern Securities Company that comprised the Northern Pacific, Union Pacific, and Burlington Railroads. More significantly, he guided the merger of the CYRUS MCCORMICK and JOHN DEERE farm implement companies, along with three smaller firms, to form the International Harvester Company. This huge corporation controlled nearly 85 percent of the American harvester and reaper market. After it initially lost money, he implemented reforms that made it efficient and strong.

Perkins thought that big corporations were beneficial to the nation as long as they acted responsibly toward society. Thus, while some reformers advocated breaking up the conglomerates, he favored keeping them and developing a cooperative relationship between the large corporations and the national government, in which the latter could act to curb abuses.

Perkins's advocacy propelled him into politics, and after leaving the House of Morgan he joined Theodore Roosevelt's 1912 campaign for the Republican presidential nomination. When Roosevelt lost and opted to form a third political party, the Progressive Party, Perkins served as chairman of its executive committee and contributed large sums of money to the campaign. Again Roosevelt lost, but Perkins remained active in the party, working to undermine radical reformers who wanted to dismantle the big corporations.

Perkins died on June 18, 1920. He had married Evelyn Ball in 1889, and they had a daughter and a son, George W. Perkins Jr., who had his own prominent career in business and entered the government in 1949 as assistant secretary of state for European affairs.

BIBLIOGRAPHY

Carosso, Vincent P., *Investment Banking in America*, 1970; Corey, Lewis, *The House of Morgan*, 1930.

Perot, Ross

(June 27, 1930–)
Computer Services Executive

In looking for business associates, Henry Ross Perot declared, "I want people who are smart, tough, self-reliant . . . people who love to win." As a computer services entrepreneur and later, a controversial politician, he exemplified these qualities along with stubbornness, self-righteousness, and imperiousness.

Ross Perot was born Henry Ray Perot on June 27, 1930, in Texarkana, Texas. His mother, Lulu May Ray Perot, was a former secretary, and his father, Gabriel Elias Perot, worked as a cotton broker. They changed young Perot's name to Henry Ross when he was in the fifth grade. Perot held numerous jobs as a child: he broke horses, sold garden seeds and Christmas cards, and, at age 12, convinced a newspaper publisher to give him a paper route in a run-down neighborhood. Perot surprised the publisher by selling a large number of subscriptions. The youngster delivered newspapers on bicycle and horseback—a story he later loved to tell audiences.

Perot's work ethic showed again in 1943 when, in an unusual feat, he achieved Eagle Scout just 16 months after joining the Boy Scouts. Four years later, he graduated from Texarkana High School with a good but undistinguished record and enrolled at Texarkana Junior College. While there, he applied to the U.S. Naval Academy and, at age 19, gained acceptance. Perot studied engineering and displayed dedication and discipline.

When the Korean War erupted in 1950, the navy assigned him to a destroyer, but combat had ended by the time his ship reached the scene. Perot served as chief engineer, but his self-righteousness, and his conviction that he was right and everyone else was wrong, caused conflict with the ship's captain, and in 1955 the navy transferred him to a lesser position on an aircraft carrier. Perot, angered by the navy's slowness in promoting him, requested and received an honorable discharge in 1957.

While in the service, Perot had met an executive with International Business Machines (IBM) who told the young man to "look him up." Perot did so and began working in Dallas, Texas, as a salesman, selling the refrigerator-sized IBM 1401 computer to businesses. A change in the company's commission system in 1961 placed limits on Perot's income and caused him to consider other opportunities. In December, while sitting in a bar-

Ross Perot (Library of Congress)

ber shop reading *Reader's Digest*, he came across a statement by Henry David Thoreau: "The mass of men lead lives of quiet desperation." Perot determined to avoid this fate, and so he left IBM.

Rather than continue with computer sales, he decided to sell data processing services—something already offered by other firms, including IBM. In June 1962, aided by money he had earned at IBM and a small loan from his wife, Margot Birmingham, whom he had married in 1956, Perot incorporated Electronic Data Services (EDS) while working part-time as a consulting data processing manager at Blue Cross–Blue Shield of Texas.

Perot appealed to businesses by telling them that using his service would enable them to avoid buying expensive computers. He would run the computer programs with which they were unfamiliar, and compile the information they needed. He made his first sale in February 1963, and operated an accounting system for Frito-Lay potato chips. Perot at first did not own any computers, so on his projects he instructed his workers to use downtime on computers owned by other companies. Like IBM, Perot enforced a strict dress code for his workers—white shirts and ties, neat hair—and insisted they be faithful to their wives.

Despite his success, Perot knew EDS stood on brittle ground, that in time cheaper computers would threaten his business and that, already, companies found they could set up their own programs and get along without EDS. So, in 1967, he developed the concept of facilities management, whereby EDS operated a company's computer center.

Near the same time, the federal government inadvertently helped EDS. In 1965, Congress had passed legislation establishing Medicare, and the resulting claims from patients overwhelmed insurance companies. EDS stepped in as a subcontractor for Blue Cross–Blue Shield, and Perot's success in establishing a system that allowed his client to issue checks on time led to contracts with other insurance companies. By 1968, annual profits at EDS reached $2.4 million, and when Perot went public with EDS stock in September 1968, he became a billionaire.

While continuing his business, Perot plunged into the first of several crusades that characterized his public life. In December 1969, he chartered a cargo plane, loaded it with food, medicine, and gifts for American prisoners of war, and took it to North Vietnam. Although the North

Vietnamese government refused permission for the aircraft to land, Perot's mission attracted international attention. One observer said: "I don't think there is any question but that his ... activities highlighted concerns ... in a way the government couldn't."

In the 1970s and into the following decade, Perot took the lead in insisting that the United States had deserted POWs when it withdrew its troops from Vietnam. For years the government denied the charge, but it later admitted that 135 servicemen had been left behind. Although Perot had raised awareness about the issue, his refusal to cooperate with government officials and his inability to verify his claims marred his work.

Perot's most dramatic public effort came in 1978. That year in Teheran, the Iranian revolutionary government arrested and imprisoned two EDS employees, Paul Chiapparone and Bill Gaylord. Perot launched a three-pronged plan to get their release: he pressured the U.S. government to intervene, he had a banking project manager in Iran negotiate with that government's leaders, and he hired Colonel Arthur "Bull" Sessions to train a team of EDS executives to rescue the men. Operation HOTFOOT, as Perot called it, had many faults, but in the end it worked. In February 1979, Sessions got EDS employees in Iran—Iranian nationals—to incite crowds that stormed the prison. During this riot Chiapparone and Gaylord escaped. The adventure, written about in the book *On Wings of Eagles* and made into a TV movie, won Perot considerable praise.

At the same time, the governor of Texas recruited Perot to head a war on drugs. Perot's recommendations caused the legislature to pass tougher sentencing laws. In 1983, Perot headed a Select Committee on Public Education that made several proposals adopted by the legislature: more money for school lunches, higher salaries for teachers, and a "no pass, no play" rule that prohibited students who failed classes from playing on athletic teams.

In 1984, Perot sold EDS to General Motors (GM) for $2.5 billion and stock in the auto manufacturer. Under the deal he remained chairman of EDS and gained a seat on the GM board of directors. Perot wasted little time in publicly criticizing what he called GM mismanagement. Relations between the Texan and GM got so bad that in 1986 GM bought Perot's shares for $700 million and severed its relationship with him. Two years later, Perot founded the Perot Systems Corporation and obtained a lucrative contract to automate the U.S. Postal Service. He invested as well in a computer company and in Texas real estate. Over the years, Perot gave more than $100 million to the Boy Scouts, Girl Scouts, Salvation Army, hospitals, and programs for low-income families.

After seeing the American public's disenchantment with both the Republican and Democratic Parties, Perot decided in 1992 to run for president. On the issues, he opposed the federal deficit and called for a balanced budget, sought to end waste in spending, and wanted to exclude wealthy retirees from Social Security and Medicare. These positions proved less important, though, than a widespread desire for a "nonpolitical" candidate, a qualification Perot seemed to fill. Consequently, efforts by his campaign organizers and by independent voters resulted in his name appearing on all 50 state ballots.

As Perot's campaign gained momentum, he startled the nation by announcing his withdrawal from the race. Then in another surprising move, on October 1 he declared his reentry. In a sensational and unsubstantiated story, Perot explained that he had withdrawn earlier because the Republicans intended to disrupt his daughter's wedding with dirty tricks. Although Perot failed to win the presidency, he got 19 percent of the popular vote—an impressive showing for an independent candidate.

Soon after his defeat, Perot organized United We Stand, America and kept a high political profile by campaigning against the North American Free Trade Agreement (NAFTA), a treaty, he claimed, that would result in the loss of American jobs to Mexico. Despite his opinion, at President Bill Clinton's urging, Congress approved NAFTA.

In 1995, Perot organized the Reform Party and the following year he again ran for president. But new difficulties confronted him when differences erupted within his own party. Richard Lamm, a former governor, opposed Perot for the nomination and some within the party accused the Texan of stifling debate. A special commission kept Perot out of the presidential debates, and his standing with the general public worsened. He won only 8 percent of the popular vote, much less than four years earlier.

Observers speculated as to whether Perot's 1996 loss ended his political crusade. After the debacle, he pushed for campaign finance reform—as he had during the election—and continued to lead the Reform Party. With Bill Clinton's popularity, he faded from public view, but few who knew Perot expected him to remain in the background.

BIBLIOGRAPHY

Mason, Todd, *Perot: An Unauthorized Biography*, 1990; Posner, Gerald, *Citizen Perot: His Life and Times*, 1996.

Pew, Joseph

(July 25, 1848–October 10, 1912)
Oil and Gas Executive

As Americans discovered oil and natural gas, Joseph Newton Pew led in realizing the importance of both to an industrializing society.

Joseph was born on July 25, 1848, in Mercer County, Pennsylvania, to John Pew, a farmer, and Nancy (Glenn) Pew. As a boy, Joseph worked for his father and in 1866 graduated from the Edinboro Normal School. After teaching school for two years, he opened a real estate broker's office, first in Mercer County, and later in Titusville, Pennsylvania. The latter proved fortuitous—oil had been discovered in Titusville in 1859, and Pew invested heavily in that region's oil lands.

Pew also realized the potential market for natural gas, and by 1877 he joined with several partners to pipe the product to Bradford, Pennsylvania, for use in homes there. In 1880, he built a pipeline to Olean, New York, and provided gas to that city through his Keystone Gas Company.

Pew organized the Penn Fuel Company in 1882 and undertook his biggest project up to that time when he laid pipelines in the streets of Pittsburgh, Pennsylvania. When pressure in the pipeline decreased, he invented and patented a pump to move the gas.

At the same time, he organized the Sun Oil Company of Delaware, served as its president, and built a refinery in Toledo, Ohio. In 1901, he formed the Sun Company of New Jersey, which had refineries in Ohio and Pennsylvania and oil wells in Ohio, Illinois, West Virginia, and Texas.

Soon after selling Penn Fuel to GEORGE WESTINGHOUSE, Pew organized the People's Natural Gas Company, which, like his previous business, supplied natural gas to Pittsburgh. He served as president of People's until 1903. Pew died on October 10, 1912, while serving as president of Sun Company-New Jersey. He had married Mary Catharine Anderson, and in addition to two daughters, they had three sons, two of whom succeeded him in the oil and natural gas business.

BIBLIOGRAPHY

Pew, J. Howard, *Faith and Freedom in the Journal of a Great American: J. Howard Pew*, 1975.

Phelps, Anson

(March 24, 1781–November 30, 1853)
Merchant

Anson Greene Phelps was a merchant with a flair for variety. Achieving success in many endeavors, Phelps tried his hand at selling saddles, manufacturing metal, mining, and construction. His propensity to lend money for land projects was critical to the formation of Scranton, Pennsylvania. As he prospered, he also became a philanthropist.

Anson, the youngest of the four sons of Thomas and Dorothy Woodbridge Phelps, was born in Simsbury, Connecticut, on March 24, 1781. His father, a descendant of British immigrants, owned a partial interest in a saw and grist mill after serving in the American Revolution. Thomas Phelps died in 1789, followed by his wife in 1795. The orphaned Anson went to live with a minister and learned the trade of a saddler from his elder brother.

Eventually, after becoming knowledgeable at the trade, Phelps moved to Hartford, where, on October 26, 1806, he married Olivia Eggleston. The couple had one son and seven daughters.

Phelps's business as a saddler began to prosper. He increased his manufacture of saddles and expanded his sales area by shipping them south. He also opened another shop in Charleston, South Carolina. The venture grew rapidly, leading Phelps to diversify, and move into the sale and trade of imported tinplate and other metals.

In 1812, the Phelps family moved to New York City, in order for Phelps to begin a partnership with Elisha Peck. The firm of Phelps, Peck & Company gained national prominence for its extensive metal importing and manufacturing infrastructure. Though the business was strong enough to expand to another region of New York, Peck and Phelps decided in 1828 to dissolve the partnership. The next few years were difficult ones for Phelps, culminating in the tragedy of one of his warehouses collapsing and killing several people.

Phelps regrouped and went into partnership with his two sons-in-law, WILLIAM DODGE and Daniel James. The firm, Phelps, Dodge & Company, moved beyond trade to develop interests in mining and railroads. Later activities included copper mining and the establishment of the factory town of Ansonia. The partnership was also a significant investor in the development of the Pennsylvania iron industry. The city of Scranton owes its existence in part to Phelps for his loans to the city's founder, George W. Scranton.

Phelps's personal interests were as diverse as his business activities. A pious man, he was a devout member of the Presbyterian Church. He also served as the director of the American Bible Society and sat on the American Board of Commissioners for Foreign Missions. Other philanthropic actions were directed at the New York Institute of the Blind, as well as the American Colonization Society of the state of Connecticut. He believed that the society's goal of returning former slaves to the African continent was the best method of abolishing slavery. Upon his death, he willed $600,000 of his fortune to religious and benevolent purposes.

Phelps suffered for some time from bad health. He died in New York on November 30, 1853.

BIBLIOGRAPHY

Dictionary of American Biography, vol. VII, 1964; Dodge, D. S., *Memorials of Wm. E. Dodge*, 1887; Phelps, O. S., and A. T. Servin, *Phelps Family*, 1899; Prentiss, G. E., *A Sermon Preached on the Death of Anson G. Phelps with Some Extracts from His Diary*, 1854.

Phillips, Frank

(November 28, 1873–August 23, 1950)
Oil Industrialist

Frank Phillips, the founder of Phillips Petroleum Company, was a legendary oil-field wildcatter and a pioneering entrepreneur of the oil industry. He revolutionized oil-processing practices, and his company grew to be a booming empire that made him a multimillionaire.

Phillips, the first son in a family of 10 children, was born in Scotia, Nebraska, on November 28, 1873. His father, Lewis Franklin Phillips, was a carpenter, and his mother, Lucinda Josephine Faucett Phillips, was a schoolteacher. In 1874, the family moved to Creston, Iowa. Phillips, the eldest, was a born leader. As a child, he believed he was destined to become a self-made hero like those in the writings of Horatio Alger, the rags-to-riches author he revered. Eager to earn a living, Phillips left school at the age of 14 and became an apprentice barber.

For several years, Phillips traveled around the West, working as a barber and occasionally securing railroad work. By 1895, Phillips returned to Iowa, where he became the owner of the Climax Shaving Parlor. Soon, he bought another branch store and began to sell "Phillips Mountain Sage," a highly popular rainwater tonic touted as a cure for baldness.

By 1897, Phillips had married Jane Gibson, the daughter of a respected Creston banker. The couple had one child, John Gibson, and later adopted two daughters, Mary and Sara Jane. In 1898, Phillips sold his barbershops and became a bond and securities salesman.

After several years of profitable sales, with commissions totaling over $75,000, Phillips, on a visit to the 1904 St. Louis World's Fair, was told that oil was "flowing out of the ground like water" in Oklahoma. Sensing the potential, Phillips moved to Bartlesville, a town in the heart of what was then known as Indian Territory.

With investors lined up by his father-in-law, Phillips formed the Anchor Oil and Gas Company. Phillips purchased oil leases and began to "wildcat," the process of drilling wells in unproven territory. After several unlucky attempts, Phillips's fourth well was a winner. Phillips then pulled off an unprecedented feat and drilled for oil 81 times in a row without a single one coming up dry.

Before this remarkable run of good luck, Phillips's brothers, Waite and L. E., had joined him in Bartlesville. The Phillips brothers were unimpressed by the conservatism of local banks, which largely opposed the financing of oil ventures. Believing that a bank that catered to the oil business could succeed in oil territory, the Phillips brothers started their own bank. In July 1905, two months before he drilled his first gusher, Phillips formed the Citizen's Bank and Trust Company. In a relatively short time, the Phillips brothers dominated the local banking market.

Encouraged by the success of Anchor Oil and Gas Company, the Phillips brothers formed additional companies, including Lewcinda Oil and Gas Company, owned wholly by the Phillips family. For a time, the brothers contemplated switching gears to focus more on banking than new oil projects. But with the automobile gaining in popularity, World War I further increasing demand for fuel, and the discovery of new fields in the Osage Indian region, more Phillips companies would follow.

On June 13, 1917, the Phillips Petroleum Company, a public company consolidating the holdings of the Phillips family, was incorporated. The company experienced immediate and phenomenal growth, expanding from assets of $3 million in 1917 to a listing on the New York Stock Exchange and a value of $34 million by 1920.

Phillips was fiercely individualistic and energetic. He maintained homes in both Bartlesville and New York City, enjoying the contrast of midwestern down-to-earth spirit and the cosmopolitan flavor of Manhattan in the 1920s. He also expanded the scope of his businesses. "Uncle Frank," as he was called by his employees, was a strong believer in research and development. Phillips Petro-

leum Company became a leader in the oil industry largely because of innovative techniques like the thermal polymerization process, which decreased inefficiency by converting waste gas into gasoline. The company's research program also developed a component of aviation fuel, as well as a process called copper sweetening to raise octane ratings of gasoline.

Phillips understood the benefits of diversification. By 1927, the company had established its own refineries, as well as a chain of gas stations. The filling stations, which carried the name "Phillips 66," completed the chain of seeing the product (i.e., oil) through from discovery to drilling to refining to marketing to the sale of the end product. The Phillips Petroleum Company was a comprehensive business organization.

Phillips continued to diversify with the purchase of the Oklahoma Natural Gas Company, a move that resulted in the sale of "Philgas" to rural areas not connected to city gas mains. The company further increased its petroleum market share with the purchase in 1930 of the Independent Oil and Gas Company. After World War II, the company produced fertilizers and chemicals. Phillips was attuned to changing trends. Lindbergh's historic flight fired both his imagination and his instinct for publicity. In 1927, he sponsored Col. Arthur C. Goebel's nonstop flight to Hawaii, publicizing his Phillips Nu-Aviation fuel and capitalizing on the public's fascination with Goebel's daredevil stunts.

By the time of Phillips's retirement in 1949, he was a multimillionaire. The Phillips Petroleum Company was the ninth largest oil company in the United States, enjoying over $625 million in assets and acting as a significant power in America and abroad.

Phillips retired to Woolaroc, a retreat he had built on ranchland near Bartlesville. He became a patron of educational institutions, and, though Methodist, gave generously to churches of differing denominations. He also established the Frank Phillips Foundation.

Philips had a colorful personality, and he was something of an enigma. Though his business was a major contributor to America's growing love affair with the automobile, he never learned to drive. He was a friendly and unpretentious man, but demanded recognition of his authority.

After several years of suffering from arteriosclerosis, Phillips died in Atlantic City, New Jersey, on August 23, 1950, from complications arising from a gallbladder operation.

BIBLIOGRAPHY

American Business, September 1937-January 1938; *New York Times*, Obituary, August 24, 1950; *Newsweek*, September 4, 1950; Wallis, Michael, *Oil Man: The Story of Frank Phillips and the Birth of Phillips Petroleum*, 1988; Wertz, W., ed., *Phillips, the First 66 Years*, 1983.

Pickens, T. Boone

(May 22, 1928–)
Financier

Everyone agrees that Thomas Boone Pickens Jr. usually referred to as T. Boone, works tremendously hard, 14-hour days, and demands much. But opinions differ as to whether, as an investor and head of the Mesa Petroleum Company, he is a financial genius or a scoundrel. He made a fortune in the 1980s as a corporate raider and was the first of that breed to make the cover of *Fortune* magazine, but in the 1990s his company fell on hard times.

T. Boone, born on May 22, 1928, in Holdenville, Oklahoma, first learned about oil from his father, Thomas Boone Pickens, a lawyer for Phillips Petroleum Company. During World War II he watched as his mother, Grace Marclen (Molonson) Pickens, took charge of the town's gasoline-rationing program. At the end of the war, T. Boone moved with his family to Amarillo, Texas, and after graduating from Amarillo High School, he received a B.S. degree in geology from Oklahoma State University in 1951.

He went to work as a well-site geologist with Phillips Petroleum, but disliked corporate conservatism and in 1955 founded his own company in Amarillo called Petroleum Exploration. His success caused him to incorporate in 1964 under a new name, the Mesa Petroleum Company. Pickens structured the firm to engage in drilling, exploration, and production, while leaving the operating of service stations, refineries, and pipelines to other companies. In 1969, he expanded when he acquired the Hugoton Production Company and its large gas field north of Amarillo.

Pickens seemed to have a keen sense of timing. For example, he divested Mesa of its operations in the North Sea in 1980 and made a profit of $65 million shortly before Britain began to levy a high tax on oil from that location. Two years later, he ventured into his first speculative corporate raid when he tried to gain control of the Cities Service Company. As in a string of other bids, Pickens failed to gain control of the company, but he made a profit of over $31 million through greenmail—the tactic of buying huge blocks of a corporation's stock with the intention of selling them back at a premium so that the company could avert a takeover.

He tried the same maneuver in late 1982 against the General American Oil Company and made $43 million, and again in 1983 against the Gulf Oil Corporation and made $760 million along with the reputation of being a "Wall Street wolf." An assault on Phillips Petroleum in 1984 netted nearly $90 million for Pickens and his fellow investors. That same year, he earned more than $20 million in salary, bonuses, and deferred compensation, making him the highest-paid corporate executive in America.

In 1985, T. Boone raided another oil firm, the Unocal Corporation, and claimed an after-tax gain of $83 million (although some investors questioned this figure). Then, in 1987, he made a daring move outside the oil business when he tried to take over Boeing, the world's largest maker of commercial jets and a producer of military aircraft and missiles. He targeted the company because its stock price had dropped below its real value. Two years later, he took his tactics over-

T. Boone Pickens (Ricardo Watson/Archive)

seas in a raid on the Japanese firm, Koito Manufacturing, a supplier of auto parts to Toyota.

In time, the heavy indebtedness incurred by Mesa to make these raids took its toll, and by 1992 the company saw its own stock drop from $90 a share to just $4. Pickens had bet on rising natural gas prices to help him—instead, they went down. As financial problems at Mesa mounted in 1996—the company's debt topped $1 billion—Pickens lost control to another investor.

Yet Pickens had changed the corporate world by promoting the then unusual idea that CEOs should own stock in their companies. His takeover bids ushered in a continuing era of such strategy. A predator or a builder, which would be Pickens's legacy? One observer said: "As he fades into the Texas sunset, let's take a moment to give T. Boone Pickens his due. Thanks to him, corporate life, especially at the top, is radically different: filled with both pressure and rewards that didn't used to exist. Like it or not—like him or not—the business landscape that exists today is one that he had no small role in painting."

BIBLIOGRAPHY

"Blitz on Boeing: Picket Chooses a New Target," *Time*, August 10, 1987; Pickens, T. Boone, *Boone*, 1987; Rowe, Frederick E., "Man vs. Message," *Forbes*, June 8, 1992; Sloan, Allan, "Going Out with His Boots On," *Newsweek*, March 11, 1996; "T. Boone's Tokyo Fling," *Time*, April 17, 1989.

Pillsbury, Charles

(December 3, 1842–September 17, 1899)
Manufacturer

Although he had no previous experience as a miller, Charles Alfred Pillsbury bought a small flour mill and within 20 years made it the largest milling company in the world.

Charles was born on December 3, 1842, in Warner, New Hampshire, to Alfred Pillsbury and Margaret Sprague (Carlton) Pillsbury. His father owned a grocery store and later worked as a purchasing agent for a railroad. After graduating from the New London Academy, young Pillsbury attended Dartmouth College, from which he received a B.A. degree in 1863. That year he moved to Montreal and joined a produce commission house as a clerk, working there for three years before marrying Mary A. Stinson and then following his uncle to Minneapolis, Minnesota.

In 1869, Pillsbury, with $10,000 in capital acquired from his uncle and father, bought a one-third interest in a five-year-old flour mill. Although he knew little about milling, he learned quickly and with foresight bought recently invented purifying equipment that allowed him to use a roller process to convert hard spring wheat into a fine white flour that was excellent for making bread.

Sales grew quickly, and in 1872 he organized C. A. Pillsbury & Company with his uncle and father as partners, later joined by his brother. He bought additional mills and by 1886 had the largest milling company in the world, making $15 million in sales a year. Despite fires that destroyed or damaged several of the mills, the Pillsbury Company's total capacity in 1889 reached 10,000 barrels a day. Charles Pillsbury's business made Minneapolis a milling center, further advanced by his building the Minneapolis, Sault Ste. Marie & Atlantic Railroad, which eased reliance on the Chicago lines, noted for their high shipping rates.

Pillsbury invested in banking and lumbering, but he always remained primarily interested in his mills and established benevolent relations with his workers. He experimented with a profit-sharing plan and helped Minneapolis coopers start cooperatives that worked with his company. He also engaged in philanthropy and entered politics in 1878, when he won the first of five terms in the state senate.

In 1889, Pillsbury sold his company to an English financial syndicate, which merged it with other firms to form the Pillsbury-Washburn Flour Mills. Charles Pillsbury stayed with the company as managing director and retained a substantial stock investment. He died on September 17, 1899, survived by two of his four children.

After Pillsbury-Washburn went into receivership in 1907, Charles Pillsbury's sons and a cousin regained control of the company for the Pillsbury family. In the 1990s, Pillsbury made more than flour; its diverse interests included frozen food and restaurants.

BIBLIOGRAPHY

Pillsbury, Philip W., *The Pioneering Pillsburys*, 1950.

Pinkerton, Allan

(July 21, 1819–July 1, 1884)
Detective Agency Entrepeneur

Allan Pinkerton founded a detective agency that became an American legend for its role in capturing outlaws and for its espionage during the Civil War.

Born on July 21, 1819, in Glasgow, Scotland, the son of William Pinkerton and Isabella McQueen, young Allan grew up in poverty as his father, a weaver, struggled to make a living during a time of mechanization in the textile industry. As it turned out, the elder Pinkerton died when Allan was only 10, at which point the youngster, who had received only basic schooling, found a job as an errand boy. He then apprenticed briefly as a weaver and finally as a barrel maker, or cooper.

Intelligent and energetic, Pinkerton joined the Chartist movement, a labor protest that aimed to advance trade unionism and reform Parliament. Pinkerton was

Allan Pinkerton (North Wind Picture Archives)

militant in his beliefs, and he engaged in numerous demonstrations, some violent. When the Chartist movement waned in 1842, he considered leaving Scotland for the United States. Although Pinkerton later said he fled his homeland with the law at his heels, his most recent biographer thinks Pinkerton left as part of a calm, rational decision to seek opportunity. In any event, Pinkerton married Joan Carfae (they would have six children), and in April 1842 the couple set sail.

By the following year, Pinkerton had settled in Dundee, Illinois, a small town near Chicago, where he opened a cooper's shop, advertising as the "Only and Original Cooper of Dundee." His cooperage prospered, and by 1846 he had eight employees.

Pinkerton's entry into detective work occurred accidentally. In June 1846, he took his raft up the Fox River to a small island near Dundee, where he felled trees for his shop. While there, he noticed a blackened patch indicating someone had been camping in that spot. He returned several more times to the island and on one occasion hid among the trees and discovered counterfeiters making dimes and other coins. He alerted the sheriff, and the subsequent capture of the criminals earned Pinkerton fame.

A short time later, several Dundee merchants approached Pinkerton about capturing another counterfeiter. He agreed and by using a sting operation, caught the man red-handed in Chicago. Stirred by his success, Pinkerton ran for county sheriff in 1847, but lost, whereupon he accepted an offer from the Cook County sheriff to move to Chicago and work as his deputy. In 1849, the mayor appointed him the city's first full-time detective.

Political disagreements caused him to quit the following year, however, and he joined the U. S. Post Office as special U.S. mail agent. His sleuthing led to the arrest of the Chicago postmaster's nephew for stealing bank drafts and money orders.

Pinkerton then formed his own detective agency with several partners, named the North-Western Detective Agency (later Pinkerton's National Detective Agency), and for an emblem adopted a wide-awake human eye with the slogan "We Never Sleep." By 1856, he had established branch offices in other states and had signed several lucrative contracts with midwestern railroads. In an era noted for local police corruption, companies turned to Pinkerton for honest investigative work. In addition, Pinkerton offered a nationwide service, one unhampered by state boundaries.

By the time of the Civil War, Pinkerton had gained prominence, and as his business expanded he formed important political connections. He also continued his reform ways, this time as an ardent abolitionist. In fact, in the late 1850s, his house in Chicago often teemed with runaway slaves, and he formed a friendship with fanatical abolitionist John Brown.

As the Civil War loomed, Pinkerton was asked by the Wilmington & Baltimore Railroad to investigate rumors that secessionists planned to sabotage the line. After Pinkerton began his investigation, he discovered evidence that a group of secessionists intended to assassinate President-elect Abraham Lincoln on his way to Washington. Pinkerton warned Lincoln and devised a plan whereby the president-elect would travel through Baltimore earlier than expected, during the night. After Lincoln (code-named "Nuts" by Pinkerton) arrived safely in Washington, Pinkerton (code-named "Plum") sent a telegram to a colleague stating "Plums arrived with nuts this morning." Later, newspapers ridiculed Lincoln for having sneaked into Washington, and he regretted his action.

Beginning in 1861, Pinkerton organized a secret service for Union General George McClellan, who wanted spies to infiltrate the South. Pinkerton and his agents provided meticulous, although sometimes inaccurate, reports about military installations, roads, and railroads, and evidence he gathered personally led to the arrest of a prominent Washington socialite as a rebel spy.

During Pinkerton's later years his agency pursued bank robbers in the West, the most notorious episodes involving shoot-outs with the James and Younger gangs. By that time, however, Allan Pinkerton had been superseded at his agency by his sons, William and Robert, and by the end of 1877 they ran the business with little interference from their father.

Pinkerton died on July 1, 1884, his principles of detective work so effective that they were adopted by many private and public agencies. In the mid-1990s, Pinkerton's agency, renamed Pinkerton, Inc., operated 250 offices around the world and employed 50,000 people, with the greatest part of its business providing security services.

BIBLIOGRAPHY

Horan, James D., *The Pinkertons: The Detective Agency That Made History*, 1967; Horan, James D., and Howard Swiggett, *The Pinkerton Story*, 1952; Lavine, Sigmund, *Allan Pinkerton: The First Private Detective*, 1963; MacKay, James, *Allan Pinkerton: The First Private Eye*, 1996.

Post, Charles

(October 26, 1854–May 9, 1914)
Manufacturer

Charles William Post converted a cereal beverage into a food empire based on dubious health claims.

Charles was born on October 26, 1854, in Springfield, Illinois, to Charles Rollin Post and Caroline (Lathrop) Post. After graduating from public school, he briefly attended the University of Illinois before holding several different business positions. At age 26, he managed a plow factory in Springfield, but health problems caused him to leave Illinois for Texas, where he rode the range and invested in real estate and a woolen factory.

Post then went to Battle Creek, Michigan, in 1891 and checked into the famous sanitarium run by John Harvey Kellogg and WILL KELLOGG. The Kelloggs placed him on a diet heavy in fruits, nuts, and grains. With his meals he received one of the latest experimental foods developed by the Kelloggs, a cereal beverage they served as a substitute for coffee.

Charles Post (Library of Congress)

Post recovered his health and stole ideas from the Kelloggs who had yet to aggressively market the products they were developing at the sanitarium. He took the cereal beverage and began selling it as Monk's Brew, and then in 1896, as Postum. Masterful at using advertising hyperbole, he launched a campaign for Postum that called the beverage a builder of "red blood." Then, in 1898, he marketed Grape Nuts, a product similar to the granola served by the Kelloggs to sanitarium patients. Post followed this in 1904 with corn flakes he called Elijah's Manna, which were also similar to cereal flakes developed by the Kelloggs. After he renamed the flakes Post Toasties, sales increased dramatically.

All along Post appealed to an urbanizing nation by emphasizing the convenience of his foods and the health benefits derived from eating them. City dwellers, who worried about declining health as the nation distanced itself rapidly from its rural roots, found comfort in Post's claims. One magazine thought otherwise, however, and in 1910 *Collier's* sued Post for issuing dishonest advertisements. A jury ruled in the magazine's favor and gave it a cash award.

Post had no sympathy with unions; he hated them. While he spent money to make his factories spotlessly clean and to help his workers in buying homes, he doggedly fought the labor movement. He issued many antiunion advertisements that discussed violence at union demonstrations. In 1902, he formed the Citizens' Industrial Alliance to fight the labor movement, and served as its president from 1905 to 1908. Two years later, the National Trades' and Workers' Association succeeded the Alliance and was promoted as a substitute for trade unions.

In his later years, Post traveled frequently to Europe and acquired an impressive art collection. He and his second wife, Leila D. Young (his marriage to Ella Merriwether had ended in divorce), had three homes—one in Washington, D.C., another in Santa Barbara, California, and a third, a 200,000-acre ranch, in Garza County, Texas. When Post's health failed in 1914 and he had to have an appendicitis operation, the accompanying strain caused him to commit suicide on May 9 at his Santa Barbara home.

The Postum Cereal Company remained independent until 1925, when it merged with the Jell-O Company to form General Foods. Philip Morris Companies acquired General Foods in 1985, and four years later combined it with Kraft Foods. Another reorganization occurred in 1995, forming Kraft General Foods.

BIBLIOGRAPHY

Major, Nettie Leitch, *C. W. Post—The Hour and the Man: A Biography with Genealogical Supplement*, 1963.

Preston, Andrew

(June 29, 1846–September 26, 1924)
Merchant

As president of the United Fruit Company for 25 years, Andrew Woodbury Preston virtually invented the banana trade, increasing the volume of trading from around 500,000 bunches of bananas imported into the United States in the 1870s to around 35 million bunches per year by the time of his death in 1924. Preston's system of buying up large tracts of tropical land in Central America, instituting a massive infrastructure for farming and distribution, and then influencing local politics to engineer a corporate-friendly climate established the precedent for interference that would eventually sully the United Fruit Company name.

The son of Benjamin and Sarah Lee Pollard Preston, Andrew was born in Beverly, Massachusetts, on June 29, 1846. Though he originally entered the business world as a shoe manufacturer in partnership with Augustus Williams, he began his career in the fruit trade in the late 1860s. In 1869, he married Frances E. Gulbertson, with whom he would eventually have one daughter.

With a new family to support and an enterprising spirit that chafed at being an employee, Preston was intent on seeking the right opportunity to go into business for himself. In his work for a fruit and produce commission firm in Boston, he periodically sold bananas. As many Americans at this time had not even seen, let alone eaten, a banana, the fruit was seldom available. By 1882, Preston decided to establish his own fruit commission business with plans to focus on the importation of bananas. Shortly thereafter, he enlisted nine other investors and formed the Boston Fruit Company. During the first few years, all profits were reinvested in the company.

The company was very successful in creating a market demand for bananas. By 1898, Americans were eating around 16 million bunches each year. In 1899, Preston merged the company with the interests of a New Yorker, Minor C. Keith, who had become the primary owner of Central American railroads. As president of the newly incorporated United Fruit Company, Preston set out to own and cultivate large areas of Central American land using modern techniques to ensure predictable harvests of bananas. Keith, who controlled virtually all of the region's railroads, provided the link for transporting the produce to the coast for shipment to the United States.

Under Preston, United Fruit developed a highly organized system of cultivation, distribution, and marketing. The scale of its efforts in any given nation of Central America was so large that many of these countries, dubbed "Banana Republics," developed economies based almost solely on the banana crop. Though United Fruit employed large numbers of local workers and established hotels, hospitals, and homes in each country, its system for ownership and cultivation of lands and for distribution of the fruit was so self-sufficient that little of the profit associated with the banana trade was reinvested in the local economy. In later years, after Preston's death, United Fruit became such a powerful entity that it sought to control the governments of the countries in which it operated. Though much of the controversy surrounding the company, which in 1969 became United Brands, occurred after Preston's death, his highly efficient attempts to establish monopolistic control set the stage for the events to follow.

By the time of his death in 1924, the company was capitalized at $100 million, employed 67,000 people, owned over 1.6 million acres of land, and operated a fleet of 80 steamships. There were also thousands of miles of railroad, telegraph, and telephone lines under its control. Preston was president of the parent company, as well as its international subsidiaries. The subsidiaries, as well as United Fruit, also sold a number of other tropical products such as sugar and cacao.

Preston was active in other areas as well, serving as president of First National Bank of Boston; the U.S. Smelting, Refining and Mining Company; and the First National Corporation of Boston. He died on September 26, 1924.

BIBLIOGRAPHY

Adams, Frederick U., *The Conquest of the Tropics*, 1914; McCann, Thomas, *An American Company: The Tragedy of United Fruit*, 1976; Moskowitz, Milton, et al., eds., *Everybody's Business*, 1980; O'Connor, *The Corporations and the State*, 1974.

Pritzker, Jay

(August 26, 1922–)
Hotel Executive

Through a welter of holding companies, Jay Pritzker and his brother Robert built an empire known for its ownership of the Hyatt Regency hotels.

Born on August 26, 1922, in Chicago, Illinois, the son of Abraham Nicholas Pritzker and Fanny (Doppelt) Pritzker, Jay grew up in a wealthy family. His father founded a law firm in 1902, and young Jay continued in that profession. After receiving a B.S. degree from Northwestern University in 1941 and then serving in the navy during World War II, he returned to Northwestern and received a law degree in 1947. The same year, he married Marian Friend, with whom he had five children.

In 1948, Pritzker joined his father's law firm, but as a financial wizard he preferred investments, and so used his father's credit to conclude several deals. He founded his most prominent business in 1957 when he opened a Hyatt hotel. Over the succeeding years, he and his brother Robert expanded the chain, invested in other real estate, and held shares in numerous industries.

In 1984, Pritzker acquired Braniff, a bankrupt airline. At first he tried to revive it by making it a full-fare airline in competition with larger companies. But after Braniff lost $86 million, he changed tactics and made it a no-frills line, lowering fares and replacing hot food with cold box lunches. Braniff then began to show a profit.

Pritzker's fortune in 1997 stood at some $3 billion, and he continued as chairman and CEO of the Hyatt Corporation. The company owned more than 100 luxury hotels and resorts in North America and the Caribbean and operated another 70 hotels and resorts elsewhere. In addition, Hyatt managed casinos and owned a golf course.

Although Pritzker was known for such indulgences as trying to make his son a star by pumping $1 million into the young man's rock band, he also earned a reputation for philanthropy. He and Robert gave $60 million to the Illinois Institute of Technology, and contributed to more than 200 organizations, including the Boy Scouts of America and the Chicago Art Institute.

The Pritzker children have continued in the family businesses, with Jay's son Thomas serving as president of Hyatt. According to a colleague, "The Pritzker family are not quitters. They have rarely failed in anything they've attempted."

BIBLIOGRAPHY

Simon, Ruth, "The Eagles and the Gnat," *Forbes*, November 4, 1985.

Procter, William

(August 25, 1862–May 2, 1934)
Manufacturer

Through his devotion to humanitarian principles, William Cooper Procter established profit sharing and other enlightened policies at his family's company, Procter & Gamble, and helped develop the firm into one of the largest consumer businesses in the nation.

William was born on August 25, 1862, in Glendale, Ohio, to William Alexander Procter and Charlotte Elizabeth (Jackson) Procter. In 1830, his grandfather had founded a candle factory in Cincinnati, a city known for its hog butchering, and thus one with a plentiful supply of the animal fat used in making candles. Seven

William Procter (Library of Congress)

years later, Procter merged with a soap-making business owned by his wife's brother-in-law, James Gamble, to form Procter & Gamble.

The business expanded considerably under the elder William Procter, who emphasized making soap over candles. In 1879, the company introduced Ivory Soap, the popularity of which resulted from an accident when a worker inadvertently stirred a batch of the soap too long, producing air bubbles that made each bar float. Consumers began requesting more of the "soap that floats," and Procter & Gamble had a hit. A short time later, the company promoted Ivory with the slogans "It floats," and with "99 44/100 percent pure."

In 1883, soon after Ivory's appearance, the younger William entered the firm, having graduated from Princeton Univer-sity. He worked in all the company's departments, and in 1890, one year after marrying Jane Eliza, he became general manager. After his father died in 1907, he was named president, and held the post until 1930.

During his tenure as general manager and as president, Procter instituted policies that reflected his strong humanitarianism. His was the first large business to give its workers a half-day off on Saturdays. He began a profit-sharing plan and a stock-ownership system, provided his workers with pensions, allowed his employees to be represented on the board of directors, and guaranteed work for 48 weeks every calendar year.

While president, Procter directed the company to much higher sales—from $20 million at the beginning of his term to $200 million at its end. The company built additional factories in New York, Georgia, Texas, Maryland, California, Canada, and England, and it introduced several new products, including Crisco, the first vegetable shortening.

Procter took civic responsibility seriously, and engaged in many community endeavors, such as leading the Cincinnati Red Cross and donating money to the local children's hospital and to Princeton University. He died of bronchial pneumonia on May 2, 1934.

Procter & Gamble achieved its greatest market triumph shortly after World War II when its laboratories produced a new detergent that pulled oil and grease from clothes. The company called the product Tide. In the 1990s, Procter & Gamble had operations in more than 70 countries, and even a partial list shows that its consumer products have pervaded American society. Cascade, Comet, Charmin, Pampers, Cover Girl, Old Spice,

Secret, Crest, Scope, Crisco, Hawaiian Punch, and Pringles are just a few of the products manufactured by Procter & Gamble that are used throughout the country every day.

BIBLIOGRAPHY

Feis, Herbert, *Labor Relations: A Study Made in the Procter and Gamble Company*, 1928.

Pulitzer, Joseph

(April 10, 1847–October 29, 1911)
Publisher

The teeming masses of urban America in the late 1800s presented a lucrative market for newspaper publishers who appealed to their interests. Through a combination of sensationalist reporting, solid stories, and attractive features, Joseph Pulitzer built the *New York World* into the nation's first modern, mass-circulation newspaper.

Joseph was born on April 10, 1847, in Mako, Hungary, to Philip Pulitzer, a grain merchant, and Louise (Berger) Pulitzer. He was educated by private tutors and decided to pursue a military career. After poor eyesight caused the thin, bespectacled young man to be rejected by armies in Europe, a recruiter for the Union army in the United States convinced him to sign up. He thus immigrated to Boston in 1864 and joined a New York regiment, but since the Civil War ended in less than a year, he saw limited combat.

He then set out for St. Louis, learned English, read law, and gained admittance to the Missouri bar. His newspaper experience began in 1868 when he worked as a reporter for the German-language *Westliche Post*. Pulitzer developed an interest in politics, especially as a crusader against corruption, and in 1869 won election to the Missouri state legislature as a Republican. In a heated dispute, he shot and wounded a lobbyist. Friends helped him pay the court fine.

Pulitzer continued as a reporter at several different newspapers, and in 1878 married Kate Davis. They had seven children. Later that year, he bought the struggling *St. Louis Dispatch*, merged it with the *Post*, and launched investigative stories and campaigns against lotteries, gambling, and tax evasion. After the *Post-Dispatch* began making a profit, Pulitzer visited New York City in 1883 and bought another struggling paper, the *New York World*. He continued to own the *Post-Dispatch*, but moved to New York City and gave most of his attention to the *World*.

With the *World* he used sensational stories to attract readers from among the city's growing working class. Prior to his purchase, the *World* carried lead stories with such headlines as:

ELECTION OF AN EXECUTIVE COMMITTEE OF THE AMERICAN COCKER SPANIEL CLUB

After his purchase, the headlines read "THE DEADLY LIGHTNING," a story about a fire in New Jersey that destroyed an oil refinery and killed six people, and for a story about an execution in Pittsburgh:

WARD M'CONKEY HANGED SHOUTING FROM UNDER THE BLACK CAP THAT HIS EXECUTIONERS ARE MURDERERS

For the first time, Pulitzer spread headlines along several columns and used large typeset.

Pulitzer's stories emphasized abortion, murder, and mayhem, and had profuse illustrations, including maps in which "X" marked the spot of a dastardly deed. Other newspaper publishers had used illustrations before Pulitzer, but he employed them more extensively and prominently, later stating, "I had a small paper which had been dead for years and I was trying in every way I could think of to build up its circulation.... What could I use for bait? A picture, of course.... On page one, in a position that would make the *World* stand out as the paper lay on the newsstand."

Pulitzer, who believed the *World* should be both informative and entertaining, also created a sports page, an innovation since newspapers tucked sports stories away in obscurity if they reported sports at all. Pulitzer devoted another page to "women's news." His Sunday edition carried features and color comics, presaging modern Sunday papers and their hefty supplements. Between 1884 and 1885, circulation for the Sunday edition jumped from 15,000 to 150,000.

Pulitzer promoted his newspaper with contests and gimmicks. He launched a campaign to raise money for erecting the Statue of Liberty, for example, which had been given as a gift to the United States by France. Pulitzer collected $100,000 from 120,000 contributors to build the statue's pedestal. A poetry contest that accompanied the fund-raiser resulted in the selection of a poem by Emma Lazarus, whose words "Give me your hungry, your tired, your poor," were emblazoned on the pedestal.

In 1887, he founded the *Evening World* to go with his morning *World.* The two papers, however, differed in content, with the evening paper pursuing sensationalism, and the morning one usually taking a more objective and cerebral path. After WILLIAM RANDOLPH HEARST arrived from San Francisco in the late 1890s and bought the *New York Journal,* intense competition erupted. In the effort to build mass circulation, the two publishers lowered the price of their papers to a penny and pursued "yellow journalism" (exploitive, sensationalist stories) with a vengeance. Some observers claim that Pulitzer and Hearst contributed significantly to the outbreak of the Spanish-American War in 1898, since both kept stirring hatred toward Spain in their call for liberating Cuba, a Spanish possession.

The contest with Hearst put enormous amounts of money at stake, for the two men had changed the way newspapers made a profit. Rather than relying on the price of the paper, they now depended primarily on the profit generated by advertising revenues, and advertisers wanted to reach a large number of readers. "If a newspaper is to be of real service to the public," said Pulitzer, "it must have a big circulation ... because circulation means advertising, and advertising means money, and money means independence."

In his later years, Pulitzer suffered from declining health, especially bad eyesight that made him nearly blind. After having surrendered to yellow journalism during the Spanish-American War crisis, the morning *World* gained a reputation for serious journalism and exerted a strong influence in politics, waging battles against what it called privilege and corruption.

When he died on October 29, 1911, Pulitzer left $2 million to create a school of journalism at Columbia University in New York City and money in a trust to encourage through prizes—what became known as the Pulitzer Prizes—"public service, public morals, American literature, and the advancement of education." The *World* was sold in the 1930s, and two decades later it folded. Pulitzer's son, Joseph Pulitzer II, succeeded his father as editor and publisher of the *St. Louis Post-Dispatch* and directed the paper to national and international prominence through careful, well-researched stories.

BIBLIOGRAPHY

Barrett, James Wyman, *Joseph Pulitzer and His World*, 1941; Juergens, George, *Joseph Pulitzer and the New York World*, 1966; Rammelkamp, Julian, *Pulitzer's "Post-Dispatch," 1878–1883*, 1967; Seitz, Don C., *Joseph Pulitzer: His Life and Letters*, 1967.

Pullman, George

(March 3, 1831–October 19, 1897)
Railroad Executive

George M. Pullman, an inventor and businessman, founded the Pullman Palace Car Company, the world's largest manufacturer and operator of railroad sleeping cars, dining cars, and parlor cars in the nineteenth and early twentieth centuries. His business sense enabled him to operate a national network of luxury cars on existing trains, and his ability to clearly focus on what the customer wanted (convertible sleeping cars and practical dining cars) made him one of the most important industrialists of the nineteenth century.

Pullman was born on March 3, 1831, in what is now Brocton, New York, south of Buffalo. George's father, Lewis, was a carpenter by trade but also moved buildings and operated a farm on his property. George attended school until the fourth grade, then dropped out in 1845 and worked as a clerk in a general store, earning $40 a year. In 1848, he moved to Albion, New York, and became a cabinetmaker in his brother's factory. After his father died in 1853, George took over his house-moving business. A nationwide financial depression, starting in 1857, hurt his moving business, but in the spring of 1859 he moved to Chicago to work on a job to elevate a five-story, brick hotel.

At the time of Pullman's move, Chicago was in the process of raising its entire downtown area by several feet to lay water and sewer lines and to get the streets out of the mud. For Pullman and his

George Pullman (Library of Congress)

partner, Charles Moore, their business elevating buildings boomed. They also explored other opportunities, starting a business in Colorado to operate stamping mills for crushing gold-bearing rocks. Pullman left Chicago on June 19, 1860, to manage the new business in Central City, Colorado, leaving his brother, Albert, and his partner, Moore, to manage the Chicago business. With several partners, Pullman purchased and operated numerous mills, ran a miner's supply store, operated a freight-hauling business, and owned some gold mines in Colorado. Though his business ventures were profitable, they did not meet Pullman's expectations and on April 9, 1863, he moved back to Chicago. He did not return to the business of elevating buildings, however, but concentrated on starting a new business of manufacturing railroad sleeping cars.

Even while Pullman was still living in New York, he had been interested in ways to improve railroad sleeping cars. On a short train trip from Albion to Buffalo in 1858, he bought a sleeping car ticket and analyzed the design of the car in some detail, producing an extensive list of shortcomings, first and foremost that beds could not be converted into chairs for passengers' daytime use. Pullman and a New York friend, Benjamin Field, formed a partnership just before Pullman moved to Chicago to redesign the cars.

Once in Chicago, Pullman made an arrangement with the Alton and St. Louis Railroad to rebuild one of their older coaches into a sleeping car. He and Field demonstrated their car to the railroad on August 15, 1859, then built two more cars and operated them on the Alton and other midwestern railroads for several years to demonstrate their capabilities and gauge public response to them. The public loved the sleeping cars, prompting Pullman to concentrate more of his energy on the business when he returned from Colorado.

Demand quickly exceeded the three renovated cars, compelling Pullman to produce his first sleeping car from his own shop, the Pioneer, in May 1865. Within a year, Pullman and Field had built and were operating 48 sleeping cars on railroads in the Midwest. That same year, Field left the partnership to pursue political interests.

With a workable design established, Pullman incorporated the Pullman Palace Car Company on February 22, 1867, to manufacture and operate sleeping cars for railroads across the nation. The Pullman Company's formation occurred at the same time that long-distance rail travel was becoming enormously popular. In May 1869, two years after the company was formed, the first transcontinental railroad service started between Chicago and Sacramento, a trip of more than five days. Pullman cars were a part of the transcontinental trains from the first day and made cross-country travel more comfortable and popular. The company also started building and operating parlor cars and dining cars.

Pullman handled most of the marketing for the company, while his brother Albert managed the employees and most of the car construction. The success of their combined efforts resulted in dramatic growth for the business over the next 20 years.

On June 13, 1867, Pullman married Harriett (Hattie) Sanger in Chicago. The couple had four children: two daughters (Florence and Harriett) and twin sons (George Jr. and Sanger). With the success of the Pullman Company, Pullman's personal fortune flourished, and the family joined the ranks of the upper class, owning a private railroad car and mansions in Chicago, New York City, upstate New York, and Florida.

In 1880, the increased demand for Pullman cars convinced Pullman to consolidate assembly operations into a single manufacturing plant. The Pullman Company built the town of Pullman just south of Chicago to house both the plant and Pullman workers. The "company town" provided rental houses, stores, banks, and a church for Pullman employees. The plant was huge, with shops and assembly areas representing some of the largest single-floor buildings ever built. By 1890, the town had more than 10,000 residents, and many Americans considered it a great success that benefited both workers and owners.

Initially, Pullman himself was given many accolades for establishing the town and being sensitive to the needs of his workers. Throughout the 1880s, however, Pullman spent much of his time consolidating the business and fighting legal battles to protect his monopoly on sleeping car services. The demands on his time meant that he lost contact with his employees and their situation in the town. When Albert left the company in 1886, Pullman's last trusted link with his employees was broken, and he became increasingly isolated from them.

In 1894, relations between Pullman and his employees reached a low point, culminating in the Pullman strike, the first truly national strike, in May of that year. The main impetus for the strike was that the Pullman Company had reduced employee wages because of a nationwide financial depression following the Panic of 1893. The company had not seen fit, however, to reduce the rents that employees paid for their company homes. Although Pullman had always fancied himself a benevolent father figure to his employees, after the strike many Americans came to see him as a greedy businessman, bent on paying his workers as little as possible in an effort to increase his profits. Pullman's concept of a company town, so popular before the strike, was dead. His personal reputation never recovered from the labor dispute.

After the strike, the Pullman Company continued to grow. Pullman, however, was worn out. He grew increasingly irritable, had trouble getting along with his family, and tended to go his own way. On October 19, 1897, at the age of 66, Pullman died in Chicago of a massive heart attack. Although his image was damaged by the strike, and automobiles and airplanes eventually destroyed rail travel and the company he had founded, Pullman ranks as one of the most significant industrialists this country has produced.

BIBLIOGRAPHY

Carwardine, William H., *The Pullman Strike*, 1973; Leyendecker, Liston E., *Palace Car Prince*, 1992.

Queeny, Edgar

(September 29, 1897–July 7, 1968)
Manufacturer

Edgar Monsanto Queeny—a dour man nicknamed "stone face"—took the Monsanto Chemical Company founded by his father JOHN QUEENY, and made it a giant in the industry.

Edgar was born on September 29, 1897, in St. Louis, Missouri, to John Queeny and Olga Mendez (Monsanto) Queeny. He was educated in St. Louis public schools and at a private school in New York. After attending Cornell University from 1915 to 1917, he enlisted in the navy and served in World War I. After his discharge in 1919, he married Ethel Schneider and joined Monsanto as the company's first advertising manager. The elder Queeny had founded Monsanto in 1901 to make saccharin, a sweetener, and by the end of the war it had become a major chemical company.

Edgar Queeny earned promotion to assistant general manager and second vice president in 1923, to general manager the following year, and to president in 1928. Over the next 30 years, he increased Monsanto's assets from $12 million to $857 million and boosted the number of employees from 3,000 to 30,000.

Meanwhile during the Great Depression, the conservative Republican Queeny criticized the New Deal and what he called big government. His political position did not stop him, however, from lobbying for government assistance for his business in the form of protective tariffs. Interestingly, while Queeny distrusted modern social developments, he promoted technological ones that changed American society. During World War II, Monsanto led the nation in making styrene, an essential ingredient in artificial rubber. In addition to heavy chemicals, Monsanto produced fine and intermediate chemicals, medicines, and coal-tar derivatives.

Through Queeny's acquisition of other chemical companies and through its diversified product line, Monsanto's sales passed $1 billion in 1962—just two years after Queeny had stepped down from the company. Soon after that, it dropped "chemical" from its name in a move intended to reflect its heterogeneous nature. Queeny died on July 7, 1968.

BIBLIOGRAPHY

Forrestal, Dan J., *Faith, Hope, and $5,000: The Story of Monsanto*, 1977; Haynes, William, *American Chemical Industry: The Chemical Companies*, 1949.

Queeny, John

(August 17, 1859–March 19, 1933)
Manufacturer

John Francis Queeny developed Monsanto into a leading chemical company from its beginning as a manufacturer of saccharin.

Born on August 17, 1859, in Chicago, Illinois, to John F. Queeny, a building contractor from Ireland, and Sarah (Flaherty) Queeny, John Queeny began his business career in 1872 working for various wholesale druggists. He continued in that endeavor until the mid-1890s, when he joined Merck and Company, chemical manufacturers in New York City. Queeny worked as a purchasing agent for Merck and Company until 1897, when he relocated to St. Louis and joined the Meyer Brothers Drug Company.

Queeny left Meyer Brothers in 1906 to open a St. Louis branch of another drug firm, but the following year he quit to devote all his energy to his previously part-time business, the Monsanto Chemical Company. Queeny had founded Monsanto—named after his wife, Olga Mendez Monsanto—in 1901 to produce saccharin, a calorie-free sweetener. He expanded it a few years later to make caffeine and vanillin. In 1915, one year after he relinquished the presidency to become chairman of the board, total sales reached $1 million.

World War I forced Queeny to innovate. The war disrupted chemical shipments from Germany, and to survive he had to make his own basic ingredients for his finished products. His was the first American company to make carbolic acid, used in making pharmaceuticals and other items. When the German patent for aspirin expired in 1917, he began making that product as well. (Today, Monsanto makes more aspirin than any other company.)

After the war, Queeny diversified his product line further, producing a wide variety of chemicals. He had laid the foundation for the giant that Monsanto became after World War II. After his death on March 19, 1933, his son EDGAR QUEENY headed the company.

BIBLIOGRAPHY
Forrestal, Dan J., *Faith, Hope, and $5,000: The Story of Monsanto*, 1977.

Raskob, John

(March 19, 1879–October 15, 1950)
Financier

John Jakob Raskob devised financial methods that shaped the development of the modern corporation. His political activities illustrated the interdependence of politics and the business community. Raskob's most notable physical legacy was the construction of the Empire State Building.

John, the son of John Raskob and Anna Frances Moran Raskob, was born in Lockport, New York, on March 19, 1879. John, his sister, and two brothers had a devout Catholic upbringing. After high school, he studied accounting and stenography at a business college.

In 1898, after a brief stint as a lawyer's secretary, Raskob was hired by the Holly Manufacturing Company as a stenographer. His next job, with Arthur Moxham (the head of a steel company in Nova Scotia) enabled Raskob to meet PIERRE DU PONT, who hired him as a bookkeeper and personal secretary.

Du Pont took note of Raskob's aptitude in finance. In 1902, when Du Pont and his cousins took over their family's explosives business, Raskob's financial talent was unleashed. With Raskob's counsel, the Du Ponts bought out Laflin and Rand, their largest competitor. He was instrumental in assisting Du Pont with the merger's financial aspects. The new E. I. du Pont de Nemours Powder Company grew, and by 1904 the company controlled over two-thirds of the black powder and dynamite capacity in the United States. Raskob worked with Du Pont to assure this expansion was accomplished with minimal expense and with all three cousins retaining control.

Pierre Du Pont became treasurer of the company, and Raskob served as his assistant. Together, they introduced modern financial accounting and auditing methods to the explosives industry, creating policies to maintain the influx of capital and devising methods of determining returns on investments. These innovations were significant in the evolution of modern corporate finance.

On June 18, 1906, Raskob married Helen Springer Green, with whom he had 13 children. The marriage eventually soured, but, as devout Catholics, the couple separated though never divorced. Raskob continued to live in New York, while Helen moved to Arizona.

In 1909, Raskob took over from Du Pont as treasurer, although he did not officially receive the title for five years. In 1914, Raskob and Du Pont, as investors in General Motors, became involved in a dispute between the founder of General Motors (WILLIAM DURANT) and his bankers. Raskob and Durant became friends. The two had much in common, from their shared status as financiers rather than manufacturers to their diminutive physical stature and stylish manner of dress. Raskob counseled regulating the price of General Motors stock; when his counsel paid off, Durant agreed to turn financial management over to the DuPont group.

In 1918, Raskob left DuPont to become the chairman of the General Motors Corporation finance committee. His tenure at General Motors was significant for his introduction of accounting techniques and for his adept handling of the company's finances during the post–World War

I recession. Immediately after the end of the war in 1918, Raskob had launched a great expansion by selling large blocks of stock to several companies. In September 1919, a recession hit, and Raskob used the money from the stock sales to keep the company afloat. Working with Pierre Du Pont, Raskob arranged for the DuPont Company and J. P. MORGAN JR.'s company to provide funds to General Motors, in exchange for additional blocks of General Motors stocks and the resignation of Durant as president.

After Du Pont succeeded Durant as president of the General Motors Company, Raskob's influence slowly decreased. He had contributed materially to the company's success, however, mandating the use of modern accounting and auditing methods and initiating the General Motors Acceptance Corporation in early 1919 to encourage the practice of providing credit to dealers and customers. This program, with its "buy now, pay later" mentality, stimulated the market for the company's lower-cost vehicles. In addition, he advised Du Pont in the development of the company's financial structure and implemented an executive stock bonus plan, the Management Securities Company, that made millionaires out of the 80 General Motors executives who participated.

By 1928, Raskob's wealth was estimated at $100 million. As his interest in General Motors waned, he turned to politics and its role in business. He had dabbled in the political arena in 1926, but became involved in earnest with the presidential campaign of 1928. After the Democratic Party's presidential candidate, Alfred Smith, began to position the Democratic Party as the choice for businessmen, Raskob became chairman of the Demo-cratic National Committee. Though Smith lost the presidency to Republican Herbert Hoover in November 1928, Raskob continued to serve as party chairman. He resigned his post at General Motors that same year, amid concerns that the company should send a strong message that it was not involved in partisan politics.

As a guiding force in the Democratic Party, Raskob strove to expose Hoover's failure to devise effective financial policies to halt the economic collapse of 1929, which marked the beginning of the Great Depression. With the backing of the Democratic Party, Raskob pushed for economic reforms such as tax cuts and a five-day workweek. In addition to his political activities, he remained active in private financial dealings, joining with Alfred Smith to build the Empire State Building in New York City. The project for the tallest building in the world was planned during the booming 1920s, but despite the depression, Raskob and Smith decided to begin construction as planned in 1930 as a gesture of confidence in the U.S. economy. Climbing to 1,245 feet, the Empire State Building was considered an architectural triumph.

In 1932, Raskob left his position as chairman of the Democratic National Committee. His investments, including the Empire State Building, were not doing well. In addition, he objected to newly elected President Franklin D. Roosevelt's New Deal program and formed in response the American Liberty League, a group designed to combat Roosevelt's plans to expand the economic role of the federal government.

After starting the league, Raskob began to travel and make new investments in mining. As these investments proved successful, he turned his attention to philanthropy. His contributions throughout his life to both civic and Catholic causes earned him in 1928 the title of Private Chamberlain in the Papal House. He would later be knighted twice by the Pope. In 1945, he established the Raskob Foundation for Catholic Activities.

Raskob died of a coronary occlusion on October 15, 1950, at his Eastern Shore estate near Centerville, Maryland.

BIBLIOGRAPHY

Chandler, Alfred D., Jr., and Stephen Salsbury, *Pierre S. du Pont and the Making of the Modern Corporation*, 1971; Crowther, Samuel, "Everybody Ought to Be Rich: An Interview with John J. Raskob," *Ladies Home Journal*, August 1929; *New York Times*, Obituary, October 16, 1950; Zilg, Gerard Colby, *Dupont: Beyond the Nylon Curtain*, 1974.

Redstone, Sumner

(May 27, 1923–)
Entertainment Executive

A media mogul with interests in video stores, movie studios, and cable systems, Sumner Redstone began his business career after working several years as a lawyer.

Sumner was born on May 27, 1923, to Michael Rothstein and Belle (Ostrovsky) Rothstein in Boston, Massachusetts. (The family later changed its surname.) He grew up in a Jewish neighborhood where his father sold linoleum before owning two nightclubs. After Redstone completed his education at Boston Latin School in 1940, where he obtained the highest grade-point average in the school's history, he entered Harvard. He obtained his B.A. degree in only two and a half years, and then joined the army and worked as a cryptographer. Redstone decoded Japanese military and diplomatic messages, achieved the rank of first lieutenant, and received two commendations.

After the war ended in 1945, he returned to Harvard and entered its law school. He graduated in 1947 and then began a clerkship with the United States Court of Appeals in San Francisco, while teaching at the University of San Francisco. From 1948 to 1951, Redstone served as special assistant to the U.S. attorney general in Washington, D.C., during which time he married Phyllis Gloria Raphael. The couple had a son and daughter. He became a partner in the law firm of Ford, Bergson, Adams, Borkland & Redstone in 1951.

Redstone eventually tired of law. He saw it as a business, and if he were to engage in business he wanted to make more money. Thus, in 1954, he quit his law practice and joined Redstone Management. A firm begun by his father many years earlier, it owned 12 drive-in theaters in the northeastern United

States. Redstone boosted the company's business when he took several movie studios to court and forced them to allow drive-ins access to first-run films.

In the 1960s, Redstone added more theaters to the business—renamed National Amusements—and by mid-decade owned 35 screens. He expanded this number to 125 a decade later, and then made an important decision. Realizing that drive-ins were losing popularity, he converted his locations into huge indoor multiscreen theaters that he called multiplexes.

Redstone almost died in 1979 when he was trapped in a hotel fire in Boston and received severe burns. He recovered, though, and plunged back into business. In the early and mid-1980s, he sold his shares in Twentieth Century–Fox, Columbia Pictures, and MGM/UA for profits in the millions. At the same time, he obtained a 24 percent interest in WMS Industries, a maker of video-arcade games and slot machines.

In 1986, Redstone began buying into Viacom International, a giant entertainment company that owned a cable-TV system, television and radio stations, and the USA, MTV, VH1, Nickelodeon, Showtime, and Movie Channel networks. Although Redstone's National Amusements had over 250 screens, he believed the future lay in cable television and in videos, and thought Viacom the company through which the future could be achieved. Consequently, he gained control of Viacom in the late 1980s, a move that cost $3.4 billion and left him heavily in debt. Under Redstone, MTV generated a larger audience and more revenues, and as a result

Viacom earned a profit exceeding $60 million in 1992.

Redstone wanted to extend his ownership into Hollywood, and in 1993 bought a 90 percent interest in Paramount Pictures for $10 billion. Paramount then made a fortune with two hit movies, *Forrest Gump* and *Clear and Present Danger.*

In another deal, Redstone brought Blockbuster Video, owned by Wayne Huizenga, under Viacom's control, and soon added Simon & Schuster Publishing. Frank Biondi served as Viacom's CEO, but in 1997 Redstone convinced the board of directors to fire him. Why he ousted Biondi remains unclear, although his decision was probably linked to a downturn in revenues at Blockbuster and at Paramount. Blockbuster's sales had declined as consumers turned in greater numbers from renting videos to buying them, or to watching them over satellite systems. Paramount's revenues suffered from several movie flops, notably *Sabrina, Jade,* and *A Vampire in Brooklyn,* although it produced some hits, too. With Biondi gone, Sumner took direct control.

By that time, according to *Forbes* magazine, Redstone ranked among the 20 wealthiest Americans. "Great successes are built on taking the negatives in your life and turning them around," he said.

BIBLIOGRAPHY

"Play, Pause, Eject?," "A Firing at Fort Sumner," *Time,* January 29, 1996; Ressner, Jeffrey, *Forbes,* December 1, 1997; Sloan, Allan, "$600 Million Dollar Man," *Newsweek,* July 8, 1996.

Revson, Charles

(October 11, 1906–August 24, 1975)
Manufacturer

Charles Revson's biographer said of him: "No one who grows up in a tenement, starts a business in the middle of the depression, and ultimately builds a half-billion-dollar global corporation, is ordinary, or even 'normal.' . . . His business style was so abrasive, his personal style so eccentric, and his success so stunning, that he became something of a legend." The business Revson founded and built, Revlon, ranked by the 1970s among the 300 largest companies in the nation.

Revson was born on October 11, 1906, in Somerville, Massachusetts. He grew up in Manchester, New Hampshire, where his father, a Jewish immigrant from Russia, worked as a cigar packer, and where his family lived in a six-unit tenement house. After graduating from Manchester Central High School in 1923, Revson moved to New York City and sold dresses for a company owned by his cousin. Although Revson's family wanted him to become a lawyer, his job introduced him to women's fashions, which fascinated him.

After leaving his cousin's firm—some sources say Revson was fired for buying too much of a material he liked—he married Ida Tompkins, which was the first of several marriages that ended in divorce. In 1932, he moved back in with his family, and with $300 of capital, joined his brother Joseph and Charles Lachman, a chemist, to form Revlon. Lachman had developed a formula for a different kind of nail polish that was nonstreak, creamy, and opaque.

Despite the Great Depression then under way, Revson shrewdly linked his

Charles Revson (Archive Photos)

company to beauty salons that were expanding as women flocked to get permanent waves. His nail polish and eventually his other beauty products sold briskly. He immersed himself in his company, working long hours, walking around the office wearing different colors of nail polish, and with lipstick streaks on his arm as he tested the various products. A complex man, Revson's associates used many adjectives to describe him: crude, lonely, brilliant, insecure, generous, honest, and ruthless. He had a nasty streak and often belittled people in public.

Already noted for his creative magazine advertising, Revson expanded to television in the 1950s, and his sales skyrocketed after he sponsored the hit quiz show *$64,000 Question.* Unfortunately for Revson, the show was pulled from the air amid accusations that contestants were given answers (under pressure from Revlon which wanted higher ratings). An investigation failed to tie Revson to the fix, but the controversy tarnished his company.

Still, Revson marketed a profusion of new products: cosmetics, skin-care lotions, shampoos, hair sprays, perfumes, and men's toiletries. In 1973, he introduced one of his best-sellers, Charlie cologne for women, advertised as "a most original fragrance." By then, Revlon was listed among the 200 most profitable companies in America. Revson died on August 24, 1975.

BIBLIOGRAPHY

Tobias, Andrew, *Fire and Ice: The Story of Charles Revson, the Man Who Built the Revlon Empire,* 1976.

Reynolds, Richard J.

(July 20, 1850–July 29, 1918)
Manufacturer

Prince Albert tobacco, Camel cigarettes, Reynolds Wrap—all three products captured American consumers, and all were produced from the diverse interests of the Reynolds family.

Richard J. Reynolds was born on July 20, 1850, in Patrick County, Virginia, to Nancy (Cox) Reynolds and Hardin W. Reynolds, a prosperous merchant and tobacco manufacturer who owned a large plantation and many slaves. Although R. J. attended college beginning in 1868, he disliked it and left in 1870 to work in his father's tobacco factory and sell tobacco from a wagon, which he steered through North Carolina, Kentucky, and Tennessee. After a brief stint at the Bryant and Stratton Business College in Baltimore, Maryland, R. J. returned to the tobacco factory, where his father made him superintendent. The two men formed a partnership as H. W. Reynolds & Son. Wanting to be closer to the farms that produced flue-cured leaf tobacco, R. J. moved the factory in 1875 to Winston, North Carolina. There he built a 38-x-60-foot, two-story, red-brick building and went into competition with three other tobacco manufacturers who had already established themselves in the town.

By 1887, the R. J. Reynolds Tobacco Company, as it had been renamed, was producing several brands of chewing tobacco, among them Old Reliable, Black Crook, and World's Choice. Facing formidable competition from the huge Tobacco Trust operated by JAMES BUCHANAN DUKE, and needing capital, R. J. sold out to Duke's Continental Tobacco Company in 1899, a move that made R. J. Reynolds Tobacco a subsidiary of the larger firm.

After marrying Mary Catherine Smith in 1905 (the couple eventually had four children), R. J. took his business in a new direction when in 1907 he defied Duke's orders that he sell only chewing tobacco and instead introduced Prince Albert smoking tobacco. R. J. developed the idea to sell the tobacco using an image of King Edward in a Prince Albert coat. R. J.'s company perfected a machine that packed Prince Albert in tins, and by 1917—six years after the federal courts had dissolved the Tobacco Trust—500,000 two-ounce packages were being shipped daily.

At the same time, Camel cigarettes appeared, introduced in 1913 and made popular when R. J. distributed them free during World War I to American soldiers fighting in France. Shortly after the war, more than half of all cigarettes sold in the United States were Camels, a feat achieved by innovative advertising, using such pitch-es as: "Why Man—We Made the Cigarette for You," "Compare Camels with Any Cigarette at Any Price," "I've Tried Them All but Give Me a Camel," and the well-known "I'd Walk a Mile for a Camel." Reynolds created the modern cigarette industry. One observer said: "In town after town when they introduced Camels, other cigarette brands were swept to one side."

R. J. died on July 29, 1918, leaving his brother William to assume the company presidency.

BIBLIOGRAPHY

Tilley, Nannie M., *The R. J. Reynolds Tobacco Company*, 1985.

Reynolds, Richard S.

(August 15, 1881–July 29, 1955)
Manufacturer

After the R. J. Reynolds Company was founded by RICHARD J. REYNOLDS in the late nineteenth century, it came to dominate the tobacco industry with such products as Camel cigarettes.

The Reynolds involvement with aluminum began with Richard S. Reynolds, son of Abram David Reynolds and Sarah Ann (Hoge) Reynolds, and nephew of Richard J. Reynolds. Richard was born on August 15, 1881, in Bristol, Tennessee. He graduated from that town's King College and enrolled in law school at the University of Virginia. However, his uncle R. J.

convinced him in 1902 to quit school and join the Reynolds Tobacco Company.

Richard served as secretary and developed the moisture-saving tin container for Prince Albert tobacco. He resigned, however, in 1912 to pursue his own business and founded the Reynolds Corporation to make soap powder. The firm faltered until he invented a waterproof ammunition container and during World War I obtained a government contract for it.

In 1919, Richard founded the U.S. Tin Foil Company and made rolling tin for cigarette and gum packages. Convinced that a big market existed for aluminum foil, he formed the Reynolds Metal Company and began making the product in 1928. During World War II, he manufactured aluminum for the war effort, much to the dismay of the leading producer, Alcoa, headed by ARTHUR VINING DAVIS, who disliked the challenge to his near monopoly. After the war, Richard returned to the consumer market with Reynolds Wrap, a kitchen foil. By 1953, he had made Reynolds Metals the second largest aluminum company in the nation.

Richard, who died on July 29, 1955, had married Louise Parham in 1905 and had four children, one of whom, Richard S. Reynolds Jr., born on May 27, 1908, headed Reynolds Metals. In fact, the company experienced its greatest expansion under the younger Reynolds when he spent $40 million to build new plants.

BIBLIOGRAPHY

Tilley, Nannie M., *The R. J. Reynolds Tobacco Company*, 1985.

Rickenbacker, Edward

(October 8, 1890–July 23, 1973)
Airline Executive

Having cheated death numerous times as a race car driver and fighter pilot in World War I, Edward Vernon Rickenbacker seemingly led a charmed life, but his hard work and optimistic attitude were largely responsible for his success in business. He worked in automotive engineering and sales before moving into the aviation industry as president and general manager of Eastern Airlines.

The third of eight children, Edward was born as Edward Richenbacher on October 8, 1890, in Columbus, Ohio. He changed his name to Edward Vernon Rickenbacker at the time of World War I. His parents, William and Elizabeth Barcler Richenbacher, were both Swiss-born, and they instilled in Edward a stern work ethic. The family lived in a rough neighborhood in Columbus, and William worked long hours at the Panhandle Railroad yard to support his large family.

Rickenbacker only finished six grades of schooling before his father's death forced him to help support his family by taking a job working 12-hour days at a glass factory at age 11. He worked his way through several other jobs, each with slightly better wages, until he joined the Frayer-Miller Automobile Company. Lee Frayer admired Rickenbacker's enthusiasm and encouraged him to study all the workings of the internal combustion engine.

Frayer also introduced Rickenbacker to the relatively new field of automotive racing. Rickenbacker began as Frayer's racing mechanic and soon was racing alongside him. From 1909 to 1914, Rickenbacker worked as an automotive engineer at the Columbus Buggy Company and dabbled in car sales. His improving record at the racetrack brought him national attention. At the outbreak of World War I, though eager to join the war effort as a pilot, at the age of 26 he was one year older than the limit for military service. He settled instead for being a driver for Col. Billy Mitchell. Mitchell shared Rickenbacker's enthusiasm for aviation and helped him fake his age so that Rickenbacker could join the 94th Aero Pursuit Squadron. Once in the air, he earned a reputation as a flying ace and became a national hero. He was awarded several medals for his service, including the Congressional Medal of Honor.

Upon returning to the United States, Rickenbacker launched his own car company, the Rickenbacker Motor Company. At the New York automobile show in January 1922, he unveiled three new models that incorporated advanced safety features like those found in racing cars. The Rickenbacker cars were praised by critics but sold poorly, and Rickenbacker resigned as vice president and director of sales in 1926. One year later, he bought a majority share in the Indianapolis Speedway, which he owned for nearly 20 years. He married Adelaide Frost Durant on September 16, 1922, and the couple subsequently had two sons.

Rickenbacker moved into the aviation industry, at first bouncing between executive positions at several young aviation companies, some of which failed. He finally settled in as vice president and general manager of Eastern Airlines in 1935, and three years later was elected president.

During World War II, Rickenbacker was called upon to lend his technical expertise to the inspection of American air bases overseas. On his second such mis-

Edward Rickenbacker (Library of Congress)

sion, bound for the Pacific, Rickenbacker found himself, along with six others, stranded in rubber rafts after their plane missed its destination and was forced to land in the ocean. He survived the ordeal by catching fish and drinking rainwater before finally being rescued 23 days later.

Near the end of the war, Rickenbacker proposed a massive expansion of the commercial airline industry, led by his own Eastern Airlines, to absorb many of the American pilots returning from military service. This program was particularly profitable for Eastern in the late 1940s as demand for air transportation surged.

Problems arose in the early 1950s, however, as Rickenbacker's tough management style and cost-cutting philosophy took a toll on the quality of Eastern's service. Competition from other airlines, particularly Delta, compounded these difficulties, and Eastern Airlines gradually declined through the decade. In 1959, Rickenbacker stepped down as president but remained chairman of the board until retiring from that post in 1964. In addition to his numerous military commendations, Rickenbacker received several honorary doctoral degrees in aeronautical science from major universities. He died on July 23, 1973, in Zurich, Switzerland.

BIBLIOGRAPHY

Adamson, H. C., *Eddie Rickenbacker*, 1946; Forbes, B. C., *America's Fifty Foremost Business Leaders*, 1948; Moskowitz, Milton, et al., eds., *Everybody's Business*, 1980; Rickenbacker, Edward V., *Seven Came Through*, 1943.

Ringling, Charles

(December 2, 1863–December 3, 1926)
Entertainer

Considered the genius behind the Ringling Brothers, Barnum & Bailey Circus, Charles Ringling went from performing simple skits to creating "the greatest show on earth."

Charles was born on December 2, 1863, in McGregor, Iowa, to August F. Rungeling, a harness maker, and Marie Salome (Juliar) Rungeling. (The name was changed to Ringling at a later date.) Charles moved with his family to Baraboo, Wisconsin, while still a child, and grew up there along with his six brothers. In 1882, he and four of his brothers, Otto, Albert, Alfred, and John, began presenting skits in Baraboo and nearby towns. They danced, played musical instruments, and sang, calling their troupe the Ringling Brothers Classic and Comic Concert Company.

They desired, however, to enter the circus business, and in 1884 they organized their first performing company, traveling about in a wagon with a trained horse and a dancing bear. Charles Ringling pushed himself and his brothers to expand and become more creative. Beginning in 1888, they bought an elephant and their business grew rapidly.

The Ringling brothers first used railroad cars for transportation in 1890, and by 1900 had one of the largest traveling shows. Charles then led in acquiring other circuses: Forepaugh-Sells in 1906, and in 1907 the Barnum & Bailey Circus for $410,000. This gave them the world's largest circus.

Although Charles Ringling had other business interests—a bank and real estate—he loved the circus and traveled with it each year from spring to autumn. He died on December 3, 1926, at Sarasota, Florida, where he had a winter home and had begun developing facilities, including a civic center. One of Charles Ringling's nephews, John Ringling North, changed the circus even more when, during the 1950s, he elevated it from a tent show into a stadium and indoor attraction.

BIBLIOGRAPHY

Adams, Bluford, *E Pluribus Barnum: The Great Showman and the Making of U.S. Popular Culture*, 1997; Harlow, Alvin F., *The Ringlings: Wizards of the Circus*, 1951; North, Henry Ringling, *The Circus Kings: Our Ringling Family Story*, 1960; Plowden, Gene, *Those Amazing Ringlings and Their Circus*, 1967.

Rockefeller, John D.

(July 8, 1839–May 23, 1937)
Oil Industrialist

Reform journalist Ida Tarbell pilloried him; others called him, as many still do, the greatest business leader in American history. John Davison Rockefeller reshaped American industry in creating the Standard Oil Company, and in doing so amassed a fortune. Early in his career, he said prophetically to a banker, "Some day I'll be the richest man in the world."

Born on July 8, 1839, in Richford, New York, the son of William Avery Rockefeller and Eliza (Davison) Rockefeller, John first attended school in Monrovia, New York, where his father owned a farm. In 1850, he moved with his family to Oswego, New York, and three years later to Cleveland, Ohio. After graduating from Cleveland High School he had hopes of going to college, but his father insisted on a business career, and the serious, reserved young man took courses for three months at a commercial school.

After that, he joined a commission merchant firm, where he received important training and made contacts with Cleveland businessmen. In 1859, he formed a partnership with Maurice B. Clark, and with $4,000 in capital the two entrepreneurs traded in grain, hay, and

John D. Rockefeller (Library of Congress)

meats. According to one biographer, "success seemed to come quickly and easily to Rockefeller" in this enterprise.

During the Civil War, Clark & Rockefeller made considerable money provisioning the Union army; in fact, the early 1860s brought Rockefeller the capital he needed to expand into other businesses. He did not see military service during the war. Instead, he paid $300—as many wealthy young men did—to excuse himself from combat.

While the war raged, Rockefeller surveyed the developing oil frenzy in northwestern Pennsylvania. New opportunities appeared with the rapid growth of petroleum refining and with the building of a railroad between Cleveland and the oil fields. As the oil arrived in Cleveland, refineries sprang up to process it, and Rockefeller decided this would be the endeavor that would bring him fame and fortune. After all, it cost little to acquire the new technology—a person could build a small refinery for as little as $1,000. In 1863, he and several partners constructed the Excelsior refinery near the Cuyahoga River. The following year, in September 1864, he married Laura Celestia Spelman, daughter of a Cleveland businessman. They later had four children.

Putting his future prospects in oil, Rockefeller quit the merchant business, and in February 1865 bought out all his partners except Samuel Andrews, a move he later referred to as having "determined my career." Before the end of the year, Rockefeller & Andrews was operating the largest of Cleveland's 30 refineries. He then brought his brother, WILLIAM ROCKEFELLER, into the business and built a second refinery.

Higher prices for oil meant more refineries, until a postwar drop in the market in 1867. While other refineries collapsed, Rockefeller's remained strong, a credit to his efficiency and his commitment. He always saw himself as engaged in a high calling; the oil deposits, he said, "were the gifts of the great Creator, the bountiful gifts of the great Creator." That year, Rockefeller took in another talented businessman, HENRY FLAGLER, as a partner. Flagler brought with him capital and an ability to negotiate lower shipping rates with the railroads, as well as an austere, puritanical attitude that complemented Rockefeller's.

To provide a more flexible organization, in 1870 Rockefeller and Flagler founded the Standard Oil Company of Ohio. Previously unaccustomed to corporations, the nation was experiencing their formation on a large scale as industrialization proceeded in the late nineteenth century. Standard Oil both reflected this development and furthered it.

Transportation posed a crucial challenge for all oil refineries, including Standard Oil. High shipping rates along the railroads could put a company at a disadvantage with it competitors. Thus, Standard Oil and other refineries reached agreements with several railroads whereby they would ostensibly pay the published shipping rates but receive a secret rebate in return. In 1870, Rockefeller made a deal with the New York Central-Lake Shore system, agreeing to replace his shipments along the Great Lakes with shipments along the railroad at special low rates.

When, in the following year, a recession dropped oil prices, Rockefeller joined several competitors and railroad executives, led by THOMAS ALEXANDER SCOTT of the Pennsylvania Railroad, to form the South Improvement Company.

Intended to crush those firms not a part of it, South Improvement fell victim to opposition from oil producers, the public, and the Pennsylvania legislature, which revoked its charter. The public interpreted South Improvement as a scheme to create a greedy monopoly, and Rockefeller's reputation suffered.

Early in 1872, Rockefeller acquired nearly all the oil refineries in Cleveland. Over the next two years, he added to his holdings refineries in Pittsburgh, Philadelphia, and Long Island. As the technology of oil pipelines developed, he gained control of these, too. Thus, by the late 1870s, his Standard Oil Company had a near monopoly in the industry.

All the while, Rockefeller pursued a vigorous campaign to integrate vertically, meaning he tried to dominate not only the refining of oil but also the source and its distribution, including its support industries such as cooperage plants and warehouses. Thus, when new oil fields opened in Ohio and Indiana during the 1880s, Rockefeller acted to gain control of them. He entered the export market, too, shipping oil and kerosene to Asia, Africa, and South America. Throughout his career, he insisted that his goal was to bring order to a chaotic industry known for its boom and bust cycles. He intended to provide the nation with a reliable energy source, and although he made money, accrued power, and crushed competitors, he saw these as secondary to his greater service.

In 1881, a Rockefeller attorney devised a new system called the trust that placed Standard Oil stock, and that of its subsidiaries, in the hands of nine trustees. Since the trustees rather than the company held the stock, this allowed Standard Oil to circumvent laws that gave it no right to own property outside Ohio. Within a short time, "trust" came to mean any big business combination—a recognition of the drive toward mammoth corporations accelerated by Rockefeller.

Newspapers, politicians, and the public increasingly attacked trusts, especially Standard Oil. Many suspected that Rockefeller and his associates had used ruthless and even illegal tactics. Indeed, they had. Although Rockefeller paid fair market value for many companies he acquired, others he drove into submission through cutthroat attacks, such as selling oil at a loss and then, after the competitor collapsed, driving up prices. He was also directly involved in bribing politicians. One observer commented that Standard Oil had done everything with the Pennsylvania legislature except refine it.

Antitrust legislation by Congress and a decision by the Ohio Supreme Court forced Rockefeller in 1892 to disband his trust. But he didn't miss a beat in maintaining centralized control—he simply transferred properties to groups of companies in several different states and then used interlocking directorates. Then, in 1899, he turned over Standard Oil to   a New Jersey holding company, with himself as president and Flagler as vice president.

While the public criticized and even condemned Rockefeller, he quietly gave much of his money away through philanthropy, often under the guidance of the Baptist Church in which he had long been a lay leader. He gave money to Spelman College in Georgia to educate African-American women, and founded the University of Chicago (ultimately giving it $80 million). After he retired from Standard Oil in 1897, he spent a good deal of his time establishing philanthropic institutions, most prominently the Rockefeller Institute for Medical Research, founded in 1901, and the Rockefeller Foundation, chartered in 1913 "to promote the well-being of mankind and the world." The Rockefeller Foundation helped eliminate yellow fever, gave money to hospitals overseas, and provided relief after World War I.

Rockefeller's wealth peaked at about $900 million—a considerable sum at that time, more than the entire federal budget, and more than 2 percent of the gross national product, qualifying him by those criteria as the wealthiest man in America's history. He gave away more than $500 million.

By the time Standard Oil suffered the widely read attacks from Ida Tarbell in her *History of the Standard Oil Company* in 1904, and the Supreme Court ordered the breakup of Standard Oil in 1911 as a company in restraint of trade, Rockefeller had little to do with the corporation. He died on May 23, 1937, an enigmatic business leader who denied a desire for great wealth, but obtained it; who praised competition, but crushed it; who shunned the public that scorned him, but contributed lavishly to help it.

BIBLIOGRAPHY

Chernow, Ron, *Titan: The Life John D. Rockefeller, Sr.*, 1998; Flynn, John T., *God's Gold: The Story of Rockefeller and His Times*, 1932; Fosdick, Raymond B., *The Story of the Rockefeller Foundation*, 1953; Holliday, W. Trevor, *John D. Rockefeller, 1839–1937: Industrial Pioneer and Man*, 1948; Nevins, Allan, *John D. Rockefeller: The Heroic Age of American Industry*, 2 vols., 1940; Nevins, Allan, *Study in Power: John D. Rockefeller, Industrialist and Philanthropist*, 2 vols., 1953; Rockefeller, John D., *Random Reminiscences of Men and Events*, 1909; Tarbell, Ida M., *History of the Standard Oil Company*, 2 vols., 1904.

Rockefeller, William

(May 31, 1841–June 24, 1922)
Financier, Oil Indusrialist

Brother of the famed industrialist JOHN D. ROCKEFELLER, William Rockefeller helped make the Standard Oil Company one of the nation's most powerful corporations.

William was born on May 31, 1841, in Richford, New York, to William Avery Rockefeller and Eliza (Davison) Rockefeller. Young William moved with his family several times during his childhood, eventually settling in 1853 in Cleveland, Ohio, where he attended the public schools. At age 16, he entered business—his father wanted both brothers to pursue business careers—by working as a bookkeeper for a miller. In 1862, he entered into a partnership to form Hughes & Rockefeller, a commission merchant business similar to that owned by his brother.

When oil discoveries expanded in Pennsylvania, William got involved in the industry through John. His older brother had established an oil refining firm, Rockefeller & Andrews, in Cleveland and then invited William to join it for the purpose of handling exports from New York. William Rockefeller & Company was thus formed in 1867, with headquarters in New York City, as a subsidiary of Rockefeller & Andrews, that would later become known as Standard Oil.

William helped guide the many mergers of Standard Oil with other refineries in the 1870s and 1880s. He differed from John Rockefeller in that he engaged in many stock speculations and invested heavily in other corporations. He became a director in several of them, and with a partner, Henry H. Rogers, controlled the Consolidated Gas Company of New York and the United Gas Improvement Company of Philadelphia.

After the U.S. Supreme Court ordered the breakup of the Standard Oil Company in 1911, William withdrew from the oil industry. He continued to supervise his investments, however, and built a large estate in Tarrytown, New York, adjoining his brother's. He died on June 24, 1922, survived by his four children. Unlike John Rockefeller, William, who amassed a fortune of about $200 million, gave little to philanthropy.

William Rockefeller (UPI/Corbis-Bettmann)

BIBLIOGRAPHY

Chernow, Ron, *Titan: The Life of John D. Rockefeller, Sr.*, 1998; Flynn, John T., *God's Gold: The Story of Rockefeller and His Times*, 1932; Nevins, Allan, *John D. Rockefeller: The Heroic Age of American Industry*, 2 vols., 1940; Nevins, Allan, *Study in Power: John D. Rockefeller, Industrialist and Philanthropist*, 2 vols., 1953; Tarbell, Ida M., *History of the Standard Oil Company*, 2 vols., 1904.

Rockwell, Willard

(March 31, 1888–October 1, 1978)
Manufacturer

Representative of the close ties between the federal government and corporate America, Willard Frederick Rockwell engaged in myriad acquisitions and mergers to form an industrial complex that made items as diverse as automobile springs and space rockets.

Born on March 31, 1888, in Dorchester, Massachusetts, to Frederick Joshua Rockwell, a contractor, and Catherine (Herr) Rockwell, Willard graduated from Mechanical Arts High School in Boston and received a B.S. degree in 1909 from the Massachusetts Institute of Technology. The previous year, he had married Clara Whitcomb Thayer with whom he would have five children.

After graduation, Rockwell worked for Scovell and Company, an industry survey firm, as an efficiency engineer. He quit in 1915 to join the Torbenson Axle Company in Cleveland, Ohio, as factory manager. During World War I, he made contacts with the federal government, which would later benefit him when he worked as a civilian specialist in the Motor Transport Division of the Quartermaster Corps.

After the war, he returned to Torbenson, but left again during a dispute in 1919 and bought a small axle company, Wisconsin Parts, in Oshkosh, Wisconsin. There he invented a double reduction gear for axles, an invention beneficial to trucks, and in 1928 reached a deal with the Tinken-Detroit Axle Company to buy him out and make him president of its subsidiary, Wisconsin Parts.

At the same time, the ANDREW MELLON family of Pittsburgh recruited Rockwell to lead the Equitable Meter and Manufac-turing Company as president. The company made gas, water, and gasoline meters and valves. In 1933, while still with Tinken-Detroit and Equitable, he became chairman of the Standard Steel Spring Company in Coraopolis, Pennsylvania.

Over the following years, Rockwell brought together companies that made automobile parts. During World War II, Tinken-Detroit provided 80 percent of the U.S. Army's axle needs, and Standard Steel provided 75 percent of the heat-treated armor plate for tanks.

Convinced that the industrial future lay in conglomerates, Rockwell pursued additional combinations after the war. In the late 1940s, he acquired the Delta Manufacturing Company, makers of power tools; the Crescent Machine Company; the Monessen Foundry and Machine Company; and others. By 1947, his businesses had annual sales exceeding $62 million and operated 15 manufacturing plants.

In 1953, he combined Tinken-Detroit with Standard Steel to form the Rockwell Spring and Axle Company, renamed the Rockwell Standard Corporation in 1958, which became one of the largest suppliers of auto parts in the nation. In 1967, he merged it with North American Aviation to form North American–Rockwell. Through this company, which in 1973 became Rockwell International, Rockwell again established close ties with the federal government by providing the high technology needed for America's space program. Rockwell International emerged as the prime contractor for the space shuttle, although it received enormous criticism for supposedly deficient work when, in 1986, the shuttle *Challenger* exploded in flight.

Paradoxically, given his ties to the federal bureaucracy, Rockwell, a staunch Republican, criticized big government and praised private enterprise. He died on October 1, 1978. His son, Willard F. Rockwell Jr., had been appointed chairman of the board and CEO at Rockwell International in 1973, and continued in that position until 1979, when he lost control of the company in a power struggle.

BIBLIOGRAPHY

Kaufman, Richard F., *The War Profiteers*, 1972; Melman, Seymour, *Pentagon Capitalism*, 1970; Rockwell, Willard F., *The Rebellious Colonel Speaks*, 1964.

Rosenthal, William

(October 28, 1881–April 12, 1958)
Manufacturer

With his wife Ida Rosenthal, William Rosenthal built a company best known for its advertising slogan: "I dreamed I went shopping in my Maidenform Bra."

William was born on October 28, 1881, in Racow, Russia, to Solomon Rosenthal, a teacher, and Sarah (Botwinick) Rosenthal. He immigrated to the United States in 1905 and went to night school in Hoboken, New Jersey, where he took courses in design. The following year, he married Ida Cohen and worked at odd jobs. From 1906 until 1916, while raising the couple's daughter, Ida made dresses. In 1916, William Rosenthal joined her, and they opened the Rosenthal Dressmaking Establishment. In 1918, they moved their business from Hoboken to New York City.

During the 1920s, women's fashions changed, and the Rosenthals took advantage of the new style that shifted from a boyish look with flattened chests to a fuller bosom. They designed a brassiere, the first modern uplift bra, which gave women a different rounded shape.

The design sold well, and in 1923 the Rosenthals founded the Maidenform Brassiere Company, which they operated for several years along with their dressmaking business. In 1924, they moved Maidenform to larger facilities in Bayonne, New Jersey, and William became president, a position he held until his death, while Ida served as treasurer. The company expanded its line in the 1930s to include women's girdles, lingerie, and swimwear.

Already prominent in the garment industry, Maidenform gained wider attention with its advertising campaign in 1949 that produced the famous "I dreamed I went shopping" slogan. By 1958, the company had facilities in five states plus Puerto Rico, Trinidad, Canada, and England, with yearly sales that exceeded $30 million. William Rosenthal died on April 12, 1958, at which time Ida became president. The following year, she relinquished the presidency and became chair of the board, a position she held until 1966. She was honorary chair until her death in 1973. In 1996, Maidenform, a private company, had sales exceeding $400 million.

BIBLIOGRAPHY

Fontanel, Beatrice, *Support and Seduction: The History of Corsets and Bras*, 1997.

Rosenwald, Julius

(August 12, 1862–January 6, 1932)
Merchant

Julius Rosenwald took the mail-order business founded by RICHARD SEARS, modernized it, and with the money he made engaged in extensive philanthropy, for which he is best known.

Born on August 12, 1862, in Springfield, Illinois, to Samuel Rosenwald and Augusta (Hammerslough) Rosenwald, Julius Rosenwald obtained an education in the city's public schools, and in 1879 began his business career at Hammerslough Brothers, a wholesale clothier in New York City. After six years at that firm, he formed with a partner his own clothing business, Rosenwald & Weil in Chicago.

His move to Chicago came at a time when the railroad had connected the city to rural America. That development had led Richard Sears to locate his mail-order business in Chicago, a terminus for the all-important rail network needed to take goods to farmers. Rosenwald first discovered Sears's booming business when the entrepreneur ordered from him a large number of pants. When Rosenwald asked how he was going to sell all the pants, Sears surprised him by saying they had already been sold.

Intrigued, Rosenwald began investigating Sears's business and discovered a mixed situation: prosperity, but also extensive disorder and a need for capital to fund expansion. Rosenwald provided the capital and in 1895 became vice president and treasurer of Sears, Roebuck & Company. From 1910 to 1925, he served as president and from 1925 to 1932 as chairman of the board after Sears had retired. Rosenwald brought Sears into the era of department stores, and thus developed a more urban appeal.

But for all his success at Sears, Rosenwald earned his greatest reputation in philanthropy. Rather than use his fortune strictly for investment, he gave heavily to charities and community groups. He helped found the Federation of Jewish Charities in Chicago in 1923 and as a member of the American Jewish Committee helped protect Jews from discriminatory practices. Through the Julius Rosenwald Fund—chartered to promote "the well-being of mankind"—he provided moneys to feed starving children in postwar Europe. Believing strongly in education, he contributed more than $3 million toward the construction of several thousand black schools in the South.

Rosenwald died on January 6, 1932, survived by his second wife, Adelaide Goodkind (his first wife, Augusta Nusbaum, had died in 1929), and several children.

BIBLIOGRAPHY

Embree, Edwin R., *Investment in People: The Story of the Julius Rosenwald Fund*, 1949; Jarrette, Alfred G., *Julius Rosenwald: A Biography Documented*, 1975; Werner, M. R., *Julius Rosenwald: The Life of a Practical Humanitarian*, 1939.

Rubinstein, Helena

(December 25, 1871–April 1, 1965)
Manufacturer

The modern beauty industry owes its origins to Helena Rubinstein, the Polish woman who launched a company based on skin-care products and cosmetics. Rubinstein's innovations, marketing style, aggressive business sense, and personal charisma had a tremendous impact, both internationally and in the United States. Her business savvy not only made her a multimillionaire but also sweetened the profits for many of the secondary businesses, like department stores, that benefited from her products' popularity. Rubinstein was also an avid collector of art, befriending (and often painted by) numerous famous artists.

Helena, the "Empress of Beauty," was born in Krakow, Poland, on December 25, 1871, the eldest of eight daughters of August and Horace Rubinstein. The dark-haired, strong-featured Helena was strong-willed from an early age. After briefly studying medicine in Switzerland, she traveled to Australia in 1902 to stay with

Helena Rubinstein (Archive Photos)

relatives. As she was fond of saying later in life, the Helena Rubinstein empire was built from seven jars of a Polish face cream she carried with her to Melbourne. Having secured a loan from a woman she befriended on the journey, Helena sent for a large supply of a family face cream, hand-lettered new labels for the jars, and established a modest salon. After good press and experimentation with new types of cream for different skin types inspired by the dry, weather-beaten skin of Australian women, Helena's "Valaze Cream" made the salon very successful.

A year and a half later, in search of new opportunities, Rubinstein left the Australia business in the hands of a sister and went to Europe to study dermatology with the leading practitioners of the time. In 1908, she launched the Helena Rubinstein salon in London. The salon, which was very exclusive and catered to the aristocratic upper class, helped to change social customs for all women of the day. Largely due to Rubinstein's efforts, cosmetics became acceptable for every woman (for many generations, the wearing of lipstick, eye makeup, and rouge had been common only among actresses and prostitutes).

Another momentous event in Rubinstein's busy year of 1908 was her marriage to Edward William Titus, a Polish-American chemist who had courted Helena since her days in Australia. The couple eventually had two sons, Roy Valentine and Horace Gustav, both of whom would someday work for their mother's company.

After her success in London, Rubinstein, exhibiting the drive for expansion that became synonymous with her company name, opened a new salon in Paris in 1914. In 1916, she turned her attention to the United States, and in two years, there were salons in New York, Chicago, Boston, Los Angeles, and other metropolitan areas. She also authorized the sale of her products in department stores, a move she made reluctantly not only because of the perceived loss of prestige but also because of quality control concerns. To address those worries, she insisted that the departments employ trained Helena Rubinstein salon professionals.

The huge organization continued to grow, with new salons popping up in Italy, Canada, Argentina, Brazil, and Tokyo. Rubinstein was an extremely demanding employer who worked long hours and involved herself with seemingly boundless energy in every phase of the business. She was a micromanager who insisted on perfection. Nevertheless, it was her colorful and forceful personality, social connections, and lavish lifestyle as much as her work ethic that made her a multimillionaire.

Within the beauty industry, and to the amusement of outsiders, the feud between Helena Rubinstein and her competitor ELIZABETH ARDEN was legendary. The two companies battled fiercely for control of the public's beauty dollars and escalated the conflict to the personal level of raiding each other's corporate personnel ranks.

As her fortune grew, Rubinstein, a longtime devotee of art and friend to many famous artists such as Pablo Picasso and Salvador Dali, became a feverish art collector. Her vast collection, which overflowed her five homes and the salons, was remarkable for its diversity of style and value and was widely regarded as one of the best in the world. She was also an avid jewelry collector, and her eccentric yet endearing habit of storing her gems in an office file cabinet under the appropriate letter was noted frequently in interviews.

In 1937, Rubinstein and Titus divorced after a 25-year marriage. A year later, she married Prince Archtil Gourielli-Tchkonia, a recent American immigrant of Georgian nobility. In 1942, the couple launched the House of Gourielli for Men, Rubinstein's first venture targeting men. It was a novel experiment, a combination of clothing boutique, salon, and lunchroom that served as an upscale gathering place for businessmen, complete with ticker tapes to track the doings of Wall Street. While popular, the salon proved too elite and did not enjoy the tremendous success of Rubinstein's other ventures.

In 1953, Rubinstein established the Helena Rubinstein Foundation, an institute for research in health and medicine. She continued to involve herself closely in the business until the death of her younger son Horace in 1956, a loss that affected her greatly.

While Rubinstein relinquished some control over her business as she grew older, she continued to remain involved, often conducting meetings and telephone business transactions in her bedroom. By the time of her death, she had amassed a fortune in the neighborhood of $150 million. On April 1, 1965, Rubinstein died in New York City after being hospitalized several days earlier for a severe stroke and blood clots.

BIBLIOGRAPHY

Life, July 21, 1941; *New York Times*, Obituary, April 2, 1965; *New Yorker*, June 30, 1928; O'Higgins, Patrick, *Madame: An Intimate Biography of Helena Rubinstein*, 1971; Rubinstein, Helena, *The Art of Feminine Beauty*, 1936; Rubinstein, Helena, *My Life for Beauty*, 1964.

S

Sachs, Walter

(1884-August 1980)
Banker

Walter Edward Sachs played a crucial role in developing Goldman, Sachs into one of the world's largest investment-banking houses.

Born in 1884 in New York City to Samuel Sachs and Louisa (Goldman) Sachs, Walter obtained a B.A. degree from Harvard in 1904, where he edited the *Harvard Crimson* and had on his staff a future president, Franklin D. Roosevelt. After dropping out of law school in 1905, Sachs joined the firm of Goldman, Sachs. Sachs's grandfather, Marcus Goldman, had founded the company in 1869 to buy and sell the IOUs held by New York jewelers and leather merchants. He then brought Samuel Sachs, his son-in-law, into the business, creating Goldman, Sachs. Now Samuel brought in Walter, although without enthusiasm, for he had wanted his son to finish law school.

As a full partner Walter Sachs was one of the first American financiers to establish contacts with the Communist Soviet Union in 1925, and, importantly, he guided the firm through the shock of the 1929 stock market crash and the ensuing travails of the Great Depression. Under his leadership, and that of another partner, Saul Weinberg, Goldman, Sachs ranked among the world's major investment-banking houses.

In the 1940s and 1950s, the firm's growth brought antitrust suits from the federal government, and between 1947 and 1953 Sachs spent much of his time fighting the accusation that Goldman, Sachs had, in cooperation with several other Wall Street houses, monopolized the nation's securities business. A federal court ruled in favor of the defendants.

In addition to his business, Sachs was active in the National Association for the Advancement of Colored People and was chair of the executive committee of the New York State Chamber of Commerce. He died at his home in Darien, Connecticut, in August 1980, survived by his wife, Virginia Carver, three children, five grandchildren, and four great-grandchildren.

In June 1998, as the firm earned record profits exceeding $2 billion early in the year, Goldman, Sachs ended its status as a private company and went public. Critics of the plan said it would make the company susceptible to a takeover by a large financial institution; supporters believed it would enable the company to expand its investments and acquire American and foreign finance companies. The *New York Times* said of the decision that it "would make Goldman a prime player in the financial industry's rush to consolidate, a trend that has turned nearly all of America's venerable finance partnerships . . . into homogenized financial giants in less than two decades."

BIBLIOGRAPHY

Sachs, Walter Edward, *The Reminiscences of Walter E. Sachs*, 1972.

Sage, Henry

(January 3, 1814–September 18, 1897)
Merchant, Lumberman

In his early dealings with the lumber trade, Henry William Sage realized the great potential that would be created for the lumber industry as the United States grew. Having been successful as a merchant, Sage used his capital to launch successive logging businesses, first in Canada and then in Michigan. Throughout his career, Sage also acquired large quantities of real estate and invested his fortune in railroads and other industries.

Henry, the son of Charles and Sally Williams Sage, was born in Middletown, Connecticut, on January 3, 1814. Charles was an inept businessman and lost money on almost every venture he undertook, making Henry's childhood one of perpetual poverty. Henry attended the Bristol Academy in Connecticut and planned to attend Yale, an aspiration that was crushed when the family moved to Ithaca, New York. For two years after the move, he lacked access to formal education. After a few months of study with Dr. Austin Church, he decided to go into business. He was unsuccessful in finding work as a clerk until he was hired at age 18 by his uncles, Timothy and Manwell Williams, who were established shippers and merchants in the Ithaca area.

Sage worked for his uncles for five years, keeping the books and loading canal boats. By 1837, he had learned much about the mercantile trade, but he was unsatisfied with his advancement in his uncles' business. Sage joined with Joseph E. Shaw and Frederick Barnard to launch their own business in Ithaca dealing in general merchandise, ranging from

Henry Sage (North Wind Picture Archives)

produce and grain to lumber. Their business served mainly as a trading depot with canal boats running shipments to New York City, Albany, and Buffalo. In 1840, Sage married Susan Elizabeth Linn, who bore him two sons, Dean and Henry William.

The business prospered in its first decade, making Sage a man of considerable means. He began investing in real estate in the Ithaca area and also tried his hand in the lumber business by purchasing timberlands and a small sawmill in Tioga County in 1847 with his new partner C. B. Chauncey. Through this experience, Sage recognized that an enormous demand for lumber would arise as the country began rapidly expanding westward. After four years with Chauncey, Sage dissolved their partnership, and in 1853 opened his own steam-powered sawmill in Ithaca. One year later, he constructed a similar mill next to the large tracts of land he had purchased near Lake Simcoe in Canada, and he invited William Grant to join him as his partner. This enterprise launched a new phase in Sage's career, as he became a full-scale lumber producer.

It was necessary for Sage and Grant to import labor for their logging and milling operations, so they established a company town at Bell Evart complete with housing and stores. The mill operated successfully for 15 years. In 1869, Sage sold the property and facilities for $120,000. The new owners were not as successful and defaulted on over half the payment to Sage. Nevertheless, the venture provided Sage with an operational framework for his next lumber endeavor in Michigan.

Sage joined with John McGraw to establish a mill on the shores of the Saginaw River opposite Bay City, Michigan. Three years after the mill was erected in 1865, Sage was joined by his two sons in the business and bought out his partner's stake for $461,000. By 1870, the mill was one of the largest in the world, producing 34 million feet of lumber that year.

The village of Winona sprung up around the mill and was similar to the company town Sage had helped to create at Bell Evart. Sage used his control as the main landlord in the village, as well as the employment of scab labor, to break the strikes that broke out during the depression years in the 1870s. In the early 1880s, however, the Knights of Labor began organizing the workers in Sage's em-

ploy. In the Great Strike of 1885, workers again demanded shorter working hours. This time, the workers succeeded in shutting down the milling operations through mob actions, and it took six weeks for the situation to be resolved.

The timber supplies surrounding Sage's Michigan mill were gradually depleted and the plant shut down in the early 1890s. In 1893, he organized the Sage Land and Improvement Company to manage the vast pieces of real estate that he had accumulated over the preceding 30 years. His properties included over half a million acres in seven states, most of it timberlands. Sage also invested heavily in railroad and industrial securities and held a portfolio valued at $4.5 million at the time of his death.

Sage was affiliated with several churches throughout his lifetime, and he fancied himself an amateur philosopher. In the later years of his life, he worked to improve education and served on the board of trustees of Cornell University. He also created the Sage College for Women and the Sage School of Philosophy in 1870 and 1875, respectively. He died in Ithaca on September 18, 1897.

BIBLIOGRAPHY

Defenbaugh, James E., *History of the Lumber Industry in America*, 1907; Goodstein, Anita S., *Biography of a Businessman: Henry W. Sage, 1814–1897*, 1962; Hotchkiss, George W., *History of the Lumber and Forest Industry of the Northwest*, 1898.

Sanders, Harland

(September 8, 1890–December 1, 1980)
Restaurant Executive

Sporting a white goatee and dressed in a white suit and string bow tie, Harland Sanders played the part of a southern colonel to promote his Kentucky Fried Chicken (KFC), the product that made him a millionaire at age 66.

As a child, Harland knew severe poverty. He was born on September 8, 1890, on a farm near Henryville, Indiana, and because his father died while Harland was only six, the youngster's mother had to take jobs peeling tomatoes and sewing. With his mother working long hours, Harland had to cook for himself and his two siblings.

When Sanders reached age 12, his mother married again, and since his stepfather disliked children, the youngster was sent to work on a farm in Green-wood, Indiana. He quit school after the seventh grade, left the farm at age 15 for other jobs, and over the next two decades worked as a buggy painter, streetcar conductor, ferryboat operator, and insurance salesman. After Sanders managed to earn a law degree through a correspondence school, he worked as a justice of the peace.

Harland Sanders's life took yet another turn, this one toward prosperity, in 1929 when he opened a filling station in Corbin, Kentucky. He began to serve meals to travelers, and after they raved about his food and kept coming back for more, he tore out the gasoline pumps and converted his business into Sanders' Café. In the late 1930s, he expanded his restaurant to seat 142 diners while maintaining a home-style atmosphere.

His most popular dish was southern fried chicken, but he had a hard time making it quickly enough and maintaining the quality he desired until 1939, when he used a new invention, the pressure cooker, to hold in the moisture and flavor. Over the years he developed a mix of 11 herbs and spices that he added to the recipe, which he kept secret.

Sanders made a good income from his café, but in 1956 he had to sell it when a new interstate highway bypassed it and diverted traffic. At the age of 66, Sanders feared retiring on meager savings, so after having sold his chicken recipe to a restaurant in Utah and seeing how it had proved popular there, he decided to travel the country and sell it to other restaurants under an arrangement to collect four cents for every piece of chicken sold.

Harland Sanders (UPI/Corbis-Bettmann)

Sanders called his chicken "finger lickin' good," and by 1960 had contracts with 200 outlets. While his wife kept the books and mixed the seasonings for KFC, he continued to travel and get more contracts. Three years later, he had over 600 outlets, but the crushing pace made him receptive to selling his business. That occurred in 1964 when John Y. Brown, a Kentucky businessman, and Jack Massey, a Tennessee millionaire, bought KFC for $2 million—but only after Sanders had extracted from them a promise to abide by his recipe and the quality he had established.

Brown used revised franchise contracts and takeout service to expand KFC. He used also heavy advertising that relied on Sanders, who for $75,000 a year continued to work for the company as an adviser. Sanders traveled the nation in his trademark suit and appeared frequently in television commercials.

But in 1971, Brown sold KFC to Heublein, Incorporated, and the restaurants quickly deteriorated under poor management. By 1976, KFC operated in the red, and Colonel Sanders, retained by Heublein for $200,000 per year, stunned the company when he walked into a New York City KFC and, in front of a reporter, tasted the chicken and declared, "That's the worst fried chicken I've ever seen."

Sanders died on December 1, 1980, in Shelbyville, Kentucky, so revered that his body lay in state in the rotunda of the state capitol, and flags in Frankfort flew at half mast. Since then, KFC has enjoyed a comeback in quality and customers under its new owner, Pepsico.

BIBLIOGRAPHY

Pearce, John Ed, *The Colonel: The Captivating Biography of the Dynamic Founder of a Fast-Food Empire*, 1982; Sanders, Harland, *Life as I Have Known It Has Been Finger Lickin' Good*, 1974.

Sarnoff, David

(February 27, 1891–December 12, 1971)
Entertainment Executive

The visionary and the practical combined in the personality of David Sarnoff, who promoted radio and television networks well before others thought them feasible. As a result, he reshaped society and made the Radio Corporation of America (RCA) a leader in communications technology.

Born in Uzlian, Russia, on February 27, 1891, to Abraham Sarnoff, a house painter, and Leah (Previn) Sarnoff, David emigrated with his family to Albany, New York, and later to New York City, where he lived in a Jewish neighborhood on the Lower East Side. As a boy, David studied to become a scholar of the Jewish Talmud, but his father's illness and his family's poverty forced him to work at odd jobs. He left school after the eighth grade and began working as a messenger boy at the Commercial Cable Company, his first job in direct contact with communications, a technology then poised to undergo dramatic change.

In September 1906, the Marconi Wireless Telegraph Company of America hired Sarnoff as an office boy at a salary of $5.50 a week. He had been teaching himself telegraphy at home, however, and soon began working as a wireless operator at several Marconi locations. Legend has it that Sarnoff, while working the telegraph at the Marconi office in Manhattan on April 14, 1912, received the signal from a wireless operator reporting the sinking of the cruise liner *Titanic.* Once he learned about the sinking he stayed at his post for 72 hours straight, copying down the names of survivors telegraphed to him from a rescue ship.

Sarnoff, a workaholic who considered sloth a sin, rose up through the ranks at Marconi. In 1914, the company made him contract manager, a position that gave him responsibility for investigating inventions in communication. Sarnoff liked the position, for he had great faith in technology, was thrilled with discovery, and wanted more power. In 1916, he proposed to the company that it make radios that could receive music. His memo, titled "Subject: Radio Music Box," stated, "I have in mind a plan of development which would make radio a 'household utility' in the same sense as the piano or phonograph. The idea is to bring music into the home by wireless. . . . A radio-telephone transmitter having a range of say 25 to 50 miles can be installed at a fixed point where the instrumental or vocal music or both are produced. The receiver can be designed in the form of a simple 'Radio Music Box' and arranged for several wavelengths, which should be

changeable with the throwing of a single switch or pressing of a single button."

Sarnoff did not create the idea; rather, as he often did, he took half-formulated concepts and brought them together into a unified plan. In 1906, Reginald A. Fessenden had transmitted speech and music from his experimental station in Massachusetts to ships at sea. In any event, Sarnoff's general manager rejected the proposal.

After the Marconi Company sold its stock to General Electric (GE), Sarnoff pursued his "Radio Music Box," trying to get a GE subsidiary, RCA, to broadcast radio programs into homes. Partly through his efforts, but substantially through other experimenters in radio, on July 2, 1921, RCA broadcast the Jack Dempsey–Georges Carpentier fight and captured the nation's attention. The following year, Sarnoff proposed a full-scale radio network to provide entertainment and news on a regular schedule, and in 1926 RCA incorporated the National Broadcasting Company (NBC) for that aim.

In 1928, while serving as executive vice president of RCA, Sarnoff joined JoSEPH KENNEDY to create a motion picture company, Radio-Keith-Orpheum (RKO), that used sound equipment made by RCA for new "talkie" movies. Meanwhile, RCA sold more than $800 million worth of receivers, and in 1929 Sarnoff reached a deal with General Motors creating a company to make car radios for the auto manufacturer.

Sarnoff became president of RCA in 1930 and immediately faced a U.S. Justice Department lawsuit charging the company with antitrust violations for having created a communications monopoly. Sarnoff reached a settlement with the government that allowed him to end RCA's relationship with GE and gain its independence—a move he had long desired anyway.

Although the Great Depression hurt RCA's radio sales, Sarnoff never wavered in his faith in the technology. In 1933, he opened the RCA Building at Rockefeller Center, and installed his office on the thirty third floor. In 1942, he founded the RCA Laboratories to explore innovations in communications.

He had already met with Vladimir T. Zworykin in 1929. Zworykin had been broadcasting pictures, and Sarnoff hired him to further develop television (the inventor, Philo Farnsworth, and Zowrykin engaged in numerous patent disputes). In 1939, using an experimental station, Sarnoff broadcast two speeches from the New York World's Fair. NBC aired the first commercial television broadcast on July 1, 1941. Of such early television, the famed essayist E. B. White presciently remarked: "I believe television is going to be the test of the modern world, and that in this new opportunity to see beyond the range of our vision, we shall discover a new and unbearable disturbance of the modern peace or a saving radiance in the sky. We shall stand or fall by television—of that I am quite sure."

During World War II, Sarnoff was called to active duty, worked in London as special assistant for communications, and built a radio station that transmitted to Allied forces in Europe. He helped restore the French broadcast system in 1944, and was made a brigadier general. When he returned to RCA after the war, he preferred to be called "General."

As television expanded in the late 1940s, Sarnoff lagged behind a competing network, the Columbia Broadcasting System, whose executive, WILLIAM PALEY, paid big money to lure stars away from NBC. Red Skelton, George Burns and Gracie Allen, Jack Benny, and Groucho Marx, among others, jumped ship. During the following decade, RCA led in developing color television, and NBC broadcast the first network shows in color, but Sarnoff failed in his effort to outdo International Business Machines in building computers.

As head of NBC, he had a reputation for terse orders and for pursuing the bottom line, neither understanding popular culture nor seeing television as, to use White's words, a "saving radiance." He once said about the TV networks, "We're in the same position of a plumber laying a pipe. We're not responsible for what goes through the pipe."

In 1955, Sarnoff's oldest son, Robert, became president of NBC. Sarnoff continued as chief executive officer at the parent company, RCA, until 1965 when he retired to serve as chairman. That same year, Robert Sarnoff was appointed president of RCA. David Sarnoff died on December 12, 1971, in New York City, remembered as a radio and television pioneer who, in promoting the new media, had forever changed American society. One observer stated, "Some say his relentless drive left a wake of uneasiness and fear among his employees and colleagues alike. But for every detractor there are many who remember David Sarnoff as a tough but fair-minded boss, an autocrat whose decisions were right far more often than wrong. Through his singleness of purpose, Sarnoff helped build the electronics industry."

BIBLIOGRAPHY

Bilby, Kenneth, *The General: David Sarnoff and the Rise of the Communications Industry,* 1986; Dreher, Carl, *Sarnoff,* 1977; Kittross, John, *Stay Tuned,* 1990; Lyons, Eugene, *David Sarnoff,* 1966; Tebbel, John, *David Sarnoff,* 1963; Wiesner, Jerome B., ed., *Looking Ahead: The Papers of David Sarnoff,* 1968.

Saunders, Clarence

(December 1881–October 14, 1953)
Merchant

In his financially tumultuous life, Clarence Saunders revolutionized food shopping in America when he founded his Piggly Wiggly stores.

Born in Amherst County, Virginia, in December 1881, Saunders grew up in Clarksville, Tennessee. The son of a poor tobacco farmer, he received little formal schooling and as a boy worked as a grocery clerk, earning $4 a month. After laboring in an Alabama coke plant and a Tennessee sawmill, he returned to the grocery business as a salesman for a wholesaler. By 1915, he had his own successful wholesale company in Memphis, Tennessee.

The following year, Saunders, ever flamboyant and innovative, opened a revolutionary new grocery store at 79 Jefferson Street in Memphis. Until that time, shoppers typically obtained their groceries by handing the store clerk a list and waiting for the items to be retrieved. Saunders considered this procedure wasteful. He wanted to reduce costs, save time, and expose consumers to a wider variety of products. Thus, when he opened his Piggly Wiggly store—the name, he said, "just came out of my noodle"—he set it up so that shoppers would enter through a turnstile and, basket in hand, walk along a continuous aisle lined with open shelves. They would retrieve the desired items themselves and have to walk by the entire stock before reaching a checkout counter. No more clerks, no more cracker barrels, and every item was packaged and priced.

Saunders's "self-service" method attracted shoppers in droves. Whereas a typical grocery store grossed about $400 a week, a Piggly Wiggly grossed $7,000. Saunders opened nine stores within a year, and by 1922 he had 1,200 stores in 29 states, half owned by him and the others franchised.

That phenomenal growth shook the grocery industry and caused unexpected changes throughout the economy. Saunders had elevated the importance of packaging as a sales tactic and had stimulated impulse buying since consumers, attracted by the goods before them, bought items they had never intended to buy. One historian has observed that Piggly Wiggly "established a new relation between each buyer and everything offered for sale."

As his business prospered, Saunders married Carolyn Walker and became the father of five children. He also started building a mansion. But, in 1923, he lost $10 million in a Piggly Wiggly stock transaction. Financially ruined, he lost his mansion and his wife, who divorced him in 1928. He later married Patricia Bomburg, and they had one daughter.

Saunders tried another innovation in 1937, an automated store he named Keedoozle. He placed all merchandise behind glass doors. Shoppers selected the items they wanted by inserting a key into a corresponding slot, at which point the product would travel down a conveyor belt to a loading dock for pickup. Constant breakdowns with the technology doomed Keedoozle, and it folded before World War II.

Saunders opened a new Keedoozle in 1948 but with no better results. He tried yet a third time in 1953, under the name Foodelectric, but he died that year, on October 14 before the store could establish itself. Today, Piggly Wiggly operates more than 700 franchised supermarkets, primarily in the South.

BIBLIOGRAPHY

Boorstin, Daniel, *The Americans: The Democratic Experience*, 1973; Saunders, Clarence, *The Piggly Wiggly System*, 1917.

Schiff, Dorothy

(March 11, 1903–August 30, 1989)
Publisher

Though her career as a newspaper publisher came about almost by accident, Dorothy Schiff was instrumental in the success of the *New York Post* from 1939 until 1976. Under her direction, the nation's oldest continuously published newspaper (started by Alexander Hamilton) was saved from financial ruin. Her ownership of the *Post* was also distinctive in that as she was the sole stockholder, her corporate books were not subject to public scrutiny. During her reign, the paper became a champion of liberal causes and eventually pioneered the sensational tabloid style that has greatly impacted the shape of today's journalism.

Dorothy, the daughter of Mortimer L. and Adele Neustadt Schiff, was born on March 11, 1903, in New York City. Because of Adele's fear of infectious diseases, Dorothy and her brother, John, were educated at home by tutors. Schiff later attended the Brearley School in Manhattan, followed by a year at Bryn Mawr College.

In 1921, Schiff was officially presented to society, spending her next few years enjoying the lifestyle of a wealthy debutante. On October 17, 1923, she married Dick Hall. During the course of their unhappy marriage, the couple had two children, Morti and Adele. Schiff eventually divorced Hall, renounced her conversion to Christianity from Judaism, and in 1932

Dorothy Schiff (Archive Photos)

married George Backer. The couple had one child, Sarah Ann.

Despite her upbringing as a Republican, Schiff found herself increasingly aligned with Democratic President Franklin D. Roosevelt's administration and the New Deal program. Her resulting work with the labor movement and the Democratic Party earned her the attention of Roosevelt. Over the years, they formed a close and unusual relationship; while Schiff demurred on questions of the exact nature of the relationship, it was clear that her companionship was eagerly sought by the president. According to interviews later in life, he assured her accessibility to him by having her buy property next to his vacation home.

Early in their marriage, Backer had prevailed upon Schiff to purchase the *New York Post*, which she did in 1939. While she retained the titles of director, vice president, and treasurer, Backer was the president and publisher. During these years, the relationship between Schiff and her husband grew distant, and she became uncomfortable with Backer's direction of the newspaper. Backer suffered a debilitating illness in 1942, during which time Schiff took over as publisher and president.

After writing several political columns and acquiring more knowledge of the business end, Schiff decided the newspaper needed a different emphasis. In 1943, she and Backer divorced, making Schiff both owner and president. She pursued her intent to make the *Post* a more popular, less intellectual newspaper.

During that same year, Schiff and her editor, Theodore O. Thackery, made major changes to the newspaper, as well as to their relationship. They were married in the summer of 1943, and it was a relationship defined by their joint ambition for the *Post*. Together, they created the new tabloid style of the newspaper and began to incorporate numerous feature columns. The *Post* became increasingly more leftist.

While both Schiff and Thackery were liberal, they eventually began to veer in different ideological directions. The popular and contentious "Appeal to Reason" editorial column of the *Post* frequently ran letters by each of them that spotlighted their contrasting points of view. After a temporary transfer of editorial power to Thackery, the financial decline of the newspaper compelled Schiff to dissolve her professional and personal association with him in 1949.

By 1950, Schiff was devoting all of her attention to the *Post*. She tightened the structure of the publication, confining news reporting to news columns and editorializing to an editorial section, and diversifying the content of the regular feature columns. She also became more savvy about attracting advertising money. After the first year of Schiff's solo leadership, the newspaper regained its financial footing.

In reporting the news, Schiff always attempted to treat friends and strangers on an equal level. The *Post* tended toward exposés, and Schiff was not immune to the occasional social or political fallout from a story. Gradually, Schiff moved the *Post* in a less liberal direction. Believing that the paper should express both humor and public interest, she and her staff heightened the use of a sensational style, frequently trumpeting the more scandalous aspects of breaking news stories. Despite this bent, the *Post* remained respected for its blunt treatment and condemnation of the staunch conservatism of the McCarthy era.

One of the most popular features of the newspaper was a column penned by Schiff herself. Originally called "Publisher's Corner," but commonly known as "Dear Reader," Schiff drew upon her many social and political connections to write shrewd commentaries on a wide array of people and happenings. These memos transcribed numerous conversations with notable personalities, including Fidel Castro, Winston Churchill, and Albert Einstein.

Schiff's circle of acquaintances widened in 1953 with her marriage to Rudolph Sonneborn, a wealthy businessman. Though initially fascinated by each other, Schiff and Sonneborn grew apart. Their years of marriage were dominated by Sonneborn's recovery from a stroke. By 1965, the two had parted ways.

In 1976, Schiff sold the *Post* to Australian publishing magnate Rupert Murdoch, though she continued to consult for the paper until 1981. She died on August 30, 1989.

BIBLIOGRAPHY

McHenry, Robert, ed., *Her Heritage: A Biographical Encyclopedia of Famous American Women*, 1994; Nevins, Allan, *The Evening Post: A Century of Journalism*, 1968: Potter, Jeffrey, *Men, Money & Magic: The Story of Dorothy Schiff*, 1976.

Schumacher, Ferdinand

(March 30, 1822–April 15, 1908)
Manufacturer

While working as a grocer, Ferdinand Schumacher became convinced of the nutritional value and commercial potential of oatmeal. He was one of the pioneers of oatmeal milling and distribution, and succeeded in building his own company, the German Mills American Oatmeal Factory, into the leading oatmeal producer of his time. As oatmeal grew in popularity, however, competition in the oatmeal and cereal industry surged, and much of the latter part of Schumacher's career was spent waging price wars or bickering with other members of the industry over consolidation arrangements.

The son of a well-to-do commission merchant, Ferdinand Schumacher was born on March 30, 1822, in Hanover, Germany. He received a quality education in the schools of Hanover and began a five-year unpaid apprenticeship at age 15 to learn the grocer's trade. Schumacher joined his father's office in 1842, and after five years he became the shipping clerk for Egestaff and Hurtsig, the largest sugar refining plant in Hanover.

In 1850, he decided to immigrate to America to join his brother Otto in working on a farm in Euclid, Ohio. One year later, on September 7, he was married to his cousin Hermine. Only two of Schumacher's seven children lived to survive him. In 1852, he finally settled his new family in Akron, Ohio, which would remain his home for the remainder of his life.

In Akron, Schumacher opened his own grocery store. By 1854, Schumacher had become convinced that oatmeal was a potentially great product, rich in protein and many nutrients. That year, he began his oatmeal production with a small man-powered mill in the back room of his grocery store. His initial market consisted of the influx of recent immigrants from Germany, workers who found oatmeal to be an inexpensive yet hearty substitute for meat. Demand was strong, and in 1856 he opened his first mill and organized the German Mills American Oatmeal Factory. In 1863, he constructed a second mill and shortly afterward greatly expanded the company's capacity with the purchase of the Cascade Flour Mills.

As a new wave of German and Irish immigrants entered the United States in the 1870s and 1880s, demand for his product grew quickly. Americans, however, for the most part still shunned oatmeal because it was associated with animal feed. Although he did not advertise directly in newspapers, Schumacher became an outspoken advocate of the benefits of oatmeal and responded with editorial letters to any criticisms of the new oatmeal craze. A major victory in his fight for the acceptance of oatmeal came in 1874 when Schumacher's recipe for breakfast oatmeal was included in a popular standard cookbook.

With increasing demand, Schumacher continued to expand his production operations, but competition increased as well. To stay ahead, he introduced in 1875 the first substantial modernization of the milling process by using a machine to convert hulled kernels into coarse meal. In 1878, he imported porcelain rollers to produce rolled oats, which became popular so quickly that he converted the whole production line to the rolled variety by 1881.

By 1886, Schumacher was the largest employer in Akron and was selling 360,000 pounds of oatmeal per day. That same year, however, all of his mills and stored grain were destroyed in a tremendous fire, and the company's future became uncertain. With this crippling blow to the company's dominance, the fire also gave competitors an opportunity to renew attempts to organize the industry to stop the ruinous price wars that had plagued them in recent years. Schumacher's closest competitors, Henry Parsons Crowell (owner of the Quaker Oats Company) and Robert Stuart, led these organization efforts. Schumacher was able to reorganize after the fire by buying out his local competitor, the Akron Milling Company, and thereby forming the new F. Schumacher Milling Company. In November 1886, he finally agreed to meet with the organizers of the consolidation movement in Chicago. Out of this meeting was born the Consolidated Oatmeal Company, which attempted to control pricing and production through sales quotas based on market share.

This pool of milling companies ultimately failed, for it did not control enough of the total oatmeal market to be effective in controlling production levels. However, the seven largest cereal mills reorganized under a holding company called the American Cereal Company near the end of 1888. Schumacher controlled 50 percent of the new firm and installed himself as president with Crowell as vice president and Stuart as treasurer. Over the next few years, Crowell and Schumacher clashed over many marketing and sales issues. Crowell wanted to market worldwide with a single oatmeal brand based on his trademarks of the highly successful Quaker Oats, but Schumacher stubbornly insisted on continuing to market his own F. S. brand alongside Quaker Oats. Quaker Oats gained in popularity over F. S., but Schumacher refused to budge and instead offered rebates and discounts to continue the wasteful self-competition.

In 1893, Schumacher's wife died. Schumacher's battle with Crowell became the central to his life until he was remarried, on August 1, 1899, to Mary Zipperlan. During this same year, a proxy fight for control of the company ensued, and Schumacher was ousted by Crowell and Stuart. In 1901, the company was renamed the Quaker Oats Company.

In addition to his business interests, Schumacher was a member of the Universalist Church and an ardent supporter of Prohibition. In 1883, he ran as the gubernatorial candidate in Ohio for the Prohibition Party, receiving the largest vote any candidate had ever earned with that party, although he failed to win the election. Schumacher died in Akron on April 15, 1908.

BIBLIOGRAPHY

Chandler, Alfred D., Jr., *The Visible Hand*, 1977; Moskowitz, Milton, et al., eds., *Everybody's Business*, 1980; Storck, John, and W. D. Teague, *Flour for Man's Bread*, 1952; Thornton, Harrison J., *The History of the Quaker Oats Company*, 1933.

Schwab, Charles

(February 18, 1862–September 18, 1939)
Manufacturer

Few men rose more quickly, or fell from wealth more resoundingly, than did Charles Schwab. Within 10 years he went from store clerk to leadership at Carnegie Steel, and late in life lost everything he had earned.

Born on February 18, 1862, to John A. Schwab and Pauline (Farabaugh) Schwab in Williamsburg, Pennsylvania, Charles grew up in nearby Loretto, a small town where his father owned and operated a livery stable. After graduating from high school in 1880, Schwab worked as a grocery clerk in Braddock, site of the Edgar Thomson Steel Works owned by ANDREW CARNEGIE. Within a short time, the plant's superintendent, William Jones, offered Schwab a job as a stake driver for $1 per day.

Charles Schwab (Library of Congress)

Schwab's friendly, outgoing personality, and his intelligence and hard work led Jones to promote the 19-year-old to chief engineer and assistant manager within six months. In 1883, Schwab married Emma Dinkey of Loretto.

Schwab emerged as a Carnegie favorite, and the steel magnate soon made him superintendent of the company's newest acquisition, the Homestead Works in Homestead, Pennsylvania. After Jones died in an accident in 1889, Schwab returned to the Thomson Works as superintendent. Three years later, a bloody strike at Homestead damaged Carnegie's reputation and soured labor relations. In response, Carnegie instructed Schwab to improve conditions at the plant, which he did. This led to Schwab's appointment as president of Carnegie Steel in 1897, and in that capacity he earned more than $1 million per year, fulfilling what many considered a storybook rise from his dollar-per-day beginnings.

In 1901, Schwab facilitated one of the most important economic developments in American history when he convinced Carnegie to sell his steel business to J. P. MORGAN SR. This created the United States Steel Company, the nation's largest corporation. Schwab served as its president until 1903, when policy differences with Morgan and the board of directors forced his resignation.

Schwab continued his involvement in the steel industry, however. In 1904, he acquired the U.S. Shipbuilding Company and the Bethlehem Steel Company, both of which were experiencing financial difficulties. He merged these to form the

Bethlehem Steel Corporation, and used his own money, along with other investments, to make it a profitable business. Bethlehem provided steel girders for the skyscrapers just then beginning to pierce city skylines.

When World War I began, Bethlehem Steel benefited greatly, first by providing submarines for Britain, and then, after the United States entered the conflict, building ships for the American navy. President Woodrow Wilson appointed Schwab director general of the Emergency Fleet Corporation. By war's end, Bethlehem Steel challenged United States Steel for supremacy in the industry. But Schwab's later years brought a dramatic change in his fortunes. Worth $200 million at one point, he lived lavishly and invested unwisely. Schwab died insolvent in New York City on September 18, 1939.

BIBLIOGRAPHY

Hessen, Robert, *Steel Titan: The Life of Charles M. Schwab*, 1975.

Scott, Edward

(1846–1931)
Manufacturer

When Americans replaced privies with bathrooms in the late 1800s, Edward Irvin Scott replaced sheets of scrap paper with sheets of toilet paper, creating Scott Tissue.

Irvin, as he liked to be called, was born in 1846 in rural Saratoga County, New York, and went into business in 1879 when he and his brother, Clarence, borrowed $2,000 and opened a paper jobbing business in Philadelphia, Pennsylvania. From pushcarts they sold wrapping paper, scratch pads, and bags. As they made money they bought a horse-drawn wagon and decided that to be more efficient they needed to specialize in one product.

At that time, with urbanization and improvements in plumbing, the outdoor privy was giving way to bathrooms. The Scotts concluded that a market existed for a classy tissue that would replace the sheets torn from old catalogs and newspapers typically used in the outhouse. So they began buying large rolls of tissue from paper factories and converting them into smaller rolls, thus producing toilet paper. Back in 1857, Joseph Gayetty had manufactured a similar product, but he had done so as separate sheets rather than on rolls. The Scott product had a greater appeal, and before long the brothers were producing thousands of rolls under various store labels or wrapped in plain brown paper.

Then, in 1896, Irvin's son, Arthur H. Scott, convinced his father and uncle to apply their own brand name to the tissue. In 1902, the Scotts labeled and sold their tissue as Waldorf. Soon after, the company moved to larger headquarters in Chester, Pennsylvania, and in 1913, one year after Clarence Scott's death, Irvin Scott introduced the first paper distinctively labeled Scott Tissue, protected by a dustproof wrapper, and bearing the slogan (also Arthur Scott's idea) "soft as old linen."

Scott began advertising, too, breaking through the modesty that formerly made the topic taboo. An early advertisement said, "A highly-absorbent, snow-white, soothing tissue soft as fine old linen. Kind to the most sensitive skin. Peculiarly adapted to the needs of women of intuitive daintiness. Ask your doctor. No conversation. Just say 'Scott Tissue' to your storekeeper and receive a big, economical, dustproof roll." Meanwhile, the Scotts came upon another product by accident. One day in 1907, they received an order of paper too heavy to use as toilet tissue. At first they thought about throwing it out. But then they decided to perforate it and sell it as towels. Initially sold only to hotels and restaurants, Scott

Towels appeared in grocery stores beginning in 1931.

Irvin Scott retired from the company in 1921. His son Arthur, who became its new leader, died in 1927. Thomas McCabe then became president and guided the business to greater growth. Irvin Scott died in 1931, after having made Scott Tissue a household necessity. In 1995, Scott Paper, under the leadership of the controversial AL DUNLAP, merged with Kimberly-Clark, a company founded by JOHN KIMBERLY. The $9.4 billion deal created a company with annual revenue of more than $13 billion.

BIBLIOGRAPHY

Fucini, Joseph J., and Suzy Fucini, *Entrepreneurs: The Men and Women behind Famous Brand Names and How They Made It*, 1965.

Scott, Thomas Alexander

(December 28, 1823–May 21, 1881)
Railroad Executive

Thomas Alexander Scott presided over the Pennsylvania Railroad and through his guidance shaped the career of industrialist ANDREW CARNEGIE.

Thomas was born on December 28, 1823, in Fort Loudon, Pennsylvania, to Thomas Scott and Rebecca (Douglas) Scott. As a boy, Thomas worked at a general supply store. At 17, he moved to Columbia, Pennsylvania, and clerked in the office of a brother-in-law, who collected tolls for the state road system.

Scott's involvement with railroads began in 1850, when the Pennsylvania Railroad made him a station agent in Duncansville. America's rush to build more railroads had contributed to a managerial revolution within railroad companies that created large bureaucracies with promotion based on a person's ability to make decisions. Scott advanced quickly in these circumstances. In 1852, he was appointed third assistant superintendent of the Pennsylvania Railroad's western division, with his office in Pittsburgh. Six years later, he was promoted to general superintendent, and in 1860 to first vice president.

During these years, Scott formed a close relationship with Andrew Carnegie. Scott had hired the young man as his personal telegrapher in 1852, and Carnegie soon served as his assistant. Scott was Carnegie's mentor and taught him about the railroad. Together they developed effective business methods. As vice president, Scott recommended Carnegie for the superintendent's position, and his protégé gloried in getting it. In addition, Scott taught Carnegie about investments, persuading him to buy stock, and even lending him the money for that purpose.

After the South seceded from the Union to begin the Civil War, Scott firmly supported the federal government. In 1861, he advised President-elect Abraham Lincoln to enter Washington secretly so as to avoid assassination, a plan that Lincoln adopted. During the Civil War, Scott coordinated railroads for the shipment of troops, and moved 13,000 men with their artillery, wagons, and horses from Nashville to Chattanooga, Tennessee.

Along with J. Edgar Thomson, the Pennsylvania Railroad's president, Scott directed the company's continued expansion in the 1860s. When Thomson died in 1874, Scott succeeded him as president, and worked to consolidate and strengthen the system. At the same time, he served as president of the Texas and Pacific Railway Company.

Scott suffered a stroke in 1878 that partially paralyzed him. For some time he continued his duties, but then resigned on June 1, 1880. Less than a year later, on May 21, 1881, he died at his home near Darby, Pennsylvania. His wife, Anna Dike Riddle, survived him, as did four children, two from a previous marriage.

BIBLIOGRAPHY

Livesay, Harold C., *Andrew Carnegie and the Rise of Big Business*, 1975.

Scripps, Edward

(June 18, 1854–March 12, 1926)
Newspaper Owner

Today as more and more mergers occur in the media, Americans have grown accustomed to newspaper conglomerates. The hometown paper is now owned by a distant company. This development owes much to Edward Wyllis Scripps, for he began the nation's first newspaper chain.

Edward was born on June 18, 1854, on a farm near Rushville, Illinois, to James Mogg Scripps and his third wife, Julia (Osborn) Scripps. After attending both public and private schools, Edward began working in 1872 as an office boy at the *Detroit Tribune*, a paper managed by his half brother, James Edmund Scripps.

When James founded the *Detroit Evening News* in 1873, Edward worked there, first as a reporter and then as city editor.

In 1877, Edward quit his position to travel to Europe with another half brother, George H. Scripps. During that journey, Edward decided to start his own newspaper. With $10,000 borrowed from his two half brothers and a cousin, in 1878 he started the *Cleveland Penny Press* (later the *Cleveland Press*), a cheap, mass-circulation newspaper he produced in a four-room shack. As with his later newspapers, Edward geared the *Penny Press* to what he called "the 95 percent," or the common people.

In the early 1880s, he and his half brothers bought papers in St. Louis and Cincinnati. Combined with the ones they owned in Detroit and Cleveland, they formed the first newspaper chain in the United States. By decade's end, after a dispute with James, Edward sold him his interest in all the newspapers, except the *Cincinnati Post*.

In 1894, he joined George and Milton Alexander McRae to found the Scripps-McRae League of Newspapers. He followed this three years later with the Scripps-McRae Press Association, begun to obtain telegraph news. In 1904, he bought a similar organization, the Publishers' Press, and three years later combined it with his association to form the United Press (later United Press International). At about the same time, he organized the Newspaper Enterprise Association, the first syndicate to supply newspapers with feature articles, illustrations, and cartoons.

Scripps founded another newspaper chain in the early 1900s, the Scripps Coast League, comprised of papers along the West Coast. Eventually he owned 34 newspapers in 15 states. In 1903, Edward Scripps and his half sister Ellen Browning Scripps endowed the Scripps Institution for Biological Research in La Jolla, California (later the Scripps Institution of Oceanography.)

Scripps retired in 1908 and turned over ownership of his papers to his eldest son, James. The Scripps newspapers were merged with those owned by Roy W. Howard in the 1920s to form the Scripps-Howard chain. Edward Scripps died on his yacht off the coast of Liberia on March 12, 1926.

BIBLIOGRAPHY

Cochran, Negley Dakin, *E. W. Scripps*, 1972; Gardner, Gibson, *Lusty Scripps: The Life of E. W. Scripps*, 1932; Preece, Charles, *Edward Willis and Ellen Browning Scripps: An Unmatched Pair*, 1990; Trimble, Vance H., *The Astonishing Mr. Scripps: The Turbulent Life of America's* Penny Press *Lord*, 1992.

Sears, Richard

(December 7, 1864–September 27, 1914)
Merchant

Richard Warren Sears combined his ambition, boastful talk, and accidental encounter with unsold watches to form the largest mail-order business in the early twentieth century: Sears, Roebuck & Company.

Richard was born on December 7, 1864, in Stewartville, Minnesota, to James Warren Sears and Eliza (Burton) Sears. When Richard was a child, the family relocated several times to other towns in Minnesota. At age 17, Richard got a job as station agent at a small train depot in North Branch, where he operated the telegraph, sold tickets, and handled shipments.

In 1883, he relocated to the depot in Redwood Falls. His drive and opportunistic nature showed when he sold wood to farmers who journeyed into town to sell their produce. An even greater opportunity appeared when a shipment of watches arrived at the depot and went unclaimed. Sears decided to sell the watches for the company that had sent them. He made a quick profit, but more importantly discovered his salesmanship, for as one banker said of Sears: "He could sell a breath of air!"

In 1886, Sears moved to Minneapolis, began the R. W. Sears Watch Company, and hired A. C. Roebuck as a watch repairer. The following year, Sears sold his watches through the mail, using COD (cash on delivery), a common practice that seemed unique when he advertised it as "send no cash now." Sears worked from 7:00 in the morning until late at night, and his watch company grew rapidly. In 1892, he issued stock, and the fol-

Richard Sears (Library of Congress)

lowing year adopted a new name for his firm, Sears, Roebuck & Company.

Sears published his first catalog in 1893, and its many products showed that he had expanded well beyond watches. That same year, he moved his headquarters to Chicago, a booming city and a more central location for mail-order shipments. From there, Sears sold largely to customers in rural areas, people who wanted city goods but could not travel far to get them. His business expanded so rapidly, he often failed to fill all the orders that came in. This pace disturbed Roebuck to the point that he withdrew from the firm in 1895, although he returned several years later as an employee.

Needing more capital, Sears turned to Aaron Nusbaum and JULIUS ROSENWALD who joined him as partners. Sears captivated consumers with his advertisements and catalog. He wrote his own sales copy—every word—and true to the exaggerated language of the day, advertised his products in such terms as "the finest sewing machine in the world." To assure a steady supply of goods, Sears bought several manufacturing companies. His 1906 catalog proudly described "factories that we own or control in addition to our 40-acre plant."

At the same time Sears blanketed magazines with his advertisements, his catalog grew larger. After initially charging for it, he distributed it for free—aided by the federal government that had recently begun delivering mail directly to farmers' homes. Many rural dwellers awaited the catalog and called it the Dream Book or Wish Book. But country shopkeepers hardly considered it a dream; they hated it for cutting into their business, and they sometimes offered discounts to people who would bring the catalogs in and allow them to be burned.

Sears told his customers: "You cannot do us a greater favor than to show this catalog to your friends and allow them to use it for sending us orders." And send they did, ordering sewing machines, ovens, dolls, clothes, cream separators, Bengal tiger plush robes, and the famous Heidelberg electric belts, guaranteed to cure ailments. Sears said: "What we want above all is a satisfied customer. We want his permanent trade. To get this we must give the right goods at the right prices. In this mail-order business we can't afford to fool any of the people any of the time." Toward that end, he offered a money-back guarantee on everything he sold.

As the company grew larger, however, Sears's partners, especially Rosenwald, considered his ideas outdated. When a depression hit the nation in 1907, for the first time in its history Sears & Roebuck experienced a decline in sales. Disagreements between Rosenwald and Sears worsened. On November 21, 1908, Sears resigned, and never again took an active part in the company.

A millionaire, Sears had little time left to enjoy his fortune. He died on September 27, 1914, at age 50. Rosenwald presided over the next phase in Sears & Roebuck's expansion when the company opened its own department stores.

BIBLIOGRAPHY

Asher, Louis E., and Edith Heal, *Send No Money*, 1942.

Shoen, Leonard

(February 29, 1916–)
Truck and Trailer Rental Entrepreneur

America's increasingly mobile population after World War II needed a cheap way to move household goods, and Leonard Shoen provided it by founding a trailer rental business called U-Haul. With little competition he made millions, only to find his business empire embroiled in the 1990s in fistfights, lawsuits, and accusations involving murder.

Born on a farm near McGrath, Minnesota, on February 29, 1916, Shoen learned about business at an early age from his father, who engaged in numerous enterprises, none highly successful. In 1937, after graduating from Moler Barber College, Shoen enrolled at Oregon State University in Corvallis, and to earn money for his education leased a barbershop in a local hotel. Within a year, he had four barbers working for him and opened a second shop. With the outbreak of World War II, however, Shoen lost his employees, and after he was suspended from college in 1942, he enlisted in the navy.

Shoen got his idea for U-Haul in 1944, while in the hospital recovering from scarlet fever. He had seen people renting trailers from trailer lots. These typically old conveyances often broke down on the road. Shoen determined to build his own durable trailers, and in 1945, with $5,000 in savings, he started putting them together on a ranch in Ridgefield, Washington.

Shoen's quick success in the business resulted from three developments. First, as World War II ended, former servicemen wanted an inexpensive way to move their household goods, as did many other Americans. Second, Shoen invented a low-cost method for operating his business. To advertise, he painted the covered trailers a distinctive orange with the U-Haul name in grey. As people pulled the trailers, they promoted the company. He avoided high overhead costs by placing the trailers at service stations, and having the station owner rent the trailers and handle the paperwork for a percentage of the rental fee. Third, he had no substantial competition.

U-Haul trailers rented for $2 a day, and by 1949 Shoen had expanded his network, making it possible to rent a trailer one-way from city to city throughout most of the United States. To help in his business endeavors, Shoen obtained a law degree in 1955 from Northwestern University. At U-Haul, he added trucks to his fleet, and in 1968 moved his headquarters to Phoenix, Arizona. Difficulties occurred in the 1970s, however, when a gas shortage dampened rentals, and then other companies provided stiff competition. Still, U-Haul and its holding company, AMERCO (also involved in real estate investments), recovered and prospered.

Shoen married four times, had several children, and decided to distribute the bulk of company stock to them—a decision that led to enormous problems. Shoen retired from the company in 1986—voluntarily he said, although others claimed that some of his children forced him out. Three years later, a vicious struggle erupted among the children as one faction attempted to reinstate Shoen as head of the company. A fistfight marred the stockholders' meeting in March 1989 and caused Shoen to remark: "I created a monster." About Joe Shoen, who then controlled U-Haul, he said: "My son . . . I think is incompetent. I'm not very pleased with his behavior."

Then, in 1990, when Eva Shoen, wife of Samuel Shoen, was found murdered, Leonard Shoen stated that he thought Joe and another of his sons, Mark, had plotted the killing. Adding to the turmoil, a lawsuit by Sam Shoen against his brother Joe over control of the company resulted in Sam collecting millions of dollars in damages. Perhaps Leonard had created a monster. But U-Haul rolled on with 14,000 independent dealers in 1998, and 1,100 company-owned moving centers.

BIBLIOGRAPHY

"It's a Family Feud at U-Haul," *Miami Herald,* March 7, 1989; Reisner, Mel, "U-Haul Family in Dispute over Control," *Miami Herald,* January 29, 1989; Shoen, L. S., *You and Me,* 1980; Silver, A. David, *Entrepreneurial Megabucks: The 100 Greatest Entrepreneurs of the Last Twenty-Five Years,* 1985.

Shubert, Lee

(March 15, 1873–December 25, 1953)
Entertainment Executive

After breaking through a monopoly that existed in the early 1900s, Lee Shubert established his own empire of theaters and stage productions.

Shubert was born Levi Szemanski in Shirvinta, Russia, to David Szemanski, a Jewish pack peddler, and Catarina Szemanski, most likely on March 15, 1873. When David Szemanski immigrated to the United States in 1882, customs officials recorded his last name as Shurbent, and he, in turn, changed it to Shubert. The rest of David's family joined him in New York City the following year.

If David Shubert came to America thinking the move would make him successful, he was mistaken. He failed as a storekeeper and turned to alcohol. The family's poverty forced Lee Shubert to begin work at age 10 and prevented him from obtaining a formal education. After jobs selling newspapers, shining shoes, rolling cigars, and cutting shirts, he and a younger brother, Samuel, with financial help from a clothier, obtained the road rights to the play *A Texas Steer* and took it on a tour through the Northeast that earned them a good profit. Over the next three years, additional profitable plays followed, and in April 1890 Lee, Samuel, and a third brother, Jacob, obtained a lease on New York City's Herald Square Theater. In doing so, they challenged and eventually broke the theater monopoly of the Klaw-Erlanger syndicate.

By 1902, Lee Shubert was handling the financial affairs for the Shubert Theatrical Corporation, and by 1906 the company owned 13 theaters. Within the next 10 years, Lee and Jacob Shubert (Samuel had died in 1905) dominated American theaters. In the 1920s, they gained a reputation for staging low-budget "Viennese-American" operettas, such as *The Student Prince,* and they built several Broadway theaters, including the Winter Garden. During that same decade, they placed all their business interests—among them 86 theaters in the United States and Canada, and 6 in London—under a holding company, the Shubert Theater Corporation. The Shuberts were producing 25 percent of all American plays and controlled numerous other bookings.

Then the Great Depression hit, sending the Shubert Theater Corporation into bankruptcy. Lee Shubert, however, revived the theatrical business, and, while expanding his real estate investments, produced several popular musicals, such as *Hellzapoppin',* along with such dramas as *Ten Little Indians.*

In 1950, the federal government filed an antitrust suit against the Shubert brothers. Five years later, a consent decree resulted in the Shuberts selling 12 theaters and giving up their booking business.

Meanwhile, Lee Shubert had married Marcella Swanson after a widely publicized legal battle between them. Shubert died on December 25, 1953, with an estate valued at $16 million. In the 1950s and 1960s, Jacob Shubert's son John ran the company, and after that a great-nephew took it over.

BIBLIOGRAPHY

Hirsch, Foster, *The Boys from Syracuse: The Shuberts' Theatrical Empire,* 1998; McNamara, Brooks, *The Shuberts of Broadway: A History Drawn from the Collections of the Shubert Archive,* 1990; Stagg, Jerry, *The Brothers Shubert,* 1968.

Silverman, Fred

(September 13, 1937–)
Entertainment Executive

Fred Silverman worked magic at the CBS and ABC television networks, in each instance taking low ratings and turning them around. He seemed invincible, until he failed at NBC and pundits wrote him off as a has-been—a premature judgment, as it turned out.

Silverman was born on September 13, 1937, in New York City and after attending public schools in the borough of Queens, he obtained a B.A. degree in 1958 from Syracuse University. He continued his studies at Ohio State University, from which he received a master's degree in broadcasting. For his thesis, Silverman analyzed programming at ABC and concluded that in order for that television network to rise above its last place position in the ratings, it would have to change its corporate mentality and become more profit-driven.

Soon after graduating from Ohio State in 1959, Silverman obtained his first job in broadcasting when he joined WGN-TV in Chicago. Here he began applying his seemingly intuitive ability to know what viewers wanted to watch. After boosting WGN's ratings, in 1963 he moved to WPIX-TV in New York City, where he did the same for that station.

A scant six weeks later, CBS hired Silverman to overhaul its daytime programming, especially its children's shows. His addition of *Children's Film Festival* won the network a Peabody Award, while his scheduling of new soap operas boosted daytime ratings and advertising revenues along with them. The network reacted by promoting Silverman in 1970 to vice president of program planning and development.

Silverman confronted the challenge of raising prime-time ratings at CBS. These had been sliding because of the shows with rural themes that were unpopular with younger viewers, the kind sponsors preferred. As a result, Silverman gutted the schedule, canceling such shows as *Petticoat Junction*, *Green Acres*, and the long-running *Beverly Hillbillies*. Among the replacements were *All in the Family*, a caustic, original comedy that raised controversial issues, reached number one in the ratings, and won several Emmys. In a short while, Silverman added other critically acclaimed ratings winners: *Maude*, *Good Times*, *The Jeffersons*, *The Mary Tyler Moore Show*, *The Bob Newhart Show*, and *M*A*S*H*. He added dramas, too, such as *Cannon* and *Kojak*, and a sentimental depiction of life in the 1930s, *The Waltons*.

CBS won 35 Emmys in 1974–1975 and had 9 of the nation's top 10 shows. Silverman had his flops, such as *Me and the Chimp*, *Big Eddie*, and *Planet of the Apes*, but he had restored CBS to its

number-one position among the networks, an accomplishment that led ABC—the very same last-place network he had criticized in his master's thesis—to lure him away by offering him the presidency of its entertainment division. Silverman accepted, and in June 1975 put together a schedule (using shows picked by his predecessor) that began moving ABC ahead of CBS. For ABC, he scheduled fast-paced comedies—derided by critics as shallow. He also borrowed the miniseries concept from the Public Broadcasting System (PBS), and presented *Rich Man, Poor Man* in installments.

With some exceptions, the quality of Silverman's programming lagged well behind that at CBS—vacuous fare such as *The Love Boat*, and *Fantasy Island*, *Charlie's Angels*, and *Three's Company*. But in January 1977, he presented the critically acclaimed miniseries "Roots," and opened the fall season with "Behind Closed Doors," a riveting political drama.

Silverman jumped to a third network, NBC, early in 1978 after it offered him the company presidency. But at NBC he failed, partly due to strikes by writers and actors. In 1981, the network, stuck in third place, fired him. Many observers considered Silverman finished, and for a while he disappeared from the entertainment scene. But he made a comeback in 1985 by producing a two-hour "Perry Mason" special and by forming Fred Silverman Company, an independent production firm, that sold several hit shows to the networks—*Matlock*, *In the Heat of the Night*, and *Father Dowling Mysteries*. In 1989, *Forbes* magazine estimated that Silverman had made more than $3 million from his programs.

Later that year, Silverman joined television executive Fred Pierce to form

PierceSilverman Company, which produced original live and taped programming. Silverman seemed invigorated and commented, "When I started out there were three networks and PBS, and that was it. There are so many more opportunities now. I wish I were 20 years younger."

About more recent television shows, Silverman commented in 1996, "I think that the most distinguished series programming has been in the hour form, with shows like *NYPD Blue, ER, Murder One*, ensemble pieces. I just don't think that TV comedy has progressed. If anything, it's taken several steps backward."

BIBLIOGRAPHY

Bedell, Sally, *Up the Tube: Prime-Time TV and the Silverman Years*, 1981; Gubernick, Lisa, "'I'm Not Rumpled Anymore,'" *Forbes*, May 6, 1989; "PierceSilverman: Former Top ABC Executives Team Up," *Broadcasting*, March 27, 1989.

Simplot, Jack

(1909–)
Manufacturer

While driving around Idaho with "MR SPUD" on his license plate, John Richard "Jack" Simplot described himself as "an old potato farmer." Simplot, however, ranked among the nation's billionaires, making his fortune at first from processing potatoes, and then from diversifying into other food items and even computer technology.

Born in 1909—some sources say in Idaho, others in Iowa—Simplot grew up on his father's 120-acre hardscrabble farm near Delco, Idaho. Simplot left school and home at age 14, and he worked at odd jobs while renting 40 acres of potato land from his father. With money he saved, he bought hogs and soon owned several hundred of them that he sold at a profit.

Then, in 1928, he learned about a potato- sorting machine. Lacking the money to buy it, he formed a partnership with a local farmer, acquired the machine, and used it to sort not only his potatoes but those of other farmers, who were charged a fee for the service. Now an entrepreneur, in 1931 he married the daughter of a wealthy hardware merchant.

The times worked in Simplot's favor. When the Great Depression began, the demand increased for potatoes, a relatively cheap food. By 1940, he owned nearly 30,000 acres of farm and grazing land scattered throughout Idaho. That year, he stumbled into the onion-drying business when he and the dissatisfied customer of a California onion processor arranged a deal whereby Simplot dried onions, converted them into powder and flakes, and shipped them west.

Successful with onions, he decided to dehydrate his potatoes. Few such facilities existed, so Simplot had little competition. In 1941, he devised a way to easily remove the peel by soaking the potatoes in a lye wash to soften the skin, and then using high-pressure water jets to strip them. During World War II, the army ordered large quantities of Simplot's dried potatoes, and between 1942 and 1945 he produced about 33 million pounds annually.

From potatoes he built a diversified empire. In one instance, he constructed a large box plant near his processing factory, and when it became difficult to acquire lumber at the price he wanted, he erected sawmills, owning three of them by the late 1960s. He also founded a million-dollar phosphate plant in Pocatello, Idaho to produce fertilizer, earning some $2 million from that product in 1967 alone.

But Simplot's greatest earnings from food awaited the rise of a fast-food chain headed by RAY KROC, namely McDonald's. Simplot had, in the 1940s, developed a process to freeze-dry French fries, and in the 1950s he sold the product as a frozen food in supermarkets. Then, in the 1960s, he convinced Kroc to use his frozen French fries in the rapidly expanding McDonald's. By the late 1960s, Simplot was selling 550 million pounds of frozen fries to McDonald's each year, and by the late 1980s, 700 million pounds.

Simplot pursued a radically different enterprise in 1980 when he backed twin brothers who decided to make not potato chips but computer chips with their Micron Technology firm. Although Simplot relinquished the chairmanship of the J. R. Simplot Company to his youngest son in 1994, he remained active in his eighties as a director, and as the largest single stockholder in Micron, controlling shares worth $1.8 billion in 1996. He said about Micron: "It's my baby, I guess. I'm going to stick with it as long as I can."

BIBLIOGRAPHY

Gilder, George, *The Spirit of Enterprise*, 1984; Zuckerman, Laurence, "From Mr. Spud to Mr. Chips," *New York Times*, February 8, 1996.

Singer, Isaac

(October 27, 1811–July 23, 1875)
Manufacturer

An inventor and manufacturer, Isaac Merrit Singer developed sewing machines and marketed them so successfully that soon after his death his company proclaimed: "On every sea are floating the Singer Machines; along every road pressed by the foot of civilized man this tireless ally of the world's greatest sisterhood is going upon its errand of helpfulness."

Singer had a restless life. He was born on October 27, 1811, in Pittstown, New York, and grew up in Oswego, where his father worked as a millwright. He received only limited schooling, and at age 12 began wandering from town to town, usually working as a machinist, although he also held jobs as an actor and theater manager. He obtained his first patent in 1839 for a rock-drilling machine, but sold it and quickly spent the money he had earned. Singer obtained another patent in 1849 for a wood and metal-carving machine. A boiler exploded in his factory, however, destroyed his invention, and cost him what little money he had.

By this time, sewing machines had appeared, first in Europe and then in the United States, but their limitations made them impractical for widespread use until 1845, when Elias Howe invented a machine that used an eye-pointed needle and oscillating shuttle. Howe tried to get consumers interested in his machine by demonstrating its utility. At one point he held a contest with expert seamstresses that showed his invention could sew quicker and better than they could, but its high price worked against him.

Singer stepped into the situation in 1851 when, in just 11 days, he built a sewing machine that improved on Howe's by providing continuous stitching. He patented his invention that August, and using borrowed money, he and attorney Edward Clark founded I. M. Singer & Company to manufacture and distribute the sewing machines.

In 1854, Howe sued Singer for patent infringement. After a sensational trial, widely reported in newspapers, the court ruled in Howe's favor, and Singer had to pay his rival $15,000. In addition, Howe was to receive a 25 percent royalty on every machine sold by Singer and by other companies. That arrangement proved short-lived. As patent disputes continued, Singer and several other competitors formed the Sewing Machine Combination in 1856 to eliminate the battles.

Isaac Singer (North Wind Picture Archives)

They pooled patents, and inventors shared in the royalties. Howe received $5 for each machine sold, and eventually earned $2 million.

By this time, Singer's company led in making sewing machines. This was partly due to the numerous improvements Singer had made to his machines, for which he obtained 20 patents between 1851 and 1863, including those for the continuous wheel feed and yielding presser foot. It was also due to Singer's salesmanship. Together with Clark, he developed installment buying on a scale previously unknown. A consumer could buy a $125 Singer for just $5 down, with the remainder paid in small monthly installments. By 1860, I. M. Singer sold more sewing machines than any other company in the world.

Although Singer still held considerable stock in his company, he retired from active involvement in 1863 and moved to Europe. In 1865, he married Eugenia Summerville (he had been married to

Catherine Maria Haley, but divorced in 1860), and they had two daughters. He died on July 23, 1875, in Torquay, England.

Singer sewing machines changed the way Americans looked and the way they shopped. Better-fitting clothes could be made at home, or they could be mass-produced, resulting in standardized ready-to-wear styles.

BIBLIOGRAPHY

Eastley, Charles M., *The Singer Saga*, 1983.

Slater, Samuel

(June 9, 1768–April 21, 1835)
Manufacturer

Samuel Slater has been called the founder of American industry. He built the first modern textile mill in the United Sates, doing so by importing secrets from his native country, England.

Samuel was born on June 9, 1768, in Belper, Derbyshire, England, to William Slater, a farmer, and Elizabeth (Fox) Slater. During his schooling, Slater displayed a talent for mathematics, and at age 14, when his father died, he began an apprenticeship with Jeddah Strutt, then developing cotton manufacturing machinery. Samuel learned about mechanics from Strutt, and wanted to take cotton manufacturing further. Strutt, however, thought that the enterprise had only limited value. Consequently, after Samuel learned of money being offered by state legislatures in America for experienced textile makers, he decided to emigrate.

Given his expertise, however, leaving England posed a problem. The British government did not want any plans for textile manufacturing to leave the country out of fear other nations would use them to gain an industrial advantage. Slater circumvented the English restrictions in two ways. First, he supervised the construction of Strutt's new textile works and memorized the details about its machinery. Second, when he departed in September 1789, he did so without telling anyone, not even his mother, and he wore a disguise.

Slater reached New York later that year, and in April 1790 contracted with Almy & Brown in Providence, Rhode Island, to make cotton machinery. A water-powered spinning frame of 24 spindles that produced cotton yarn went into operation in 1791. Machine industries such as Slater's solved the problem in America of a scarce supply of skilled labor able to make finished goods. The machines enabled Slater to use cheap unskilled labor, mainly women and children.

Later that year, Slater married Hannah Wilkinson. In 1793, Slater and his partners formed Almy, Brown & Slater and built a factory in Pawtucket. Five years later, while continuing in his position with Almy and Brown, he formed another partnership to begin Samuel Slater &

Company. After opening a manufactory in Pawtucket, he opened yarn-spinning plants in Smithfield, Rhode Island (later Slatersville), and East Webster, Massachusetts, along with cotton mills at Jewett City, Connecticut, and Amoskeag Falls, New Hampshire, of which the latter stimulated manufacturing along the Merrimac River.

Slater died on April 21, 1835, survived by his second wife Esther Parkinson, whom he had married in 1817 after his first wife's death, and six sons.

BIBLIOGRAPHY

Cameron, Edward Hugh, *Samuel Slater: Father of American Manufactures*, 1960; Tucker, Barbara M., *Samuel Slater and the Origins of the American Textile Industry, 1790–1800*, 1984.

Samuel Slater (North Wind Picture Archives)

Sloan, Alfred

(May 25, 1875–February 17, 1966)
Manufacturer

In order to compete effectively with the Ford Motor Company, Alfred Pritchard Sloan Jr. developed a system at General Motors, called the "ladder of consumption," that reshaped the American economy.

On May 25, 1875, Alfred was born into a comfortable family setting in Brooklyn, New York, son of Alfred Pritchard Sloan and Katherine (Mead) Sloan. His father had numerous business investments and at one point was a partner in a tea and coffee importing company. Sloan received his B.S. degree in electrical engineering from the Massachusetts Institute of Technology in 1895, after only three years of study. He then began work as a draftsman at the Hyatt Roller Bearing Company, a firm in Harrison, New Jersey, in which his father had invested.

Appointed Hyatt's president and general manager in 1901, Sloan held the position for 15 years. Shortly before his promotion, he began linking the company to an emerging technology that he thought would captivate America, the automobile. Sloan perfected steel roller bearings; learned the workings of the automobile industry, including the names of its leaders; and hit the road, selling roller bearings to car companies. He sent a letter to Henry Ford in 1899 asking him to consider using "our Flexible Roller Bearings." Before long, Ford agreed and installed the bearings in rear axles.

Sloan secured another important customer when General Motors (GM) began using his roller bearings. But he worried that these companies might start making their own roller bearings, and in 1916 he agreed to make Hyatt a division of GM, selling it for $13.5 million, while continuing as its president.

From there, Sloan rose within the ranks of GM and in 1930 was put in charge of operations as vice president, and shortly after, was named president. Sloan decided to restructure GM, to change the way it made and marketed cars. "The great problem of the future," he wrote an associate, "is to have our cars different from each other and different from year to year."

Sloan's "ladder of consumption" idea was developed to solve the problem of how to manufacture several cars that overlapped in their market appeal. He designed each make for a different income group, an arrangement that invited consumers to buy upward as their wealth increased. Thus, for example, Chevrolet cars were aimed at a lower income bracket than Buicks, and Buicks lower than Cadillacs. A person who bought a Chevrolet could aspire to one day own a Buick, and after that a Cadillac.

The price gap between each level was set to make it possible for a consumer to move upward without much difficulty. Thus, a Cadillac, while more expensive than a Buick, would not be exorbitantly so. According to one historian, "Sloan developed a new form of industrial organization in which a giant corporation was split into semi-autonomous divisions that at times competed with one another"— much like Chevrolet and Pontiac, which competed at the borders of their price ranges.

To produce a different model each year, Sloan established a styling department and introduced colors and gadgets. He instructed designers to think about making appeals to women. "The 'laws' of the Paris dressmaker have come to be a factor," he said.

Under Sloan GM prospered, and its executives received high salaries and bonuses. Yet there were problems. For one, Sloan had poor relations with labor, partly because he opposed all government attempts to set minimum wages, partly because he despised unions and such proposals as a five-day workweek, and partly because labor received little in terms of pay or security from GM's prosperity.

For another, Sloan's emphasis on new models strained the industry, burdened by constant replanning and retooling. As each GM division competed to offer new gadgets on its models, Chevrolets began looking more like Cadillacs. And the gadgets often took precedence over quality—making GM and other car companies vulnerable to foreign competition.

Sloan, who sponsored philanthropic endeavors such as the Sloan-Kettering Cancer Center (with Charles Kettering), relinquished the presidency of GM in 1937 and served as chairman of the board from that year until 1956. He died on February 17, 1966.

Bibliography

Boorstin, Daniel J., *The Americans: The Democratic Experience*, 1973; Douglass, Paul, *Six upon the World: Toward an American Culture for an Industrial Age*, 1954; Sloan, Alfred P., *My Years with General Motors*, 1964.

Smith, Fred

(August 11, 1944–)
Shipping Executive

While in college, Frederick Wallace Smith submitted a paper to his economics professor that outlined a bold idea to develop an express letter and package delivery company. He got a C for the paper, but turned the concept into a multimillion-dollar business, Federal Express.

Frederick was born into wealth on August 11, 1944, in Marks, Mississippi. His father, Frederick Smith, owned large tracts of farmland in northern Mississippi and founded Dixie Greyhound Bus Service and Toodle House Restaurants. When the elder Smith died in 1948, he left his wife, Sally (Wallace) Smith, and children with adequate means of support. A trust fund assured that young Fred would never know financial hardship.

As a teenager, Fred attended an exclusive prep school in Memphis, Tennessee, played sports, and learned to fly. He entered Yale in 1962, but spent more time socializing than studying, and earned only average grades—including the one for his economics paper. He graduated in 1966 with a bachelor of arts degree, and then served in the Marine Corps as an officer. He fought in the Vietnam War and earned a Silver Star, a Bronze Star, and two Purple Hearts.

After his return to the United States in 1969, Smith decided to pursue flying, his main interest, and with money from his trust fund, which by then exceeded $13 million, he purchased an ailing firm, Arkansas Aviation Sales. The Little Rock–based business provided maintenance service to corporate airplanes, but Smith made it profitable by having it handle the purchase and sale of used jets.

Still, Smith felt unfulfilled. He wanted to revolutionize business, and so returned to his idea for express mail. At that time, only United Parcel Service, and to a lesser degree Emery Air Freight and Flying Tiger, provided a service similar to what Smith had in mind. But even they fell short, since they were too slow and unreliable. Before starting his venture, Smith hired consultants who studied a prospective market. They reported that a transportation network involving 100 cities would be profitable, and that businesses would pay a premium price for quick package delivery.

The need for reliable package transport was increasing as more high-tech companies existed in scattered locations rather than being concentrated in a few areas. In June 1971, Smith incorporated Federal Express, but he had yet to establish his transportation network.He had to create an air cargo fleet, purchase warehouses, and establish truck connections. He raised $96 million from venture capitalists on Wall Street, established his headquarters in Memphis, bought 33 Dassault Falcon aircraft, and in April 1973 began service to 25 cities. On the first night, FedEx handled only 186 packages—a bruising disappointment. Over the next few months, the company struggled near bankruptcy, and Smith dug deeper into his trust fund. Some on the FedEx board talked about removing Smith, but he had established an excellent rapport with his executives and workers, and in 1975 business began to pick up.

Then, in 1977, the federal government deregulated the airline industry, which freed Smith to buy bigger planes and enter more markets. With money obtained from the sale of public stock, he bought Boeing 727s. He also launched a successful advertising campaign by using identifiable colors on his trucks—orange, purple, and white—and by promoting the slogan "absolutely positively overnight."

In the mid-1980s, businesses began using FedEx regularly.

Smith tried to broaden his company's appeal by adding ZapMail, a system that used satellites to send facsimile copies across the nation in seconds. The endeavor foundered, however, when fax machines became common, and he closed it in 1986 after it lost $300 million.

Despite that setback, FedEx continued its sensational growth, and in 1987 its revenues topped $3.5 billion. Two years later, Smith purchased a major competitor, Flying Tiger International, the world's largest air cargo firm, and as the 1980s ended, Smith's personal wealth reached $395 million.

BIBLIOGRAPHY

Morgenson, Gretchen, ed., *Forbes: Great Minds of Business*, 1997; Sigafoos, Robert A., *Absolutely, Positively Overnight*, 1983.

Smith, Roger

(July 12, 1925–)
Manufacturer

A controversial leader of General Motors for nearly 10 years, Roger Bonham Smith earned notoriety for the firm's plunging profits, his autocratic style, and his vilification in a popular movie.

Born in Columbus, Ohio, on July 12, 1925, to Emmet Quimby Smith and Bess Belle (Obetz) Smith, Roger moved with his family to Detroit, Michigan, around 1930, where his father worked for an auto parts supplier. After graduating from Detroit University School, a secondary school, in 1942, Smith entered the University of Michigan and paid for his education by working part-time. World War II interrupted Smith's studies, and in 1944 he joined the U.S. Navy. After his discharge in 1946, he returned to college, receiving his B.A. degree from the University of Michigan in 1947 and his M.B.A. in 1949.

He then joined General Motors (GM) as a senior clerk, and over the next two decades climbed the corporate ladder through the company's financial departments, gaining a reputation as a "bean counter." In 1970, he was elected treasurer, and the following year the company made him vice president in charge of financial staff. Smith departed the financial sector in 1972, when he advanced to the vice presidency of the nonautomotive and defense group. When he discovered two GM units losing money—Frigidaire, makers of appliances, and Terex, makers of earth-moving equipment—he sold them.

Sitting also on the board of directors in 1974, Smith directed the corporation's adoption of strategic planning. Then, in 1981, as a gasoline shortage and competition from Japanese automakers rattled the industry, Smith became GM's tenth chairman and CEO. With a mandate to act quickly and decisively to reshape a moribund corporate bureaucracy, he cut costs by laying off workers and jettisoned several new product programs. Controversy struck immediately when amid all the layoffs he announced a new bonus plan for executives. Although Smith later abandoned the plan, many workers lost confidence in him.

Smith's three most substantial changes involved reorganization, acquiring additional companies, and founding a new car manufacturing plant. In 1984, hoping to promote efficiency, he reduced GM's five divisions to two. By many accounts the move slowed rather than sped vehicle production, and it angered dislocated workers. Later that year, he purchased Electronic Data Systems, and, as a result, placed that firm's founder, ROSS PEROT, on GM's board. There ensued two years of divisive wrangling between Smith and Perot, until the latter left GM.

Smith continued to diversify in 1985, when he merged GM with the Hughes Aircraft Company (founded by HOWARD HUGHES). At the same time, he launched the subsidiary Saturn Corporation, to make cars under a system that paid workers based on performance rather than an hourly wage, to produce four-door sedans through modular construction.

Smith's iron-fisted tactics earned him the attention of a neophyte movie director, Roger Moore, who in 1989 released the movie *Roger & Me*, a humorous, satirical, and biting evaluation of GM. Critics praised the film, and it placed the largely unknown Smith in the national spotlight.

Overall, Smith failed to reinvigorate GM. Inefficiency and complacency remained strong, and his diversification drained profits. One analyst considered his reign among "the most turbulent periods in GM history." Smith retired as chairman and CEO in 1990 but remained on the GM board. "You're seeing a turnaround in market penetration," he said at the time.

Smith continued to exert authority as a board member, but many within the company opposed him. In 1993, under pressure to resign, he retired from the board. According to one newspaper, GM's outside directors had "found it increasingly difficult to erase his management legacy while he continued to sit by their side on the board."

BIBLIOGRAPHY

Levin, Doron P., "GM Chief Defends His Record as His Retirement Nears," *New York Times*, June 25, 1990; Levin, Doron P., "Roger Smith Is Leaving GM's Board," *New York Times*,

January 28, 1993; Woutat, Donald, "Can Stempel Get GM Back on Right Road?," *Los Angeles Times*, December 15, 1991.

Soros, George

(August 12, 1930–)
Financier

In recent years, George Soros has earned a reputation less for his business interests than for his philanthropy. He has given away so much money that many rank him with JOHN D. ROCKEFELLER, ANDREW CARNEGIE, and JULIUS ROSENWALD as among the great philanthropists in American history. Soros's generosity, however, has included some controversial programs dedicated to the promotion of what he calls an open society. "When I was offered an honorary degree at Oxford," Soros recently said, "they asked me how I wanted to be described, and I said I would like to be called a financial, philanthropic, and philosophical speculator."

Born in Budapest, Hungary, on August 12, 1930, the son of Tivadar Soros and Elisabeth (Szucs) Soros, as a Jewish youth George experienced two oppressive regimes that bred in him a distaste for totalitarianism: Nazism and communism.

Soros emigrated to England in 1947 and graduated from the London School of Economics in 1952. He moved to the United States in 1956 and began accumulating a large fortune through a private investment firm, Soros Fund Management, which advised the Quantum Group of Funds. In 1960, he married Annaliese Witschak, and they had three children. (That marriage ended in divorce in 1983, and Soros married Susan Weber in 1983, with whom he had two children.)

In finance Soros displayed an incredible ability to anticipate international economic shifts and subsequently direct investments into profitable channels, especially regarding currencies. As one example, in 1992, he concluded that the British pound would lose value, and so he borrowed billions of pounds and converted them to German marks. When the pound collapsed, Soros repaid the

George Soros (Reuters/Jim Bourg/Archive Photos)

pounds to the Bank of England at the lower rate and pocketed a profit of $1 billion. Financiers called him "the man who broke the Bank of England."

With his fortune estimated anywhere from $2 billion to $5 billion, Soros, slightly built but fervent in his ideas, had begun the Open Society Fund in 1979. He said that the philosopher Karl Popper, his professor at the London School of Economics, influenced him greatly with his condemnation of Nazism and communism as equivalents. Popper advocated free societies, and Soros started his fund to promote them. He gave heavily to projects in Eastern Europe and established a foundation in Hungary in 1984 and in the Soviet Union in 1987.

Soros spent his money on everything from photocopiers for groups in Hungary to millions of dollars to help Soviet, and later Russian, science to millions more in an effort to save Sarajevo from Serb depredations. In 1996 alone, he gave more money to Hungary than did the U.S. government. Rather than supporting libraries, museums, and colleges, he gave his money to humanitarian, educational, and scientific programs that he believed would promote democracy. He funded scholarships in South Africa to help the victims of apartheid, for example, and his donations to Russia aimed to improve the standard of living there in order to stimulate an open, progressive government.

In 1993, he began funding programs in his adopted country, the United States. "I do not see this as an emergency intervention," he said. "But I do think that to have a reasonably just society, there should be ongoing concern and intervention in issues that are troubling and undermining our society."

His giving raised a storm of controversy, primarily from conservatives who accused him of supporting liberal programs that undermined middle-class values. He provided $50 million to the Emma Lazarus Fund, a project started in 1996 to help legal immigrants adjust to American society. Soros said he gave the grant as a response to the "outrageous" laws denying such immigrants several types of public assistance and benefits. He gave $15 million to a program that enhanced relief and dignity in dying, and $12 million to the Algebra Project to improve the math skills of children in rural and inner-city schools.

Soros has called U.S. drug policy a failure for being more punitive than educational, and through grants he has backed needle exchange programs to help prevent the spread of AIDS. He supports campaign finance reform to maintain an open society, and abortion rights to maintain women's freedom of choice. He has criticized the corruption of professions such as medicine by materialism, and what he calls a government preoccupation with helping business rather than helping the disadvantaged. "The core of an open society is under attack in our laissez-faire society," he claimed.

Soros continued to make money, too, as evident with his heavy investments in Russia (more than $2.5 billion), an endeavor he expected to continue as a sign of his confidence in the government. He said: "Let me make it absolutely clear that as an investor my decisions are guided by profit considerations. For instance, I would have no hesitation in selling my shares at the appropriate time. But the decision to become engaged in investing was influenced by what is good for Russia."

Soros insisted he wanted to give away all his money before he died. A prolific writer, he has authored several articles and books, including *The Alchemy of Finance*, *Underwriting Democracy*, and *Soros on Soros*. Despite all his giving, in 1997 he portrayed his philanthropy as falling short: "Open society will prevail only if people believe in it as a desirable goal. That is where the open societies of the West are failing today—you need only to look at Bosnia—and that is where I have failed so far, both as a philosopher and an activist."

BIBLIOGRAPHY

Soros, George, *The Alchemy of Finance*, 1987; Soros, George, *Opening the Soviet System*, 1990; Soros, George, *Soros on Soros*, 1997; Soros, George, *Underwriting Democracy*, 1991.

Spalding, Albert

(September 2, 1850–September 9, 1915)
Manufacturer

An outstanding player in the early days of baseball, Albert Goodwill Spalding dominated the business side of the sport as well. His company, A. G. Spalding & Brothers, developed a monopoly in sporting goods.

Born on September 2, 1850, on a farm in Byron, Illinois, to James Lawrence Spalding and Harriet Irene (Goodwill) Wright Spalding, Albert attended public schools in his hometown and in nearby Rockford, and as a boy learned how to play baseball from a Civil War veteran. By age 17, Spalding was already large in size and commanding in personality, and had earned a reputation for his pitching and hitting. His talents corresponded with the emergence of baseball as a professional sport.

Spalding joined the Boston team of the National Association of Professional Ball Players in 1871 and compiled an amazing record. As a pitcher he won 37 games and lost only 8 in 1874, and won 41 and lost only 15 in 1875. An excellent batter, he hit .320 from 1871 to 1875.

The following year, he jumped to the Chicago White Stockings of the National League and continued his domination by compiling a 47–13 pitching record with a 1.75 ERA (earned run average) while batting .312. He pitched eight shutouts that year, and opposing teams almost always counted on recording a loss when going up against him. While posting those numbers, Spalding managed his ball club, too, winning the 1876 championship. He played mainly first base and second base in 1877 and 1878, and then retired from the game.

He had already entered business in 1876 when he opened a large baseball goods store in Chicago. Spalding shrewdly used his status as a player to build his sales. For example, in 1877, he became one of the first players to wear a baseball glove. The glove protected his hand, but it did more. As intended, it started a trend in which players regularly wore gloves manufactured and sold by Spalding. And when youngsters wanted to emulate the players, they, of course, turned to Spalding's gloves.

Operating as A. G. Spalding & Brothers (in partnership with his brother and brother-in-law), in 1878 Spalding was named the official supplier of baseballs for the National League after he agreed to *pay the league* $1 per dozen balls. Spalding reasoned that although he would lose money to the league, he would reap profits from being able to advertise his product as the "official baseball of the National League."

While building his business, Spalding served as president of the Chicago White Stockings (later renamed the Cubs) from 1881 to 1892. In 1888, he organized a trip around the world by the club. They played exhibition games in Australia, Ceylon, Italy, France, Britain, and Egypt, where the players tossed balls among the pyramids. Spalding realized the tour would win few foreign converts to baseball, but he wanted the publicity so the National League would grow at home and with it the demand for Spalding products.

Spalding expanded his business further by secretly acquiring competing companies, a popular practice of the era. In 1892, he merged with six other firms, forming a conglomerate capitalized at $4 million. Spalding & Brothers swallowed Wright and Ditson, A. J. Reach, and three other companies, while outwardly they appeared to still be competing with one another. The monopoly he developed in sporting goods resembled that established by JOHN D. ROCKEFELLER in oil and reflected an era in which big business had come of age.

Ambitious, materialistic, organizational, and individualistic, Spalding believed that anyone with willpower and brains could succeed. He praised competition while seeking its elimination. He lived in urban America, yet gloried in baseball's connection to a virtuous rural setting.

At a time when baseball suffered from rowdiness and gambling, he insisted on a clean sport, one that children could attend. Ever the salesman, from 1878 to 1880, he edited *Spalding's Official Base Ball Guide*, and in 1911 he wrote *America's National Game*, a history of the sport that promoted a myth many accepted as truth: baseball had been invented by Abner Doubleday at Cooperstown, New York. Spalding's story was intended to make baseball a completely American sport devoid of any foreign influences and thus deny that it had actually derived from a British game called "rounders."

Spalding died on September 9, 1915, in Point Loma, California. He had married Sarah Josephine Keith in 1875, and after she died in 1899, Elizabeth Churchill Mayer in 1900. She and a son from his first marriage survived him. For his tireless promotion, the nation remembered Spalding as the "Father of Baseball."

BIBLIOGRAPHY

Bartlett, Arthur, *Baseball and Mr. Spalding*, 1951; Levine, Peter, *A. G. Spalding and the Rise of Baseball*, 1985; Seymour, Harold, *Baseball: The Early Years*, 1960; Spalding, Albert G., *America's National Game*, 1911.

Spencer, Henry

(December 16, 1872–July 4, 1956)
Financier, Railroad Executive

Henry Benning Spencer enjoyed a noteworthy career in railroad management before achieving success with his lucrative concept of owning and operating refrigerated railway cars that were leased to the major railroads to transport fresh produce. This profitable venture illustrated the enormous potential for the rapidly expanding railroads to unify the nation.

Henry, the son of another noted railroad executive, SAMUEL SPENCER, and Louisa Virginia Benning Spencer, was born on December 16, 1872, in Long Branch, New Jersey. After a secondary school education at Baltimore public schools and the Berkeley School in New York City, Henry attended Harvard, graduating in 1855.

Spencer began his railroad career as a clerk for the superintendent of the Elgin, Joliet and Eastern Railroad in Joliet, Illinois. By 1897, he had risen to the rank of superintendent of the Alabama Great Southern Railroad, which was headquartered in Birmingham, Alabama. Just one year later, he moved to Kentucky for a new post as superintendent of the Louisville Division of the Southern Railroad Company. From 1901 until 1905, Spencer was the assistant general manager of the St. Louis–Louisville line of the Southern Railroad. At some point during his Louisville years, Spencer met and married Katharine Price, with whom he had two daughters and a son. Their son, Samuel Spencer II, despite pursuing a legal career, would later continue the family legacy of railroad management by serving as president and chairman of the board of the Tennessee Railroad Company.

Earning a promotion to general manager of the Southern Railroad, Spencer and his family relocated to Washington, D.C., in 1905. By the following year, he was named vice president of the Southern Railway System, a post he held until 1917. The expansion of the railroad system, combined with technological advances in refrigeration, provided the capability for Spencer's next successful venture.

In 1920, Spencer founded the Fruit Growers Express, a company established by major railroads with routes west of the Mississippi River to provide refrigerated as well as ventilated railroad cars for the transportation of perishable food items. The enterprise, which owned all of the repair shops and the cars that it rented to the railroads, proved enormously profitable. Between 1920 and 1947, revenue climbed from an already respectable annual yield of around $6 million to about $34 million, and the personnel ranks swelled from 650 employees to 5,000. At the same time, the number of refrigerated cars in service increased from just over 5,000 to more than 20,000.

Spencer capitalized on the obvious demand for this type of service by heading up a similar organization, the Western Fruit Express Company, from 1923 until 1948 in Washington, D.C. This company primarily serviced the West in conjunction with the Great Northern Railway Company. He was also the organizer for an analogous firm in 1926, the Burlington Refrigeration Express Company.

Spencer was an active manager, and he was always involved in a number of projects simultaneously. He served as a director of the Northern Pacific Railroad for 20 years. During World War I, Spencer was chairman of the Central Coal Commission and was also placed in charge of purchasing for the U.S. Railroad Administration. At one time, he was director of the prominent Riggs National Bank in Washington, D.C. Spencer served as president and chairman of the board of the Tennessee Railroad Company from 1918 until his death on July 4, 1956.

BIBLIOGRAPHY

Ingham, John N., ed., *Biographical Dictionary of American Business Leaders*, 1983; Klein, Maury, *History of the Louisville and Nashville Railroad*, 1972; Stover, *Railroads of the South, 1865–1900*, 1955; Zipley, William Z., *Railroads: Finance and Organization*, 1915.

Spencer, Samuel

(March 2, 1847–November 29, 1906)
Railroad Executive

Samuel Spencer, one of the few railroad executives to have practical engineering savvy, was integral to the reorganization of the southern railroad system in the late 1800s, a change that factored significantly in the economic development of the post–Civil War New South.

Samuel, born on March 2, 1847, in Columbus, Georgia, was the only child of Lambert and Verona Mitchell Spencer. Samuel attended elementary school in Columbus and the Georgia Military Institute in Marietta before leaving school to join the Confederate army in 1863. He served initially as a private in the Nelson Rangers and then with a cavalry unit. He left the military in April 1865, resuming his education by enrolling in the University of Georgia at Athens. In 1867, Samuel, who had entered with junior-year standing, graduated with full honors and was accepted to the graduate engineering program at the University of Virginia.

After two years of engineering studies, Spencer began to acquire practical experience through several engineering positions with the Savannah & Memphis Railroad. By 1872, he was a principal engineer. On February 6 of that same year, he married Louisa Virginia Benning. The couple had two sons and a daughter. One of his sons, HENRY SPENCER, would follow in his father's footsteps. After the wedding, he spent two months in the employ of the New Jersey Southern Railroad as a clerk, followed by a four-year stint in charge of one of the transportation divisions of the Baltimore & Ohio Railroad (B&O). Though he left the B&O briefly from 1876 until 1879 to serve as the general superintendent of the Long Island Railroad, he returned to become the assistant to the president.

Spencer's standing with the B&O grew, and in December 1887, after holding a succession of vice presidential appointments, he became the president of the

Samuel Spencer (North Wind Picture Archives)

railroad company. The position was short-lived, however. Spencer was forced to resign when board members feared that he had a role in the attempt by Drexel, Morgan & Company to gain control of the railroad.

After being ousted as president of the B&O, Spencer was hired by Drexel, Morgan & Company as their expert railroad analyst. By the end of 1890, he had become a partner in the firm. The company, with Spencer's input, played a leading role in the reorganization of southern railroads that took place in the late 1800s. In 1893, he served as one of the treasurers for both the Richmond & Danville Railroad and the East Tennessee, Virginia & Georgia Railway. When Drexel, Morgan & Company consolidated the Richmond & Danville and other smaller southern railroads into the Southern Railway, Spencer was appointed the first president of the new company.

Under Spencer's management, the new railroad underwent tremendous expansion, multiplying the mileage of the service area, increasing freight contracts, and greatly increasing passenger traffic. Between 1896 and 1906, the company's annual earnings skyrocketed from $17.1 million to $53.6 million. Employees of the railroad had great affection for Spencer. The Southern Railway was an integral part of the economic development of the region that was becoming known as the "New South."

With business booming, Spencer turned his attention to appearing before congressional committees to protest rate regulation. He conceded that railroads had a responsibility to acknowledge public interest and maintained that discriminatory (and often secret) price-fixing practices within the industry were wrong. He asserted, however, that further government control would be tantamount to enacting a "commercial lynch law."

After years of service in various aspects of the railroad industry, it is ironic that Spencer's death, on November 29, 1906, was the result of injuries from a rear-end collision of two fast passenger trains on his own road in Campbell County, Virginia.

BIBLIOGRAPHY

Hungerford, Edward, *The Story of the Baltimore & Ohio Railroad, 1827–1927*, 1928; *In Memorium: Samuel Spencer*, 1910; *New York Tribune*, February 1 and October 12, 1905, November 30 and December 1 and 8, 1906; Page, Rosewell, ed., *University of Virginia: Its History, Influence, Equipment and Characteristics*, 1904; *Poor's Manual of the Railroads of the U.S., 1869–1906*; Spencer, Samuel, "Railway Rates and Industrial Progress," *Century Magazine*, January 1906.

Sperry, Elmer

(October 21, 1860–June 16, 1930)
Engineer

A prolific inventor and keen businessman, Elmer Ambrose Sperry applied his talents to a strikingly diverse range of engineering problems throughout his career. In his early years, his interests centered around electric machines for use in transportation and the generation of electricity. Later in his career, Sperry turned his attention to electrochemistry and ultimately to the principles of the gyroscope and its practical application in navigation for which he is best known.

Elmer was born to Mary Burst and Stephen Decatur Sperry on October 21, 1860, near Cortland, New York. His mother died tragically just a few hours after the difficult delivery. Although Elmer never knew his mother, he may have inherited her talent for science and mathematics; her few possessions that were left to him included an astronomy chart and her science books. His father traveled frequently for work, which involved the manufacturing, transportation, and dealing of lumber. Elmer was primarily raised by his paternal grandparents and his aunt, Helen Burst.

Sperry attended the local public school, but his thirst for knowledge led him to spend his extra time studying machinery at the shops and factories in Cortland and at the laboratories of nearby Cornell University. A truly inspiring event in Sperry's life was his 1876 visit to the Centennial Exhibition in Philadelphia, where he saw many mechanical exhibits and experiments. Upon finishing his public school education, he spent three years at the State Normal and

Elmer Sperry (Library of Congress)

Training School and one year at Cornell in 1878.

While at Cornell, Sperry studied the engineering of electric dynamos and saw great possibilities for improving the machine. With the financial backing of an interested Cortland manufacturer, Sperry was sent to Syracuse, New York, to build a large dynamo for operating arc lamps. After successfully completing the project by 1880, he moved to Chicago and founded the Sperry Electric Company for the manufacture of his improved dynamos, arc lamps, and other appliances. The company's factory opened on Sperry's twentieth birthday.

Sperry married Zula A. Goodman on June 28, 1887. Zula's enthusiasm was a constant source of encouragement for Sperry, and she served on the board of directors for the Elmer A. Sperry Company, established as a clearinghouse for Sperry's many other patents. Though the couple had four children, three sons and a daughter, one of the sons was later tragically killed while flying an airplane over the English Channel.

After a few years of success with the Sperry Electric Company, Sperry turned his interests toward the application of electricity to transportation. In 1888, he began by creating the Sperry Electric Mining Machine Company, which initially produced new types of cutting and drilling equipment for coal-mining operations. Sperry then designed new electric generators and electric locomotives for transporting coal out of mines. This work led him to create the Sperry Electric Railway Company in 1890 for manufacturing electric street-railway cars in Cleveland, Ohio. The company, which included all of Sperry's patented improvements to the streetcars, was eventually sold to the General Electric Company in 1894. From 1894 to 1900, Sperry applied the knowledge gained in his streetcar endeavors to the design of a new electric automobile. His patented storage battery allowed the vehicles to travel an impressive distance of 100 miles on one charge.

While developing the improved battery, Sperry became interested in other aspects of electrochemistry. In 1900, he formed a research lab in Washington, D.C., and over the next 10 years, he and his associates researched new chemical processes for the production of pure caustic soda, hydrogen, and chlorine compounds, and developed a tin recovery process for recycling tin from old cans and scrap metal. During this period, Sperry also experimented with a type of compound internal combustion engine that used diesel fuel. He developed a machine for producing electric fuse wire and created yet another company, the Chicago Fuse Wire Company, to manufacture fuses.

Sperry is best remembered for his contributions to the technology of navigation by making use of gyroscopic principles. For centuries, the gyroscope had been merely a curious toy, but around 1896 Sperry began to envision its applications in navigation. His vast experience in diverse fields had equipped him well to deal with both the electrical and mechanical difficulties in creating gyroscopic compasses and stabilizers for ships and airplanes.

In 1910, the Sperry Gyroscope Company was established in Brooklyn, New York. Later that same year, his first prototype compass was tested on the battleship *Delaware*. The compass was soon adopted by the U.S. Navy, and after World War I, the device was adopted by over 60 steamship lines. In 1914, his stabilizer for airplanes won first prize as a safety device from the French Aero Club. In 1929, he closed out the Sperry Gyroscope Company but continued research on many other topics under a new company, Sperry Products, Incorporated.

In the course of his life, Sperry received hundreds of patents and formed eight companies to manufacture his inventions with annual revenue of over $8 million. He was awarded numerous prizes and medals for his innovations as well as honorary degrees from Stevens Institute of Technology, Lehigh University, and Northwestern University. He was a member of numerous engineering and scientific societies. Sperry died on June 16, 1930.

BIBLIOGRAPHY

Hughes, Thomas Parker, *Elmer Sperry: Inventor and Engineer*, 1971; Hughes, Thomas Parker, *Science and the Instrument-Maker: Michelson, Sperry, and the Speed of Light*, 1976; Hunsaker, Jerome Clarke, *Elmer Ambrose Sperry, 1860–1930*, 1955.

Spreckels, Claus

(July 9, 1828–December 26, 1908)
Manufacturer

Claus Spreckels, known as "the Sugar King," held a monopoly on the manufacture and sale of refined sugar on the Pacific Coast of the United States in the late 1800s. The millionaire was both renowned and reviled for his role in turning Hawaii into a wide-scale exporter of sugar. Viewed by many as a domineering opportunist who swept over the island kingdom and interfered with local politics and culture, he is nonetheless recognized as the catalyst for rapid economic development in the area.

Born on July 9, 1828, in Lamstedt, Germany, Claus was the eldest of the six children of Diedrich and Garinna Back Spreck- els. At the age of 18, he left the region of Hanover to immigrate to the United States. In 1846, he began working at a grocery store in Charleston, South Carolina, a store that he soon bought. With business doing well, in 1852 he married Anna Christina Mangel, with whom he had four sons and a daughter.

Claus Spreckels (North Wind Picture Archives)

In 1855, the family sold the grocery store and opened a new wholesale and retail grocery store in New York City. Though the venture was immediately profitable, Spreckels sold it just one year later, and at the advice of his brother Bernard, moved the family to San Francisco, California. By 1863, after years of owning small grocery stores, Spreckels reentered the business world on a larger scale, as owner, along with Bernard, of the Bay Sugar Refining Company. The raw sugar was imported from the Hawaiian Islands. Spreckels became very involved in the industry but sold his interest in the company in 1865 in order to move to Europe to study all aspects of the manufacture of sugar.

Upon his return to San Francisco in 1867, Spreckels established the California Sugar Refinery, building it in the following five years into a large-scale operation with an output of 50 million pounds of sugar per year. On July 28, 1874, he earned a patent for his invention of a method for producing loaf, or hard, sugar. During the next decade, he continued to ramp up production, constructing by 1883 the largest refinery on the Pacific Coast. He also diversified, branching out into the farming of sugar beets in Salinas, California, and opening a sugar-beet refinery. In order to facilitate transportation between Salinas and San Francisco, Spreckels financed the Pajaro Valley Railroad, which was completed in 1898.

Though Spreckels himself held the Pacific Coast monopoly on the manufacture and sale of refined sugar, he was enraged by the competition of the Sugar Trust, centered in the eastern United States, and spent $3 million on the construction of a refinery in Philadelphia. With the project completed in 1889, he compelled the trust to purchase the refinery at a higher cost.

In addition to Spreckels's frenetic drive to achieve dominance in the U.S.

sugar industry, he was equally determined to control the market at its source: the Hawaiian Islands. In 1876, President Ulysses S. Grant signed a reciprocity treaty between the United States and Hawaii, enabling the entry of duty-free sugar into America. This move was strongly resisted by Spreckels and other refiners, who worried that Hawaii's high-grade sugars, which went directly to merchants, would drive out the market for the American refiners' second-grade products known as "coffee sugars." Spreckels traveled to Hawaii just before the full price rise caused by the treaty could take effect. Resolving his own problem (and generating tremendous animosity from Californian competitors and Hawaiian planters), Spreckels bought up over 50 percent of the anticipated sugar crop for 1877. With his new Hawaiian Commercial Company, Spreckels bought existing plantations and established new ones, for the first time owning all stages involved in the manufacture of sugar.

In the decade that followed, Spreckels allied himself closely with the highly corrupt government of Hawaii's last king, David Kalakaua, and the premier, Walter Murray Gibson, a former missionary who by then owned much of the islands. Spreckels amassed a great deal of political influence before the Hawaiian Revolution of 1893 ended the career of his cronies. By the early 1890s, a falling-out with Kalakaua and Gibson left Spreckels with economic holdings but no ability to extend them by government connections. His Hawaiian holdings gradually declined. The control of the Hawaiian Commercial Company was also the subject of a bitter family dispute. In 1899, after long financial and legal battles, Spreckels's sons, Rudolph and Claus, wrested control of the company away from him and his other sons, Adolph and John Dietrich.

While sugar was the dominant player in Spreckels's business world, he also energetically rallied against other monopolies that drove prices up and discouraged competition. He financially assisted the development of the San Francisco & San Joaquin Valley Railway to compete against the dominant Southern Pacific Railroad. In 1899, he organized the Independent Light & Power Company, followed by the Independent Gas and Power Company in 1903, with the aim of compelling the San Francisco Gas & Electric Company to lower its rates, improve service, and eventually buy him out.

Spreckels, considered by many to be one of the principal "robber barons" of his time, was also known as a generous benefactor of San Francisco and its institutions. He invested widely in real estate, building the first skyscraper in San Francisco—the Spreckels Building on Market Street. On December 26, 1908, three years after reconciling with his sons, Claus Spreckels died in San Francisco.

BIBLIOGRAPHY

Adler, Jacob, *Claus Spreckels: The Sugar King in Hawaii*, 1966; Cordray, William Woodrow, "Claus Spreckels of California," unpublished Ph.D. dissertation, 1955; *San Francisco Call*, March 24, 1906, and December 27, 1908; *San Francisco Chronicle*, December 27, 1908.

Stanford, Leland

(March 9, 1824–June 21, 1893)
Railroad Executive

Leland Stanford had no qualms about conflicts of interest. As governor of California, he mixed politics with his own investments, helping build the mighty Central Pacific Railroad and tying it to a transcontinental rail system.

Born on March 9, 1824, in Watervliet, New York, the son of Joshua Stanford, a wealthy farmer and builder, and Elizabeth (Phillips) Stanford, Leland attended the Clinton Liberal Institute in Clinton, New York, and the Cazenovia Seminary in Cazenovia, New York, before beginning law studies in Albany in 1844.

In 1847, after obtaining his degree, Stanford opened a law practice in Port Washington, Wisconsin, where his father had bought for him a law library considered the best in the state. Three years later, Stanford married Elizabeth Lathrop, daughter of a prominent businessman in Albany. Stanford's professional life changed in 1852 when his office and library burned to the ground. At that point, he decided to join his five brothers who

Leland Stanford (Archive Photos)

had moved to California and started merchant businesses selling supplies to the miners involved in the gold rush.

After running a moderately successful store in a gold-mining town, Stanford settled in Sacramento and there met three other businessmen—Charles Crocker, Mark Hopkins, and Colis P. Huntington—who would later join him, forming a group called the "Big Four," to start the Central Pacific Railroad. While involved in his merchant business, Stanford entered politics. In 1859, he ran for governor but lost. The following year, he served as a delegate to the Republican National Convention that nominated Abraham Lincoln for the presidency.

Stanford had joined the party more for economic reasons than for any principles about slavery. He believed the Republicans would be friendly toward his, and

California's, desire for railroad development—and indeed the party platform strongly supported internal improvements. Stanford again ran for governor in 1861 and prevailed over a splintered Democratic Party.

All during that year, he pursued his desire for a transcontinental railroad that would connect California with the East. His efforts, and those of other railroad supporters, convinced Congress to pass the Pacific Railway Act, which provided federal subsidies for a railroad from Iowa to California. President Lincoln signed the bill in 1862.

While governor, Stanford invested in the Central Pacific Railroad, and at the same time he convinced the legislature and local governments to pass several acts that resulted in the company receiving more than $800,000 in subsidies. In one instance, elections in Placer and Sacramento Counties were marred by charges of fraud and vote buying.

At the same time, Stanford worked with Mormon leader Brigham Young to make sure the Central Pacific had access to Utah's Wasatch Mountains. It was also his suggestion that led to the railroad exploiting Chinese laborers to build the line.

Stanford left the governorship in 1863 and devoted his full energy to building the Central Pacific, serving as president of the company from 1863 until 1893. The railroad built eastward from California, exacting an enormous toll on the Chinese workers, while the Union Pacific built westward from Nebraska. Stanford and the rest of the Big Four earned huge profits from their investments in companies supplying the Central Pacific—a practice later condemned by an investigating commission.

On May 10, 1869, the Central Pacific and Union Pacific joined in Utah, and Stanford helped drive the golden spike that marked the accomplishment. Stanford and his colleagues in the Big Four then gained control of railroad transportation in southern California by building lines down the coast and through the San Joaquin Valley. With a monopoly in place, they charged the highest railroad rates in the nation.

In the mid-1870s, the Big Four created the Southern Pacific Company (Stanford served as its president from 1885 to 1890) as a holding company for the Central Pacific and other properties, and for years the Southern Pacific dominated the California legislature. When reformers advocated governmental controls on railroads in California and elsewhere, Stanford called the plans "communistic." For him, governmental power was good when it provided his businesses with subsidies and evil when it engaged in social reform.

By the 1880s, Stanford had clearly been relegated by Huntington to a secondary status at the Southern Pacific. Stanford returned to elective politics in 1884 and won a seat in the U.S. Senate. The election displayed a rift between Stanford and Huntington, who had supported another Republican for the office.

In addition to his railroad activities, Stanford developed vineyards and a large ranch where he bred fine racing stock and raised the quality of California horses. In 1885, he endowed Leland Stanford Junior University—later Stanford University—and over the years spent more than $20 million on the college. Stanford died at his home in Palo Alto on June 21, 1893.

BIBLIOGRAPHY

Klein, Maury, *Union Pacific: The Birth of a Railroad*, 1987; Lewis, Oscar, *The Big Four*, 1938.

Steinberg, Saul

(August 13, 1939–)
Financier

Although Saul Steinberg said in 1969, "I'm no takeover artist," he engaged in numerous corporate raids, and as such received a storm of criticism from those who thought that his actions ruined companies.

Born in Brooklyn, New York, on August 13, 1939, the son of a plastics manufacturer, Steinberg began reading the *Wall Street Journal* when he was still in high school, and decided then that he would become a millionaire. After graduating, he enrolled in the Wharton School of Business. As a senior, he began dealing in the stock market, buying shares in O'Sullivan Rubber. He demonstrated what would become a pattern for him in his investments when he threatened to use proxies in order to take over the company. His move forced O'Sullivan to buy him out at three times the original value of his stock.

In 1961, a couple of years after graduating from Wharton, Steinberg obtained a loan from his father and founded the Ideal Leasing Corporation, later called the Leasco Data Processing Equipment Corporation. He bought computers from IBM and then leased them to businesses at rates lower than IBM—in effect using the computer corporation's own product to undersell it. By 1965, Leasco's assets reached $5.4 million, and in the late 1960s its stock sold at considerably more than earnings.

Steinberg then bought other companies, generally small ones until 1968, when he took over Reliance Insurance, merged it with Leasco, and served as its CEO. He then stunned the financial world by pursuing Chemical Bank, a $9 billion corporation and a pillar of the national economy. Protests from within the business community and from among politicians who saw the takeover as dangerous to the economy forced Steinberg to relinquish this quest, but not until he had made a $36 million profit.

Steinberg spent most of the 1970s working to pull Reliance through a difficult financial period. Then he again raided other companies, acquiring their stock, striking fear into them that he would take them over, and compelling them to buy back his shares—all at a substantial profit for Steinberg. He pursued that strategy, for example, with Lomas & Nettleton, a giant mortgage-banking house, and Chris-Craft Industries, a boat manufacturer. Then he tried to take over the Walt Disney Company. Disney agreed to buy back Steinberg's stock to prevent the takeover, paying him $325 million and thus leaving him with a profit of over $30 million. The 1990s found Steinberg continuing his investments, joined by his son.

BIBLIOGRAPHY

Allison, Eric W., *The Raiders of Wall Street*, 1986; Fisher, Katherine D., *The Computer Establishment*, 1981; Taylor, John, *Storming the Magic Kingdom: Wall Street, the Raiders, and the Battle for Disney*, 1987.

Steinem, Gloria

(March 25, 1934–)
Editor

A leading feminist and journalist, Gloria Steinem, activated by the 1960s counterculture, founded *Ms.* magazine.

Gloria was born on March 25, 1934, in Toledo, Ohio. Her father, Leo Steinem, worked at one point as an antique dealer and operated a summer resort, but for the most part he lived as an itinerant and traveled in a house trailer with his family, barely able to keep the household together. In 1946, he and Gloria's mother, Gloria Nunevillar Steinem, divorced, and young Gloria then lived with her mother in a poor district of East Toledo. For years she took care of her mother, a near invalid who suffered from anxiety and depression. As a teenager, Gloria tap-danced at the neighborhood Elks Club and entered and won a local television talent contest, hoping this might lead to an escape from her environment in Toledo.

Then, in 1952, she was accepted to Smith College in Massachusetts. She worked hard, won scholarships, and graduated magna cum laude in 1956 with a degree in political science. That summer, Steinem traveled to India under a fellowship she had received to study in Delhi and Calcutta. Little did she realize the trip would have a transforming impact on her, helping to shape her social outlook. In fact, the journey proved so eventful that one of her biographers, Carolyn G. Heilbrun, says Steinem discovered in India "the political focus of her life," namely, a strong concern for the disadvantaged. Steinem also discovered, as she published freelance articles in Indian newspapers, that she could earn a living through writing and advocacy.

Upon her return to the United States in 1958, Steinem tried to find work as a reporter, but to no avail. She eventually was hired as codirector of the Independent Research Service in Cambridge, Massachusetts. This organization operated in conjunction with the National Student Association (NSA), which brought together leaders in college student governments.

Steinem landed her first job with a magazine in 1960, but did not have her first article published until two years later, when *Esquire* carried her story about the sexual revolution. In 1963, Steinem wrote an article that appeared in *Show*, based on her work as an undercover Playboy Bunny. The article preceded her conversion to feminism by six years, but it presaged her later observations that women were sex objects, worth something to men only as bunnies.

Steinem's writing gained little recognition however, until her "City Politic" column appeared in *New York* magazine in 1968. According to Heilbrun, with this column Steinem "was on her way to becoming a serious journalist, reporting events affecting women, as well as other dispossessed groups, but not recognizing that she was noticing women in any special way."

The counterculture affected Steinem greatly, stimulating her feminist outlook. Her feminist viewpoints first emerged in March 1969 when she attended a meeting on abortion organized by the radical feminist group Redstockings. Steinem spoke out and confessed she had once had an abortion, and she said that women should not have to feel criminal about undergoing the procedure.

Following this meeting, Steinem wrote an article, "After Black Power, Women's Liberation," in which she took an openly feminist stand. Her writing ability and the knack she had for presenting ideas without being confrontational moved her to the forefront of the emerging women's liberation movement. In 1971, she joined Betty Friedan, Bella Abzug, and Congresswoman Shirley Chisholm in founding the National Women's Political Caucus (NWPC), which recruited women to run for public office.

At the same time, her journalistic career took a new turn when she worked to found a feminist magazine. At first, she doubted she would get any advertisers for the project, but her enthusiasm grew when she contacted women editors, journalists, and opinion makers and found them all supportive. Publisher Clay S. Felker then agreed to run a 30-page sample publication, called *Ms.*, as an insert in the December 1971 issue of his magazine *New York.* After this proved successful, he financed the first full issue of *Ms.*, which appeared in January 1972. Steinem served as editor for both publications.

During the following summer, *Ms.* appeared on a regular monthly basis and featured articles such as "Down with Sexist Upbringing," and "Why Women Fear Success." Within a few months, the magazine's circulation reached half a million.

Steinem believed that the oppression of women prevented men from living fuller lives, and she carried that view into her work at *Ms.* She believed, as well, that men and women should share equal responsibility for child rearing and household obligations.

In 1972, Steinem campaigned to get the necessary number of states to ratify the Equal Rights Amendment, an effort that eventually failed. At the same time, radicals within the women's liberation movement attacked her and *Ms.* for selling out to the male-dominated corporations that pay for most magazine advertising. In 1987, *Ms.*, in the midst of financial troubles, was purchased by an Australian communications conglomerate, and in the 1990s the magazine raised its price in order to publish without any advertisers at all. Steinem continued for several years as a consultant while also working as a contributing editor at Random House publishers.

BIBLIOGRAPHY

Heilbrun, Carolyn G., *The Education of a Woman: The Life of Gloria Steinem,* 1995; Steinem, Gloria, *Outrageous Acts and Everyday Rebellion,* 1983; Steinem, Gloria, *Revolution from Within,* 1992; Stern, Ladensohn, *Gloria Steinem: Her Passions, Politics, and Mystique,* 1997.

Steinway, Henry

(February 15, 1797–February 7, 1871)
Manufacturer

First in Europe and then in the United States, Henry Steinway made the grandest of the concert grand pianos.

Born Heinrich Steinweg on February 15, 1797, in Wolfshagen, Germany, Steinway suffered considerable tragedy as a youth. During the Napoleonic Wars, his mother and most of his siblings died from cold and hunger as they fled the French troops. Several years later, during a severe thunderstorm, lightning struck the shelter in which he, his father, and his three surviving brothers had huddled and killed all except Heinrich.

In 1815, Steinway, now an orphan, joined the army of the duke of Brunswick and served as a bugler. He entertained as well, by playing the zither and piano-forte, and shortly before leaving the army began making mouth organs. Upon returning to civilian life, he decided to learn the wood-making skills needed to craft musical instruments, and for several years worked as a cabinetmaker. By 1825, he was employed as an organ maker in the village of Seesen, while in the kitchen of his small home he made pianos on his own. They gained such a reputation for quality that he soon had enough orders to start a business. Before long, his sons joined him, and they flourished until a revolution in 1848 ruined the economy.

Seeking to start anew, Steinway and all but one of his sons emigrated to the United States in 1850 (at that time he changed his name from Steinweg to the anglicized Steinway). To improve their finances and learn more about the American piano market, they worked for three years in various New York City piano-building shops. They opened the House of Steinway & Sons in Manhattan in March 1853, and a year later gained prominence when one of their square pianos that featured cross-strings and a full cast-iron frame won first prize at the American Institute Fair.

International recognition came in 1867 when a Steinway piano won the Grand Gold Medal of Honor at the Paris Exhibition—the first time an American company had received the award. Before long, Steinways became the piano of choice for serious musicians and concert pianists.

In 1866, the Steinways opened Steinway Hall that comprised showrooms and a 9,225-square-foot, 2,000-seat concert hall that, until Carnegie Hall opened in 1891, housed the New York Philharmonic Orchestra. Shortly before Henry died, he and his sons started building Steinway Village in the borough of Queens, complete with its own foundries, factory, post office, and housing for employees.

Henry Steinway died on February 7, 1871, at which time his sons Theodore and William took over the company. By 1909, Steinway & Sons had a showroom in London, a factory in Hamburg, and a retail outlet in Berlin. Today, Steinway & Sons—still at Steinway Village—makes about 5,000 pianos a year carefully crafted from maple and spruce with a 340-pound cast-iron plate that provides the rigid foundation needed to hold 40,000 pounds of string tension. More than 90 percent of all concert piano performances worldwide use Steinway grand pianos.

BIBLIOGRAPHY

Dodge, Alfred, *Pianos and Their Makers*, 1911; Hubbard, Elbert, *The Story of the Steinways*, 1911.

Stern, Leonard

(March 28, 1938–)
Manufacturer

After entering his father's Hartz Mountain Company and enlarging its product line to over 1,200 items for pets, the tough-talking, quick-tempered Leonard Stern encountered legal problems that included charges of antitrust violations and perjury.

Born on March 28, 1938, in New York City, the son of Max Stern and Hilda (Lowenthal) Stern, as a child Leonard often accompanied his father to work. Having emigrated from Germany in the 1920s, Max Stern opened a shop where he sold birdseed, cages, and water dishes. Leonard's parents divorced when he was 12, and Max Stern married Ghity Amiel Lindenbaum. At age 17, Leonard enrolled in New York University's School of Commerce, from which he graduated in 1957. He earned his M.B.A. degree from New York University in 1959 after combining his studies with jobs selling vending machines and safety locks.

By that time, Max Stern had built his shop into the Hartz Mountain Company and was making millions of dollars annually selling birds, bird food, and bird accessories. He invited Leonard to join the firm, and within a short time the young man expanded Hartz's product line to include cat litter, dog and cat shampoos, flea collars, artificial bones, fake mice, and tropical fish food. Sales in the 1970s reached $135 million a year, and earnings $14 million. At the same time, through stock transfers, Leonard Stern obtained all of the family's 13.6 million shares. Meanwhile, Stern had married Judith Falk in 1962, and they had three children.

In the 1970s, Stern diversified Hartz Mountain by merging it with Sternco, a fish supply company owned by him and his brother. He also involved the company in a lucrative real estate deal, buying 1,300 acres in the New Jersey Meadowlands and developing the property into condominiums and offices.

Stern's legal problems began in the late 1970s, after Hartz had cornered 75 percent of the pet supplies market. The A. H. Robins Company—owner of Sergeant's pet products—charged Hartz with using bribery, coercion, and kickbacks to ensure that distributors gave preference, and even exclusive rights, to Hartz products. In October 1979, Hartz agreed to an out-of-court settlement and paid Robins $42.5 million.

More trouble ensued when a U.S. attorney's office began investigating Stern and other Hartz executives. In March 1984, the Hartz company pleaded guilty to obstructing justice, committing perjury, and suborning perjury, and paid a $20,000 fine. *American Lawyer* magazine slammed Stern and sneered at the judgment's leniency when it published an article titled "The Hartz Mountain Guide to Committing Perjury, Suborning Perjury, Obstructing Justice, Locking Up the Market, and Paying a $20,000 Fine."

While maintaining his ownership of Hartz but distancing himself from its daily operation, Stern bought the *Village Voice* newspaper from Australian businessman Rupert Murdoch in 1985. Stern allowed the liberal publication to maintain its editorial independence, while he boosted its circulation and its profits and increased staff salaries. He later acquired a 50 percent interest in the Hudson Reporter Group, a chain of seven New Jersey weekly newspapers. In the 1990s, Stern Publications owned not only the *Village Voice* but also the *Los Angeles Weekly, Orange County Weekly, Seattle Weekly, Long Island Voice, Minneapolis City Pages*, and the *Cleveland Free Times.* "My work is a smorgasbord of excitement," he claimed.

Stern, who had divorced his first wife in 1980, in 1987 married Allison Maher, a film producer and former model, and they lived in a six-story mansion overlooking Central Park. Stern gave millions of dollars in the 1990s to New York's Yeshiva University and additional money to various charities, including the Homes for the Homeless, which he founded to operate shelters in New York City.

BIBLIOGRAPHY
Alpert, Mark, "The Battle of the Billionaires," *Fortune*, September 25, 1989; Perry, Nancy, "From Birdseed to the Meadowlands," *Fortune*, September 28, 1987.

Stettinius, Edward

(February 15, 1865–September 3, 1925)
Financier

Edward Stettinius gained national prominence for his leadership of the Diamond Match Company and for his work in the defense industry during World War I.

Born on February 15, 1865, in St. Louis, Missouri, the son of Joseph Stettinius and Isabel (Riley) Stettinius, Edward grew up without his father, who died when the boy was three years old. He obtained his secondary education in the college preparatory departments at St. Louis University, and after graduating from there in 1881 he worked for several local businesses. When his mother died in 1891, he moved to Chicago and became treasurer of Stirling & Company, a machine business. In 1905, he became the company president.

By 1911, Stettinius was the president of the Diamond Match Company, which

Edward Stettinius (FDR Library)

gave to the public its patent on a new substance that replaced the white phosphorous previously used in making matches. The phosphorous had been proved poisonous and a great danger to workers at rival match companies.

In 1915, Britain and its allies engaged in World War I retained the banking firm of J. P. Morgan & Company to buy war supplies in the United States. J. P. MORGAN SR., in turn, searched for someone to lead the undertaking and chose Stettinius, who left Diamond Match to coordinate the production of war goods. The project required him to direct the modernization of plants and see that needed materials could be produced in great quantities in record time.

As a reward for his work, J. P. Morgan & Company made him a partner in the firm in 1916. After the United States entered the war, President Woodrow Wilson appointed Stettinius surveyor-general of purchases and, in 1918, assistant secretary of war under Newton D. Baker. In that capacity, he went to France and handled the orders for war materials needed by American forces.

Stettinius returned to the United States after the war, and in January 1919 left government service to resume his work with J. P. Morgan & Company. He died on September 3, 1925, survived by his wife, Judith Garrington, whom he had married in 1894, and four children. A son, Edward Stettinius Jr., served on the board of directors of United States Steel and as U.S. secretary of state under Presidents Franklin D. Roosevelt and Harry Truman.

BIBLIOGRAPHY

Clarkson, G. B., *Industrial America in the World War*, 1923; Lamont, T. W., *The Record of a Useful Life*, 1933.

Stevens, John

(1749–March 6, 1838)
Inventor, Transportation Executive

Through his early experiments with steam engines, John Stevens laid the foundation for America's steamboat and railroad development.

John was born in 1749 in New York City to John Stevens and Elizabeth (Alexander) Stevens. The elder Stevens, a merchant and shipowner, lived in Perth Amboy, New Jersey, and the youngster grew up there in comfortable surroundings. In 1762, after completing his early schooling, he entered King's College (today Columbia University) in New York City. He graduated in 1768 and in 1771 received an appointment to practice law. He never did enter the profession, however, and instead involved himself in the political activities leading to the American Revolution.

Commissioned a captain in the Continental army in 1776, Stevens served as loan commissioner for Hunterdon County, New Jersey, and collected money for the military. A few months later, he was appointed treasurer of New Jersey. After his service in the war, in 1782 he married Rachel Cox, and two years later bought a huge tract of land near Hoboken. There he managed his estate and built a home.

In the late 1780s, he developed an interest in the work of John Fitch and James Rumsey, then experimenting with building a steamboat. From that point on, Stevens poured enormous amounts of his own wealth into trying to develop steam power. In August 1791, two years after Rumsey had obtained a grant from the New York legislature to build a steamboat, Stevens received patents for his inventions, an improved steam boiler and steam engine.

He hoped to build a steam ferry that would run along the Hudson River, and in the late 1790s constructed and successfully tried an experimental boat on the Passaic River. While continuing his work and building the first screw-drive steamboat, he promoted turnpikes and that year became president of the Bergen Turnpike Company, organized to construct toll roads across Bergen County in New Jersey.

In 1803, Stevens obtained a patent on yet another improved boiler, and his small steamboat, *Little Juliana*, plied the Hudson. He then started building a larger boat, but before he could complete it, in 1807 Robert Fulton sailed his paddlewheel steamboat *Clermont* up the Hudson to Albany and back. Because Fulton possessed a monopoly to use the Hudson, Stevens sent his ship, the 100-foot *Phoenix*—a much sturdier ship than the *Clermont*—to Philadelphia, its voyage in the Atlantic making it the world's first seagoing steamboat. He briefly operated another steamboat, the *Juliana*, as a ferry across the Hudson until Fulton threatened a lawsuit.

About the same time, he turned his attention to rail transportation, and in 1815 secured from New Jersey a railroad charter—the first issued in the nation—for a line from Trenton to New Brunswick. In 1828, at his urging, the Pennsylvania legislature appropriated $2 million to build the Philadelphia & Columbia Railroad, which began service in 1834 as part of Stevens's company, the Pennsylvania Railroad.

Stevens did not employ steam power on these railroads. In 1825, he built an experimental steam locomotive, the first in the United States, which operated on his Hoboken estate along a circular track. But he left the employment of steam on the Pennsylvania to others, who developed the locomotives after Stevens had retired from his engineering work, and who, in using them on railroads, overcame farmers' complaints that the sparks set fire to barns and the noise frightened hens and cows.

Stevens died on March 6, 1838, survived by his wife and seven children and remembered as a leader in railroad development.

BIBLIOGRAPHY
Turnbull, A. D., *John Stevens: An American Record*, 1838.

Stewart, Martha

(August 3, 1941–)
Entertainment Executive

Called a "taste maker for the masses," Martha Stewart has made millions of dollars through books, magazines, TV shows, and videos dedicated to homemaking.

Martha Stewart was born Martha Kostyra on August 3, 1941, in Jersey City, New Jersey, daughter of Edward Kostyra, a pharmaceuticals salesman, and Martha (Ruszkowski) Kostyra, a schoolteacher. As a girl, Martha showed an inclination

Martha Stewart (David P. Allen/Corbis)

for cooking and gardening and while still in grammar school organized birthday parties for neighborhood children. At age 13, she began modeling and continued

doing so during her years at Barnard College in New York City. She appeared in numerous television commercials for Clairol hair-care products, Lifebuoy soap, and Tareyton cigarettes. She married Andrew Stewart, a law school student, and graduated from Barnard in 1963 with a degree in art and history.

After modeling for another two years, she left to take care of her only child, a daughter. A few years later, Stewart, known for her energy and drive, grew restless and decided to enter her father-in-law's profession, stock brokerage. She joined a small Wall Street firm and earned more than $100,000. But she quit in 1972, and she and her husband moved to Westport, Connecticut, to restore an old farmhouse they had bought.

In 1976, Stewart founded a catering business that specialized in gourmet meals, often prepared with fresh herbs she had grown in her garden. Before long, she had a staff of full-time and temporary workers cooking in her basement kitchen. In 1981, she catered 19 parties and attracted corporate clients. As her business topped $1 million in annual sales, she contributed articles to the *New York Times* and wrote a column for a magazine.

The following year, Crown Publishing asked Stewart to produce an oversized, heavily illustrated recipe and decorations book. Titled *Entertaining*, it received mixed reviews (much like her career) but sold widely. Critics said the book contained many errors, and that she used recipes without crediting her sources. During the rest of the decade and into the early 1990s, she wrote nine more books, ranging from *Martha Stewart's Quick Cook: 200 Easy and Elegant Recipes* to *Martha Stewart's Gardening, Month by Month.* They usually contained profuse photographs, many of her as she promoted herself as a "brand name."

In addition to her books, Stewart appeared in television specials and produced video and audiotapes. In 1987, she signed with Kmart as the company's official spokesperson, and her appearance in magazine ads and television commercials made her ubiquitous. That same year, her husband moved out, and in 1990 the couple divorced.

Also in 1990, Stewart began publishing a bimonthly magazine called *Martha Stewart Living* as part of a $15 million contract she had signed with the media company Time-Warner. The magazine contained articles about how to stencil a tablecloth, marbleize a pumpkin, fix a crystal chandelier, make beeswax candles, and the like. She promoted herself through her column "Martha's Calendar" that listed dates for her upcoming lectures, book signings, and television appearances. By 1995, the magazine's circulation topped 1 million, while her syndicated TV shows reached 5 million viewers a week.

She had, by then, a vast array of products: six videos; signature sheets, towels, and paints; a recipe collection; and mail-order items, and her book sales had topped 5 million copies. Supporters praised her for her ability to understand middle-class tastes; others called her an opportunist who stole ideas, represented recipes from other cooks as her own, and acted testily toward coworkers. All agreed she was a hardworking perfectionist with incredible stamina, able to handle several projects at the same time. When a friend asked her how she managed to do it, she replied: "Oh, I do several things at once. I'm Windexing the phone as we speak."

BIBLIOGRAPHY

Hoge, Sharon King, "The Place Settings of Kilimanjaro," *Forbes,* October 23, 1995; Kasindorf, Jeanie Russell, "Martha, Inc.," *Working Woman,* June 1995; Leyner, Mark, "Martha Stewart," *Esquire,* August 1995; Oppenheimer, Jerry, *Martha Stewart—Just Desserts: The Unauthorized Biography,* 1997.

Stiegel, Henry

(May 17, 1729–January 10, 1785)
Manufacturer

Henry William Stiegel was a glassmaker in Pennsylvania who made—and lost—one of the largest fortunes in the colonial era. His work, which included intricate bottles, drinking glasses, and flasks, was highly praised by his contemporaries and is still noted by leading art museums for its craftsmanship.

Henry William Stiegel, originally named Heinrich Wilhelm Stiegel, was born near Cologne, Germany, on May 17, 1729. His father, John Frederick, died in 1741, leaving six children in the care of their mother, Dorothea Elizabeth. Henry, the eldest, was 12 at the time.

In 1750, Stiegel, his mother, and one brother sailed from Rotterdam for Philadelphia, settling in Schaefferstown. Stiegel worked in Lancaster County for Jacob Huber, an ironmaster. Two years later, he married Elizabeth, Huber's daughter. The couple had two daughters in the course of their short marriage, which ended with Elizabeth's death on February 13, 1758.

Several months later, Stiegel entered into a partnership with Charles and Alexander Stedman to purchase the ironworks from Stiegel's father-in-law. They renamed the business Elizabeth Furnace. In October of that year, Stiegel was married to Elizabeth Hölz, with whom he had one son.

The primary function of Elizabeth Furnace was to make stoves, kettles for potash and soap works, and equipment for sugar refineries. The ironworks prospered, and Stiegel purchased thousands of acres of surrounding land, in part to erect tenant houses. He built several personal residences, shops, a mill, and a malt house. On April 10, 1760, Stiegel, a new citizen of England, anglicized his name to Henry William Stiegel.

By this time, Stiegel was one of the most successful iron casters in the country. He bought another iron foundry, Charming Forge, in Berks County. In 1762, he bought a partial interest in 720 acres of Lancaster County land and developed the town of Manheim. Within Manheim, he built houses for sale, as well as another residence for himself. His ostentatious lifestyle earned him the nickname "Baron von Stiegel."

In 1763, a visit to England altered the course of Stiegel's business legacy. When he returned from his trip in 1764, he brought with him from London and Bristol a number of skilled glass workers. He began construction of a glass manufactory in Manheim and also conducted experiments at the Elizabeth Furnace factory to learn the skills necessary to create bottles and windows.

By 1767, his glassmaking factory was operating full force to turn out windows and sheet glass. Two years later, he built a second factory, the American Flint Glass Manufactory. A highly successful enterprise, the business had agents in Philadelphia, New York, Boston, and Baltimore, as well as in a number of smaller cities. He diversified his product line, introducing the popular glassware that is still highly prized by art collectors today. Stiegel flasks, perfume bottles, and toys were often engraved or enameled, and etched with various colors. Their delicate, finely proportioned lines; well chosen colors; and smooth, even surfaces earned Stiegel a reputation for craftsmanship that is immortalized in the collections of the Metropolitan Museum of Art.

Though Stiegel had the business acumen to make him one of Pennsylvania's wealthiest citizens, he was an overly confident man who embarked on a number of risky, and often unsuccessful, business ventures. These errors in judgment were compounded by his extravagant lifestyle. He was a carefree, happy individual whose slide into financial ruin was as rapid as his original meteoric rise to wealth. He sold many of his land and business holdings to focus on the glassworks, but by 1774 the American Flint Glass Manufactory had closed its doors, and Stiegel was bankrupt.

After a short stint in debtor's prison, Stiegel was employed for a while by the new owner of Elizabeth Furnace. In 1779, he became a schoolmaster and music teacher in Schaefferstown. He had always been a passionate lover of music. In earlier, happier times he had often organized performances by a band of musicians culled from the ranks of his employees. Stiegel died in poverty in Charming Forge, Pennsylvania, on January 10, 1785, three years after the death of his wife.

BIBLIOGRAPHY

Brendle, A. S., *Henry William Stiegel*, 1912; Faris, J. T., *The Romance of Forgotten Men*, 1928; Heiges, George L., *Henry William Stiegel and His Associates: A Story of Early American Industry*, 1948; Heiges, George L., *Henry William Stiegel: The Life Story of a Famous American Glass-Maker*, 1937; Hunter, F. W., *Stiegel Glass*, 1914.

Strauss, Levi

(February 6, 1829–September 26, 1902)
Merchant, Manufacturer

From making work pants for miners and teamsters, Levi Strauss founded the clothing company that today leads the blue jeans industry.

Little is known about Levi's youth, but he was born to Hirsch Strauss and his second wife, Rebecca (Haas) Strauss, on February 6, 1829, in Bavaria, Germany. Levi, or Loeb as he was originally named, along with his mother and two sisters, immigrated to the United States in 1847 after the elder Strauss had died from tuberculosis. They settled in New York City, and Levi joined his two half brothers who had established a dry-goods business.

In 1853, after obtaining U.S. citizenship, Strauss moved to San Francisco during the California gold rush. With a small amount of capital, he opened a shop on Sacramento Street near the waterfront and sold dry goods to the burgeoning population. Operating as Levi Strauss & Company, Strauss obtained his stock from auctions held when ships arrived at port, and from his brothers who shipped items to him from New York City.

By 1856, Strauss had moved to a larger shop, and while continuing to sell dry goods retail, he increasingly wholesaled shipments from the East. He sometimes packed samples in large trunks, loaded them on a wagon, and peddled them to retail outlets located in the gold-mining towns.

Because of his marketing techniques, Jacob Davis, an immigrant from Eastern Europe, became acquainted with Strauss's products. Davis had a tailor shop in Reno, Nevada, where he made horse blankets and tents with materials purchased from Strauss. In 1869, when teamsters, surveyors, and miners complained to him about their inability to buy clothes durable enough for their work, he cut an oversized garment and, instead of thread, used metal rivets to hold the pockets to the material. He made 10 pair of riveted pants in 1871, and soon the demand convinced him he had found his own gold mine.

The following year, Davis approached Strauss about joining him to manufacture the pants. Strauss agreed and discovered he could get $36 for a dozen of the riveted pants, as opposed to $10 for the regular pants he had been selling. Strauss called the riveted pants overalls. (The company did not call them jeans until 1960.) At first, under Davis's supervision, Strauss had seamstresses make the pants in their homes, but he later established a factory. The overalls boosted his profits, and enabled him in 1875 to spend $785,000 to buy the Pacific Woolen Mills, a company that provided him with woolen blankets and yarns.

Beginning in 1877, Strauss made his overalls with indigo blue denim and, using orange linen thread, sewed two curving Vs on the back pockets. (He made some of the overalls with brown duck, which the company discontinued in 1911.)

He attached to the back of each pair an oilcloth patch showing two teamsters whipping a pair of dray horses that were straining to tear the pants apart. In 1890, he designated the blue denim overalls lot number 501.

In the 1890s, Strauss emerged as a leading California businessman with several investments and with personal wealth that exceeded $6 million. Yet he said, "I don't think large fortunes cause happiness to their owners, for immediately those who possess them become slaves to their wealth. They must devote their lives to caring for their possessions." Strauss never married but lived with his sister and nephews. He died on September 26, 1902, after which Levi Strauss & Company continued to expand. Beginning in the 1940s, college students adopted denim pants as the style for young men. There followed an enormous surge in the popularity of blue jeans among young American men and women in the 1960s and a heavy demand for them overseas as well.

BIBLIOGRAPHY
Cray, Ed, *Levi's*, 1978.

Strong, William

(May 16, 1837–August 3, 1914)
Railroad Executive

The story of the development of the nation's railroads consists of numerous rags-to-riches successes, colorful anecdotes of the trials of life in the Wild West, and descriptions of overcoming the elements. William Barstow Strong merits his chapter in the story for his organizational ability that enabled the expansion of the Atchison, Topeka, & Santa Fe Railroad.

William, the son of Elijah Gridley and Sarah Ashley Partridge Strong, was born on May 16, 1837, in Brownington, Vermont. After public schooling in Beloit, Wisconsin, William moved to Chicago to attend Bell's Business College.

After graduating in 1855, Strong went to Milton, Wisconsin, to work as a station agent and telegraph operator for the Milwaukee & St. Paul Railroad. He married Abby Jane Moore on October 2, 1859, and continued to work for the Milwaukee & St. Paul in various capacities for the next eight years. Strong and his wife raised one daughter and two sons.

In 1867, Strong left Wisconsin, moving to Council Bluffs, Iowa, for his new job as the general western agent for the Chicago & Northwestern Railway headquarters. Over the next few years, his reputation as a skilled, practical manager enabled him to rise quickly in the profession. From 1870 to 1872, he was employed by the Chicago, Burlington, & Quincy Railroad as assistant general superintendent. By 1874, Strong was general superintendent for the Michigan Central Railroad, but left the position a year later to return to the Burlington line as general superintendent.

In 1877, Strong was offered a job that would enable him to fully realize his potential as an administrator. By accepting the role of directing the extension program of the Atchison, Topeka, & Santa Fe Railroad, Strong's career soared. It was largely due to his guidance that this small railroad became a vast and important transportation system.

When Strong started with the Santa Fe as vice president and general manager, the railroad comprised a total of 786 miles of track located principally within Kansas. In 1881, Strong assumed the presidency, and by the time he resigned in 1889, the railroad comprised almost 7,000 miles of track, placing the Santa Fe among the largest lines in the country. Strong was held in high regard for the energy and business acumen he brought to the expansion of the railroad. He oversaw construction from Kansas through Colorado, along with arrangements for connecting lines through to the Pacific coastline, a route to Chicago, and connection with the Gulf Coast.

Colleagues and employees believed him to be a very skillful organizer, characterizing him as an "honest, honorable, large-hearted man . . . and a practical railway manager of the highest ability." Despite his hard work, the company suffered from high construction costs and found itself mired in the general economic recession of the late 1880s. The business was reorganized after Strong resigned.

Strong returned to Beloit, Wisconsin, where he lived on his farm and served as president of a Beloit bank. In 1907, he moved to Los Angeles, where he died on August 3, 1914.

BIBLIOGRAPHY

Armitage, Merle, *Operations Santa Fé: Atchison, Topeka, & Santa Fé Railway System*, 1948; Bryant, Keith L., *History of the Atchison, Topeka & Santa Fe Railway*, 1982; Daggett, Stuart, *Railroad Reorganization*, 1908; Dwight, B. W., *The History of the Descendants of Elder John Strong, of Northampton, Mass.*, 1871; *Los Angeles Times*, Obituary, August 4, 1914.

Studebaker, Clement

(March 12, 1831–November 27, 1901)
Manufacturer

Clement Studebaker, a blacksmith and wagon maker, guided his business to national prominence with his diligence and skill at securing government and corporate contracts. His early work in the Studebaker Brothers Manufacturing Company paved the way for the company's eventual success with the automobile, a shift in focus that came near the end of Studebaker's life.

Clement Studebaker (Library of Congress)

Clement, the son of John and Rebecca Mohler Studebaker, was born on March 12, 1831, in Pinetown, a small town near Gettysburg, Pennsylvania. His parents, the descendants of German immigrants, suffered financial hardships. In 1836, they moved their five children in wagons made by John Studebaker to Ashland, Ohio. John rented a small patch of land and set up trade as a blacksmith and wagon maker.

Young Studebaker, known throughout his life as "Clem," worked for his father and on neighboring farms during his early years of schooling. At age 19, he moved to South Bend, Indiana, to teach district school, working in his free time as a blacksmith. In 1852, with little money and a few tools, Clem and his older brother Henry established the firm of H. & C. Studebaker. They were blacksmiths, and, as their father had done, took on extra work making wagons. Soon the demand for wagons exploded; H. & C. Studebaker would eventually make over 750,000 wagons.

As agricultural activity in the Midwest increased, the Studebakers faced a growing demand for their high-quality wagons. The growth of the railroad also served as an impetus for building new horse-drawn vehicles. By the mid-1850s, the brothers had received their first of many government contracts. Their productivity and their insistence on quality was earning them a good reputation in the business. Studebaker also shrewdly thought to burn the name Studebaker onto each of the government wagons, a move that increased the name recognition of their product and general demand for the vehicles.

In 1863, Studebaker's first wife, Charity M. Bratt, died. Their marriage had been fraught with sadness from the loss of two children who both died in infancy.

A year after Charity's death, Studebaker married Ann Milburn Harper, with whom he had three children.

John M. Studebaker replaced his brother Henry in the partnership with Clem in 1857. It was ultimately John who catapulted Studebaker into national prominence as an automobile manufacturer after Clem's death.

In 1868, the Studebaker Brothers Manufacturing Company was established, with Clem at the helm as president. The business expanded as two more Studebaker brothers, Peter and Jacob, joined the fold. Soon the business became the largest maker of horse-drawn vehicles in the world.

Credit is due Studebaker for his intuition in experimenting early in 1897 with different versions of self-propelled vehicles. His early insight led to the company's manufacture of electric and gasoline automobiles, although this step was not taken until after Studebaker's death.

Studebaker was considered a man of high standards, with sound judgment and a refinement that exceeded his limited education. A social man, he entertained in his home leaders in science, arts, and literature, as well as political leaders, including Presidents Ulysses S. Grant, Benjamin Harrison, and William McKinley. His other interests outside of work included active participation and leadership in the Methodist Church. Studebaker was also a staunch Republican and served as a delegate to the Republican National Conventions of 1880 and 1888. He was chosen by President Harrison to be a delegate to the Pan-American Congress in 1889 and by the state of Indiana as its representative to the World's Columbian Exposition in Chicago in 1893.

Studebaker remained active in business, educational issues, and his other interests until his death on November 27, 1901.

BIBLIOGRAPHY

Betz, I. H., "The Studebaker Brothers, the Wagon-Builders of South Bend, Ind.," *Pennsylvania-German*, April 1910; *Biographical History of Self-Made Men of the State of Indiana*, 1880; Carlock, Walter, *The Studebaker Family in America, 1736–1976*, 1976; *Chicago Tribune*, Obituary, November 28, 1901; Erskine, A. R., *History of the Studebaker Corporation*, 1924.

Swearingen, John

(September 7, 1918–)
Oil Industrialist

Cantankerous and outspoken, demanding and dictatorial, John Eldred Swearingen Jr. converted Standard Oil of Indiana into one of the more aggressive companies in the petroleum industry.

Born in Columbia, South Carolina, on September 7, 1918, to John Eldred Swearingen and Mary (Hough) Swearingen, young John—whose father was the state commissioner of education—received his B.S. degree from the University of

South Carolina in 1938 and a master's degree in engineering from the Carnegie-Mellon Institute in 1939. He joined Standard Oil of Indiana that year and began working in the company's research department as a chemical engineer. Eight years later, he was transferred to the production department, a move he considered crucial to his subsequent career, for it was in that department that Swearingen helped the company to determine how much to invest in recent gas discoveries. His analysis led to his being named head of production in 1951.

Swearingen became executive vice president in 1956, at which time he realigned and consolidated Standard Oil's subsidiaries. Two years later he became president. He boosted the company's production by avoiding high-cost explorations in well-publicized regions, opting instead for buying drilling rights at bargain prices in lesser-known locales. During Swearingen's tenure, Standard Oil of Indiana acquired onshore leases in the United States covering more than 60,000 square miles—greater than any other oil company. He later engaged in offshore drilling, too, and cut costs by automating departments and reducing the number of employees by several thousand. His policies caused labor strife and provoked five strikes, one that lasted 241 days, but in each instance the company prevailed.

In addition, Swearingen boosted the company's overseas presence. Whereas in 1960 the firm had been producing only a minuscule amount of crude oil in foreign countries, by 1984 it was conducting explorations in 30 nations, and nearly half its total oil production came from those sources.

Critics complained about Standard Oil's excessive profits, especially during a severe national gas shortage in the mid-1970s. Swearingen proposed that domestic drilling be increased by providing revenues for oil companies through a 30-cent-a-gallon tax hike on gasoline. When told this might unduly burden lower-income families, he replied: "I'm sympathetic to poor people, but for heaven's sake, let's not ruin our future to take care of a relatively few people. . . . What is a man on relief doing owning an automobile? Let's not let our sympathies run away with us."

Coworkers often called Swearingen difficult, but he insisted: "The whole point is to get everybody working together for some common objective and to have a feeling of pride. . . . Our company has achieved that." Swearingen, who after a divorce had remarried in the late 1960s, left Standard Oil of Indiana in the mid-1980s and became CEO of Continental Illinois, a bank holding company.

Standard Oil of Indiana, meanwhile, changed its name to Amoco in order to promote a clearer brand identification. Today, it is a leading petroleum and chemical producer operating worldwide.

BIBLIOGRAPHY

"John Eldred Swearingen, Jr.," *Fortune*, April 2, 1984.

Swift, Gustavus

(June 24, 1839–March 27, 1903)
Meat Packer

Founder of Swift and Company, Gustavus Franklin Swift revolutionized the meatpacking industry and the greater economy when he developed refrigerated transportation, vertical integration, and assembly-line production.

Swift was born on June 24, 1839, on his father's farm near Sandwich, Massachusetts. At age 16, he showed an interest in business when, with $25, he purchased a heifer, slaughtered it, and sold the meat door-to-door. Four years later, in 1859, he opened his first butcher shop in Eastham, Massachusetts. The shop soon prospered, and after turning it over to his brothers, he opened others in Barnstable, Clinton, and Freetown, from which he sent out wagons to deliver meat to his customers.

Swift's volume at the Clinton market exceeded $35,000 a year, and with that he looked for new outlets. Swift had a daring streak, and although he never took foolish risks, he often pursued ideas others rejected as dubious. At Clinton, he noticed more and more meat arriving from the western states, with wholesale slaughterers and meat dealers playing a larger role in transactions.

As a result, he moved beyond retailing, and, in 1872, entered a partnership with James Hathaway, acting as cattle buyer for this leading Boston meat merchant. Three years later, Swift moved to Chicago, the nation's railroad hub. There he recognized the disadvantages to shipping cattle back east: steers frequently died during the trip, and shipping the entire steer reduced profits since only a portion—about 600 pounds from a 1,000-pound animal—could be processed as meat. Swift wanted to ship the cattle already dressed, but faced a problem in that an adequately refrigerated railroad car had not been developed. He experimented with a refrigerated car in the winter of 1877. Hathaway opposed Swift's plan to expand this business and dissolved their partnership. Swift then invited several New England butchers to invest in his venture.

At this point, he worked with Andrew J. Chase, an engineer, to develop a refrigerated railroad car. They modified an existing one, packing ice under its roof and circulating cool air through its interior, but this method worked only sporadically, and often caused Swift to lose money. He solved his technical refrigeration problem in 1879, only to meet opposition from railroad companies that refused to transport his cars. They made more money from the poundage involved in shipping cattle on the hoof, and thus resisted change. Swift, however, found a railroad that would cooperate, and in 1881 he sent his first refrigerated car from Chicago to Boston. When competitors told consumers to avoid Swift's meat as contaminated, he toured New England and promoted his product through speeches and by selling beef from railroad cars directly to retail butchers.

Swift's refrigerated transport was an important step in vertical integration, a technique developed as well by Standard Oil and other big businesses in an era when industries expanded rapidly. With vertical integration, companies sought to control sources, processing, and distribution. Thus, in addition to developing transportation, in the 1880s Swift opened packing plants near the western cattle regions, and bought stockyards, including one in Kansas City, Kansas. To aid in distribution, he built refrigerated storage buildings in the Northeast, each with a sales staff and wagons that delivered meat directly to grocery stores.

Swift incorporated in 1885 as Swift and Company, and developed assembly-line butchering—probably the first assembly line in American industry. No longer would one person butcher an entire steer; now a worker would be responsible for only a single procedure, such as removing the head. At the same time, Swift developed by-products in order to process and sell more of the entire animal. Fertilizer, glue, and soap came from his plants.

Swift guarded every penny. He frequented Bubbly Creek in Chicago, into which his company's sewer line emptied, and watched for waste, such as fat, coming out. If he saw any, he reprimanded his superintendent. Swift's criticism often involved sarcasm. Once, when he spotted a foreman in the plant wearing a new tan overcoat, he asked him: "Do you work here?" "Yes, sir, I'm the foreman," the man replied. Swift's retort: "I guess you didn't come down to stay all day."

Shortly before his death, Swift began shipping meat overseas, and, along with J. O. Armour and EDWARD MORRIS, founded the National Packing Company, a trust capitalized at $15 million. The courts, however, ruled the company in restraint of trade and ordered its breakup. By that time, Swift employed over 25,000 people and each year slaughtered millions of cattle, hogs, and sheep.

Swift, who married Annie Marie Higgins in 1861, had 11 children. Four of his

Gustavus Swift (Library of Congress)

sons worked in his company. After his death on March 27, 1903, Swift and Company continued to grow, and in 1920 the government charged it and several other meatpacking firms with creating a monopoly and fixing prices. The companies agreed to desist from buying certain businesses, such as restaurants. Today, Swift and Company continues in business as Esmark, and although it still processes meat, it has diversified its holdings and earns its profits primarily from making bras through the International Latex Company, oil products through STP, and car stereos through Pemcor.

Swift did more than found a company. His refrigeration and assembly-line techniques, along with his vertical integration, hastened corporate growth and changed the way Americans ate, shopped, and worked.

BIBLIOGRAPHY

Swift, Louis F., *The Yankee of the Yards: The Biography of Gustavus Franklin Swift*, 1927, reprt. 1970.

Tandy, Charles

(1928–November 5, 1978)
Merchant

Charles Tandy transformed his family's leather business into Radio-Shack, an electronics chain-store company with thousands of outlets in the United States and overseas.

Born in 1928 in Fort Worth, Texas, Charles entered business at the age of 12, when he began helping his father, David L. Tandy, sell leather goods at the Hinckley-Tandy Leather Company, founded in 1919. Charles served in the navy during World War II, and when he noticed sailors being taught knitting and needlepoint as therapy, he promoted leather work as more appealing to men and established a system that used it among hospitalized service personnel.

After the war, as do-it-yourself hobbies became popular in America, Tandy, gregarious and friendly, transferred his system to his father's business. He directed the Tandycraft division, and sold leather craft supplies by mail order and in chain stores. Soon he was outselling the rest of the company.

In 1955, the Tandy Leather Company (the name used after the firm split with Hinckley in 1950) was sold to American Hide & Leather Company, a New England firm. Charles Tandy and other Tandy Leather Company stockholders purchased enough stock in American Hide, however, to gain control of the firm. In 1960, Charles Tandy, then chairman of the board, moved the business to Fort Worth and changed its name to the Tandy Corporation.

He then started looking for ways to diversify and in 1963 heard about a Boston-based chain of nine electronics stores called RadioShack, whose customers were mainly ham radio hobbyists. Financial advisers told him to stay away—RadioShack was awash in debt and likely to drag him down. But Tandy bought the chain, cut its inventory, and directed it away from the ham radios to products with more widespread appeal—stereos, speakers, and stereo equipment.

RadioShack expanded rapidly, from 172 stores in 1968 to 2,294 in 1973. Tandy combined his new product line with massive advertising, and he leased rather than bought space to open stores at the rate of two per working day. In addition, he increased profits by making many of his products—almost half of them by the mid-1970s—mainly at factories in Asia.

Tandy had a reputation for paying low salaries but hardly ever firing anyone, and for establishing a rewarding bonus system. In the mid-1970s, he built Tandy Center in downtown Fort Worth, a complex that encompassed eight square blocks and included two 19-story buildings. When he heard about the oncoming computer revolution, he made plans to enter that field. Before he could do so on a large scale, however, he died on November 5, 1978. He was survived by his wife Anne Burnette Tandy.

In the late 1970s and mid-1980s, RadioShack reaped large profits from its computers, particularly the best-selling TR 1000. In 1998, there were nearly 7,000 RadioShack stores (with $3.2 billion in sales) that, along with 96 Computer City stores, formed the Tandy Corporation.

BIBLIOGRAPHY

Moskowitz, Milton, et al., eds., *Everybody's Business*, 1980; Silver, A. David, *Entrepreneurial Megabucks: The 100 Greatest Entrepreneurs of the Last Twenty-Five Years*, 1985.

Tartikoff, Brandon

(January 13, 1949–August 27, 1997)
Entertainment Executive

Called a "boy wonder," Brandon Tartikoff led the NBC television network out of the ratings doldrums and introduced some of the most influential programs in the history of the medium.

Born on January 13, 1949, in Freeport, New York, Tartikoff seemed destined for a career in television even as a child, when he analyzed shows for his family and friends and showed an uncanny ability to pick hit programs. After graduating from Lawrenceville Preparatory School in New Jersey, he enrolled at Yale, from which he received his B.A. degree with honors in 1970. Following a short stint with an advertising agency, in 1972 he joined WTNH-TV, an American Broadcasting Company (ABC) affiliate in New Haven, Connecticut, as director of advertising and promotion. The following year, he moved to Chicago, where he obtained a similar job with another ABC affiliate, WLS-TV.

There he made an impression that changed his career when, in 1976, he boosted the station's ratings for its afternoon movies by packaging them around humorous themes, such as a week of *King Kong* and other "ape movies" that he titled "Thrilla Gorilla." FRED SILVERMAN, head of ABC network's programming, noticed Tartikoff's work and brought him to New York City as director of dramatic development. Tartikoff left ABC, however, the following year to join the National Broadcasting Company (NBC) as director of comedy programming.

Soon Silverman jumped to NBC as its president, and he named Tartikoff president of entertainment—a surprising move, given that Tartikoff was only 31. Under Silverman, though, Tartikoff had little authority. Not until Grant Tinker succeeded Silverman as NBC's president in 1981 did Tartikoff make his mark on programming and take the network out of the ratings basement.

In 1982, Tartikoff introduced a prime-time schedule that showed his desire to mix shows of greater intelligence than those at the number-one network, ABC, with shows that appealed to a less serious audience. For example, he combined the quality comedies *Family Ties* and *Cheers*, and the acclaimed drama *St. Elsewhere*, with the action-adventure series *The A-Team*. In time, all of these shows became ratings hits.

Tartikoff also had his failures, especially in 1983 with the flops *Mr. Smith*, *The Yellow Rose*, and *Buffalo Bill*. But in

1984, he scored another ratings hit and gained critical acclaim for *The Cosby Show*, featuring comedian Bill Cosby. He added to the schedule a police drama known for its visuals and rock music score, *Miami Vice*. The idea for the show originated with Tartikoff, who at a lunch with producer Anthony Yerkovich, gave him a napkin on which he had scribbled the phrase "MTV cops."

NBC finally claimed first place in the ratings in 1986. At a later date, the *New York Times* commented about Tartikoff: "No other television programmer was so closely identified with a network's success as Mr. Tartikoff was in the 1980s. NBC, which had been widely regarded as the laughingstock of the television industry when he began, ended the decade with the longest laugh in network history: a streak of dominance never equaled, as [it] finished first in the Nielsen ratings 68 weeks in a row."

Tartikoff became chairman of NBC Entertainment in 1990, but surprised the industry the following year when he quit to become chairman of Paramount Pic-tures. Although he developed several hit movies, including *Wayne's World*, *The Firm*, and *Patriot Games*, his achieve-ments failed to equal the lofty level he had recorded at NBC. Tartikoff left Para-mount in 1992, after he and his eight-year-old daughter, Calla, were hurt in a car accident, and he moved with his fam-ily to New Orleans to be near hospitals where Calla could recover.

Then, in 1997, the cancer that Tartikoff had contracted in 1981, but which had been in remission, overtook him. He died on August 27, 1997. Tartikoff had built his career on a reputation for creativity and as one of the best-liked executives in the entertainment industry. Said a col-league: "He believed in everything he was doing and more than that he believed in the medium and the people who watched it."

BIBLIOGRAPHY

Bedell, Sally, *Up the Tube: Prime-Time TV and the Silverman Years*, 1981.

Taylor, Moses

(January 11, 1806–May 23, 1882)
Merchant, Banker

As a banker and investor involved in railroads, Moses Taylor amassed one of the larger for-tunes in early America.

Born on January 11, 1806, in New York City to Jacob B. Taylor and Mary (Coo-per) Taylor, Moses grew up in a wealthy family and attended private schools. At age 15, however, his formal education ended, and he entered the merchant field as a clerk at C. G. & S. Howland, an im-porting house.

With a strong drive to accumulate ad-ditional wealth and with a mastery of even the most minute business de-tails, by 1832 Taylor established his

Moses Taylor (Archive Photos)

own merchant business, dealing mainly in sugar imports from Cuba. That same year, he married Catherine A. Wilson and they eventually had five children.

Although a fire destroyed Taylor's office in 1835, his business continued to expand, and with the capital he accumulated in 1855 he quit his import house and became president of the City Bank. In that capacity, Taylor took advantage of the financial Panic of 1857. While other bankers suffered from the downturn, Taylor bought stock in the Delaware, Lackawanna & Western Railroad at a bargain price. He well knew the importance of railroads to an industrializing nation and had faith that when the panic ended the stock price would climb, which it did. Stock he bought at $5 a share in 1857 sold in 1862 for $240.

Taylor linked his investments to yet another development in modern technology, the telegraph, and provided much of the capital needed by CYRUS FIELD to start the Atlantic Cable Company and lay a cable across the ocean from Newfoundland to Ireland. Although the first completed cable in 1858 broke, another one in 1867 began transatlantic telegraph service.

Taylor expanded his investments after the Civil War to include public utilities, but he remained most heavily involved in the Delaware, Lackawanna & Western Railroad and its allied coal and iron company. At his death on May 23, 1882, Taylor had an estate estimated at $40 million.

BIBLIOGRAPHY

Hodas, Daniel, *The Business Career of Moses Taylor: Merchant, Finance Capitalist, and Industrialist*, 1976.

Thomas, Dave

(July 2, 1932–)
Merchant

One of the most visible of all corporate executives, Americans know David R. Thomas from his humorous "I'm Dave" appearances in commercials for his fast-food restaurant company, Wendy's.

David had a difficult childhood. Soon after he was born, on July 2, 1932, in Atlantic City, New Jersey, his parents gave him up for adoption. He was then raised by Rex and Auleva Thomas, but his adoptive mother died when he was five years old. Rex Thomas, a construction worker, then drifted from town to town, resulting in Dave never having a permanent home as a boy or establishing firm friendships.

Thomas began working at odd jobs at age 12 and spent considerable time eating in low-priced restaurants. That experience, he later said, gave him the idea to enter the restaurant business. He quit school in the tenth grade, and enrolled in the army. As a cook and staff sergeant in Germany, he learned about feeding large numbers of people.

Upon his discharge in 1953, he took a job as a short-order cook at a Hobby House restaurant in Fort Wayne, Indiana. When the owner opened a second restaurant, he made Thomas assistant manager. Later, the owner opened four Kentucky Fried Chicken (KFC) restaurants, and after they lost money he asked Thomas to make them profitable in return for a 45 percent share in the business. Thomas agreed, turned the restaurants into moneymakers, and met several times with the founder of KFC, HARLAND SANDERS. The two established a friendship, and Thomas even gave Sanders advice, suggesting

Dave Thomas (Reuters/Colin Braley/Archive Photos)

he attract more customers by using a revolving sign resembling a chicken bucket.

In 1968, Thomas sold his share of the chicken franchises back to KFC for $1 million in stock. He then used some of the money to open his own restaurant. He decided it would feature hamburgers, but unlike McDonald's and Burger King, he would make his hamburgers from fresh rather than frozen meat patties, and make them to order rather than letting them sit under heating lamps. He chose Wendy's as the name for his restaurant because Wendy was the nickname for one of his daughters, Melinda Lou, who, he said, "embodied the image I wanted for a restaurant that offered old-fashioned hamburgers." Thomas opened his restaurant in Columbus, Ohio, in November 1969.

Wendy's was an immediate hit with its fresh burgers, French fries, chili, Frosty Dairy Desert, and old-style interior decor. Thomas expanded his business rapidly, opening additional restaurants by selling franchises for entire cities or regions. By the late 1970s, Wendy's seemed to be everywhere.

Thomas resigned as Wendy's CEO in 1982, but when the restaurants began losing money in the late 1980s, he returned to help lead them out of trouble. He hired an effective CEO and worked with an advertising agency to put together new commercials, leading to his appearances in them. The revived management and effective advertisements made Wendy's profitable again.

Thomas, who in 1954 married Loraine Buskirk, had five children and several grandchildren, and in the early 1990s returned to high school and earned his general equivalency diploma.

BIBLIOGRAPHY

Thomas, Dave, *Dave Says Well Done!: The Common Guy's Guide to Everyday Success*, 1994; Thomas, Dave, *Dave's Way: A New Approach to Old-Fashioned Success*, 1991.

Thompson, Jere

(January 18, 1932–)
Merchant

"Oh Thank Heaven for 7-Eleven!" went the commercial jingle in the 1970s, and 7-Eleven convenience stores by that time had become a pervasive feature of the American landscape.

7-Eleven began under JOE THOMPSON JR. who developed the convenience store idea near his home in Texas in the early part of the twentieth century under the company name of Southland. Beginning in the early 1950s, Thompson expanded 7-Eleven beyond north Texas and in 1954 went outside the state when he opened a store in Miami, Florida. Three years later, he took 7-Eleven into the North, and before he died of cancer on June 11, 1961, Southland operated more than 600 stores.

The 7-Eleven stores expanded most rapidly, though, under Thompson's two sons, JOHN THOMPSON, born on November 2, 1925, and Jere Thompson, born on January 18, 1932, both of whom had graduated from the University of Texas with degrees in business administration—John in 1948 and Jere in 1954. Upon Joe Thompson's death in 1961, John assumed the presidency and Jere the vice presidency. During the 1960s, they opened 7-Elevens in the nation's fastest-growing state, California, where they began franchising their stores, a move that earned praise from franchisees who could obtain a 7-Eleven with little capital outlay and criticism from those franchisees who believed Southland took too high a percentage of store profits.

In the early 1960s, the Thompsons opened the first 24-hour 7-Elevens in Austin, Texas, and Las Vegas, Nevada, a strategy that has since expanded so that today about 95 percent of all 7-Elevens are open around the clock. And in 1965, Southland acquired the rights to a new drink developed by two inventors in Dallas, a frozen carbonated beverage called Icee. 7-Eleven sold it as Slurpee—a big hit with youngsters—and enhanced its sales by taking ordinary flavors such as cherry and lemon-lime and calling them by "Fulla Bulla," "Firewater," and other such attention-grabbing names.

In 1968, Southland acquired the prestigious Gristede Bros. Grocery chain in New York, and the company soon acquired an auto parts chain and candy stores, and opened 7-Elevens in Europe. By the end of the 1960s, Southland operated more than 3,500 convenience stores.

With growth came problems, notably increased competition from Circle K Stores, and trouble with the Internal Revenue Service that resulted in Southland being fined for tax fraud. In 1991, the Thompson family sold its interest in Southland, and since that time 7-Eleven has been operated by the IYG Holding Company, a subsidiary of the Ito-Yokado Company and Seven-Eleven Japan.

BIBLIOGRAPHY

Liles, Allen, *Oh, Thank Heaven! The Story of the Southland Corporation*, 1976.

Thompson, Joe, Jr.

(1901–June 11, 1961)
Merchant

The 7-Eleven convenience stores began under Joe C. "Jodie" Thompson Jr., who was born in 1901 in Waxahachie, Texas, but grew up in Dallas. While attending Oak Cliff High School, Thompson worked in the summer, loading ice onto wagons for the Consumers Ice Company. After graduating in 1922 from the University of Texas with a degree in business administration, Thompson worked full-time at Consumers. He soon got the idea to sell chilled watermelons from the docks where customers picked up their ice, an idea that proved so successful it earned him a bonus—money he needed to marry Margaret Philp in 1922.

Thompson's ambition led to a rapid rise up Consumers' ladder. He became secretary-treasurer in 1926, and the following year, after the Southern Ice Company acquired Consumers and renamed the new firm the Southland Ice Company, Thompson became a director. In the summer of 1927, John Jefferson Green, an ice dock manager, began selling bread and milk to customers. He earned a profit that impressed Thompson and convinced him to develop the concept, thus giving birth to the first convenience stores.

Under Thompson's leadership, Southland expanded its ice plants—by 1928, it had 12 in Dallas—but, importantly, renamed its ice docks Tote'm stores, advertised with an Alaskan Indian totem as a symbol, and sold items people wanted in a hurry. Speed, in fact, emerged as the modus operandi for Thompson's convenience stores—sell cigarettes, dairy products, and magazines that people did not want to wait in line for, and provide quick service for which they would pay a high price. With the first Tote'm stores, customers remained in their cars while an attendant filled their order and handed it to them.

Southland tied its growth to the rise of automobiles and grocery stores. Car-habituated customers liked the way they could pull up to a Tote'm front door. And as grocery stores grew larger and larger, customers went to Tote'm as a place where they could find items without having to search amid long aisles.

In the early 1930s, though, Southland suffered when the Great Depression worsened, and Thompson, by then president of the company, had to place it in receivership. A turnaround began in 1933 when the federal government ended Prohibition, thus allowing Southland to sell beer in its stores. Two years later, Southland decided to control its own source of dairy products and founded Oak Farm Dairies.

Thompson renamed the Southland Ice Company in 1945 as the Southland Corporation, and as Americans moved to the suburbs after World War II, he de-emphasized selling ice while developing his convenience stores. In expanding, he hired an advertising agency to create a new name for his stores. Since most of them would be open from 7 A.M. to 11 P.M., the agency suggested the name 7-Eleven, and Thompson agreed. Thus, in 1946, Tote'm became 7-Eleven.

Beginning in the early 1950s, Thompson expanded 7-Eleven beyond north Texas and in 1954 went outside the state when he opened a store in Miami, Florida. Three years later, he took 7-Eleven into the North, and before he died of cancer on June 11, 1961, Southland operated more than 600 stores.

The 7-Eleven stores expanded most rapidly, though, under Thompson's two sons, JOHN THOMPSON and JERE THOMPSON.

BIBLIOGRAPHY

Liles, Allen, *Oh, Thank Heaven! The Story of the Southland Corporation*, 1976.

Thompson, John

(November 2, 1925–)
Merchant

The 7-Eleven convenience stores began under JOE THOMPSON JR., who developed the convenience store idea near his home in Texas during the early part of the twentieth century under the company name of Southland. Beginning in the early 1950s, Thompson expanded 7-Eleven beyond north Texas, and in 1954 went outside the state when he opened a store in Miami, Florida. Three years later, he took 7-Eleven into the North, and before he died of cancer on June 11, 1961, Southland operated more than 600 stores.

The 7-Eleven stores expanded most rapidly, though, under Thompson's two sons, John Thompson, born on November 2, 1925, and JERE THOMPSON, born on January 18, 1932, both of whom had graduated from the University of Texas with degrees in business administration— John in 1948 and Jere in 1954. Upon Joe Thompson's death in 1961, John assumed the presidency and Jere the vice presidency. During the 1960s, they opened 7-Elevens in the nation's fastest-growing state, California, where they began franchising their stores, a move that earned praise from franchisees who could obtain a 7-Eleven with little capital outlay and criticism from those franchisees who believed Southland took too high a percentage of store profits.

In the early 1960s, the Thompsons opened the first 24-hour 7-Elevens in Austin, Texas, and Las Vegas, Nevada, a strategy that has since expanded so that today about 95 percent of all 7-Elevens are open around the clock. In addition, in 1965, Southland acquired the rights to a new drink developed by two inventors in Dallas, a frozen carbonated beverage called Icee. 7-Eleven sold it as Slurpee— a big hit with youngsters—and enhanced its sales by taking ordinary flavors such as cherry and lemon-lime and calling them by "Fulla Bulla," "Firewater," and other such attention-grabbing names.

In 1968, Southland acquired the prestigious Gristede Bros. Grocery chain in New York, and the company soon acquired an auto parts chain and candy stores, and opened 7-Elevens in Europe. By the end of the 1960s, Southland operated more than 3,500 convenience stores.

With growth came problems, notably increased competition from Circle K Stores, and trouble with the Internal Revenue Service that resulted in Southland being fined for tax fraud. In 1991, the Thompson family sold its interest in Southland, and since that time 7-Eleven has been operated by the IYG Holding Company, a subsidiary of the Ito-Yokado Company and Seven-Eleven Japan.

BIBLIOGRAPHY

Liles, Allen, *Oh, Thank Heaven! The Story of the Southland Corporation*, 1976.

Thornton, Charles

(July 22, 1913–November 24, 1981)
Corporate Executive

Considered a pioneer of the modern corporate conglomerate, Charles Bates Thornton led Litton Industries to 25 mergers, creating a multimillion-dollar company.

Born on July 22, 1913, in Haskell, Texas, Thornton showed business savvy at age 12 when he began buying land with money he saved from odd jobs. Raised by his mother—his father had abandoned the family soon after Charles was born—the youngster owned 40 acres of land by age 14. After graduating from high school, he enrolled in 1932 at Texas Tech in Lubbock, Texas. He left two years later, to work in the Interior Department in Washington, D.C., as a clerk. At the same time, he attended George Washington University and graduated with a B.S. degree in 1937, the same year he married Flora Laney. They later had two children.

Thornton—nicknamed "Tex"—gained the attention of his superiors in the government when he wrote a report about financing low-cost federal housing that showed his ability to analyze vast amounts of statistics. Robert Lovett, the assistant secretary of war, then invited Thornton to join the army air force during World War II, and he quickly won promotion from lieutenant to colonel. Thornton devised the first statistical control system in the military and headed a team of management officers stationed at Harvard University. When asked about what statistical control meant, he humorously replied, "[it's] a fancy name for finding out what the hell we had by way of resources, and when and where it was going to be required."

After the war, Thornton and his colleagues at Harvard, among them ROBERT MCNAMARA, offered their services to the Ford Motor Company, then suffering financially. Ford accepted, and the "Whiz Kids," as they were called, applied their statistical analyses to make the company efficient and profitable. They profited from the venture, as did Ford. McNamara stayed at Ford and eventually became president, but Thornton left in 1948 to join HOWARD HUGHES at Hughes Aircraft Company. While vice president there, Thornton increased its sales from $150 million to $200 million, but he felt constrained by Hughes's opposition to diversification and quit to begin his own business.

In 1953, he and a partner, Roy L. Ash, founded the Electro-Dynamics Corporation, and the next year they acquired a small microwave tube producer, Litton Industries. Thornton believed the company could be used for diversification, and he assured financiers that within five years he would raise its sales from $3 million to $100 million. As it turned out, he reached his goal in just three years.

During that time and into the 1960s, Thornton diversified Litton by manufacturing submarines, automating ships, building oil rigs, and designing and producing educational materials. He developed close ties to the military, securing defense contracts crucial to Litton's prosperity. In 1968, Litton had 100 operating units, but that year, with Thornton spending most of his time as a government adviser, the company suffered a reversal when it experienced massive cost overruns in a contract to build destroyers and other ships for the navy.

As a result, Thornton returned to active management in 1972 and led the company to recovery. He sold money-losing subsidiaries and placed a greater emphasis on advanced technological systems, such as seismic exploration equipment.

Thornton died on November 24, 1981, from cancer. In 1998, Litton Industries was a $4.2 billion company involved in defense and commercial electronics, information technology, and shipbuilding. A primary builder of large combat ships for the navy, it employed more than 31,500 workers.

BIBLIOGRAPHY

Lay, Beirne, *Someone Has to Make It Happen: The Inside Story of Tex Thornton, the Man Who Built Litton Industries*, 1969.

Tiffany, Charles

(February 15, 1812–February 18, 1902)
Jeweler

Many Americans today identify the jewelry store founded by Charles Lewis Tiffany with wealth, and they recognize it through the novel *Breakfast at Tiffany's*, written by Truman Capote, or the subsequent movie of the same title. The movie's heroine, Holly Golightly, explains that she expunges worry by getting into a taxi and going to the famous establishment. "It calms me down right away," she says, "the quietness and the proud look of it. . . ."

Charles was born on February 15, 1812, in Killingly, Connecticut, to Comfort and Chloe (Draper) Tiffany. He attended public school, and later a private academy in Plainfield. His father owned a cotton factory and a general store, and at age 15 the precocious youngster managed the latter.

In 1837, Tiffany obtained $1,000 in capital from his father, moved to New York City, and, with his friend John B. Young, opened a stationery and notions store. They sold unusual items, including Japanese papier-mâché, terra-cotta ware, walking sticks, fans, and pottery. In 1841, Young traveled to Europe where he bought porcelain, cutlery, clocks, and jewelry for the store. That same year, the business was named Tiffany, Young & Ellis, after its partners, and Tiffany married Young's sister, Harriet Olivia Young. They had six children.

By 1848, Tiffany had gained a reputation for selling expensive items, and he added fine gems to his merchandise. These he imported from Europe, and they included crown jewels from France. At the same time, Tiffany began manufacturing gold jewelry, an endeavor enhanced in 1850 by the gold strike in California.

Tiffany opened a Paris branch in 1850, and three years later when Young and Ellis retired, he and his new partners renamed their business Tiffany & Company. In the 1850s, he began advertising in newspapers and developed a minimalist style that used few adjectives. One advertisement simply said, "Tiffany & Co., Pearls, Pearl necklaces." Among his exclusive productions, he made, for Abraham Lincoln, a jeweled inkstand, and for Ulysses S. Grant, a sword whose gold scabbard sparkled with embedded rubies, sapphires, and diamonds.

Tiffany opened a London branch in 1868, the same year he merged with John C. Moore's Silverware Company. By that time, Tiffany ranked as the leader in America's jewelry trade and counted more than 20 foreign monarchs among his customers. When he died on February 18, 1902, in Yonkers, New York, his estate was valued at $35 million. His son, Louis Comfort Tiffany, continued in the business as the store's vice president, and in 1905 Tiffany's erected a seven-story building on New York City's exclusive Fifth Avenue. "Tiffany's isn't just a place of business," said one observer. "It's part showplace, part museum, part institution, and part legend."

BIBLIOGRAPHY

Purtell, Joseph, *The Tiffany Touch*, 1973.

Tisch, Larry

(March 5, 1923–)
Financier

Frugal and opposed to risks, Lawrence "Larry" Tisch made his money by buying undervalued assets. He earned his greatest fame as head of Loew's theaters and the Columbia Broadcasting System (CBS) television network.

Born on March 5, 1923, in Brooklyn, New York, Larry grew up in New York City, the son of Al Tisch, a boys' clothing manufacturer, and Sadye (Brenner) Tisch. He earned his B.S. degree at New York University at the young age of 18 and in 1942 obtained a master's degree in industrial engineering from the University of Pennsylvania. After serving three years in the army, he entered law school at Harvard, but quit after a semester to help run his family's new business, a run-down hotel in Lakewood, New Jersey. In 1948, he married Wilma Stein; they had four children.

With his younger brother Bob, Tisch used attractions such as an indoor swimming pool, an outdoor ice-skating rink, and sleigh rides to make the Lakewood hotel a success. He went on to buy hotels in Atlantic City, New York City, and elsewhere, and in 1956 built the 780-room Americana Hotel in Bal Harbour, Florida, at a cost of $1.7 million.

In 1961, Tisch and his brother gained total control of Loew's, a leading movie theater chain, and merged it with their hotels. (They eventually sold the theaters to Sony.) The brothers used Loew's to invest in numerous companies they believed had unrealized financial value, among them Lorillard cigarette makers in 1968, CAN Insurance in 1974, and the Bulova Watch Company in 1979.

Again through Loew's, Tisch made his first investment in CBS in 1985 and 10 years later controlled about 20 percent of the network's stock. After a stint as U.S. postmaster general from 1986 to 1988, Tisch returned to Loew's. In 1990, during his acquisition of stock in CBS, the network's board of directors elected him chairman to succeed WILLIAM PALEY. Tisch had previously served as president and CEO and continued in those positions.

Tisch earned a reputation for his investment prowess, and by 1994 Loew's ranked among the top 100 companies in America with revenues of $13.5 billion. His tenure at CBS, however, raised considerable controversy. Some said he cut too deeply into the budget and that his reductions in the news bureau seriously damaged a prestigious part of the network. Others said he had little feel for the entertainment world and made a major blunder in 1994 when he let the Fox Network outbid CBS for the broadcast rights to National Football League games. Furthermore, his critics argued, when he sold CBS's recorded music and publishing business, he left the network without a diversified income.

Ratings dropped substantially at CBS in 1995 and with them, earnings. Tisch, however, remained confident: "If I thought that we could not increase our earnings every year for the next five years, I would say, 'Jeez, maybe we have to be a little more daring or something.' But we see a clear path for increased

Larry Tisch (Victor Malafronte/Archive Photos)

earnings every year." And a writer for *Fortune* magazine praised him, "As his CBS investment demonstrates . . . Tisch excels at finance. He has nearly the power of a sole proprietor, yet less than 3 percent of CBS stock actually is attributable to his personal ownership: Loew's owns just 18 percent of the broadcaster, and Larry Tisch, in turn, owns just 16 percent of Loew's. That's leverage. Loew's has dramatically reduced its financial investment in CBS without losing its clout. Since 1986, Loew's has taken $800 million in cash out of CBS—more than it initially invested—while remaining by far the largest shareholder."

In 1995, Tisch sold CBS to Westinghouse, making a pretax profit of $1 billion on the buyout that cost over $5 billion. He continued leading Loew's, making investments and considerable money from Lorillard and oil-drilling operations.

BIBLIOGRAPHY

Harris, Kathryn, "In the Eye of the Storm," *Los Angeles Times*, June 3, 1994; Zoglin, Richard, "Is CBS Sunk?," *Time*, November 27, 1995.

Totino, Rose

(1915–1994)
Manufacturer

Rose Totino took what she learned from her mother about Italian cooking, used it to make frozen pizzas, and captured the American desire for fast food.

Totino was born Rose Cruciani in 1915 to Peter and Armita Cruciani, recent immigrants, in the Italian neighborhood of northeast Minneapolis, Minnesota, where her father worked as a laborer for the city. Since the family struggled financially, as a little girl Rose sold milk from the family cow. At age 16, she quit school to work full-time at the Hollywood Candy Factory, where she made 17 cents an hour. Three years later, she met Jim Totino, a 23-year-old baker, and they soon married.

Totino concentrated on raising her daughters, and on several occasions made pizza for her neighbors, who liked it so much that they urged her to open a pizza shop. She and her husband agreed, and using their car as collateral obtained a $1,500 loan. In 1951, they began serving pizzas at Totino's Italian Kitchen. At that time, few pizza shops existed, so customers flocked to the novel and delicious food. Originally, the Totinos ran their business as a take-out eatery, but they soon changed it to a restaurant. Within three months, the business made enough money for Jim to quit his job as a baker and work full-time at the restaurant. Both Totinos put in 20-hour shifts, and on their busiest days made 400 to 500 pizzas.

By 1961, they had saved $50,000 and decided they could make more money by selling their pizza as a frozen food. After all, America's booming young population wanted easy-to-make foods, and few pizzas existed, frozen or otherwise, in a nation accustomed to hamburgers and other standard fare. But after the Totinos found they lacked the money to buy dough-making equipment, they shifted course and started their new business by making frozen manicotti and mostaccioli. With a faulty advertising campaign and other mistakes, they quickly lost $150,000.

At that point, they discovered that they could buy premade crust and thus make pizza without expensive equipment. Totino disliked the idea because she thought the crust tasted like cardboard, but she decided to counteract that liability with her superior toppings, and in 1962 the Totinos began making frozen pizza.

The business succeeded immediately, and in 1970 they built a new $2.5 million plant, complete with a bakery that allowed them to make their own crust. Totino obtained strong loyalty from her employees and later explained her management technique: "I never ruled with an iron hand. I find that if you tell people what you expect of them and that you depend on them, they will do the job."

Her company managers said:

> The Totinos gave us 100 percent responsibility. We never thought about doing anything that would somehow reflect poorly on the company.

> Around Rose you have a feeling that things are going to work out.

> She's extremely bright and intuitive. She gives [people] complete authority. You'd die before you'd mess up their business.

By 1975, the Totinos were in their sixties and wanted to lessen their workload. At the same time, other larger companies were moving into the increasingly popular pizza market and providing stiff competition. As a result, in November of that year—as sales of their pizzas exceeded $35 million—they sold their company to Pillsbury for $22 million. As part of the deal, Pillsbury made Rose Totino a corporate vice president.

Soon after, Pillsbury applied its resources to improving the Totino pizza crust—which consumers still criticized as tasting too much like cardboard—and advertised the product as "Totino's Crisp Crust Pizza." Totino died in 1994, having survived her husband by more than a decade.

BIBLIOGRAPHY

Pine, Carol, and Susan Mundale, *Self-Made: The Stories of 12 Minnesota Entrepreneurs*, 1982.

Trippe, Juan

(June 27, 1899–April 3, 1981)
Airline Executive

Starting with one mail route, Juan Terry Trippe pioneered the modern international airline industry. Trippe built Pan American Airways into the "world's longest airline," with over 80,000 miles linking 85 countries. Under his leadership, Pan Am established the first significant overseas commercial routes; supported the development of larger, faster, longer-range passenger planes; and established safety and service standards for the industry. His belief in providing services at affordable rates made international travel available to the average person.

On June 27, 1899, in Seabright, New Jersey, Charles White and Lucy Adeline Terry Trippe named their newborn son Juan Terry, in memory of Lucy's aunt, Juanita Terry. Most of Juan's childhood was spent in New York City, where Charles worked as an investment banker. Juan's devotion to aviation materialized at an early age with his principal childhood hobby of building model airplanes for flight in Central Park.

In 1917, Trippe entered Yale University, where he embarked on a series of private flying lessons. He soon left school to join the Naval Flying Service for training as a naval aviator. Trippe achieved the rank of ensign but did not see overseas service in World War I. Trippe returned to Yale, where he founded the Yale Flying Club. After graduating in 1921, he became a bond salesman for Lee, Higginson and Company, with the intention of eventually joining his father's brokerage firm.

In just two years, however, a chance business opportunity arose that rekindled Trippe's love of flying and paved the way for his ascension into the annals of aviation history. In 1923, Trippe and some of his Yale Flying Club friends purchased seven surplus navy planes for $500 and quickly established Long Island Airways, Inc., a charter service for sightseers. By 1924, he had secured the investment of a group of Boston bankers to form the Colonial Air Transport Company, a service between New York and Boston that was awarded the first contract for official airmail service in the United States.

By 1926, Trippe, frustrated with the conservative banking group's refusal to allow him to expand the route to Miami and Havana, left Colonial. By the next year, he had formed the Aviation Corporation with Cornelius Vanderbilt Whitney and John T. Hambleton. With a capital investment consisting of a single Fokker three-engine plane, the trio secured the contract to establish a Florida-Cuba route as the first U.S. international airmail route. In 1927, shortly after earning the contract, the three partners merged their new corporation with Pan Ameri-

can Airways, Inc., creating the new Pan American Airways Corporation. By early 1928, with Trippe as president, Pan Am was also carrying passengers on the Miami-Havana route.

Both the airmail and the passenger services proved popular, and Pan Am moved quickly to expand its theater of operations. By the end of 1929, the airline had become a major international carrier, with a 12,000-mile system linking 23 countries. As the business soared, Trippe's personal life, stalled for years by the disapproval of his intended wife's family, took off as well. He married Elizabeth Stettinius, the sister of future Secretary of State Edward Stettinius Jr., on June 16, 1928.

Confident that his Latin American experiments boded well for continued global expansion, Trippe in 1930 engaged Charles Lindbergh as a consultant to explore potential transoceanic commercial air routes. Lindbergh, who had completed his historic solo New York–Paris flight, surveyed a route to Asia across the Pacific by way of Alaska, the Soviet Union, Japan, and China. Though Lindbergh's test flight was successful, political considerations led the leadership of Pan Am to develop an alternative commercial route via Hawaii and Guam. As planes still lacked the capability for long-range direct flights, bases were established on various Pacific islands along the proposed route.

Trippe, who was a firm believer in encouraging technological innovation, encouraged the aircraft companies Boeing and Martin to develop planes capable of transoceanic flights. Soon both companies exceeded Trippe's expectations. On November 22, 1935, Pan Am's Martin M-30 (the China Clipper) flew 8,200 miles from San Francisco to the Philippines, becoming the first scheduled transpacific commercial flight. Almost four years later, Pan Am's Yankee Clipper (a Boeing B-314) flew the first scheduled commercial transatlantic flight, from New York to Marseilles, France, by way of the Azores and Lisbon, Portugal. The Clippers, known as "flying boats," were just one stage in the development of what Trippe envisioned as "great ocean airliners."

The outbreak of World War II curtailed Pan Am's commercial transatlantic flights, but Pan Am Clippers played an important role in the transport of diplomatic and military personnel and cargo. After the bombing of Pearl Harbor in December 1941, Trippe assigned all of Pan Am's resources to the war effort.

Commercial routes were reestablished after the war ended, and Trippe intensified his efforts to make international air travel appealing and accessible to the ordinary person. By 1948, the year after completing the goal of establishing around-the-world service, Trippe introduced Tourist Class on the New York–San Juan flight. This low-fare option was immensely popular, and with Trippe's support, the option of First Class or Tourist Class was adopted as an industry standard.

Pan Am, with Trippe at the helm, continued to embrace new and better technology, updating its fleets with each new aircraft improvement. By 1958, the company's use of the Boeing 707 and Douglas DC-8 jets enabled Pan Am to offer the first nonstop service between the United States and Europe. Trippe's role as an innovator, already well established, intensified in 1966 with the order for 25 Boeing 747 jumbo jets, to be designed by Boeing in conjunction with Pan Am engineers. The 747 doubled passenger capacity while allowing increased speed and lower operating costs.

In 1968, Trippe retired but was still an active member of the board of directors when the first Pan Am 747 made its maiden flight in 1970 from New York to London. On April 3, 1981, a year after a stroke forced him to completely retire from business activities, Trippe died in New York City.

BIBLIOGRAPHY

Daley, Robert, *An American Saga: Juan Trippe and His Pan Am Empire*, 1980; Davies, R. E. G., *A History of the World's Airlines*, 1964; Josephson, Matthew, *Empire of the Air*, 1944; Time, March 28, 1949; Trippe, Juan, "Now You Can Take That Trip Abroad," *Reader's Digest*, January 1949.

Trumbull, Jonathan

(March 26, 1740–August 7, 1809)
Financier

Jonathan Trumbull played a prominent role in the administration of the Continental army during the American Revolution. After the war, he became an influential figure in national and state politics. Serving as Connecticut's governor for 12 years, Trumbull vehemently objected to the policies of the Democratic-Republican Party and became one of the Federalist Party's staunchest defenders.

Trumbull was born on March 26, 1740, in Lebanon, Connecticut, into a prominent family. He graduated from Harvard College in 1759. Three years later, he was awarded a master's degree. In March 1767, he married Eunice Backus, with whom he had five children. In 1774, 1775, 1779, 1780, and 1788, Trumbull represented Lebanon in the state legislature. He was Speaker of the House in the latter year.

Trumbull occupied several important noncombatant roles in the American Revolution. From July 1775 until he resigned to look after the accounts of his brother, Gen. Joseph Trumbull, Trumbull acted as paymaster of the patriot troops. In November 1778, he was the unanimous choice of Congress to be the comptroller of the treasury, but he held this post for only six months before resigning. Two years later, in June 1781, he accepted an appointment as Gen. George Washington's secretary. He served on Washington's staff until the end of the war in 1783.

When the first national elections were held under the new Constitution, Trumbull was elected to the U.S. House of Representatives. He served in the House from 1789 to 1795, the last two years as Speaker. In 1794, he was elected to the U.S. Senate but resigned two years later to become the deputy governor of Connecticut. When Governor Oliver Wolcott Sr. died in 1797, Trumbull succeeded him. He was reelected annually every year for the rest of his life.

Trumbull was a staunch Federalist and adamant opponent of Thomas Jefferson's Democratic-Republican policies. While governor, Trumbull did everything he could to undermine the enforcement of the Embargo Act of 1807. In 1809, he even refused to authorize the use of the state militia by the secretary of war to enforce the embargo on the grounds that

Jonathan Trumbull (Library of Congress)

it was an unconstitutional infringement of states' rights. Shortly after his refusal, Trumbull died on August 7, 1809.

BIBLIOGRAPHY

Trumbull, Jonathan, *Jonathan Trumbull: Governor of Connecticut, 1764–1784*, 1919; Weaver, Glenn, *Jonathan Trumbull: Connecticut's Merchant*, 1913.

Trump, Donald

(June 14, 1946–)
Real Estate Developer

With his lavish style and heavily mortgaged deals, Donald Trump personified life in the flashy, materialistic 1980s, when he built an empire of apartment buildings, hotels, and casinos.

Born on June 14, 1946, Donald came from a wealthy family. His parents, Fred C. Trump and Mary Trump, raised him in a 23-room house located in the exclusive Jamaica Estates section of Queens, New York. The elder Trump had made his money in real estate, and encouraged his son to do likewise. After graduation from the New York Military Academy at Cornwall-on-the-Hudson, Donald enrolled in 1964 at Fordham University in the North Bronx. Two years later, he transferred to the Wharton School of Finance at the University of Pennsylvania, where, in 1968, he earned a bachelor's degree in economics. He later reported, though, that college had bored him, for his real estate courses stressed single-family dwellings rather than large, impressive buildings.

After college, Donald Trump went to work for his father's company, the Trump Organization. He managed thousands of apartments, and spent most of his time collecting rents. He also oversaw the leasing of space to New York State's Off-Track Betting Corporation on land that his father had earlier acquired from New York City at no expense.

In October 1973, the U.S. Justice Department sued the Trump Organization for discriminating against African Americans in its rental practices. Donald Trump denied the charges, going so far as to insist he had no involvement in renting the apartments, some 14,000 units, all occupied by whites. But he eventually signed a consent decree.

Using ties to New York Governor Hugh Carey and New York City Mayor Abraham Beam, men to whose campaigns the Trumps had contributed heavily, Donald Trump persuaded the city to build its new convention center at the defunct Penn Central railroad yards along West 34th Street, land on which he held options. Trump and his father handled the sale of this land in 1974 to the city's Urban Development Corporation for a $500,000 commission. Donald Trump initially demanded $4.4 million, but relented when it turned out he was not legally entitled to that amount.

Two years later, Trump joined with the Hyatt Corporation and bought the old Commodore Hotel, also in New York City. With Mayor Beam's support he obtained a long-term tax abatement worth $45 million. "Whatever Donald and Fred want," the mayor once said, "they have my complete backing." Renovated and renamed the Grand Hyatt, the hotel opened in 1980 with a sleek steel and glass exterior, 1,400 rooms, a ballroom, a shopping arcade, and five restaurants. While that work was in progress, he married Ivana Zelniak in 1977, a union that produced three children.

Trump pulled off another major deal in 1979 when, with the Equitable Life Assurance Company, he acquired the site of a former department store next to the exclusive Tiffany & Company on Fifth Avenue, and built Trump Tower. With another tax abatement, this one worth $50 million, he completed the structure in 1982, the largest and most expensive reinforced concrete building in the city. Trump Tower contained posh apartments and shops, and brought in rents of $1 million per year.

In the early 1980s, Trump purchased the Barbizon-Plaza Hotel and an adjacent apartment house for $13 million. He also completed work on Trump Plaza, a $15 million apartment complex on 61st Street.

Over the next few years, Trump concentrated on real estate in Atlantic City, New Jersey, where he used risky financial deals in a drive to dominate the emerging casino scene. Joining with Harrah's, the famed hotel-casino in Las Vegas, Trump began building another Trump Plaza in 1982. Construction costs ran well over budget and reached $220 million, but the casino opened in 1984. At 39 stories it was the tallest building in Atlantic City, and housed hotel rooms, the casino, a theater, seven restaurants, and a health club, all heavily adorned with marble and mirrors. In 1986, Trump borrowed $250 million and bought out Harrah's interest in Trump Plaza. Very soon thereafter, he purchased Atlantic City's Hilton Hotel and Casino.

In 1987, Trump attempted to purchase a controlling interest in Resorts, a company building a new casino, the Taj Mahal, and facing deep financial problems. Much to Trump's chagrin, however, a bidding war for Resorts ensued with Hollywood impresario Merv Griffin. A deal between the two men allowed Trump to purchase the Taj Mahal for $280 million. To obtain financing for the purchase, and for the continuing construction, Trump had to issue shaky bonds and borrow $75 million from a New Jersey bank. When he finished building the Taj Mahal in 1990, he did so with a large cost overrun, further draining his resources.

Trouble followed. As the economy faltered, Trump's situation worsened, and, in order to prevent his fall into bankruptcy, several banks agreed to loan him $65 million, while deferring interest and principal payments on $850 million. The loan package was secured by every asset in Trump's real estate and casino holdings. During this struggle, Trump faced a personal crisis. His affair with Marla Maples, a model and actress, caused his marriage to end in divorce in 1991. Although he married Maples in 1993 and they had one child, they divorced four years later.

Yet Trump weathered the storms, both professional and personal, and in the 1990s plunged into real estate development in Florida. He transformed Mar-A-Lago, a huge Palm Beach estate he had bought several years earlier, into a private club, even though some of the area's wealthy neighbors objected to the development. Today, his rejuvenated casinos earn him over $1 billion per year. To some, Trump represents a real estate genius, to others an impetuous businessman driven by selfish pursuits.

BIBLIOGRAPHY

Barrett, Wayne, *Trump: The Deals and the Downfall*, 1992; O'Donnell, John R., *Trumped!: The Inside Story of the Real Donald Trump—His Cunning Rise and Spectacular Fall*, 1991.

Turner, Ted

(November 19, 1938–)
Entertainment Executive

Nicknamed "The Mouth of the South," Robert Edward "Ted" Turner reshaped television broadcasting by creating the first cable superstation, TBS, and the first cable news network, CNN.

Born on November 19, 1938, in Cincinnati, Ohio, the son of Ed Turner, a former Mississippi cotton farmer, and Florence (Rooney) Turner, at age nine Ted moved with his family to Savannah, Georgia. There his father bought an outdoor advertising agency that he renamed the Turner Advertising Company. Ted attended the Georgia Military Academy near Atlanta and later the McCallie School in Chattanooga, Tennessee. During the summers he worked for his father, trimming grass and cutting back trees around billboards and applying creosote to the support poles.

Turner attended Brown University in Providence, Rhode Island, and in rebellion against his father decided to study the classics. The elder Turner promptly reprimanded him: "I almost puked on the way home today. . . . I think you are rapidly becoming a jackass, and the sooner you get out of that filthy atmosphere, the better it will suit me." Turner changed his major to economics, but never received a degree—he got expelled for breaking the rules that forbade females from visiting men's dorm rooms.

After Turner returned home in 1960, his father made him the general manger of the Turner Advertising Company's branch office in Macon, Georgia. Two years later, however, Ed Turner overextended himself when he bought an interest in the Outdoor Advertising Company, and in 1963 he put into motion plans to sell his business.

Ted Turner strongly disagreed, and he and his father had heated arguments about the future of the business. In March 1963, Ed Turner shot himself, and Ted Turner promptly stopped the sellout plans. Instead, he sold the family's plantations in Georgia and South Carolina, arranged financing, and took over as president and CEO. He quickly revived the advertising agency, and in 1970, against the wishes of his financial advisers, bought a small, money-losing television station, UHF-channel 17 in Atlanta.

The station lost another $2 million after Turner's purchase, but two developments changed the situation. First, the Federal Communications Commission relaxed its restrictions on the access of independent stations to cable-TV systems. Second, in 1975, RCA launched a communication satellite that started transmitting television signals. Turner signed onto it in December 1976, and by the end of 1978 his station was reaching 2 million cable homes and adding 50,000 new ones each month. The station, WTCG, had increased in value to $4 million, and was appreciating at the rate of $1 million a month.

Turner filled his broadcast time with old movies and sports, the latter enhanced when he bought the Atlanta Braves baseball team and the Atlanta Hawks basketball team. That shrewd move allowed him to show games without having to pay the teams for broadcast rights. At the same time, he boosted attendance at Braves games by improving the quality of the team's farm system.

While building his business, Turner continued his long-held interest in yachting, and in 1977 won the America's Cup. He had previously won the U.S. 5.5 Meter Championship three times.

In 1980, Turner, who had once relegated news on his station to the early morning hours and punctuated it with humorous pie throwing, launched as part of the Turner Broadcasting System (TBS) the Cable News Network (CNN). Ridiculed by journalists and investors alike as "Turner's folly," CNN was the first live, 24-hour, all-news network. In the late 1980s, profits and stature ended the ridicule—CNN earned praise for its coverage of several important events, including the explosion of the space shuttle *Challenger*, the 1989 San Francisco earthquake, and the Persian Gulf War.

In the meantime, Turner nearly lost his television empire in 1986 when he bought MGM/UA, a leading Hollywood studio and entertainment company. Although the acquisition added many old movies to his inventory, the deal put him heavily in debt. A consortium of 31 cable-TV companies bailed him out in 1987 by injecting $663 million into TBS and, in turn, acquiring 7 of the 15 seats on the company's board of directors. TBS, which employed about 4,200 people in 18 countries, was at that time worth about $7 billion.

In October 1988, Turner started another cable network, TNT, geared to showing the movies acquired from MGM. He also began a controversial project to "colorize" old black-and-white movies. In his personal life, Turner's marriage of 24 years to Jane Smith ended about the time he began TNT. An earlier, briefer marriage to July Nye had ended in divorce in the early 1960s. Turner had five children when he married movie actress and 1960s political activist Jane Fonda in 1991.

"Every time he opens his mouth," said one observer about Turner, "you've got to be there because you don't know what's going to come out. Sometimes I don't think he knows." But in the 1990s, the volatile Turner seemed to many a calmer person, perhaps a result of psychological counseling, the prescription drug lithium, and his marriage to Fonda.

Changes occurred for Turner in business, too. In 1995, with the support of JOHN MALONE, head of Tele-Communications, Incorporated (TCI) and an investor in TBS, Turner merged TBS with Time Warner, Incorporated, a giant media and entertainment company. The deal, which involved a $7.5 billion stock swap, made Turner Time Warner's biggest shareholder and vice chairman of the combined company. Later that year, Turner announced he was starting yet another cable network, CNNfn, to provide financial news.

In addition, Turner spent more time backing environmental causes that he had been partial to for years. He gave $28 million in 1996 to groups such as Worldwatch, the Bat Conservation Society, and Friends of the Wild Swan.

In 1997, Turner committed $1 billion to support the United Nations. About his donation, he said: "When I got my statement in January, I was worth $2.2 billion. Then I got another statement in August that said I was worth $3.2 billion. So I figure it's only nine months' earnings, who cares?" He once described his communications empire as "a positive force in the world, to tie the world together," and now wanted to make his money support that ideal.

BIBLIOGRAPHY

Bibb, Porter, *It Isn't as Easy as It Looks: Ted Turner's Amazing Story*, 1993; Goldberg, Robert, *Citizen Turner: The Wild Rise of an American Tycoon*, 1995; Vaughan, Roger, *Ted Turner: The Man behind the Mouth*, 1978; Whittmore, Hank, *CNN: The Inside Story*, 1990; Williams, Christian, *Lead, Follow or Get Out of the Way: The Story of Ted Turner*, 1981.

Underwood, John

(April 12, 1857–July 2, 1937)
Manufacturer

Though the first company to manufacture typewriters on a commercial scale was Remington & Sons, it was John Thomas Underwood who provided the industry with typing supplies and eventually expanded his company to become the largest typewriter manufacturer in the business by 1915.

John Thomas, the eldest son of the six children of John and Elizabeth Maire Underwood, was born on April 12, 1857, in London, England. His father was a chemist who invented the inks and special papers that made copying of handwritten papers possible. In 1872, the family moved to New Durham, New Jersey, where the elder Underwood continued to manufacture paper and ink. The young Underwood remained in boarding school in France until rejoining the family in 1873.

Underwood spent his first year in the United States working as a laborer for an iron foundry. By this time, Remington & Company had begun to make typewriters on a commercial scale. Underwood and his father decided to establish John Underwood & Company to become the first major supplier of typewriter accessories. They soon added carbon paper, ribbons, and other supplies to the product line.

In 1883, upon the death of his father, Underwood relocated the company to Brooklyn, New York, and undertook the manufacture of typewriters. Though the addition of typewriters met with moderate success, John Underwood & Company was not a serious competitor in the industry until the purchase in 1895 of the Wagner Typewriter Company. Franz Wag-

ner, a German mechanic, devised an improvement over standard typewriters that at this time did not allow a line of type to be viewed until the keystroke lifted the printing carriage. Underwood bought the rights to Wagner's patent and incorporated his company in 1898 as the Underwood Typewriter Manufacturing Company.

On April 24, 1901, Underwood married Grace Brainard, with whom he would eventually have one child, Gladys Evelyn. These were busy and active years both personally and professionally. By 1903, both of Underwood's companies were merged into a new corporation, the Underwood Typewriter Company, with Underwood as president. The combination of a well-designed product and an already-established network of typewriter supply outlets enabled the Underwood Typewriter Company to meet with great success. By 1915, the company produced almost 500 typewriters daily and employed over 7,000 workers. In 1927, the composition of the company changed again with a merger that produced the Underwood Elliott Fisher Company. Underwood served as chairman of the board of the new company for several years and then remained a director until his death.

Underwood was active in humanitarian, civic, and cultural activities. He was awarded the 1926 French Legion of Honor award for his aid to soldiers and civilians during and after World War I. He contributed to church programs and sponsored a welfare program for the poor. He was also active in the Institute of Arts and Sciences and the Academy of Music. Underwood was known as a quiet, energetic man.

On July 2, 1937, Underwood died at his Cape Cod summer home from complications caused by a heart condition.

BIBLIOGRAPHY

Current, Richard N., *The Typewriter and the Men Who Made It*, 1954; Herkimer County Historical Society, *The Story of the Typewriter, 1873–1923*, 1923; *New York Times*, Obituary, July 3, 1937; *Scientific American*, November 24, 1900; Underwood, Lucien M., and Howard J. Banker, *The Underwood Families of America*, 1913; Underwood, William Lawrence, *Notes Regarding a Branch of the Underwood Family*, 1917.

Vail, Theodore

(July 16, 1845–April 16, 1920)
Communications Executive

More than any other figure of his day, Theodore Newton Vail was responsible for structuring the telephone industry. After an early career in the telegraphic and postal services, Vail took the helm of the Bell Telephone Company and united many of the early local telephone services into a national network. After his early retirement and an 18-year hiatus, Vail was coaxed into heading the American Telephone & Telegraph Company (Bell's successor) as president. In his second term, he further strengthened the Bell system and established it as a virtual monopoly over the telephone industry.

The third of 10 children, Theodore was born to Davis and Phebe Quinby Vail on July 16, 1845, near Minerva, Ohio. In 1847, Davis moved the family back to New Jersey to return to a previous job as an ironworker at the Speedwell Iron Works near Morristown. Theodore attended the public schools and Morristown Academy for high school, where he enjoyed reading. His education in practical matters came from his first job in a drugstore at age 17. The drugstore had a telegraph machine, which Theodore quickly learned to use. After briefly studying medicine with an uncle, he moved to New York at age 19 and was employed as a telegraph operator for the Western Union Telegraph Company.

Vail's career was interrupted in 1866 when he decided to follow his family in their move to Waterloo, Iowa. For a while, he indulged in typical midwestern life, harvesting crops and enjoying the young sport of baseball of which he

Theodore Vail (Library of Congress)

would remain an avid fan for his entire life. In 1868, he returned to the telegraph service in Pinebluff, South Dakota, and finally settled in Omaha, Nebraska, soon after his marriage to Emma Louise Righter on August 3, 1869. Their only son, Davis, was born on July 18, 1870. Vail found employment as a route agent for the railway mail service. With his initiative for astute improvements to the mail-routing system, he advanced rapidly and was transferred in 1873 to the main office in Washington, D.C. By 1876, he became general superintendent of the railway mail service.

While Vail's postal career was taking off, GARDINER HUBBARD was busy organizing the rapidly developing telephone business as president of the Bell Telephone Company. From his observations of the postal service improvements, Hubbard recognized Vail's talent for organization and efficiency, and saw that these skills would be vital to the success of the fledgling telephone industry. He recruited Vail to become general manager of the Bell Telephone Company in 1878.

At that time, there were many small, local telephone systems in operation, often engaging in direct competition with each other. This meant that extended and long-distance services were completely untenable. In his first year as general manager, Vail set about revolutionizing the industry by securing financing, and then acquiring and organizing these disjointed systems. In 1885, he created the American Telephone & Telegraph Company as a subsidiary of Bell to handle long-distance service arrangements.

Having achieved many of his goals with the telephone system, Vail retired in 1889 at age 44 to a farm in Lyndonville, Vermont. Never content to be idle for long, he traveled around Europe and also became intensely interested in the development of Argentina. In fact, the improvement of Argentina's infrastructure, including a hydroelectric plant at Cordoba and an electric streetcar system in Buenos Aires, became his principal occupation from 1894 to 1907. After the deaths of his wife in February 1905 and his only son in December 1906, he sold his South American ventures and moved back to Vermont. He married Mabel R. Sanderson on July 27, 1907, and adopted his niece, Katherine Vail.

While Vail was away, Bell Telephone had blossomed from 180,680 telephones to over 2.7 million by the end of 1906. In 1900, the American Telephone & Telegraph Company took over from the Bell Telephone Company as the main corporation controlling the telephone system. The financial condition of the company, however, slowly degraded from excessive expenditures and mismanagement, and the company nearly failed in the Panic of 1907.

Vail was asked to return that same year to become president, and he accepted. He moved the company headquarters from Boston to New York City and secured financial backing for further expansion from J. P. MORGAN SR. Vail then began strengthening the network by forging agreements with all the chief officers of the independent companies linked to the Bell system. He tried to unify the communication business further by taking over the Western Union Telegraph Company, but the mating was short-lived as the federal government split the companies up in 1913 since their merger was deemed a violation of antitrust laws.

Vail also helped to advance telephone technology during his second term. His investment in scientific research resulted in technical improvements and efficient construction. On January 25, 1915, the first transcontinental telephone line was demonstrated with President Woodrow Wilson as a participant in the conversation. Later that year, radio telephony was first used to communicate between Arlington (Virginia), Paris, and Honolulu. Vail also approved plans for the construction of a telephone system in France during World War I.

Vail resigned the presidency of American Telephone & Telegraph on June 18, 1919, and became chairman of the board of directors. But less than one year later, on April 16, 1920, Vail died at the Johns Hopkins Hospital in Baltimore, Maryland.

BIBLIOGRAPHY

Paine, A. B., *Theodore N. Vail: A Biography,* 1929; Stehman, J. W., *The Financial History of the American Telephone & Telegraph Company,* 1925; *Wall Street Journal,* April 17 and 23, 1920.

Van Andel, Jay

(June 24, 1924–)
Merchant

Everything short of a hallelujah chorus runs through an Amway seminar with its revival-like atmosphere. As a multibillion-dollar company, Amway sells household products through a distribution system critics call a pyramid scheme, but its founders, RICHARD DEVOS and Jay Van Andel, along with its supporters, hail it as an exemplar of the American dream.

The lives of DeVos and Van Andel parallel each other so closely that one leading magazine has called them "Amway's Dutch Twins." The two have been lifelong friends, from their childhoods in Grand Rapids, Michigan, through their success with Amway.

Van Andel was born on June 24, 1924, in Grand Rapids, Michigan, where his father owned an automobile dealership. He became friends with DeVos in high school, and during World War II, they joined the U.S. Army Air Corps. They briefly attended Calvin College before deciding to enter business together.

In 1947, they purchased the Wolverine Air Service that operated a flying school and chartered planes from its base at Comstock Park Air Field near Grand Rapids. Although the business made money and expanded to 12 airplanes, De-Vos and Van Andel tired of it and sold the air service in 1948.

The following year, they formed the Ja-Ri Corporation and through it distributed Nutrilite Products, a food supplement marketed in capsules. Soon they embarked on direct sales. Under this system, they sold Nutrilite to customers in their homes and offices and recruited distributors, each of whom had a territory in which they sold the product. By 1955, some 5,000 independent salesmen worked for them within a large distribution network.

Four years later, however, poor relations with Nutrilite caused DeVos and Van Andel to break with the company, and in November 1959 they formed the Amway Sales Corporation to obtain such household products as laundry detergents, sell them to their distributors, and operate a marketing plan.

While DeVos and Van Andel both married women from the Grand Rapids Dutch community, had four children, and became active in the La Grave Christian Church, they developed a system of Amway distributorships that sparked controversy. Although distributors made some money selling an expanding line of products, big profits required sponsoring or bringing new recruits into the organization. One analyst explained: "The real money is made, not by what he and she personally sell, but by what their people sell. And so new distributors going into the Amway line will be encouraged to make a list of everyone they know." Thus developed a system akin to pyramid sales, although in 1979 a judge with the Federal Trade Commission ruled that Amway had not established a true pyramid system.

By the mid-1970s, Amway was selling about 150 products, and in the early 1980s some distributors reached incomes of between $200,000 and $350,000 a year. Amway held more than 200 seminars annually in about 80 cities throughout the United States and Canada. Enthusiastic, largely white participants listened to spellbinding sermons and patriotic music, and chanted in unison. One critic likened Amway to a religious cult and said, "What the revival meeting is to evangelical Christianity, the Seminar and Rally is to the world of Amway . . . a mighty coming together of the chosen to celebrate their salvation."

The Amway headquarters and plant site in Ada, Michigan, had expanded by the 1980s to 300 acres, and its laboratories and manufacturing facility exceeded 1 million square feet. Amway had an affiliate in Canada and subsidiaries around the world with more than 300,000 distributors. Later that decade, however, DeVos and Van Andel encountered problems when the Canadian government claimed Amway had avoided taxes by lying about the market value of its products. Amway had to pay more than $25 million in fines.

At the same time, the company obtained a bad reputation for trying to recruit through such deceptive tactics as when distributors invited prospects to meetings under the guise of friendly neighborhood socials. Also, some distributors developed blatant pyramid schemes. As a result, DeVos and Van Andel undertook reforms.

In politics, the two men enthusiastically supported Ronald Reagan's presidency and contributed large amounts of money to the Republican Party, believing it to be the best protector of "free enterprise."

Amway continued to grow in the 1990s, when it had, by its own account, 2.5 million distributors. In 1997, the company's retail sales reached an estimated $7 billion. Troubles still bothered Amway, though. *Consumer Reports* magazine rated several Amway products as more expensive or less effective than those of competitors. In 1997, Procter & Gamble sued Amway for operating an "illegal pyramid scheme" that had damaged its sales. In addition, Amway's distributors, perhaps cognizant of the firm's negative reputation, typically went after prospects with sales pitches that failed to mention the name Amway until late in the presentation or not until the prospect inquired. Amway refuted Procter & Gamble's charges and continued to emphasize its role in providing quality products and prosperity to distributors willing to work hard and follow its plan.

BIBLIOGRAPHY
Butterfield, Stephen, *Amway: The Cult of Free Enterprise*, 1985; Conn, Charles Paul, *The Possible Dream*, 1977.

Van Cortlandt, Oloff

(1600–April 5, 1684)
Merchant

Oloff Stevenszen Van Cortlandt was the fourth richest person in the colony of New Netherland, having built a large fortune as a merchant, brewer, and real estate investor.

Little has been documented about Van Cortlandt's childhood or parents. He is thought to have been born in 1600 in the Dutch Republic. Based on a study of Dutch traditions, it is speculated that his parents' surname was Stevens, and that his adoption in 1643 of the last name Cortlandt indicated he had been raised in or near the village of Cortlandt in the province of Utrecht.

Van Cortlandt left the Dutch Republic by securing work aboard the *Haering* as a soldier of the Dutch East India Company. He arrived in New Amsterdam (which later became New York City) in March 1638. In July 1640, he was appointed by the company as the commissioner of cargoes.

On February 26, 1642, Van Cortlandt married Anneken Loockermans, who had emigrated from the Spanish Netherlands. Loockermans's family was wealthy, and the marriage constituted the first step on Van Cortlandt's path to amassing a large fortune. He had already managed to purchase some real estate in 1641, and his new wealth enabled him to begin business as a shopkeeper in 1643.

As his business grew, Van Cortlandt became a prominent public figure. He was appointed the city treasurer for five different terms. From 1655 until 1660, he served as mayor. He was again elected mayor in 1662 and 1663. By the following year, his stature was such that he was selected to negotiate with the English in the transfer of New Amsterdam from the Dutch following the English conquest of New Netherland. For the new government of New York City, he served as alderman on four different occasions: 1665, 1667, 1670, and 1672. In 1667, Van Cortlandt served as deputy mayor.

During these years, Van Cortlandt's business expanded. He owned a brewery, financed various commercial ventures, and continued to ply a wide variety of imported goods from his store. He earned a reputation as a hardheaded business man, occasionally engaging in disputes with tax collectors. In general, he was thought to be a wise man, but opulent in his lifestyle. Van Cortlandt was also a religious leader, serving as deacon of the Dutch Reformed Church in 1646 and progressing to the office of elder by 1670.

Perhaps his most significant legacy was his role as patriarch of what would become one of the most prominent families in all of the American colonies. He fathered seven children, one of whom, STEPHANUS VAN CORTLANDT, would subsequently gain great distinction in both commercial and political affairs. With his son, Jacobus, Van Cortlandt acquired a great deal of real estate. His influence was later immortalized in the establishment of New York City's Van Cortlandt Park.

Van Cortlandt died on April 5, 1684, surrounded by his family.

BIBLIOGRAPHY

DeForest, L. E., *The Van Cortlandt Family*, 1930; Fernow, Berthold, ed., *The Records of New Amsterdam from 1653 to 1674*, 1897; Purple, S. S., *Records of the Reformed Dutch Church in New Amsterdam and New York, Marriages*, 1890; Van Rensselaer, Maria, *Correspondence of Maria Van Rensselaer 1669–1689*, 1935.

Van Cortlandt, Stephanus

(May 7, 1643–November 25, 1700)
Merchant

Stephanus Van Cortlandt was a successful seventeenth-century merchant, unrelenting in the practice of his trade even when it conflicted with colonial laws. Despite these legal infractions, he also had a long career in public office, a position that was useful in securing land and wealth.

Van Cortlandt was the eldest son of Anneken Loockermans and OLOFF VAN CORTLANDT, a wealthy merchant who was an important figure in the early history of New Amsterdam and New York. The young Van Cortlandt was born on May 7, 1643, in his father's enormous house on Brouwer Street, New Amsterdam (present-day New York City).

Raised in a religious household, Van Cortlandt attended schools run by the Dutch Reformed Church. He also spent time with his father at work and quickly demonstrated a commercial aptitude that led him to leave school. By 1664, he was deeply involved in sales, securing commissions for Jan Baptist Van Renssalaer of Amsterdam. His sister, Maria, married Van Renssalaer's son, Jeremias. Van Cortlandt traded wine, blankets, and other goods for the beaver skins that his brother-in-law obtained in Albany.

Though the English conquered the Dutch New Netherland colony in the mid-1660s, Van Cortlandt continued with his mercantile activities, locating new officials that conspired with him to import goods in violation of the newly enacted Acts of Trade. In this fashion, Van Cortlandt began to build considerable wealth in his own right. On September 10, 1671, Van Cortlandt married Gertude Schuyler. The couple had 11 children. Founded on the success of Oloff Van Cortlandt, the family dynasty remained strong and has been viewed as one of the most influential families in colonial times.

Van Cortlandt was, throughout his life, very involved in public office and services. He had a long career, with many promotions, in the militia of King's County. Summoned by New York Governor Sir Edmond Andros, he served on the governor's council in 1674. He continued to sit as a councilor for every governor for many years. In 1677, he became the first colonial-born mayor of the city of New York, a position that he held again in 1686 and 1687. Van Cortlandt's affiliation and friendship with Andros, a supporter of King James II, caused him some difficulty when England's Glorious Revolution drove James II out of power.

A resilient individual, Van Cortlandt made his way back into the good graces of the public and continued to be chosen for both administrative and judicial posts in the colonial government. In 1698, he became the commissioner of revenues as well as the commissioner of customs. He was criticized in this post by Lord Bellomont as being an honest, but overly "timorous" man, incapable of completing the necessary seizures of property required by a collections agent.

Despite the oscillations in his public career, Van Cortlandt used his offices to obtain large grants of land. Because of his connections, he was given the authority, denied to many, to negotiate with Native Americans for purchases of land. Gradually, he was established as a "lord of the manor," a designation that entitled him to the legal privilege of sending a representative of the manor to the provincial assembly.

Van Cortlandt died on November 25, 1700. His land holdings were assessed after his death to be almost 90,000 acres.

BIBLIOGRAPHY

DeForest, L. E., *The Van Cortlandt Family*, 1930; Fernow, Berthold, ed., *The Records of New Amsterdam from 1653 to 1674*, 1897; Purple, S. S., *Records of the Reformed Dutch Church in New Amsterdam and New York, Marriages*, 1890; Van Rensselaer, Maria, *Correspondence of Maria Van Rensselaer 1669–1689*, 1935.

Vanderbilt, Cornelius

(May 27, 1794–January 4, 1877)
Financier, Railroad Executive

From steamboats to railroads, Cornelius Vanderbilt built the infrastructure crucial to America's late-nineteenth-century industrialization. He ranked among that era's dominant business leaders.

Cornelius was born on May 27, 1794, at Port Richmond on Staten Island, New York, to Cornelius Vanderbilt and Phebe (Hand) Vanderbilt. His father struggled financially, farming on Staten Island and operating a boat in New York City's harbor. Young Cornelius obtained little formal schooling, and instead helped his father and learned to navigate the waters.

At age 16, he purchased a small sailing vessel and began transporting freight and passengers between Staten Island and New York City. Along the docks, people called him "Cornele the boatman."

With New York City experiencing a commercial boom, Vanderbilt's business was already prospering when the government awarded him a contract to provision forts in and around New York harbor during the War of 1812. He soon owned a fleet of schooners and personally commanded the largest one. His exploits won him a reputation for toughness as when, in the fall of 1813, he was

Cornelius Vanderbilt (Library of Congress)

the only boatman willing to brave a storm and transport messengers from Sandy Hook, New Jersey, to New York City. But Vanderbilt never enlisted in the navy, preferring to remain in business. During the war, in December 1813, he married Sophia Johnson, with whom he had 13 children.

Vanderbilt carried more than war supplies in his schooners; he used them to trade along the Hudson River and along the coast from New England to South Carolina. In 1818, when the competition from steamboats reduced his trade, he sold his ships and worked as a captain for Thomas Gibbons, who owned and operated a ferry between New Brunswick, New Jersey, and New York City. Vanderbilt moved to New Brunswick, and bought a tavern that his wife operated.

Vanderbilt convinced Gibbons to build a large steamboat, the *Bellona*. With this,

the two men challenged a New York law that had established a monopoly for Robert Fulton by banning steamboats from other states. Atop the *Bellona*'s masthead Vanderbilt flew a flag with the inscription "New Jersey Must Be Free!" Every time he entered New York's waters he risked arrest and had to outmaneuver the sheriffs. In 1823, Vanderbilt designed a steamboat in which he obtained one-third ownership, and the following year the U.S. Supreme Court struck down New York's monopolistic law as unconstitutional.

In 1829, Vanderbilt decided to sell the tavern and leave Gibbons. He moved to New York City, began a steamboat trade along the Hudson, and bested his competitors by cutting rates, often igniting prolonged rate wars. In 1834, he drove DANIEL DREW from business, and then entered the Albany trade. Soon, in an audacious arrangement, his competitors paid him handsomely to suspend his Albany route for 10 years. Vanderbilt's steamboats plied different waters and sailed to Providence, Rhode Island, and Boston, Massachusetts. He kept improving the steamboats, making them faster and more comfortable for passengers. By the mid-1840s, he earned a million dollars, and the public called him Commodore Vanderbilt.

Shortly after the California gold rush began in 1849, Vanderbilt started transporting prospectors across Nicaragua to the Pacific Ocean, enabling them to board ships headed for the promised land. He founded the Accessory Transit Company, built docks along the east and west coasts of Nicaragua and at Lake Nicaragua, and constructed a road. He then sent steamboats from New York City and New Orleans to Nicaragua, where passengers completed the journey across Central America by using his boats and wagons. His efforts shortened the travel time to California and reduced the cost of getting there.

While Vanderbilt was in Europe in 1853, the man he left in charge of Accessory Transit, Charles Morgan, manipulated company stock to gain control. In characteristic fashion, Vanderbilt responded: "You have undertaken to cheat me. I won't sue you for the law is too slow. I'll ruin you." True to his word, Vanderbilt ousted Morgan, but that was not the end of it. The American adventurer who had seized control in Nicaragua, General William Walker, took Morgan's side in the dispute and rescinded Vanderbilt's business charter. Vanderbilt reacted by assisting a military coup that, in 1857, overthrew Walker. Then in an audacious move reminiscent of his Albany route sellout, he approached two rival companies operating in Panama and got them to pay him to abandon his Nicaragua business.

At the same time, Vanderbilt initiated a passenger and cargo service between New York City and Le Havre, France. The business proved unprofitable, however, and when the Civil War began he sold it. During that conflict, he constructed warships for the federal government. He provided these without charge, but commanders complained about their poor quality.

Though nearly 70 years old, in 1862 Vanderbilt sold his steamboats and entered a new endeavor, railroads. He began buying stock in the New York & Harlem, and by 1867 controlled it. He gained control also of the Hudson River Railroad and the New York Central. On the latter, he spent $2 million to make it efficient and profitable. In 1869, the New York legislature approved his plan to combine these two lines into the New York Central & Hudson Railroad (commonly called the Central). When operated in conjunction with the Harlem, the system created an interconnected route crucial to the nation's expanding economy.

In 1868, Vanderbilt engaged in the "Erie War," an attempt by him to acquire the Erie Railroad. Several events precipitated the struggle. Earlier in the decade, Daniel Drew had gained control of the line and had nearly ruined it through stock manipulations. Despite its financially precarious condition, the Erie posed a threat to the Central, and Vanderbilt wanted to control it through measures that businessman Charles Francis Adams Jr. referred to as introducing "Caesarism into corporate life."

Vanderbilt thus entered an uneasy alliance with Drew, but Drew double-crossed him. When Vanderbilt began buying more Erie stock, Drew put the printing presses to work and produced additional shares. Vanderbilt had to spend yet more money, but the more he spent, the more the shares multiplied in number. Angered, he challenged Drew's maneuvers as illegal. The matter eventually went to the New York legislature, and after both sides had bribed the politicians, the august legislators declared Drew and his colleagues in the right. Defeated, Vanderbilt gave up his fight for the Erie, his futile effort having cost him at least $2 million.

In 1869, work began in New York City on what Vanderbilt considered a monument to himself, Grand Central Depot. Four tracks led from the building whose brick and granite structure sprawled along five acres of 42nd Street. Vanderbilt financed the project, which cost some $3 million, although the city paid for the approaches to it.

With business along the Central increasing in the 1870s, Vanderbilt decided to expand from two to four tracks between Albany and Buffalo. This allowed him to move passengers and freight more quickly and to meet his competition, but it cost nearly $40 million. Although immediately after its completion in 1874, freight volume dropped during the depression of 1893, the improvement soon paid off, and the Central returned a greater profit than its competitors. He established, too, a lucrative direct route between New York City and Chicago.

Vanderbilt made few philanthropic gifts, although he endowed Vanderbilt University in Tennessee with $1 million from his wealth, which exceeded 100 times that amount. A tough business leader, a bold financial operator, he created transportation systems that stimulated and supported America's tremendous industrial growth. He died on January 4, 1877.

BIBLIOGRAPHY

Croffut, W. A., *The Vanderbilts and the Story of Their Fortune*, 1985; Lane, Wheaton J., *Commodore Vanderbilt: An Epic of the Steam Age*, 1942.

Vanderbilt, Gloria

(February 20, 1924–)
Manufacturer

Gloria Vanderbilt got the sobriquet "poor little rich girl" during a custody battle in the 1930s, and as her life unfolded with one tumultuous episode after another, the description seemed apt. Amid her turmoil, however, she managed to found a business enterprise based on her talent for art and fashion, and Gloria Vanderbilt clothes became a brand of distinction.

A descendant of the nineteenth-century business tycoon CORNELIUS VANDERBILT, Gloria was born on February 20, 1924, in New York City to Reginald Claypoole Vanderbilt and Gloria (Morgan) Vanderbilt. When her father died the following year, Gloria inherited a trust fund of $4 million. She first made national headlines when, in 1934, her paternal aunt Gertrude Vanderbilt Whitney, on whose Long Island estate she was living, sued Gloria's mother for custody of the child. The sensational custody trial resulted in a victory for Gertrude, with Gloria's mother losing custody and three-quarters of the monetary support to which she had grown accustomed.

Vanderbilt attended the exclusive Mary C. Wheeler School in Providence, Rhode Island, and Miss Porter's School in Farmington, Connecticut. At age 17, however, she dropped out of school, much to her aunt's chagrin, to marry Pat di Cicco, an actors' agent from Hollywood. According to some reports, he beat her, and the marriage ended after only three years.

She married the famed conductor Leopold Stokowski in 1945, though he was more than 40 years her senior. After five years, she suffered what newspapers called a nervous breakdown. Yet Vanderbilt had begun exhibiting her art (14 oils and pastels) at the Rabun Studio on Madison Avenue. She followed that with a one-woman show in 1953 at another gallery in New York City and received several favorable reviews. The following year, she acted in an off-Broadway play, and through the 1950s appeared on several television programs, including a dramatization of Tolstoy's *Family Happiness.*

Her personal life remained difficult, however, and in 1955 she divorced Stokowski. While taking care of her two sons, she began writing poetry, and in 1956 married Sidney Lumet, a television director. That union lasted seven years before it ended in divorce. Vanderbilt's fourth marriage, to Wyatt Cooper, a writer, produced two sons and more happiness than she had seen in some time.

While married to Cooper, she devoted herself to painting full-time, and he encouraged her work. Then, in 1970, Vanderbilt became director of design for the Riegel Textile Corporation in New York City and began designing stationery and greeting cards for Hallmark. After her work at Hallmark ended in 1974, she entered fashion design, permitting a manufacturer to make scarves adapted from her paintings.

In 1978, Vanderbilt's husband died from a heart attack, and she plunged more intensely into her design work. Over the next few years, her name appeared on perfume, sheets, shoes, blouses, leather goods, accessories, and jeans. In a 1980 legal proceeding she disclosed that she had earned $10 million over the previous year. She once said: "I had always worn the Fiorucci jean, and it cost $100. I wanted to do one cheaper but with a good fit." Her friends said:

> Gloria didn't earn a living on her name, she got out and did it.
>
> She is not a rich woman who thinks she can paint, or design, or write. She really can do all these things and is not surprised by her successes.
>
> When you have good looks and money, people think you have nothing else.

In the 1980s, Vanderbilt began writing her autobiography. The first installment of the multivolume work appeared in 1985, and another, titled *A Mother's Story*, appeared in 1994. In it, she told of the tragic suicide of her son Carter in 1988. Twenty-three years old and with a promising future as an editor at *American Heritage*, he jumped from her fourteenth-floor apartment as she watched. In 1998, removed from the business scene, she lived in her Manhattan town house. "Tragedy," she said, "connects everyone in the world."

BIBLIOGRAPHY

Goldsmith, Bruce, *Little Gloria . . . Happy at Last*, 1980; Howard, Margo, "Gloria Vanderbilt," *People Weekly*, June 10, 1985; Saroyan, Aram, *Trio: Oona Chaplin, Carol Matthau, and Gloria Vanderbilt: A Portrait of an Intimate Friendship*, 1985; Stascz, Clarice, *The Vanderbilt Women: Dynasty of Wealth, Glamour, and Tragedy*, 1991; Vanderbilt, Gloria, *A Mother's Story*, 1994; Vanderbilt, Gloria, *Once Upon a Time: A True Story*, 1985.

Vanderlip, Frank

(November 17, 1864–June 29, 1937)
Editor, Banker

Frank Arthur Vanderlip—who is principally known for his administration of National City Bank, one of the largest banks in the United States during his lifetime—was a man of varied interests who achieved success in a number of arenas. From his post as associate editor of the *Economist* magazine to his stint as assistant secretary of the treasury to his notable role in banking, Vanderlip was a reserved and thorough professional.

Frank Vanderlip (Library of Congress)

Frank, the eldest of three children of Charles and Charlotte Woodworth Vanderlip, was born on a farm near Aurora, Illinois, on November 17, 1864. When he was 13, both his father, a blacksmith, and his sister died from tuberculosis. Frank found work at a machine shop to support his sister, mother, grandmother, and two maiden aunts. Though he had left school, he continued to be tutored in mathematics and German, as well as eventually completing a year of mechanical engineering at the University of Illinois.

In 1885, Vanderlip's career changed course when he became the city editor of the *Aurora Evening Post*. A friendship with Joseph French Johnson, the head of a financial investigating agency in Chicago, led to a new job at Johnson's firm. Working on financial data for railroads, Vanderlip gained a taste for financial reporting. By 1889, he was employed as a financial reporter for the *Chicago Tribune.*

Vanderlip did not neglect the pursuit of education during these years. Despite full-time employment, he finished a year of course work in economics and finance at the University of Chicago. As his reputation as an authority in finance grew, new opportunities emerged. From 1894 to 1897, Vanderlip was the financial editor for the Chicago weekly publication the *Economist*. He was also a favorite on the academic lecture circuit, giving talks at many colleges on finance.

After a mere three months, Vanderlip was promoted to the position of assistant secretary of the treasury, where he eventually entered the national spotlight for his role in managing the complicated financing of U.S. costs during the Spanish-American War. By the time the Treaty of Paris ended the war in 1898, U.S. expenditures on the war effort were roughly

$250 million, a sum that included the $20 million Spain received from the United States for the cession of the Philippines.

In 1901, Vanderlip returned to private industry as a vice president under James Stillman of the National City Bank of New York. He initiated a number of new approaches to banking, including the active solicitation of new accounts, bank involvement in investing, and the expansion of domestic and foreign branch networks. His monthly "bank letter" for industry news was circulated internationally.

At the age of 38, Vanderlip abandoned bachelorhood and married Narcissa Cook in early 1903. Narcissa, a college friend of Vanderlip's sister, bore six children, three girls and three boys. Vanderlip purchased a 125-acre estate called Beechwood at Scarborough-on-the-Hudson. He and his wife were active in the community, establishing and endowing the Scarborough School.

In 1909, upon Stillman's retirement, Vanderlip became the president of the bank. He continued to innovate, establishing a training program for college graduates and becoming a leading authority on foreign finance. Increased study into foreign public and private financial policies led him to expand the bank's influence abroad, establishing branches strategically in important financial centers around the world.

During World War I, Vanderlip, on a leave of absence from the bank, served at the Treasury Department as the chairman of the War Savings Committee. Vanderlip did not like the changed atmosphere of the bank upon his return, and in 1919 he sold his stock and resigned as president.

Vanderlip spent much of the rest of his life in public affairs, taking stands against isolationism, opposing and investigating the scandals that rocked the administration of President Warren G. Harding, and working on bank reform issues. In 1933, he served as chairman of the Committee for the Nation, a pulpit he used to advocate abandoning the gold standard and devaluation of the dollar.

Vanderlip was a generous but reserved man who considered himself a "wet blanket." He participated in the leadership of the Sleepy Hollow Country Club, yet never learned golf, and expressed regret that virtually no one called him Frank. Despite these impressions, he was widely respected and highly regarded as a public speaker, finance expert, and essayist.

On June 29, 1937, Vanderlip died in New York City from intestinal problems and diabetes.

BIBLIOGRAPHY

Forbes, B. C., *Men Who Are Making America*, 1917; Mayer, Robert Stanley, *The Influence of Frank Vanderlip and the National City Bank on American Commerce and Foreign Policy, 1910–1920*, 1960; Vanderlip, Frank A., *Business and Education*, 1907; Vanderlip, Frank A., *From Farm Boy to Financier*, 1935; Vanderlip, Frank A., *Tomorrow's Money*, 1934.

Vernon, Lillian

(March 18, 1927–)
Merchant

The founder of a highly successful mail-order company specializing in personalized merchandise, Lillian Vernon is one of the entrepreneurs and innovators of the catalog industry. Vernon parlayed a small investment combined with an original idea and good intuition into a multimillion-dollar company that remains an active player in the fiercely competitive world of direct-mail merchandising.

Lillian Menasche, the daughter of a successful industrialist, was born in Leipzig, Germany, on March 18, 1927. In the mid-1930s, the family left Germany, heading initially to Holland but immigrating finally to the United States. Her father opened a zipper reconditioning business in New York City. As the business prospered, he diversified his product line to include leather goods such as camera bags, purses, and belts.

In 1941, Lillian married a retailer, Sam Hochberg, and quickly chafed at the societal norm that prescribed the domestic life of child rearing and housecleaning. She worked at a number of jobs until her first pregnancy and attended psychology classes at New York University until she was expecting her second child. Frustrated and in search of extra income, Lillian settled on the mail-order business as a way to satisfy her ambition while staying home with her two children.

Lillian placed an advertisement in *Seventeen* magazine advertising leather purses and belts monogrammed in 24-carat gold. She was unprepared for the subsequent flood of orders—16,000 orders were placed within six weeks of running the advertisement, with another 16,000 pouring in shortly thereafter. Lillian continued to expand the business, placing advertisements in *Vogue* and *Redbook*. The instant success startled her husband, who facetiously commented to her in this early period that if her annual sales reached $40,000, he would close his company and join her business. The following year, Hochberg—albeit reluctantly—made good on his promise and converted his store into a warehouse for her products.

A significant area of expansion proved to be the corporate world, and the company, which was called Vernon Specialties after her Mt. Vernon, New York, home, began to accept manufacturing orders for custom-designed products from such prestigious clients as Max Factor, ELIZABETH ARDEN, Avon, and Revlon. In 1960, the first Vernon Specialties mail-order catalog was published. The 16-page black-and-white brochure with products such as combs, cuff links, and collar pins was sent to customers who had responded to previous advertisements.

The next few years were hectic at work and rocky at home, as the growth of the company contributed to tension in Lillian's marriage. In 1969, four years after Lillian changed the company name to the Lillian Vernon Corporation, she and Hochberg divorced. She was remarried in 1970 to Robert Katz, a display fixture manufacturer.

With her sons in prep school and college by this time, Lillian kicked the company's activity into high gear, taking buying trips to Europe and Asia, expanding her distribution facilities, and installing a high-tech communications center to process the 30,000 phone orders received weekly. Annual sales had exceeded $1 million by 1970. Beginning in the mid-1970s, Lillian imported extensively from other countries, acting in 1974 as one of the first American companies to conduct business with mainland China. By the mid-1980s, the various catalogs of the Lillian Vernon Corporation included products from over 33 countries. By the end of the decade, the corporation had gone public, and Lillian opened a massive new distribution center in Virginia Beach, Virginia.

The success of the Lillian Vernon Corporation is due to the business insight and tough negotiating skills of its owner. Famous among her colleagues as an autocratic individualist, she does not have many friends among her peers in the industry. She has fought a stream of criticism over the type of products she markets, reviled by some as downscale and tacky. Her response to such comments is to not only defend her taste but rally the demographic evidence that shows that her typical customer makes over $38,000 per year, spends over $34 per order, and is a repeat customer with fierce loyalty to Lillian Vernon products. An Opinion Research Poll discovered that over 47 million Americans are familiar with the Lillian Vernon name. She herself officially changed her name from Lillian Katz to Lillian Vernon in 1994.

Vernon continues to expand her marketing strategy. The corporation issues over eight distinct catalogs per year, and the firm recently launched its World Wide Web site, which features an on-line store. Assisted in the management of the company by her son, David Hochberg, Vernon nonetheless retains control of the empire she built from her kitchen table. As her son expressed in an interview, "She'll die at her desk . . . she'll never retire—it's out of the question."

BIBLIOGRAPHY

"About Lillian Vernon," http://www.lillianvernon. com/about.html; *Family Circle*, September 11, 1984; *New York Times*, August 18, 1985; Vernon, Lillian, *An Eye for Winners: How I Built One of America's Greatest Direct-Mail Businesses*, 1996; *Working Woman*, November 1986 and June 1989.

von Fürstenberg, Diane

(December 31, 1946–)
Manufacturer

Launching a business on the strength of three simple silk-jersey dress designs and the support of the fashion editor of *Vogue* magazine, Diane von Fürstenberg astonished clothing manufacturers who had disparaged her work by becoming a multimillionaire before the age of 34. Relying more on intuition about women's preferences than great understanding of fashion design, she rev-

Diane von Fürstenberg (Archive Photos)

olutionized the fashion industry by creating reasonably priced, eminently wearable dresses that captivated the American public.

Born in Brussels, Belgium, on December 31, 1946, to affluent Jewish parents Leon and Liliane Nahmias Halfin, Diane was originally named Diane Simone Michelle Halfin. Her father's background in the electronics business, combined with her mother's resilience in surviving a Nazi concentration camp, instilled young Diane with intense determination and the self-assurance needed to succeed.

After her parents divorced, Diane bounced between finishing schools in Switzerland, Spain, and England, eventually enrolling at the University of Madrid in 1965. After one year, Diane left to study economics at the University of Geneva. During her stay in Geneva, she fell in love with the heir to the Fiat fortune, Prince Edward Egon von Fürstenberg. On July 16, 1969, wearing a dress of her own design, Diane married von Fürstenberg in Paris.

Later that year, Diane launched what would become a stellar fashion career with an inauspicious start as an intern to an Italian textile manufacturer, Angelo Ferretti. Though she had not planned on a career in design, she observed the lack of basic, relatively inexpensive dresses on the market. Using the silk-jersey print fabrics made by Ferretti, Diane designed three simple dresses.

After fighting rejection by New York clothing makers, Diane won support from the editor of *Vogue* magazine, Diana Vreeland, who enthusiastically promoted one of the dresses in an issue of the magazine. At Vreeland's suggestion, she prepared a small collection of 30 items to introduce at a showing for the press at the

Gotham Hotel. The show took place in April 1970. Featuring tunics, hooded capes, and shirtwaist midi-dresses in a variety of prints and textures, her entire collection was priced between $25 to $100 apiece.

Diane was instantly inundated with orders and was overwhelmed by her inability to have the clothing, which was sewn in Italy, prepared fast enough. After unsuccessfully trying to establish her line as a division of a larger manufacturer, she secured a $30,000 loan from her father to open a showroom in April 1972. By the end of the year, Diane's designs were earning revenues of over $1 million, and within five years, gross annual income exceeded $142 million.

Diane's trademark design was her original simple, clinging dress in bold geometric patterns. All of her designs demonstrated her preference for flattering yet practical clothing. Her dresses were so popular largely because they invoked the elegance of high fashion, yet were designed with the typical woman—and her budget—in mind. Occasionally belittled by established fashion designers, Diane has been known to respond, "I never pretended I was a fabulous designer. I am a woman who makes clothes."

In the late 1970s, Diane began to diversify her product line. In addition to costume jewelry, scarves, shoes, and sunglasses, Diane, who was not allowed as a teenager to wear makeup, created a line of cosmetics and skin-care products. She has also licensed her name for use on additional products through lucrative franchising arrangements.

In 1975, Diane and her husband divorced, although she retained custody of the children, Alexandre and Tatiana. The woman who became a multimillionaire by age 34 and has led an active social life with celebrity friends now splits her time between a lavish apartment in New York City and a farmhouse in rural Connecticut. She maintains an active management role in her company.

BIBLIOGRAPHY

Cunningham, Sheila, "Success Story: Diane Von Fürstenberg," *Working Woman*, September 1980; Francke, Lynda Bird, et al., "Princess of Fashion," *Newsweek*, March 22, 1976; Kaye, D., and F. Ruffin, "How to Make a Million before You're 34," Redbook, May 1977; *Vogue*, July 1976.

Wachner, Linda

(February 3, 1946–)
Manufacturer

When Linda Joy Wachner acquired the Warnaco Group, an apparel manufacturer, she made history as the first woman to ever obtain an American corporation in a hostile takeover. A tireless worker and a demanding boss, as head of Warnaco she raised a storm of controversy while boosting company profits.

Born on February 3, 1946, in New York City to Herman and Shirley Wachner, Linda received her B.A. degree in economics from the University of Buffalo in 1966 and entered the retail business as a junior buyer at Foley's Department Store in Houston, Texas. She had determined as a child to one day own her own company, and with this start she set her sights on reaching her goal. At Foley's she frequently walked the sales floor and talked with customers about products. Her dynamic approach earned her the attention of Macy's Department Store in New York City, with the result that in 1969 she began working there as a senior buyer.

In 1974, she left Macy's to become the vice president of Warnaco's Warner Division in Bridgeport, Connecticut. Warner's manufactured and marketed women's undergarments, and Wachner soon dramatically improved the company's sales when she decided that bras in department stores should be taken out of their boxes and draped on hangers for display.

Her success at Warnaco led to other positions, most notably her appointment as president of Max Factor Cosmetics in 1982. Yet she still had not achieved her goal of ownership, so in 1986 she and a group of investors tried to buy another leading cosmetics and perfume business, Revlon. That effort failed, however, and Wachner then set her sights on Warnaco, the company for which she had worked just a few years before.

In 1987, she borrowed $3 million and directed a $480 million leveraged buyout of Warnaco, making her one of the few women to ever head a *Fortune* 500 company. She then took action to make the underachieving firm more profitable by reorganizing it into such divisions as Hathaway Shirts, Christian Dior, and Chaps by Ralph Lauren. Wachner eliminated slow-selling lines and closed most of the Warnaco outlet stores. In all, the annual savings amounted to over $30 million. She also made an effort to boost international sales, which was aimed at making Warnaco, in her words, "the foremost apparel conglomerate in the world."

Between 1991 and 1996, Warnaco stock climbed 130 percent. Wachner's worth based on her holdings in Warnaco and in another company, Authentic Fitness (makers of Speedo and Ann Cole swimwear), topped $100 million. Yet controversy surrounded her success. She earned a widespread reputation for being one of the toughest bosses in corporate America. Rumor had it that she advised an associate to fire several of his employees to show them he meant business. Turnover at her companies was high, causing one observer to comment: "Warnaco has gotten a reputation for having a revolving door in the executive suite."

Wachner earned the enmity of workers at the Hathaway plant in Waterville, Maine, when she reneged on a promise.

She had told them that if they cut costs and boosted production she would keep the low-profit company afloat. They did, but in 1996 Wachner announced she was closing the plant (while workers in Honduras sewed the shirts for a fraction of the $7.50 an hour paid at Waterville). The workers knew that if mismanagement at the plant could be corrected, the business would survive. As a result, they joined with an investment group that bought the factory, restructured operations, and restored its profitability and reputation for making quality shirts.

In 1995, Wachner reached a deal with Australian media mogul Rupert Murdoch to promote Warnaco's most popular lines, Olga bras and Fruit of the Loom underwear, over his regional television network in Asia. At the same time, she made plans to expand the number of Authentic Fitness stores in the United States from 50 to 200, and in an innovative arrangement with Bally Health Clubs she opened Speedo shops in some of its 350 establishments.

Wachner, a widow who liked to be called "Miss Linda," regularly traveled by helicopter between company headquarters on New York City's Park Avenue and her mansion in the Hamptons on Long Island.

BIBLIOGRAPHY

Barman, Sharon, "Wachner Takes on the World," *Working Woman*, February 1995; Rice, Faye, "Linda Wachner Finally Gets a Company," *Fortune*, May 26, 1986; Serwer, Andrew, "A Wachnerian Soap Opera," *Fortune*, May 12, 1997; Taylor, Alex III, "New Outfit or a Queen of Beauty," *Fortune*, January 5, 1987; Zagorin, Adam, "Short-Shirted in Maine," *Time*, June 3, 1996.

Walgreen, Charles

(October 9, 1873–December 11, 1939)
Merchant

From Charles Rudolph Walgreen came not only the drugstore lunch counter and a double-rich malted milk but also the first major drugstore chain, Walgreen's.

Born on October 9, 1873, on a farm near Galesburg, Illinois, to Charles Walgreen and Ellen (Olson) Walgreen, young Charles moved with his family in 1887 to Dixon, Illinois, where he graduated from public school and attended a local business college.

In the early 1890s, his career path was set by an accident. When he lost the first joint of a finger, the doctor who treated him influenced him to become a druggist's apprentice. In 1893, Walgreen began working at drugstores in Chicago during the day and studying pharmacology at night. By 1897, he was a registered pharmacist, but when the Spanish-American War erupted the following year, he left his job to join the U.S. Army.

After his discharge, Walgreen found work as a pharmacist with Isaac W. Blood, a druggist in Chicago. When Blood retired in 1901, Walgreen used his savings to buy the store. The following year, he married Myrtle R. Norton; they had three children.

Walgreen decided to base his prices on a percentage of profits and to sell products cheaper than his competitors. Toward this end, he began making some of his products. He also opened a soda fountain—a small marble slab, wash basin, and wall case of inverted syrup bottles. Other pharmacists operated soda fountains, too, but Walgreen soon changed the nature of them when he began selling homemade soup, hot sandwiches, and desserts prepared by his wife.

As his first store prospered, he bought a second one in 1909. That year, he began making his own ice cream, and opened a larger fountain in a vacant building next door to the new location. There his soda clerks served phosphates, banana splits, sodas, sundaes, and ice-cream cones. Another of Walgreen's food innovations occurred in 1922 when the fountain manager at his store in the Chicago Loop, Ivar "Pop" Coulsen, concocted the first double-rich chocolate malted milk by adding to the traditional drink two scoops of vanilla ice cream.

Walgreen created the nation's first drugstore chain and, by 1925, had 65 stores. In 1933, in the depths of the Great Depression, his company paid its first stock dividend. Walgreen designed his stores to be bright, as opposed to the dingy atmosphere found in most turn-of-the-century drugstores, and was among the first retailers to use window and open displays, although he still relied on clerks providing service.

When Walgreen died on December 11, 1939, his son, Charles R. Walgreen Jr., took over the company and converted the expanding chain into self-service stores. In 1969, Charles R. Walgreen III, like his father and grandfather a registered pharmacist, became company president and in 1976 chairman of the board. During the 1970s, Walgreen's suffered when it diversified into discount retailing, but the company sold those acquisitions to again focus on drugstores, and in the 1980s sales climbed. In 1997, the chain operated more than 2,400 stores in 34 states and Puerto Rico, with annual sales topping $10 billion.

BIBLIOGRAPHY

Morgan, John J. B., and E. T. Webb, *Making the Most of Your Life*, 1932; Simon, Ruth, "Pills and Profits," *Forbes*, June 30, 1986.

Walker, Sarah

(December 23, 1867–May 25, 1919)
Merchant

A pioneer African-American business woman, Sarah Breedlove Walker built a million-dollar business and promoted black pride based on her "Walker Method" of hair care.

Born on December 23, 1867, in Delta, Louisiana, to Owen and Minerva Breedlove and orphaned in early childhood, Sarah grew up in poverty. She married at age 14 and bore a daughter, A'Lelia. At age 20, Sarah's, husband died, and she moved to St. Louis, Missouri, where she worked as a washerwoman.

In 1905, she came upon an idea—she said it appeared to her in a dream—to make a formula that would improve the appearance of black women by making their hair straight and shiny. Mixing soaps and ointments and experimenting with existing treatments, she developed "The Walker Method," which consisted of a shampoo, a pomade, vigorous brushing, and heated iron combs. After trying the method on herself and friends in St. Louis, she moved to Denver, Colorado, where she engaged in more preliminary work on the method, and married Charles J. Walker, a newspaperman.

She soon began promoting her method door-to-door, and as business expanded she hired agents to help her. By 1907, she had established manufacturing headquarters in Denver and had begun traveling through the South and East, giving lectures and presenting demonstrations to African-American groups. In 1908, she opened a second office in Pittsburgh, Pennsylvania, which her daughter managed. Two years later, she combined the offices and moved them to Indianapolis as The Madame C. J. Walker Manufacturing Company. She preferred in her later years to be called Madame Walker.

As president and owner of the company, she built a business that employed about 3,000 people, mainly women called "Walker Agents." Dressed in white blouses and long black skirts, and carrying black satchels containing Walker's preparations, they made house calls in the United States and in Caribbean countries. Of all the products offered, Madame C. J. Walker's Hair Grower sold best.

Madame Walker continued her own instructional lectures, and by World War I was one of the best-known African Americans in the nation. She believed her products beneficial not only to the women who used them but also to the black community as a whole, for they encouraged racial beauty. And she taught her agents that cleanliness and loveliness were important in advancing black self-respect.

Walker invested money in real estate and in 1914 moved to New York City, where she built a town house. Three years later, she built Villa Lewaro, an exclusive country home at Irvington-on-Hudson, New York. A philanthropist, she donated money to the National Association for the Advancement of Colored People, to the needy in Indianapolis, and to Tuskegee Institute for scholarships.

Madame Walker died on May 25, 1919, at Villa Lewaro, leaving a million-dollar estate. She willed most of it, along with the ownership of her business, to her daughter, A'Lelia. In the 1920s, A'Lelia (then Mrs. A'Lelia Walker Robinson Wilson Kennedy) presided over a famous salon in Harlem that brought together white and black artists and intellectuals and helped stimulate the Harlem Renaissance.

BIBLIOGRAPHY

Bundles, A'Lelia Perry, *Madame C. J. Walker*, 1991; Doyle, Kathleen, "Madam C. J. Walker: First Black Woman Millionaire," *American History Illustrated*, 1989.

Wallace, Dewitt

(November 12, 1889–March 30, 1981)
Publisher

When asked what he wanted as an epitaph, Dewitt Wallace said, "The final condensation"—a phrase that reflected his fame in founding the leading publication of condensed articles, *Reader's Digest.*

Born on November 12, 1889, in St. Paul, Minnesota, Wallace, whose father was a Presbyterian minister, adopted strong Christian beliefs at an early age. After attending Macalester College in his hometown and the University of California at Berkeley, he wrote publicity for Westinghouse Electric in Pittsburgh, Pennsylvania. At the same time, he published a booklet that summarized hundreds of free pamphlets for farmers. When World War I erupted, Wallace joined the army and was wounded while fighting on the western front.

After his return home, he married Lila Acheson, and decided to publish a magazine that would appeal to an increasingly busy, urban population by presenting condensed versions of articles that originally appeared elsewhere. In 1920, after several publishers rejected his idea, Wallace and his wife composed a sample copy of *Reader's Digest* and mailed out thousands of subscription appeals. They received 1,500 commitments, and although Wallace was disappointed in the response, Lila convinced him to proceed with the magazine. They issued the first edition in February 1922.

From the start such articles as "How to Keep Young Mentally," "Watch Your Dog and Be Wise," and "The Firefly's Light" showed that *Reader's Digest* would appeal to a mass audience with wholesome stories emphasizing middle-class values and American pieties. Wallace intended his publication to reflect his own Christian moral upbringing and to present articles in basic English that was widely accessible. Intellectuals panned it, but Wallace had tapped the heart of middle America, and circulation rapidly increased, reaching 216,000 just seven years after the magazine's start.

In the 1930s, Wallace began using articles expressly written for *Reader's Digest* to accompany the condensations. During that decade, he moved the company's headquarters to Pleasantville, New York, and expanded overseas with editions in England, Spain, and Portugal.

During the cold war, Wallace took a strongly conservative, anti-Communist position. By the mid-1950s, *Reader's Digest* was being published in 16 languages and had over 30 million readers. Wallace expanded the company's publishing in the 1960s to produce condensed books, encyclopedias, and classic reprints through Reader's Digest Books.

Dewitt and Lila Wallace ran everything. "We do as we damn well please," he once said, "and that's close to ideal." Even after he officially retired in the 1970s, he still made the decisions. When Dewitt died on March 30, 1981, he left 50 percent of the voting stock to Lila, who already owned nearly all of the other shares. After she died three years later, the company underwent a substantial shake-up in leadership, a result of declining profits as well as the childless Wallaces' inability to keep the company in the family. Despite those problems, in the mid-1990s, *Reader's Digest* ranked as the third best-selling magazine in the nation.

BIBLIOGRAPHY

Canning, Peter, *American Dreamers: The Wallaces and* Reader's Digest: *An Insider's Story*, 1996; Heidenry, John, *Theirs Was the Kingdom: Lila and DeWitt Wallace and the Story of* Reader's Digest, 1993.

Wallace, Dwane

(October 29, 1911–December 21, 1978)
Manufacturer

Taking over the floundering aircraft company launched by his uncle Clyde Cessna, Dwane L. Wallace built the Cessna Aircraft Company into the world leader in light airplane manufacturing. Wallace was a bold designer who emphasized efficient production techniques and high-quality standards. The company's breakthrough came when Wallace secured large military contracts for his aircraft during World War II. He used these profits to realize his dreams of making and selling reasonably priced small planes to the public and businesses.

Wallace was born in Belmont, Kansas, on October 29, 1911. His uncle Clyde Cessna was one of the premier designers and builders in early aviation. Cessna got his start as an automobile salesman but fell in love with airplanes after attending an air show in Oklahoma City in February 1911. During the next 14 years, he managed his Kansas farm and spent his spare time building and flying light airplanes. Through this experience, Cessna became a master builder, and after initially failing to start his own business, he joined with Walter Beecher and others in 1925 to organize the Travel Air Company.

In 1927, Cessna sold his stake in that company to form his own, naming it the Cessna Aircraft Company. Just as the company began to take off, the Great Depression set in, and Cessna aircraft closed down in 1931.

Wallace first flew with his uncle Clyde Cessna at age nine and grew to share his uncle's enthusiasm for airplanes. Wallace attended Wichita University and earned a degree in aeronautical engineering with hopes of joining Cessna's company as an engineer. He graduated soon after his uncle's plant closed down and instead went to work for Beech Aircraft.

In 1933, Wallace convinced his uncle to reopen his aircraft factory and volunteered to manage the plant without pay. He set to work designing a fast and efficient four-seat cabin plane, the C-34. The plane was an instant success, and Wallace took over the company when Cessna retired in 1936.

Wallace promoted his plane by competing in and winning flying contests, prompting would-be barnstormers to flock to buy the aircraft. In 1937, Wallace introduced the improved C-37 model and began designing a plane that would evolve into the T-50, a light training plane that was easy to fly and construct. The ease of manufacturing the T-50 allowed Wallace to institute production-line techniques that dramatically lowered the price and availability of his planes to the public.

Despite these engineering successes, the young company and its leader were in dire financial straits in 1939. Wallace had poured literally every dollar from the company treasury into the development of the T-50 model. That same year, however, Wallace made a deal that catapulted the company into greatness.

Wallace traveled to New York City to make a presentation about the T-50 to the British Purchasing Commission, which was in charge of buying war supplies for Great Britain. His confidence persuaded the commission to grant his company a $6.8 million contract for planes, and large orders from Canada and the U.S. military soon followed. These contracts represented a major turning point for the company, allowing it to significantly expand its production facilities. During World War II, Cessna was able to supply over 5,000 T-50 trainers to the U.S. Army, and by 1943 total sales had reached $71 million. Wallace married Velma Ruth Lunt on September 8, 1941, and the couple eventually had four daughters—Linda, Karen, Diana, and Sarah.

After the war, Wallace used the wartime profits to develop his commercial private aircraft line starting with the 120/140 series. Cessna Aircraft was one of the few companies to maintain its profitability after the demand for military planes dried up. By the early 1950s, Wallace had established Cessna as one of the leaders in the light plane industry, and in the latter half of the decade, Cessna's

sales rose 112 percent, surpassing Beech Aircraft as the largest manufacturer of small private airplanes. The company delivered 6,416 planes in 1958, and Wallace had good reason to be optimistic about the next decade.

In the 1960s, Cessna enjoyed continued sales growth, but Wallace made two costly decisions. The first was his attempt to manufacture helicopters and tap what he considered to be a large, unforeseen market. There was no public demand, but it took Wallace 10 years to finally abandon the project.

Wallace's second new idea was to develop a small jet plane called the Citation, for private business needs. The development costs ran into the millions, and the Citation's success was initially doubted. Wallace firmly believed in the new jet, and his faith was finally vindicated in 1974, when the Citation began returning profits. Within 10 years, the Citation had become the best-selling business jet in the country. In the same time period, however, sales of other Cessna models had seemingly leveled off due to market saturation.

At the time of his retirement in 1975, Wallace remained optimistic that Cessna's sales would recover. After retiring, Wallace was largely forgotten by the company, and he was content to move into seats on the boards of the Coleman Company and the Fourth National Bank of Wichita until his death on December 21, 1978.

BIBLIOGRAPHY

Deneau, Gerald, *An Eye on the Sky*, 1962; *Fortune*, April 1952; Gunston, Bill, *The Planemakers*, 1980; Rosenberg, C.R., *The Challenging Skies*, 1966.

Walton, Sam

(March 29, 1918–April 5, 1992)
Merchant

"Like Henry Ford with his Model T," said a professor of rural sociology at the University of Missouri, "Sam Walton and his Wal-marts, for better or for worse, transformed small-town America." Others think he transformed the entire nation.

Born in Kingfisher, Oklahoma, on March 29, 1918, to Thomas and Nancy Walton, Samuel Moore Walton lived in several different small towns as his father, a farm-mortgage broker, moved about. Then, in 1926, the family settled in Columbia, Missouri. During the Great Depression, young Sam attended Hickman High School, from which he graduated in 1936 after having been quarterback of the football team, captain of the basketball team, and president of the senior class. He studied economics at the University of Missouri and received his B.A. degree in 1940.

At that point, Walton entered the retail business when he began working at a J. C. Penney store in Des Moines, Iowa. With the outbreak of World War II, he served as an officer in the Army Intelligence Corps, a position that kept him stateside. Soon after the war, he used his savings and a loan to franchise a Ben Franklin variety store in Newport, Arkansas.

He boosted sales through an unusual method: "It didn't take me long to start experimenting," he later recalled, "that's just the way I am. I was always looking for offbeat suppliers or sources. I started driving over to Tennessee to some fellows I found who would give me special buys at prices way below what Ben Franklin was charging me. . . . I'd stuff [my] car and trailer with whatever I could get good deals on—usually on soft lines: ladies' panties and nylons, men's shirts—and I'd bring them back, price them low, and just blow that stuff out the store."

Walton lost his store, however, in 1950 when the landlord refused to renew the lease. He then moved to Bentonville, Arkansas, where he and a younger brother franchised another Ben Franklin store. Walton employed a new self-service system, one he had discovered at two Ben Franklins in Minnesota: no clerks or cash registers around the store, only checkout lanes in the front. By 1960, Walton had 15 stores in Arkansas and Missouri and had laid the foundation for his own discount chain.

By the early 1960s, retailers had developed the discount superstore concept—Korvette, Caldor, Kmart, Zayre, and Woolworth's all opened such stores using self-service, large inventories, and massive parking lots. Walton joined them in 1962 when he opened his first Wal-Mart Discount City in Rogers, Arkansas. At least one observer called it a mess—with donkey rides and watermelons mixed together outside under a boiling sun and merchandise haphazardly arranged inside.

But Walton quickly brought order to his enterprise and pursued an important new concept: large discount stores in small towns. Walton saw cities saturated with retailers and believed he could prosper in towns that the larger companies had written off. At first, Wal-Mart grew slowly—25 stores by 1970, well behind Kmart and others. Then expansion exploded: 64 stores by the end of 1972 with sales reaching $125 million. The folksy Walton, who liked to fly in his Cessna and scout locations for new stores, owned the eighth largest retail business in America by 1983, and *Forbes* magazine estimated his worth at $2.15 billion.

At that time, Walton altered his company's direction and began building Wal-Mart stores in larger suburbs. By 1989, more than 1,300 Wal-Marts spread from the East Coast to Colorado with sales approaching $26 billion. Walton had opened Sam's Clubs, too—warehouse-style stores that sold merchandise at discount prices in bulk—and he founded Wal-Mart Super-centers, ranging from 97,000 to 211,000 square feet, that featured a supermarket and a regular Wal-Mart under one roof.

Walton often visited his stores, dropping in unannounced to check the layouts and books, and talk to his employees, or what Wal-Mart called "associates." He prided himself on a profit-sharing program and a friendly, open atmosphere. He often led his workers in a cheer—some called corny, others uplifting. He once described it, "Give me a W! Give me an A! Give me an L! Give me a Squiggly! (Here, everybody sort of does the twist.) Give me an M! Give me an A! Give me an R! Give me a T! What's that spell? Wal-Mart! What's that spell? Wal-Mart! Who's No. 1? THE CUSTOMER!"

Critics were not inclined to cheer for Wal-Mart, however. Suppliers complained that the company acted as if they owed it something. Many small-town merchants dreaded the arrival of Wal-Mart because it destroyed their businesses and converted Main Street into a deserted street.

Wal-Mart, said others, contributed to suburban sprawl, to American neighborhoods without a focus, and to ugliness as each Wal-Mart looked like every other, a drab box.

In 1991, while Walton reached a pinnacle as America's wealthiest person, Wal-Mart surpassed Sears as the nation's largest retailer. The company had stores in 43 states and Mexico. Meanwhile, Walton offered his own formula for how a large company must operate:

> Think one store at a time. That sounds easy enough, but it's something we've constantly had to stay on top of.

> Communicate, communicate, communicate: If you had to boil down the Wal-Mart system to one single idea, it would probably be communication because it is one of the real keys to our success. What good is figuring out a better way to sell beach towels if you aren't going to tell everybody in your company about it?

> Keep your ear to the ground: A computer is not—and will never be—a substitute for getting out in your stores and learning what's going on.

Walton died of leukemia in Little Rock, Arkansas, on April 5, 1992. Since then, Wal-Mart has marched on to more stores, to bigger stores, and to a ubiquitous presence.

BIBLIOGRAPHY

Teutsch, Austin, *The Sam Walton Story: The Retailing of Middle America*, 1991; Trimble, Vance H., *Sam Walton: The Inside Story of America's Richest Man*, 1990; Walton, Sam, *Sam Walton, Made in America: My Story*, 1992.

Wanamaker, John

(July 11, 1838–December 12, 1922)
Merchant

As America urbanized after the Civil War, shopping habits changed considerably and there emerged what some called "consumers' palaces," more popularly known as department stores. Along with ROWLAND MACY and a few other retailers, John Wanamaker pioneered in developing these new establishments.

Born on July 11, 1838, in Philadelphia, Pennsylvania, the son of Nelson Wanamaker and Elizabeth Deshong (Kochersperger) Wanamaker, John began working at age 13 as an errand boy at a publishing company. After a brief stint as a clothing salesman and a bout with poor health, in 1857 Wanamaker became the secretary of the Young Men's Christian Association in Philadelphia, earning $1,000 a year. In 1860, he married Mary Erringer Brown.

The following year, Wanamaker and his brother-in-law, Nathan Brown, founded a men's clothing business that within 10 years developed into the largest such store in the nation. In 1869, one year after Brown's death, Wanamaker opened a more fashionable store called John Wanamaker & Company. With a flair for publicity and showmanship, Wanamaker prepared for the upcoming Centennial Exposition in Philadelphia by converting an old railroad depot into a huge dry-goods and men's clothing store. Called "The Depot," it attracted many tourists who came to Philadelphia in 1876. After the exposition he converted The Depot into a collection of specialty shops under one roof, thus creating one of the first department stores.

By the late 1870s, Wanamaker owned three stores: the original one he had founded with Brown, John Wanamaker & Company, and The Depot. His two sons entered the business, lightening his workload and allowing him to expand further in 1896, when he opened a store in New York City.

Wanamaker also entered politics, having donated to Republican candidates in the past. In 1896, he sought the Republican nomination for the U.S. Senate, and in 1898 the governorship of Pennsylvania. He lost both electoral races.

After nearly going broke during the Panic of 1907, Wanamaker recovered and his stores again prospered. Throughout the development of his stores, Wanamaker showed a keen sense for innovative adaptation. He guaranteed money back to dissatisfied customers, engaged in massive newspaper advertising (some credit him with placing the first full-page newspaper ad), and established numerous benefits for his employees.

Wanamaker remained active in his business until his death on December 12, 1922. His son Rodman succeeded him as sole owner of the two department stores. (Wanamaker's wife had died in 1920.) Two daughters also survived him.

BIBLIOGRAPHY

Appel, Joseph Herbert, *The Business Biography of John Wanamaker*, 1930; Appel, Joseph Herbert, *John Wanamker: A Study*, 1927; Gibbons, Herbert Adams, *John Wanamaker*, 1926.

Wang, An

(February 7, 1920–March 24, 1990)
Inventor, Manufacturer

In founding Wang Laboratories, An Wang led the massive technological revolution that swept America after World War II. He ushered in the computer age by inventing the magnetic memory core that made data storage possible prior to the microchip.

An was born on February 7, 1920, in Shanghai, China, to Yin Lu Wang and Zen Wan (Chien) Wang. His father taught English at a private elementary school and later practiced herbal medicine. An Wang entered Chiao Tung University, a college highly regarded for its technological programs, at only 16 years of age. He studied electrical engineering and communications, and, using the English his father had taught him, translated articles into Chinese for a scientific digest.

After graduating with a B.S. degree in 1941, Wang remained at the university as a teaching assistant in electrical engineering, while also designing transmitters and radios for the army. He first came to the United States in 1945 as a technical observer to learn more about engineering. That September, he decided to enter the master's program at Harvard and received his degree the following year.

Following a brief stint as a clerical worker for a Chinese government office in Canada, Wang returned to Harvard and enrolled in the doctoral program in applied physics. Although his studies had little to do with computer science, he used the technology in his work, and later said that Harvard "introduced me to computers and let me in on the very early stage of their development."

By that time, China was in the throes of a Communist revolution, and Wang, fearing a dictatorial government, had no desire to return home; instead, he stayed at Harvard as a research fellow in the computations laboratory. Challenged to develop a way to store data on a computer without adding to its moving parts, he invented the magnetic memory core, doughnut-shaped rings of iron. Until the end of the 1960s, his invention—the first of several that led to his securing 40 patents—was used for computer memory.

Wang left Harvard in 1951 and founded his own company to manufacture and sell memory cores and develop other projects. With $600 in savings, he opened his business in a loft in Boston, Massachusetts. He moved the company to nearby Cambridge in 1954, and in 1955 incorporated Wang Laboratories with himself as president. The following year, Wang sold his memory core patent to International Business Machines (IBM) for $400,000. He later complained, however, that he had been victimized by IBM. The company, he said, had paid another inventor to challenge Wang's patent, creating uncertainty that drove down his asking price. True or not, the deal convinced Wang to stand firm against corporate giants.

Wang developed several other inventions over the next few years, most notably a scientific desk calculator in 1964 that sold for $6,500 and, a short time later, a desk top calculator at a lower price, intended for office use. Increasingly, he focused on inventions applicable to everyday work. He dominated the calculator market, and by 1967 his company's sales neared $7 million.

In a controversial move that caused dissension within Wang Laboratories, he decided to enter the word and data processing market in the early 1970s, going head to head with his nemesis IBM and other large corporations. He sold the 1200 Word Processing System, described as a "thinking typewriter," in 1972 and, three years later, the Wang Computer System. In terms of sales, his strategy resulted in Wang Laboratories climbing into second place, surpassed only by IBM, in small-business computers, and third place in word processing. In 1978, he launched the Office Information Systems that linked word and data processing.

Wang had a reputation for autocratic rule, but in 1981 he turned over his leadership to a management committee. Semiretired, he devoted most of his time to philanthropy. He gave $4 million in 1981 to Boston's Performing Arts Center so it could rebuild the roof of its theater, another $4 million to Harvard, $1 million to Wellesley College, and $6 million to found the Wang Institute of Graduate Studies for software engineers and China scholars. He also built a $15 million factory in Boston's Chinatown to provide jobs for inner-city residents.

In the mid-1980s, Wang Laboratories suffered reversals that caused it to lay off 1,600 workers. To confront the crisis, Wang in 1985 again took charge and addressed complaints from customers about delayed deliveries, poor service, and inadequate software. In 1986, Wang obtained a $480 million contract to provide minicomputers to the U.S. Air Force.

That same year, Wang's son, Frederick Wang, took control, but the company faltered again and, in 1989, lost more than $400 million. Frederick Wang was forced to resign, but this time, An Wang could not be a savior. Already ill from cancer, he died on March 24, 1990.

In the mid-1990s, Wang Global (the company's new name), with headquarters in Billerica, Massachusetts, achieved annual revenues of $3 billion from designing, installing, operating, and maintaining computing and telecommunications networks. For example, in 1994, Dell, the firm founded by MICHAEL DELL, awarded Wang a contract to provide on-site maintenance for the computers it sold, and in 1998 Wang and Microsoft, the software company founded by BILL GATES, reached an agreement to link Microsoft programs with Wang's business programs. Wang Global employed more than 21,000 workers and had subsidiaries in more than 40 countries.

BIBLIOGRAPHY
Wang, An, *Lessons*, 1986.

Ward, Aaron

(February 17, 1843-December 7, 1913)
Merchant

Aaron Montgomery Ward overcame the distrust of farmers toward buying goods from a catalog and established the nation's first large-scale mail-order service, Montgomery Ward.

Born on February 17, 1843, in Chatham, New Jersey, the son of Sylvester A. Ward and Julia Laura Mary (Green) Ward, Aaron moved with his parents to Niles, Michigan, while still a child and attended public school until age 14. After that time, he held a variety of jobs over several years, among them apprentice in a barrel-stave factory, laborer in a brickyard, and clerk in a general store. The occupation that changed his life, however, and propelled him into mail order was that of traveling salesman for a dry-goods wholesaler in St. Louis, Missouri.

As he traversed the countryside, Ward observed that farmers suffered from having to pay high prices, relative to their income, for goods bought at general stores. He got the idea to buy large quantities of goods at reduced cost from manufacturers, store them at a central location, and pass the savings on to farmers. As he began to formulate his plan, the Chicago fire of 1871 nearly wiped out his savings.

The following year his fortunes improved. He entered into marriage with Elizabeth J. Cobb. He also entered into partnership with C. W. Pardridge, and established their business in a 12-x-14-foot loft over a Chicago livery stable. Ward produced a single-page price sheet that listed the items he had for sale and mailed it to farmers.

Within two years, the price sheet expanded to 8 pages, and soon after that, a

Aaron Ward (Archive Photos)

72-page catalog. He sold fans, parasols, writing paper, needles, stereoscopes, cutlery, trunks, harnesses, and many other items—all advertised at great savings because he had eliminated the middleman.

In building his business, Ward had to overcome the farmers' habit of shopping at general stores, and he had to overcome their distrust in dealing with a distant company. He did so in several ways. First, he sold goods to the Grange, a populist farm organization. In earning their goodwill, he described his business on his catalog cover as "The Original Grange Supply House" and offered Grange members special discounts. Second, he provided an ironclad guarantee, promising that all goods could be returned if found to be defective or lacking. And third, he included in his catalogs drawings of most items, and of himself and those who worked at his company. The product sketches reassured farmers that they were not buying a pig in a poke; the other sketches personalized Ward's company.

He was so successful, that along with increased orders, he received personal requests that reflected the farmers' loneliness and trust. They sometimes asked him to select birthday gifts from the catalog. One asked him to find some summer boarders, and another asked him for a name of a baby to adopt.

Ward sincerely cared about his customers and about the public in general, as reflected in his successful effort to establish a park in Chicago along Michigan Avenue so as to maintain an open view of the lake. Ward died on December 7, 1913. Childless, he left his fortune to his wife, and she donated substantial sums to community projects. Ward's catalog encouraged another young man, RICHARD SEARS, to found a similar business.

BIBLIOGRAPHY

Herndon, Booton, *Satisfaction Guaranteed: An Unconventional Report to Today's Consumers*, 1972; Latham, Frank Brown, *1872–1972: A Century of Serving Consumers, the Story of Montgomery Ward*, 1972.

Warner, Albert

(July 23, 1884–November 26, 1967)
Entertainment Executive

When motion pictures first appeared in American society in the early twentieth century, the Warner brothers—Albert Warner, HARRY WARNER, SAMUEL WARNER, and JACK WARNER—developed a production company committed to realistic, often critical portrayals of society.

The three elder brothers, Albert, Harry, and Samuel, were born in Poland; Albert on July 23, 1884, Harry on December 12, 1881, and Samuel on August 10, 1887. Their parents, Benjamin Warner and Pearl (Eichelbaum) Warner, had moved there from Russia. Around 1890, the family immigrated to Canada, where Benjamin sold pots and pans. Soon after Jack's birth on August 2, 1892, the family relocated to Youngstown, Ohio, residing in decrepit housing while Benjamin struggled to make a living as a cobbler.

During a trip to Pittsburgh in 1904, Harry saw his first motion picture. Enthralled, on his return to Youngstown, he convinced Albert and Samuel to join him in traveling from town to town and showing movies in theaters. Jack, who had been a minstrel singer, soon joined them as well, as did their sister, Rosie. Jack sang before each movie—and whenever the film broke—and Rosie played the piano. Soon the Warners saved enough money to open their own theater in Newcastle, Pennsylvania.

They and many other theater operators encountered a problem, however: they could never rely on movies being shipped to them on time or being shipped at all. Consequently, Harry got the idea of forming an alliance with other theater operators to put pressure on the studios to deliver the movies on schedule. From this came the nation's first movie distributorship, the Duquesne Amusement Supply Company. The outfit suffered, though, when producers opposed it as a drain on their profits, and in 1912 the Warners sold out.

Their setback convinced them, however, to make their own movies. They began shooting slapstick comedies in New York City, calling them "Warner Features." In 1917, they decided to pay James W. Gerard for permission to make his popular book *My Four Years in Germany* into a movie. Released the following year, it won critical acclaim and attracted large audiences. Within a few months, the Warners built a studio on Sunset Boulevard in Hollywood, California, and incorporated as Warner Brothers Pictures. In 1925, they purchased a distribution company called Vitagraph, a move that gave them an advantage over their competitors. Then Harry and Sam got together with Bell Laboratories and worked on a cumbersome system called Vitaphone synchronization that allowed them to add sound to movies. In 1926, Warner Brothers released *Don Juan*, starring John Barrymore, with a musical score. The movie, however, contained no voices.

That awaited Al Jolson's *The Jazz Singer*. Released in 1927, it featured Jolson singing and thus was the first "talkie." The movie was not supposed to contain any words, but Jolson had ad-libbed before the songs, and the technical difficulties involved in using the Vitaphone system prevented the scenes from being edited. Samuel never knew the movie's huge success, however—he died from pneumonia on October 5, 1927, the day before *The Jazz Singer* premiered. He was survived by his wife, Lina Basquette, and a daughter.

The following year, Warner Brothers produced *Lights of New York*, the first all-talking motion picture. With its reputation for innovation, the studio attracted such big stars as Leslie Howard, Edward G. Robinson, and James Cagney. In the 1930s, the Warners acquired the Stanley Company of America, which owned hundreds of movie theaters. Following Harry's advice, the studio soon bought radio companies and music publishers, and paid large sums to attract actors from its competitors. Throughout the decade, Warner Brothers made spectacles and movies dealing with social issues.

During World War II, the Warners produced several war movies, for which they won seven Oscars. In 1949, the federal government charged them with monopolistic practices and forced them to relinquish their theaters. Although the studio had several box-office hits in the 1950s, notably *A Star Is Born* and *Rebel without a Cause*, many actors disliked the Warners for joining in the Red Scare—a hunt for Communists—and blacklisting those who held unacceptable political views.

In the 1960s, television greatly damaged Warner Brothers, and by 1969 it had stopped making movies and based its survival on profits from its two record companies, Warner/Reprise and Atlantic. Kinney Services then bought control of Warner, and in the 1970s started making movies again, among them the hits *Woodstock*, *The Exorcist*, and *All the President's Men*. Kinney renamed the company Warner Communications. In the late 1980s, Warner merged with Time, Incorporated, creating Time Warner, an entertainment giant. Today, in addition to its other enterprises, including cable television, Time Warner dominates the music industry with a 21 percent share of the market.

Among the surviving founders of Warner Brothers after World War II, Albert Warner served as the studio's treasurer until his death on November 26, 1967. Harry Warner served as president until his death on July 25, 1958, and was survived by his wife Rea Levinson; they had four children. Jack Warner held the vice presidency, and, after Harry's death, the presidency, and supervised the selection of scripts and hiring of actors. He married several times, and his son, Jack Jr., worked for the studio. Warner Sr. died on September 2, 1978.

BIBLIOGRAPHY

Higham, Charles, *Warner Brothers*, 1975; Roddick, Nick, *A New Deal in Entertainment: Warner Brothers in the 1930s*, 1983.

Warner, Harry

(December 12, 1881–July 25, 1958)
Entertainment Executive

The Warner Brothers movie studio owes its creation to ALBERT WARNER, Harry Warner, SAMUEL WARNER, and JACK WARNER.

The three elder brothers, Albert, Harry, and Samuel, were born in Poland; Albert on July 23, 1884, Harry on December 12, 1881, and Samuel on August 10, 1887. Their parents, Benjamin Warner and Pearl (Eichelbaum) Warner, had moved there from Russia. Around 1890, the family immigrated to Canada, where Benjamin sold pots and pans. Soon after Jack's birth on August 2, 1892, the family relocated to Youngstown, Ohio, residing in decrepit housing while Benjamin struggled to make a living as a cobbler.

During a trip to Pittsburgh in 1904, Harry saw his first motion picture. Enthralled, on his return to Youngstown, he convinced Albert and Samuel to join him in traveling from town to town and showing movies in theaters. Jack, who had been a minstrel singer, soon joined them as well, as did their sister, Rosie. Jack sang before each movie—and whenever the film broke—and Rosie played the piano. Soon the Warners saved enough money to open their own theater in Newcastle, Pennsylvania.

They and many other theater operators encountered a problem, however: they could never rely on movies being shipped to them on time or being shipped at all. Consequently, Harry got the idea of forming an alliance with other theater operators to put pressure on the studios to deliver the movies on schedule. From this came the nation's first movie distributorship, the Duquesne Amusement Supply Company. The outfit suffered, though, when producers opposed it as a drain on their profits, and in 1912 the Warners sold out.

Their setback convinced them, however, to make their own movies. They began shooting slapstick comedies in New York City, calling them "Warner Features." In 1917, they decided to pay James W. Gerard for permission to make his popular book *My Four Years in Germany* into a movie. Released the following year, it won critical acclaim and attracted large audiences. Within a few months, the Warners built a studio on Sunset Boulevard in Hollywood, California, and incorporated as Warner Brothers Pictures. In 1925, they purchased a distribution company called Vitagraph, a move that gave them an advantage over their competitors. Then Harry and Sam got together with Bell Laboratories and worked on a cumbersome system called Vitaphone synchronization that allowed them to add sound to movies. In 1926, Warner Brothers released *Don Juan*, starring John Barrymore, with a musical score. The movie, however, contained no voices.

That awaited Al Jolson's *The Jazz Singer*. Released in 1927, it featured Jolson singing and thus was the first "talkie." The movie was not supposed to contain any words, but Jolson had ad-libbed before the songs, and the technical difficulties involved in using the Vitaphone system prevented the scenes from being edited. Samuel never knew the movie's huge success, however—he died from

pneumonia on October 5, 1927, the day before *The Jazz Singer* premiered. He was survived by his wife, Lina Basquette, and a daughter.

The following year, Warner Brothers produced *Lights of New York*, the first all-talking motion picture. With its reputation for innovation, the studio attracted such big stars as Leslie Howard, Edward G. Robinson, and James Cagney. In the 1930s, the Warners acquired the Stanley Company of America, which owned hundreds of movie theaters. Following Harry's advice, the studio soon bought radio companies and music publishers, and paid large sums to attract actors from its competitors. Throughout the decade, Warner Brothers made spectacles and movies dealing with social issues.

During World War II, the Warners produced several war movies, for which they won seven Oscars. In 1949, the federal government charged them with monopolistic practices and forced them to relinquish their theaters. Although the studio had several box-office hits in the 1950s, notably *A Star Is Born* and *Rebel without a Cause*, many actors disliked the Warners for joining in the Red Scare—a hunt for Communists—and blacklisting those who held unacceptable political views.

In the 1960s, television greatly damaged Warner Brothers, and by 1969 it had stopped making movies and based its survival on profits from its two record companies, Warner/Reprise and Atlantic. Kinney Services then bought control of Warner, and in the 1970s started making movies again, among them the hits *Woodstock*, *The Exorcist*, and *All the President's Men*. Kinney renamed the company Warner Communications. In the late 1980s, Warner merged with Time,

Incorporated, creating Time Warner, an entertainment giant. Today, in addition to its other enterprises, including cable television, Time Warner dominates the music industry with a 21 percent share of the market.

Among the surviving founders of Warner Brothers after World War II, Albert Warner served as the studio's treasurer until his death on November 26, 1967. Harry Warner served as president until his death on July 25, 1958, and was survived by his wife Rea Levinson; they had four children. Jack Warner held the vice presidency, and, after Harry's death, the presidency, and supervised the selection of scripts and hiring of actors. He married several times, and his son, Jack Jr., worked for the studio. Warner Sr. died on September 2, 1978.

BIBLIOGRAPHY

Higham, Charles, *Warner Brothers*, 1975; Roddick, Nick, *A New Deal in Entertainment: Warner Brothers in the 1930s*, 1983.

Warner, Jack

(August 2, 1892–September 2, 1978)
Entertainment Executive

With his brothers ALBERT, HARRY, and SAMUEL, Jack Warner founded Warner Brothers movie studio.

The three elder brothers, Albert, Harry, and Samuel, were born in Poland; Albert on July 23, 1884, Harry on December 12, 1881, and Samuel on August 10, 1887. Their parents, Benjamin Warner and Pearl (Eichelbaum) Warner, had moved there from Russia. Around 1890, the family immigrated to Canada, where Benjamin sold pots and pans. Soon after Jack's birth on August 2, 1892, the family relocated to Youngstown, Ohio, residing in decrepit housing while Benjamin struggled to make a living as a cobbler.

During a trip to Pittsburgh in 1904, Harry saw his first motion picture. Enthralled, on his return to Youngstown, he convinced Albert and Samuel to join him in traveling from town to town and showing movies in theaters. Jack, who had been a minstrel singer, soon joined them as well, as did their sister, Rosie. Jack sang before each movie—and whenever the film broke—and Rosie played the piano. Soon the Warners saved enough money to open their own theater in Newcastle, Pennsylvania.

They and many other theater operators encountered a problem, however: they could never rely on movies being shipped to them on time or being shipped at all. Consequently, Harry got the idea of forming an alliance with other theater operators to put pressure on the studios to deliver the movies on schedule. From

Jack Warner (L) and his brothers Harry (M) and Albert (R) (UPI/Corbis-Bettmann)

this came the nation's first movie distributorship, the Duquesne Amusement Supply Company. The outfit suffered, though, when producers opposed it as a drain on their profits, and in 1912 the Warners sold out.

Their setback convinced them, however, to make their own movies. They began shooting slapstick comedies in New York City, calling them "Warner Features." In 1917, they decided to pay James W. Gerard for permission to make his popular book *My Four Years in Germany* into a movie. Released the following year, it won critical acclaim and attracted large audiences. Within a few months, the Warners built a studio on

Sunset Boulevard in Hollywood, California, and incorporated as Warner Brothers Pictures. In 1925, they purchased a distribution company called Vitagraph, a move that gave them an advantage over their competitors. Then Harry and Sam got together with Bell Laboratories and worked on a cumbersome system called Vitaphone synchronization that allowed them to add sound to movies. In 1926, Warner Brothers released *Don Juan*, starring John Barrymore, with a musical score. The movie, however, contained no voices.

That awaited Al Jolson's *The Jazz Singer*. Released in 1927, it featured Jolson singing and thus was the first "talkie." The movie was not supposed to contain any words, but Jolson had ad-libbed before the songs, and the technical difficulties involved in using the Vitaphone system prevented the scenes from being edited. Samuel never knew the movie's huge success, however—he died from pneumonia on October 5, 1927, the day before *The Jazz Singer* premiered. He was survived by his wife, Lina Basquette, and a daughter.

The following year, Warner Brothers produced *Lights of New York*, the first all-talking motion picture. With its reputation for innovation, the studio attracted such big stars as Leslie Howard, Edward G. Robinson, and James Cagney. In the 1930s, the Warners acquired the Stanley Company of America, which owned hundreds of movie theaters. Following Harry's advice, the studio soon bought radio companies and music publishers, and paid large sums to attract actors from its competitors. Throughout the decade, Warner Brothers made spectacles and movies dealing with social issues.

During World War II, the Warners produced several war movies, for which they won seven Oscars. In 1949, the federal government charged them with monopolistic practices and forced them to relinquish their theaters. Although the studio had several box-office hits in the 1950s, notably *A Star Is Born* and *Rebel without a Cause*, many actors disliked the Warners for joining in the Red Scare—a hunt for Communists—and blacklisting those who held unacceptable political views.

In the 1960s, television greatly damaged Warner Brothers, and by 1969 it had stopped making movies and based its survival on profits from its two record companies, Warner/Reprise and Atlantic. Kinney Services then bought control of Warner, and in the 1970s started making movies again, among them the hits *Woodstock*, *The Exorcist*, and *All the President's Men*. Kinney renamed the company Warner Communications. In the late 1980s, Warner merged with Time, Incorporated, creating Time Warner, an entertainment giant. Today, in addition to its other enterprises, including cable television, Time Warner dominates the music industry with a 21 percent share of the market.

Among the surviving founders of Warner Brothers after World War II, Albert Warner served as the studio's treasurer until his death on November 26, 1967. Harry Warner served as president until his death on July 25, 1958, and was survived by his wife Rea Levinson; they had four children. Jack Warner held the vice presidency, and, after Harry's death, the presidency, and supervised the selection of scripts and hiring of actors. He married several times, and his son, Jack Jr., worked for the studio. Warner Sr. died on September 2, 1978.

BIBLIOGRAPHY

Higham, Charles, *Warner Brothers*, 1975; Roddick, Nick, *A New Deal in Entertainment: Warner Brothers in the 1930s*, 1983.

Warner, Samuel

(August 10, 1887–October 5, 1927)
Entertainment Executive

Samuel Warner joined his brothers ALBERT, HARRY, and JACK to form Warner Brothers movie studio.

The three elder brothers, Albert, Harry, and Samuel, were born in Poland; Albert on July 23, 1884, Harry on December 12, 1881, and Samuel on August 10, 1887. Their parents, Benjamin Warner and Pearl (Eichelbaum) Warner, had moved there from Russia. Around 1890, the family immigrated to Canada, where Benjamin sold pots and pans. Soon after Jack's birth on August 2, 1892, the family relocated to Youngstown, Ohio, residing in decrepit housing while Benjamin struggled to make a living as a cobbler.

During a trip to Pittsburgh in 1904, Harry saw his first motion picture. Enthralled, on his return to Youngstown, he convinced Albert and Samuel to join him in traveling from town to town and showing movies in theaters. Jack, who had been a minstrel singer, soon joined them as well, as did their sister, Rosie. Jack sang before each movie—and whenever the film broke—and Rosie played the piano. Soon the Warners saved enough money to open their own theater in Newcastle, Pennsylvania.

They and many other theater operators met a problem, however: they could never rely on movies being shipped to them on time or being shipped at all. Consequently, Harry got the idea of forming an alliance with other theater operators to put pressure on the studios to deliver the movies on schedule. From this came the nation's first movie distributorship, the Duquesne Amusement Supply Company. The outfit suffered, though, when producers opposed it as a drain on their profits, and in 1912 the Warners sold out.

Their setback convinced them, however, to make their own movies. They began shooting slapstick comedies in New York City, calling them "Warner Features." In 1917, they decided to pay James W. Gerard for permission to make his popular book *My Four Years in Germany* into a movie. Released the following year, it won critical acclaim and attracted large audiences. Within a few months, the Warners built a studio on Sunset Boulevard in Hollywood, California, and incorporated as Warner Brothers Pictures. In 1925, they purchased a distribution company called Vitagraph, a move that gave them an advantage over their competitors. Then Harry and Sam got together with Bell Laboratories and worked on a cumbersome system called Vitaphone synchronization that allowed them to add sound to movies. In 1926, Warner Brothers released *Don Juan*, starring John Barrymore, with a musical score. The movie, however, contained no voices.

That awaited Al Jolson's *The Jazz Singer.* Released in 1927, it featured Jolson singing and thus was the first "talkie." The movie was not supposed to contain any words, but Jolson had ad-libbed before the songs, and the technical difficulties involved in using the Vitaphone system prevented the scenes from being edited. Samuel never knew the movie's huge success, however—he died from pneumonia on October 5, 1927, the day before *The Jazz Singer* premiered. He was survived by his wife, Lina Basquette, and a daughter.

The following year, Warner Brothers produced *Lights of New York*, the first all-talking motion picture. With its reputation for innovation, the studio attracted such big stars as Leslie Howard, Edward G. Robinson, and James Cagney. In the 1930s, the Warners acquired the Stanley Company of America, which owned hundreds of movie theaters. Following Harry's advice, the studio soon bought radio companies and music publishers, and paid large sums to attract actors from its competitors. Throughout the decade, Warner Brothers made spectacles and movies dealing with social issues.

During World War II, the Warners produced several war movies, for which they won seven Oscars. In 1949, the federal government charged them with monopolistic practices and forced them to relinquish their theaters. Although the studio had several box-office hits in the 1950s, notably *A Star Is Born* and *Rebel without a Cause*, many actors disliked the Warners for joining in the Red Scare—a hunt for Communists—and blacklisting those who held unacceptable political views.

In the 1960s, television greatly damaged Warner Brothers, and by 1969 it had stopped making movies and based its survival on profits from its two record companies, Warner/Reprise and Atlantic.

Kinney Services then bought control of Warner, and in the 1970s started making movies again, among them the hits *Woodstock*, *The Exorcist*, and *All the President's Men*. Kinney renamed the company Warner Communications. In the late 1980s, Warner merged with Time, Incorporated, creating Time Warner, an entertainment giant. Today, in addition to its other enterprises, including cable television, Time Warner dominates the music industry with a 21 percent share of the market.

Among the surviving founders of Warner Brothers after World War II, Albert Warner served as the studio's treasurer until his death on November 26, 1967. Harry Warner served as president until his death on July 25, 1958, and was survived by his wife Rea Levinson; they had four children. Jack Warner held the vice presidency, and, after Harry's death, the presidency, and supervised the selection of scripts and hiring of actors. He married several times, and his son, Jack Jr., worked for the studio. Warner Sr. died on September 2, 1978.

BIBLIOGRAPHY
Higham, Charles, *Warner Brothers*, 1975;
Roddick, Nick, *A New Deal in Entertainment: Warner Brothers in the 1930s*, 1983.

Wasserman, Lew

(March 15, 1913–)
Entertainment Executive

Brought into Music Corporation of America (MCA) at a young age, Lew R. Wasserman transformed the company from talent agency to a major movie and recording business.

Born on March 15, 1913, in Cleveland, Ohio, Wasserman grew up in a poor family. While in high school he worked at a local movie theater as an usher on the evening shift, not returning home until 2 A.M. The long hours, he later said, accustomed him to hard work. Wasserman first entered show business in 1930, the year he graduated from Glenville High School, when he promoted a Cleveland nightclub. Through that job, he met Jules Stein, who had in the 1920s founded MCA, a Hollywood agency for entertainers. Stein liked Wasserman's toughness and integrity and hired him as director of advertising and publicity. Wasserman, who had just married Edith Beckerman, began work at MCA in December 1936.

With MCA, Wasserman soon acted as agent for some of Hollywood's top stars: Bette Davis, Errol Flynn, and Tommy Dorsey. Impressed, Stein made Wasserman MCA's vice president in 1938. After developing MCA into Hollywood's leading talent agency, Stein decided in 1946 to retire from active management and appointed Wasserman president.

Wasserman then took advantage of a new technology that he found exciting, namely television, and linked MCA to its future. In the 1950s, he founded Revue Productions, an MCA subsidiary, to produce television shows, and during that decade the company turned out many hit programs, including *Alfred Hitchcock*

Lew Wasserman (Archive Photos)

Presents, Bachelor Father, and *General Electric Theater.* In addition, Wasserman bought Paramount Studio's pre-1948 film library for $50 million, thus acquiring 750 films he could rent to TV stations, and in December 1958 he bought the back lot of Universal Pictures for $11.25 million and refurbished it for Revue Productions.

In 1959, Wasserman reorganized MCA into MCA, Incorporated as its income flow shifted from mainly agency fees to production revenues. In the early 1960s, however, Wasserman encountered problems when he announced that MCA would buy Decca Records and Universal Studios. The federal government considered the combining of such large production companies with agency business a violation of antitrust laws and sued MCA. A settlement reached in 1962 allowed MCA to acquire Decca and Universal, but Wasserman had to end MCA's talent agency.

Through the 1960s and 1970s, MCA made a fortune from its TV shows and such theater movies as *The Sting, American Graffiti, Day of the Jackal,* and *Jesus Christ Superstar.* Money also rolled in from stars connected with its recording studios, led by pop star Elton John. Wasserman made a bad investment, however when he joined Phillips and Pioneer electronics to produce a "discovision" home entertainment system. Videotape technology overwhelmed his invention and caused MCA to lose millions.

Although MCA scored additional hits in the 1980s with TV shows *Miami Vice* and *Magnum P.I.*, and with the motion pictures *E. T.* and *Back to the Future,* the company's share of movie box-office receipts dropped, along with the value of its stock. In 1990, Wasserman sold MCA to the Matsushita Corporation of Japan for $6.13 billion and reportedly received $30 million a year in dividends on the new stock he received from Matsushita.

In 1996, Wasserman, chairman emeritus of Universal Studios, donated $10 million to the University of California at Los Angeles to establish the Edith and Lew Wasserman Fund for Undergraduate Support. He continued to serve on the board of trustees of the Academy of Motion Picture Arts and Sciences.

BIBLIOGRAPHY

Egan, Jack, "A Hollywood Thriller: MCA vs. the Sharks," *U.S. News & World Report,* September 7, 1987; Foisie, Geoff, "Look Who's Talking Again," *Broadcasting,* October 1, 1990; Moldea, Dan, *Dark Victory: Ronald Reagan, MCA, and the Mob,* 1986.

Watson, Thomas

(February 17, 1874–June 19, 1956)
Manufacturer

A consummate salesperson and a fanatical motivator, Thomas John Watson began with a business that made weighing scales and tabulating equipment, and developed it into the International Business Machines Company, or IBM, for years the dominant firm in computers.

Thomas was born on February 17, 1874, to Thomas Watson and Jane (White) Watson in East Campbell, New York, a small settlement where his father owned a lumber business. The family moved often, from one small town in the area to another. After graduating from high school in 1891, young Thomas went to the Miller School of Commerce, in Elmira, where he completed business courses. He then worked as a bookkeeper at Clarence Risley's butcher shop in Painted Horse. The work bored him, however, and he began selling sewing machines and pianos for Willard Bronson, a local businessman. As he traveled about the New York countryside, he discovered that, despite his shyness, he could sell.

Seeking more opportunity, Watson quit his job in 1894 and headed for Buffalo. One failure after another hindered him. At first he could not find work, then, while owning and operating a butcher shop, he sold building and loan stocks, only to have a colleague abscond with the money. This financial setback imperiled Watson's butcher shop, and he decided to sell it and work for the National Cash Register Company, called The Cash.

Watson blossomed as a salesman, and in 1899 the company's president, JOHN PATTERSON, recruited him to be an agent at a branch office in Rochester, one of the few areas where The Cash had trouble selling its machines. Watson did so well that, in 1903, Patterson chose him to work at the main office in Dayton, Ohio, on a surreptitious project to lead a task force that would work illegally to eliminate competitors selling secondhand cash registers.

Toward this end, Watson opened shops, ostensibly as a competitor to The Cash but actually backed by its money. He sold cash registers at prices intended to drastically undercut the secondhand competition, put it out of business, and allow The Cash to create a monopoly. At the same time, he trained salesmen to sell a "knockout machine"—a register made by The Cash that looked exactly like a competitor's, but sold for one-third to one-half less. Customers would buy the imitation rather than the real machine, thus undermining the competition. These activities would bring trouble.

Before they did, however, Watson married Jeannette Kittredge in 1912. That same year, Watson, Patterson, and 28 others were convicted and fined for criminal conspiracy in restraint of trade. The following year, in a management dispute, the mercurial Patterson fired Watson.

Watson quickly found a new position as president of the Computer Tabulating Recording Company in Elmira, New York. In addition to tabulating equipment, this firm made weighing scales, but had recently suffered financial reverses. Watson turned it around, partly by acquiring other businesses, and in 1917 he formed International Business Machines Limited. Six years later, he established the IBM Corporation of Delaware to take advantage of that state's corporate laws and to consolidate his operations.

After purchasing the Pierce Accounting Machine Company, Watson bought Electromatic Typewriters, Incorporated and entered the electric typewriter business. IBM continued to sell other business items, such as punched cards, check-writing interpreters, test-scoring machines, and collators. In a grand display of success, Watson opened a 20-story headquarters building for IBM in New York City in 1938.

Except in filling menial positions, Watson refused to hire women, blacks, Catholics, or Jews—he considered them incapable of absorbing his philosophy. He wanted complete company loyalty, and expected his employees to dress uniformly—generally in white shirt and tie—live within company-approved areas of cities and towns, and ascribe to his many motivational slogans. "If you are loyal you are successful," Watson said, and at another time: "Loyalty is the great lubricant of life." He developed the idea of putting the word THINK on signs and posting them throughout the company— every office and every desk. In return for his demands, Watson offered job security—few ever got fired—good pay rates, and a program that encouraged workers to put their savings in his companies. Money from this resulted in substantial returns for many as IBM and its subsidiaries continued to expand.

During World War II, Watson led IBM into heavy military production. He purchased the Munitions Manufacturing Company in Poughkeepsie, New York, opened a new IBM plant there, and built the company's first large computer. After the war, he expanded existing plants and opened new ones, including those at San Jose, California; Greencastle, Indiana; and Kingston, New York. He manufactured the company's first electronic calculator in 1946 and rapidly expanded business overseas, helped by the creation in 1949 of the IBM World Trade Corporation.

In 1953, IBM produced its first commercial computer, the 702, designed to handle payrolls, inventories, and accounts. The company quickly exceeded its competitors in the computer field, primarily through aggressive marketing and by offering superior software packages. After Watson died of a heart attack on June 19, 1956, his two sons, Thomas Watson Jr. and Arthur Watson, took charge, the former as head of IBM, the latter as head of the IBM World Trade Organization. By the 1970s, IBM controlled about 80 percent of the American computer market, giving no indication of the decline that would ensue in the 1980s, when competitors gained a larger share by offering high-quality, lower-priced models geared to household and small business use. A rejuvenated IBM in the 1990s more aggressively marketed its personal computers.

BIBLIOGRAPHY

Belden, Thomas Graham, *Lengthening Shadow: The Life of Thomas J. Watson*, 1962; Rodgers, William, *THINK: A Biography of the Watsons and IBM*, 1969.

Wenner, Jann

(January 7, 1946–)
Publisher

Sometimes called America's "hip capitalist," Jann Wenner tied his future to the baby-boom generation of the 1960s when he established *Rolling Stone* magazine.

Jann was born on January 7, 1946, in New York City to Edward Wenner and Ruth (Simmons) Wenner. While Jann was a child, the family moved to Marin County, north of San Francisco, where his parents founded a successful business. They soon divorced, however, and his mother moved to Hawaii. After attending the preparatory Chadwick School in Los

Angeles, Jann enrolled at the University of California at Berkeley. There he wrote a music column for the college newspaper before dropping out.

Infatuated with rock 'n' roll, Wenner immersed himself in the emerging San Francisco music scene, forming a friendship with Ralph Gleason, a longtime music critic for area newspapers. In 1966, Wenner was hired to edit *Sunday Ramparts* (a spin-off of *Ramparts* magazine) and applied his pen to discussing rock's revolutionary contents.

Influenced by underground newspapers and by their founders who had started them with little money, Wenner decided to begin his own rock magazine on a shoestring budget. *Rolling Stone* made its debut on October 18, 1967, with Wenner and his friend Gleason going from business to business in San Francisco selling advertisments. By early 1968, Wenner had obtained advertising from major record labels and later that year scored a controversial breakthrough when the manager of the Beatles agreed to have *Rolling Stone* publish a photograph of John Lennon and his wife Yoko Ono in the nude.

As *Rolling Stone* grew, Wenner lived lavishly, partying with rock stars and spending money on limousines, clothes, and drugs. He had little use for politics and considered his magazine a profit-making venture rather than one geared to social reform. He had, however, an excellent talent for spotting trends and knowing which rock musicians would soon make it big.

Wenner attracted writers to *Rolling Stone* who treated journalism experimentally and creatively. At first, the magazine covered only the San Francisco scene, but it soon carried articles about bands on the East Coast and earned a reputation for penetrating analysis. In 1977, Wenner moved the magazine's headquarters from San Francisco to New York City and reshaped the publication to cover less music and more politics. He changed direction again in 1984 when he reduced political coverage in favor of music news, record reviews, and interviews with rock stars.

Over the years, Wenner expanded his media investments beyond *Rolling Stone*. After beginning and then selling *Outside* magazine for a considerable profit, he founded *US*, aimed at young female readers; *Men's Journal*, geared to active men who engaged in hiking, mountain climbing, and other sports; and *Family Life*, intended for baby-boomer parents.

Wenner revamped *Rolling Stone* yet again in the early 1990s to appeal to a younger audience, one with no direct connection to the 1960s counterculture. A multimillionaire, he has a reputation for mercurial behavior, kind and considerate one moment, demanding and vengeful the next. He had married Jane Ellen Schindelheim in 1968, and they eventually had three children. In 1995, Wenner left his wife for a male model. Apparently, he had had several affairs, with both men and women, during the course of his marriage.

Many people praised Wenner for making *Rolling Stone* a leading reflector and shaper of popular culture. Some 1960s activists criticized him, however, for capitalizing on the counterculture. One said, "The spontaneity of the counterculture press was absorbed by *Rolling Stone*, and hip capitalism became the sponge used to mop up hippie originality."

BIBLIOGRAPHY

Draper, Robert, *Rolling Stone Magazine: The Uncensored History*, 1990; Leamer, Laurence, *The Paper Revolutionaries: The Rise of the Underground Press*, 1972; *Washington Post*, March 11, 1995; Whitaker, Tim, "Casting New Stones," *Adweek*, February 28, 1994.

Westinghouse, George

(October 6, 1846–March 12, 1914)
Inventor

A train crash convinced George Westinghouse to develop better brakes for the nation's railroads, and from his work emerged his most famous invention, the air brake. Westinghouse ranked among the pioneers in electricity as well, and patented many other devices.

George hailed from Central Bridge, New York, where he was born on October 6, 1846, to George Westinghouse and Emaline (Vedder) Westinghouse. In 1856, his father opened a shop in Schenectady, New York, where he made agricultural machinery, mill machinery, and small steam engines. An inventor, he obtained seven patents. Young George worked in his father's shop until, at age 16, he fought for the Union army in the Civil War. After receiving an honorable discharge in 1864, he joined the navy and obtained the rank of acting assistant third engineer before being mustered out in 1865.

After the war, Westinghouse studied briefly at Union College, but the work in his father's shop interested him more, and so he returned there. He obtained his first patent in October 1865 for a rotary steam engine, and soon invented a railway frog, a device that allowed trains to cross from one track to another. He invented, too, a car replacer for putting derailed cars or engines back on track.

In 1867, he married Marguerite Erskine Walker. The couple had one child, a son.

Westinghouse developed his air brake after a tragic collision between two trains near Schenectady. His invention used compressed air to transmit power from the locomotive to each car's brakes, thus allowing the engineer to stop the train at will, quickly. Additionally, the air brakes eliminated the time-consuming chore of having to adjust the brakes on each car individually. Westinghouse first applied his air brake to a train in September 1868, and, the following year, obtained a patent and chartered the Westinghouse Air Brake Company, with headquarters at Pittsburgh, Pennsylvania. By 1874, nearly 3,000 locomotives and 7,300 cars had air brakes. Over the next few years, he made several improvements to the device. Westinghouse's air brake allowed trains to travel faster under safer conditions, and thus had an enormous impact on the nation's transportation system and facilitated economic expansion. Around 1880, he took his air brake to England, and organized companies and shops in that country, as well as in France and Russia.

Westinghouse developed automatic railway signaling systems in the early

1880s, after he purchased signal patents and combined them with his own inventions. In the mid-1880s, he developed a system for transporting natural gas, hitherto a dangerous procedure. Westinghouse used pipes cut to varying sizes, beginning at the well, and employed safety valves. He first used his system to bring natural gas into Pittsburgh. He developed meters for houses and factories, and an automatic cutoff regulator, an important safety device.

That same decade, he improved on work being done by electrical engineers in France, and in 1886 founded the Westinghouse Electric Company to promote a new high-voltage alternating current single-phase system. Alternating current made it possible to readily change voltage by using a transformer, and this, in turn, meant electricity could be sent over long distances at reasonable cost. Opponents attacked the system as dangerous, but Westinghouse persevered. He purchased a patent from Nikola Tesla, the great inventor who had developed a motor that could run with alternating current, and then hired Tesla to perfect the entire electric system.

Westinghouse triumphed in 1893 when his electric company outbid the Edison General Electric Company to win the contract for lighting the Columbian Exposition in Chicago. Westinghouse built the largest alternating-current system to date, with 12 generators of 1,000 horsepower each, along with 500-horsepower alternators. Two years later, he installed electric generators at Niagara Falls.

The companies owned by Westinghouse expanded rapidly between 1893 and 1907, and employed 50,000 people in such diverse locations as San Francisco,

George Westinghouse (Library of Congress)

California, and St. Petersburg, Russia. But the Panic of 1907 caused financial problems, and Westinghouse had to fight to save his electric company. Under a plan devised by him, the company reverted to its shareholders, and he was allowed to continue as president, but with his power greatly curtailed. In 1911, he relinquished the presidency.

Westinghouse died on March 12, 1914, of heart disease in New York City, an inventor who had thrived while America underwent a momentous change from an agricultural to an industrial nation—a change facilitated by his actions.

BIBLIOGRAPHY

Levine, I. E., *Inventive Wizard: George Westinghouse*, 1962; Prout, Henry G., *A Life of George Westinghouse*, 1921, rep. 1972.

Wickham, Carl

(August 7, 1887–February 5, 1954)
Transportation Executive

Carl Eric Wickham bounced around between several careers in the milling and mining industries, until one year when his dabbling in the taxi business revealed a talent for organization and a keen vision of the future. Through careful planning and utilization of the opportunities in the emerging transportation business, Wickham built his one-car operation into the country's biggest integrated bus service, the Greyhound Corporation. Greyhound's success was largely due to his gradual but skillful coordination of existing small bus routes into a nationwide system, as well as his strategic alliances with the major railways.

Carl was born on August 7, 1887, in Sweden to Victor Wickham and Anna Martis. He attended public schools, and after completing high school immigrated to America in 1905. He was first employed at two sawmills in Arizona and then as a diamond drill operator in the mines of Hibbing, Minnesota. During the slow seasons in the mining business, Wickham sought extra work as a salesman for Hupmobile automobiles and Goodyear tires.

With no success selling cars, Wickam joined Andrew Anderson, a fellow Swede, in starting a shuttle service to carry miners from Hibbing to the towns nearby. When they made the pioneering decision to establish the route on a regularly scheduled basis, their business suddenly boomed. They added a second car and a second route. Soon they were building bus bodies to mount on truck chassis. By 1916, their business had grown enough that they decided to recruit new partners with capital and hire more drivers, and thus the Mesaba Transportation Company was born. The following year, earnings more than doubled to reach $40,000, and by 1918 the company owned a fleet of 18 buses with routes throughout northern Minnesota. In 1916, Wickham married Olga Rodin from Hibbing, Minnesota. The couple had a son and daughter.

In the early 1920s, bus companies were faced with stiff competition from the railway lines that began operating their own bus subsidiaries to help travelers complete their itineraries. Ralph Budd, the president of the Great Northern Railway, studied the situation and concluded that train service was more threatened by the automobile than by existing bus service. He sought to collaborate with bus lines rather than attempting to crush them through fierce competition. Thus in 1925, Budd invited Wickham to become president of the newly formed Northland Transportation Company, a subsidiary of the Great Northern Railway.

Wickham accepted the position and sold out his stake in the Mesaba Transportation Company. He moved to Duluth, Minnesota, and began buying out small bus lines, including his former company. The owner of one of these acquisitions, Orville Caesar, was named operating manager of the bus lines by Wickham. Together, Caesar and Wickham realized the importance of properly routed connection service to cover as wide an area as possible. To meet this goal, Wickham and Caesar organized the growing corporate structure and continued to acquire bus lines

In 1926, Wickham and some partners laid the basis for what became the Greyhound bus lines. The partners formed the Motor Transit Corporation, a holding company to consolidate a large number of small bus lines throughout the Midwest. Wickham continued to expand the bus lines by forging deals with railways to form bus subsidiaries for the railways that were also part of the Motor Transit bus system. These subsidiaries were initially partly funded by the railways, and in this way, Wickham was able to achieve rapid expansion of the bus lines throughout the country. In 1930, the company name was changed to the Greyhound Corporation, and Wickham was elected president that year. He held that post until 1946, was chairman of the board of directors during 1946–1951, and remained a director of Greyhound until his death three years later.

By 1952, Greyhound controlled a vast network of bus service through 48 states, the District of Columbia, and seven provinces of Canada with operating revenues of $229 million. In addition to pursuing his business career, Wickham was an active member of the Presbyterian Church and in various Swedish organizations throughout his life. He died on February 5, 1954.

BIBLIOGRAPHY

Genet, Arthur S., "Profile of Greyhound: The Greyhound Corporation," Address to the Newcomen Society, 1958; "Greyhound: Seventy-Five Years of History for an American Tradition," *Bus Ride*, vol. 25, October 1989; Moskowitz, Milton, et al., eds., *Everybody's Business*, 1980.

Wilson, Joseph

(December 13, 1909–1971)
Manufacturer

Joseph Chamberlain Wilson gambled when he used all his company's resources to develop a machine that he believed would revolutionize office work. The gamble led to the formation of the Xerox Corporation—what one historian has called "the greatest business success story of the post–World War II era. No other firm the size of Xerox has ever been built in so short a time."

Joseph was born on December 13, 1909, in Rochester, New York, to Joseph R. Wilson and Katherine (Upton) Wilson. After graduating with honors from the University of Rochester in 1931, he enrolled in the School of Business Administration at Harvard. He received his M.B.A. in 1933, and then joined the Haloid Company, a business begun by his grandfather three decades earlier to process photographic paper. In 1935, he married Marie Curran; the couple had six children.

After working in several different departments, Wilson became secretary of

Haloid in 1936 and treasurer in 1938, the same year his father became its president. In 1945, when World War II ended and Haloid lost its defense contracts, Wilson began searching for an invention that would allow the company to compete more effectively with larger firms, such as Eastman Kodak. He found one in 1945, when his research chief called attention to an article that discussed the work of Chester Carlson.

Carlson had developed a machine that made copies without using wet chemicals—such as the kind used in a photocopy already manufactured by Haloid— or special paper. He called his process electrophotography. Carlson had reached an agreement with the Batelle Memorial Institute, a nonprofit research organization, according to which Batelle continued work on the invention. In 1947, one year after succeeding his father as Haloid's president, Wilson bought the commercial rights to Carlson's machine from the institute.

The following year, Wilson devoted Haloid's resources to improving electrophotography and achieving Carlson's goal of producing a convenient machine for office use. Wilson introduced Haloid's first copier in 1949, but since it was clumsy and expensive, the machine made little impact. "In the early years," said a Wilson associate, "it was a very chintzy, unsure process. Many hundreds of thousands of dollars had to be spent before it could work. . . . This was a tremendous gamble, because the results coming out of the lab at that point were not very promising."

Over the next few years, Wilson went into debt to finance more research. He coined a catchy word to replace electrophotography, namely "xerography" (from the Greek words for *dry* and *writing*), and in a show of faith changed his company's name in 1958 to Haloid Xerox. During the 1950s, he introduced new models of his copier, but widespread acceptance did not come until the development of the Xerox 914 in 1960. A desksize machine, it made seven dry copies per minute on ordinary paper.

Sales boomed from $33 million in 1959 to $385 million in 1965. Wilson changed the company's name again in 1961 to the Xerox Corporation, and over the next several years continued to introduce new models. Carlson, meanwhile, made a fortune through stock ownership and royalties.

At the same time, Wilson diversified Xerox. In 1962, he bought University Microfilms of Ann Arbor, Michigan, the nation's main source of microfilmed copies of most printed materials. Then he bought American Education Publications, publisher of school magazines such as *My Weekly Reader*, and R. R. Bowker, publisher of *Books in Print, Library Journal*, and *Publisher's Weekly*. Xerox expanded overseas, too, with affiliates in England and Japan.

Wilson involved himself in numerous community endeavors and urged others to do the same. "We encourage Xerox people to involve themselves with issues of importance," he said. "We cannot as individuals or as a corporation isolate ourselves in a vacuum."

By the time Wilson died in 1971, Xerox had grown into a corporate giant. Beginning in the 1970s, it faced considerable competition from other companies that made copiers, and in the 1990s from a flattening of the market as people used computers more than copiers to reproduce materials. Nevertheless, the commanding position of Xerox was evident in the way the company's name had emerged in the common language—rather than asking someone to "copy" a document, they often asked that it be "Xeroxed."

BIBLIOGRAPHY

Dessauer, John H., *My Years with Xerox: The Billions Nobody Wanted*, 1971; Jacobson, Gary, *Xerox: American Samurai*, 1986.

Wilson, Kemmons

(January 5, 1913–)
Hotel Executive

Starting from the humblest of beginnings, Charles Kemmons Wilson created and managed the international Holiday Inn hotel chain. Throughout his career, he had a keen eye for recognizing opportunities and taking great advantage of them, progressing from selling popcorn to real estate to managing the giant motel franchise.

Kemmons was born in Osceola, Arkansas, on January 5, 1913, the only child of Charles Kemmons and Ruby Lloyd Wilson. When he was only nine months old, his father died, and he and his mother then moved to Memphis, Tennessee, where she found work as a dental assistant and then as a bookkeeper. Kemmons attended public school and worked after school as a delivery boy for a local drugstore. While working one day when he was 14, he was hit by a car, fracturing his leg so badly that he was forced to withdraw from school for nearly a year. Just two months before graduating from high school, Kemmons dropped out to support his mother who required hospitalization.

Set on becoming an independent businessman, Wilson got his start by buying a used popcorn machine and renting space for it in a local movie theater lobby. Movie theater popcorn was a novel idea at the time, and he was soon earning $30 per week. Wilson sold the machine to the theater owner for $50 and used this money to purchase five secondhand pinball machines, which he set up in drugstores and restaurants. He reinvested his profits to continue buying additional machines, and by 1933 had saved $1,700, which he then invested in the construction of a house. Using the house as collateral he obtained a loan to acquire more pinball machines, as well as jukeboxes and cigarette vending machines. He sold the house to buy other properties and expand his business. Before long, he owned seven movie theaters in the Memphis area.

At the start of World War II, Wilson sold all of his holdings for $250,000 and invested the money in war bonds. On December 2, 1941, he married Dorothy Elizabeth Lee whom he had met several years earlier while tending his pinball machine operations; the couple had five children. In 1943, Wilson joined the Air Transport Command and was assigned to the Asian theater, making flights over the Himalayas. Upon returning from the war, he bought a distributorship of Orange Crush soda, but lost $100,000 on the venture. Turning once more to the real estate business, he founded Kemmons Wilson, Incorporated in 1946 and the Kemmons Wilson Realty Company in 1948 to build and sell houses and apartment units.

His real estate business flourished, but while taking a cross-country trip with his wife and children, he recognized the need for higher-quality, reliable motels geared toward families. He built the first Holiday Inn in 1952 in Memphis to meet this need, and the results were impressive. The motel was popular enough to warrant the construction of three more Holiday Inns just one year later, and Wilson began to see the potential for a large franchise.

Wilson joined with real estate pioneer Wallace E. Johnson, who had nationwide connections in the home-building industry, to form Holiday Inns of America, which they incorporated in 1954. Wilson was chairman of the board, Johnson was president, and Wilson's mother Ruby, who had helped design the room decor in the original motel, served as vice president. Wilson and Johnson devised a plan to grant franchises to independent builders across the country, who would then construct the motels to the same design specifications as the four Holiday Inns in Memphis. The franchises would also be held to the strict quality standards of the parent company with regular and surprise inspections.

The team invited home builders and other investors to Memphis to hear their proposals, and the first franchised Holiday Inn was opened on June 14, 1954, in Mississippi. As the number of franchises increased rapidly, the company made a public stock offering in August 1957. By 1972, Holiday Inn had become the largest and fastest-growing motel chain in the world, with about 1,500 inns worldwide. To keep up with the demands of the expanding business, several subsidiaries were created. The Inn Keepers Supply Company was formed in 1957 to organize the purchasing of supplies for the motel chain, and a printing plant was added in 1958 as the Holiday Press. In 1969, Holiday Inn acquired TCO Industries, Incorporated, which is composed of Continental Trailways, Delta Steamship Lines, and Continental Tours.

Wilson has served on the boards of many industry and trade organizations as well as charitable organizations such as the American Heart Fund and the March of Dimes. He is a devout Baptist and has earned awards from several religious groups for both his business enterprises and his humanitarian work. In his career, he typically slept only five hours each night and enjoyed trotting the globe to find new hotel sites.

BIBLIOGRAPHY

"KWINC Online," http://www.kwilson.com; *Time*, June 12, 1972; Wilson, Kemmons, *Half Luck and Half Brains*, 1996; Wilson, Kemmons, *The Holiday Inn Story*, 1968.

Woodruff, Robert

(December 6, 1889–March 7, 1985)
Manufacturer

Heading into the 1920s, Coca-Cola was the most popular soft drink in America. The company's sales began to decline, however, until Robert Winship Woodruff supported an enormous advertising campaign and made Coke an international drink.

Robert was born on December 6, 1889, in Columbus, Georgia, to Ernest Woodruff and Emily (Winship) Woodruff. His father served as a director or president of several leading companies. Robert graduated from the Georgia Military Academy in 1908, and for two years attended Emory University. In 1910, he joined the General Pipe and Foundry Company as a machinist's apprentice. Within weeks, he earned promotion to the sales department of the parent company, General Fire Extinguisher.

The following year, the Atlantic Ice and Coal Company hired Woodruff as its purchasing agent, and in 1912—the year he married Nell Hodgson—he modernized the firm by replacing its horse-drawn carriages with trucks purchased from the White Motor Company. He so impressed White Motor's president that the company hired him in 1913 as a salesman in its Atlanta office. After Woodruff convinced the local city and county governments to purchase trucks from White Motor, he earned appointment as manager of the company's southern region, and in 1919 as vice president and general manager.

Meanwhile, in 1919, Woodruff's father led a group of businessmen who purchased the Coca-Cola Bottling Company from ASA CANDLER. In 1923, Coca-Cola's

Robert Woodruff (The Coca-Cola Company)

board of directors hired Robert Woodruff as the company's president. The board wanted him to reverse Coca-Cola's declining sales.

Woodruff did so by directing two changes. First, he pumped money into a creative advertising campaign that emblazoned Coke in the public mind as an essential American tradition. The D'Arcy Advertising Agency used drawings by Norman Rockwell and N. C. Wyeth in the ad campaign, along with the slogan, "The pause that refreshes." As a result of the successful ad campaign, profits jumped from $4.5 million in 1923 to $13 million in 1930, and syrup manufacturing plants—using the secret Coke formula, Merchandise 7X—operated in six cities, with bottling plants in many more. Woodruff made Coke the favorite drink of servicemen when, during World War II, he used government funds to open bottling plants near military bases.

Woodruff's second change entailed making Coke an international drink. Partly through American soldiers drinking Coke overseas, but mainly through aggressive advertising and marketing, under Woodruff's tenure Coke ranked as the world's single largest-selling product. The drink was sold in 135 countries.

Over the years, Woodruff showed himself to be a New South businessman by promoting the region's industrialization. He served as president and chairman of the board of the White Motor Company from 1929 to 1934, and as director of the Southern Railway Company, General Electric, Metropolitan Life Insurance, and American Express, among others. Although he left his position as chairman of the board at Coca-Cola in 1942 (a post he had held since 1939), he continued as chairman of its executive committee until his retirement in 1955, and for many years after that as chair of the finance committee, and as a substantial influence in the company right up until his death.

Critics blamed Woodruff for Coca-Cola's slow response in the 1970s to Pepsi-Cola's increasing share of the soft-drink market. Enfeebled, blind, and hard of hearing, he seemed intent on protecting tradition. He did, however, give his blessing to the selection in 1980 of a dynamic president, ROBERTO GOIZUETA, and used his influence to assure the new leader's appointment the following year as chairman of the board and CEO. In 1985, just weeks before he died on March 7, 1985, in Atlanta, Woodruff indicated to Goizueta that he would keep an open mind about introducing a new Coke formula, which eventually resulted in the failure of the New Coke venture.

BIBLIOGRAPHY

Kahn, E. J., Jr., *The Big Drink*, 1959; Moskowitz, Milton, et al., eds., *Everybody's Business*, 1980.

Woolworth, Frank

(April 13, 1852–August 8, 1919)
Merchant

Beyond a childhood interest in playing store, little else indicated that Frank Winfield Woolworth would one day found the nation's leading 5- and 10-cent business, a giant chain in the retail world.

Frank was born on April 13, 1852, to John Hubbell Woolworth and Fanny (McBrier) Woolworth on his family's farm near Rodman, New York. He attended public school in Greatbend, where his family had moved, and worked on his parent's farm at chores he hated. At age 19, he clerked for no pay at a village grocery store, gaining the experience he desired in order to pursue a retail career.

For some time, Woolworth made few advances and experienced many failures.

In 1873, W. H. Moore hired him to clerk at his store in Watertown—but for low wages. Two years later, Woolworth clerked at a "ninety-nine-cent" store in Port Huron, Michigan—but had his pay cut when he turned out to be a poor salesman. Soon after he married Jennie Creighton, a seamstress, in 1876, he returned to Watertown, and, having made no progress, again clerked for Moore. In 1878, he heard of a store that sold only nickel goods, and he convinced Moore to stock such low-priced items in his shop. The tactic succeeded, and the following year he got Moore to finance him in opening a nickel store in Utica, New York. Woolworth called it the "Great Five Cent Store"—but it closed in just three months.

Woolworth finally achieved success in 1879. That year, in Lancaster, Pennsylvania, he opened another store with Moore's backing, one stocked with nickel and dime goods. The business prospered, and over the next few years, with the help of his brother Charles S. Woolworth and his cousin Seymour H. Knox, he opened additional stores, some that did poorly, but others, such as those in Buffalo, Erie, and Scranton, that did well.

By 1900, Woolworth had 59 stores, and in 1905 he and his partners incorporated as F. W. Woolworth and Company. At the same time, Charles Woolworth and Seymour Knox opened their own stores, but they respected Frank Woolworth's territories. In 1912, F. W. Woolworth absorbed these stores, as it did those owned by Moore.

Across America, consumers identified with the Woolworth trademark—stores with red fronts (a color Woolworth copied from A&P groceries) adorned with the F. W. Woolworth name in large gold

Frank Woolworth (Corbis-Bettmann)

letters, and 5- and 10-cent items displayed on open counters. To maintain his low prices, Woolworth obtained contracts with companies that manufactured goods exclusively for his chain. He paid low wages, but gained a reputation for generosity toward his executives, several of whom became millionaires through their investments in his company.

In 1913, Woolworth completed construction on what was then the world's tallest skyscraper, the Woolworth Building located in New York City. He personally paid the $13.5 million cost. At the same time, he continued to open new stores and to hold the top price on his goods at 10 cents, excepting 15 cents in the West.

When Woolworth died on August 8, 1919, his company operated 1,081 stores, and his own worth approached $65 million. Although Woolworth's abandoned its 10-cent price cap in 1932, the stores maintained their reputation as five- and-dime shops with low-priced goods of a great variety—everything from ladies' wear to toys—and lunch counters where sodas and sandwiches could be bought at reasonable prices. Woolworth's gained political notoriety, too, when, in 1960, a racially segregated lunch counter at its store in Greensboro, North Carolina, grabbed headlines as the site of the nation's first massive civil rights sit-in led by black students.

Beginning in the 1960s, Woolworth's experienced new challenges. Many consumers deserted its stores, usually located in downtown areas, for department and discount stores located in suburban malls and shopping centers. Woolworth's tried to meet the decline by opening its own large outlets, called Woolco, but the effort failed. Through the 1970s and 1980s, Woolworth's closed many of its 5- and 10-cent stores, and in 1997 it shut down the remaining 400. The company continued, however, to operate its other profitable holdings, among them Foot Locker, Champs, and Kinney Shoes. One financial analyst commented that Woolworth's needed to take this step to save profits: "They needed to move on."

BIBLIOGRAPHY

Baker, Nina Brown, *Nickels and Dimes: The Story of F. W. Woolworth,* 1954; Winkler, John K., *Five and Ten: The Fabulous Life of F. W. Woolworth,* 1970.

Wrigley, Philip

(December 5, 1894–April 12, 1977)
Manufacturer

WILLIAM WRIGLEY and his son Philip Wrigley combined their chewing-gum empire with a love for baseball, and Philip mixed tradition in the sport with several ideas that struck many people as, at the least, strange and unorthodox.

In the late nineteenth and early twentieth centuries, William Wrigley built the largest chewing-gum manufactory in the world. Philip was born on December 5, 1894, to William and Ada Elizabeth (Foote) Wrigley in Chicago, Illinois, surrounded by wealth. In 1911, he entered Phillips Academy in Andover, Massachusetts, and prepared to attend Yale, but after he graduated from Phillips in 1914, he entered his father's business and helped found a factory in Melbourne, Australia. When the United States entered World War I, he enlisted in the U.S. Navy and before long was appointed superintendent of the aviation mechanics school at the Great Lakes Naval Training Station. During the war, he married Helen Blanche Atwater; they eventually had two daughters and a son.

In 1920, Wrigley returned to the William Wrigley Jr. Company as vice president and became president in 1925 after his father retired. He took over as chairman of the board after his father died in

January 1932 and earned a reputation for establishing progressive employee programs.

Wrigley's greatest prominence came from his connection to the Chicago Cubs. He acquired his father's holdings in the Cubs in 1934 and made himself president. Although the public often believed that Wrigley took little interest in matters concerning the players, in actuality no player trade was ever made without his knowledge or approval.

Throughout his years as president, Wrigley promoted Wrigley Field (the home of the Cubs) as a traditional ballpark. The ivy-covered brick walls stood in contrast to the emerging modern steel stadiums. Wrigley made such improvements on the park as instaling wider and more comfortable box seats and a more detailed scoreboard. He also pioneered in letting children into games for half-price admission and, on certain days, women in for free. He was steadfast in opposing an innovation appearing at other ballparks, however: the installation of electric lights that would allow the playing of night games. "I firmly believe that baseball is primarily a daytime sport," he said, "valuable largely because it brings people out into the air and sunlight. I think we can do many things to increase attendance at Wrigley Field before resorting to night baseball."

Despite his traditionalism, Wrigley tried some strange experiments to improve the Cubs as a team and to boost the sport of baseball. The Cubs won the pennant in 1935, 1938, and 1945, but fell short in other years and under Wrigley never won the World Series. At one time, Wrigley hired a retired army colonel as an athletic director who got the players to consume wheat germ and vitamin pills as a way to improve their play, but the plan failed. He hired a college professor with expertise in human reflexes to study the reactions of top baseball players and then use the specifications to draft players under the assumption reflexes alone would make them successful. But this plan, like the wheat germ, also failed.

During World War II, when it appeared baseball might be suspended, Wrigley promoted the formation of women's pro softball teams and served as a director in the American Girls' Softball League that resulted from his idea. The league used existing ballparks, and when attendance sagged in Milwaukee, Wrigley hired the city's symphony orchestra to play before several games. Needless to say, few people wanted to mix classical music with softball, and attendance remained weak. Wrigley ended his support of the women's league late in 1944, after it was clear baseball would survive the war.

When the Cubs continued to perform dismally, Wrigley resorted in 1961 to rotating among three coaches who took turns managing the team. Once again, an unorthodox experiment failed, and he discontinued it after the following season. Despite the hapless record achieved by the Cubs under Wrigley's presidency, many fans fondly remembered him at his death on April 12, 1977, in Elkhorn, Wisconsin, as a man who had loved the sport and had dedicated himself to its welfare.

BIBLIOGRAPHY

Angle, Paul M., *Philip K. Wrigley: A Memoir of a Modest Man*, 1975.

Wrigley, William

(September 30, 1861–January 26, 1932)
Manufacturer

William Wrigley and his son PHILIP WRIGLEY combined their chewing-gum empire with a love for baseball.

William was born on September 30, 1861, in Philadelphia, Pennsylvania, to William Wrigley and Mary A. (Ladley) Wrigley. As a youngster, he worked in his father's soap-making business, first, at age 10, selling soap on the streets, then stirring the huge vats filled with liquid soap and, in his late teens, traveling about the country in a bright red, horse-driven wagon, peddling soap to shopkeepers.

With money provided by an uncle, Wrigley began his own soap-making business in Chicago in 1891. He expanded his product line to include baking powder and then chewing gum. Wrigley soon emphasized the latter and contracted with the Zeno Manufacturing Company to produce gum for him. In 1899, he introduced a new flavor he called "Spearmint." The

William Wrigley (Archive Photos)

public, however, remained uninterested until he launched a huge advertising campaign in 1907 that boosted sales from about $170,000 to over $1 million.

Now the largest chewing-gum manufacturer in the world, Wrigley took over the Zeno Company and built factories in Chicago, New York City, Toronto, London, Berlin, Frankfurt, and Sydney. With his wealth, Wrigley expanded his interests by investing in hotels and mines, and purchasing Santa Catalina Island off the California coast, which he developed into a famous resort. Wrigley had married Ada Elizabeth (Foote) Wrigley in 1885, and their son, Philip, was born on December 5, 1894, in Chicago, surrounded by wealth. Philip joined his father in the family business in 1914.

Between 1916 and 1921, Wrigley bought stock in a National League baseball club, the Chicago Cubs. He loved watching the Cubs play and often sat in the stands drinking beer and talking to his friends.

In 1925, Wrigley retired, and Philip became president of the company. Wrigley died on January 26, 1932, in Phoenix, Arizona, from a heart ailment.

BIBLIOGRAPHY
Angle, Paul M., *Philip K. Wrigley: A Memoir of a Modest Man*, 1975.

Zeckendorf, William

(June 30, 1905–September 30, 1976)
Real Estate Developer

William Zeckendorf, a real estate developer known principally for his role in negotiating the purchase of the site for the United Nations (UN) in New York City, believed that unregulated growth would be the demise of many American cities. His preference for managed urban development is evident in projects such as L'Enfant Plaza in Washington, D.C., and Century City in Los Angeles.

William, the son of Arthur William and Byrd Rosenfield Zeckendorf, was born on June 30, 1905, in Paris, Illinois. When he was three, his father sold his general store and moved the family to Long Island, New York, to enter the shoe business. Ten years later, they relocated again to Manhattan, where William attended DeWitt Clinton High School.

Zeckendorf attended New York University for three years, but by 1925 had tired of academic life. He then went to work for his uncle Samuel Bochard as an assistant purchasing agent in real estate. Zeckendorf, who learned quickly, demonstrated an early flair for management. By 1926, he headed up a new department at the firm of Leonard Gans to manage commercial rental properties. Shortly after his appointment as department head, Zeckendorf became a commercial real estate broker, realizing his first sale, an East Side hotel, in 1927.

On September 20, 1928, Zeckendorf married Irma Levy. Before the couple divorced in 1934, they had two children, William and Susan. Two years after the wedding, Zeckendorf completed his first major deal, the sale of a $3 million West Side property that provided him with a $21,000 commission. With this success, Zeckendorf became Gans's partner, a position he held for nine years.

In 1938, Zeckendorf joined Webb and Knapp, Inc., an influential real estate company that owned or managed almost $50 million worth of property. Zeckendorf broke through the company's conservative veneer and expanded its holdings considerably. The next few years for Zeckendorf were characterized by the rapid growth of Webb and Knapp, as well as a new marriage on December 10, 1941, to Marion Griffin.

By May 1947, Zeckendorf had become company president. During the next two years, his purchases of property in 35 states, Canada, Mexico, and England doubled the value of the company's holdings. In 1949, he borrowed heavily to buy out the partners of Webb and Knapp, becoming the sole stockholder.

Zeckendorf not only improved the financial status of Webb and Knapp, he also diversified its role to include design, management, and construction. He expanded the firm's architecture staff, hiring I. M. Pei, an assistant professor of architecture at Harvard, and retained notable architects Wallace Harrison, Le Corbusier, and William Lescaze as consultants.

Over time, Zeckendorf acted as agent for other corporate clients looking to expand real estate holdings. He served as agent for Gimbel's and Macy's department stores, the Israeli government, the Rockefeller family, the Astor family, and the New York Philharmonic Society. He was well known for his ability to understand the potential value of a piece of property. He rejected the standard approach of searching for property with a structure in mind. "What I do," Zeckendorf was once quoted as saying, "is to recognize a great piece of land and conceive a suitable edifice for it."

In 1946, Zeckendorf spent what seemed an enormous sum, $6 million, for an eight-acre piece of property on the East River occupied by slaughterhouses and tenements. He envisioned a lavish facelift for the area, with office buildings, hotels, and concert and convention halls. Instead, hearing the UN was hoping to set up headquarters in New York City, he generously offered the site at any price that the UN could pay. Though willing to take a financial loss to provide a civic service, Zeckendorf ultimately made a $2 million profit on the deal when the site was bought by John D. Rockefeller Jr. as a gift to the UN.

Many of Zeckendorf's transactions were based on his ideas for transforming the urban landscape so that form and function would be integrated and growth was planned. The style of several of his large urban projects in the 1940s and 1950s reflect his modernist architectural preferences.

Zeckendorf was an active participant in professional associations, such as the Real Estate Committee of New York and the First Avenue Association. He also held directorships of the Manhattan Hospital and the American Broadcasting Company. In 1952, he served as the chairman of the fund-raising campaign of the New York Heart Association.

Zeckendorf remained active in business and community affairs in New York City, where he died on September 30, 1976.

BIBLIOGRAPHY

Business Week, August 16, 1947; *Fortune*, April 1946; *Life*, October 28, 1946; *New York Post*, December 5, 1946; *New York Star*, August 29, 1948; *New York Times*, Obituary, October 2, 1976; Zeckendorf, William, with Edward McCreary, *The Autobiography of William Zeckendorf*, 1970.

Leaders Arranged by Field of Endeavor

Advertising Executives
Bernbach, William
Lasker, Albert

Airline Executives
Bethune, Gordon
Braniff, Thomas
Burr, Donald
Hughes, Howard
Lewis, David
Lorenzo, Frank
Rickenbacker, Edward
Trippe, Juan

Bankers
Belmont, August
Brown, Alexander
Cooke, Jay
Drexel, Anthony
Giannini, Amadeo
Lamont, Thoma
Mellon, Andrew
Morgan, J. P., Jr.
Morgan, J. P., Sr.
Perkins, George
Sachs, Walter
Taylor, Moses
Vanderlip, Frank

Brewers
Busch, Adolphous
Coors, Adolph

Cattle Rancher
McCoy, Joseph

Communications Executives
Cornell, Ezra
Field, Cyrus
Geneen, Harold
Hubbard, Gardiner
Malone, John
McGowan, Bill
Vail, Theodore

Computer Services Executive
Perot, Ross

Corporate Executives
Dunlap, Al
Thornton, Charles

Detective Agency Entrepreneur
Pinkerton, Allan

Editors
Bennett, James Gordon, Jr.
Bennett, James Gordon, Sr.
Steinem, Gloria
Vanderlip, Frank

Employment Company Founder
Kelly, William

Engineers
Bechtel, Stephen
Gibbons, Fred
Hooker, Elon
Kaiser, Henry
Moody, Paul
Sperry, Elmer

Entertainers
Barnum, P. T.
Ringling, Charles

Entertainment Executives
Barden, Don
Bronfman, Edgar
Clark, Dick
Davis, Marvin
Disney, Walt
Eisner, Michael
Goldenson, Leonard
Laybourne, Geraldine
Loew, Marcus
Mayer, Louis
Ovitz, Michael
Paley, William
Redstone, Sumner
Sarnoff, David
Shubert, Lee
Silverman, Fred
Stewart, Martha
Tartikoff, Brandon

Turner, Ted
Turner, Ted
Warner, Albert
Warner, Harry
Warner, Jack
Warner, Samuel
Wasserman, Lew

Financiers
Bache, Jules
Baruch, Bernard
Boesky, Ivan
Buffett, Warren
Butterfield, John
Drew, Daniel
Duer, William
Eaton, Cyrus
Fisk, Jim
Flint, Charles
Girard, Stephen
Gould, Jay
Harriman, Edward
Hill, James J.
Icahn, Carl
Inman, Samuel
Kennedy, Joseph
Kerkorian, Kirk
Kluge, John
Lamont, Thomas
Lewis, Reginald
Ling, James
Lynch, Peter
Milken, Michael
Moore, William
Morris, Robert
Perelman, Ronald
Pickens, T. Boone
Raskob, John
Rockefeller, William
Soros, George
Spencer, Henry
Steinberg, Saul
Stettinius, Edward
Tisch, Larry
Trumbull, Jonathan
Vanderbilt, Cornelius

Hotel Executives
Hilton, Conrad
Johnson, Howard
Marriott, J. Willard

Pritzker, Jay
Wilson, Kemmons

Insurance Executives
Knapp, Joseph F.
Dryden, John
Perkins, George

Inventors
Edison, Thomas
Kettering, Charles
Stevens, John
Wang, An
Westinghouse, George

Investors
Dodge, William
Mellon, Andrew

Jeweler
Tiffany, Charles

Journalist
Ayer, Harriet

Lumberman
Sage, Henry

Manufacturers
Arden, Elizabeth
Armstrong, Thomas
Ash, Mary Kay
Ayer, Harriet
Ayer, James
Ball, Frank
Barber, Ohio
Barden, Don
Birdseye, Clarence
Boeing, William
Boit, Elizabeth
Borden, Gail
Bradley, Milton
Bronfman, Edgar
Bulova, Arde
Burroughs, William
Candler, Asa
Carnegie, Andrew
Carrier, Willis
Chrysler, Walter
Claiborne, Liz
Clark, Catherine
Coffin, Charles

Cohen, Ben
Coker, James
Colgate, William
Colt, Samuel
Corliss, George
Crane, Richard
Daniel, Jack
Davis, Arthur Vining
Deere, John
Dell, Michael
Dorrance, John
Douglas, Donald
Dow, Herbert
Dreyfus, Camille
Du Pont, Pierre
Duke, James Buchanan
Durant, William
Eastman, George
Edison, Thomas
Fairbanks, Erastus
Fields, Debbi
Firestone, Harvey
Fisher, Herman
Ford, Henry
Frick, Henry C.
Galvin, Paul
Galvin, Robert
Gardner, Edward
Gates, Bill
Gerber, Daniel
Gillette, King
Goizueta, Roberto
Goodrich, B. F.
Greenfield, Jerry
Gregg, William
Grove, Andrew
Hall, Joyce
Handler, Elliot
Hassenfeld, Stephen
Heinz, H. J.
Hershey, Milton
Hillman, Thomas
Hooker, Elon
Houghton, Amory
Hunt, H. L.
Iacocca, Lee
Jackson, Patrick
Jobs, Steven
Johnson, George
Johnson, Herbert
Johnson, Robert
Kellogg, Will

Kendall, Donald
Kendall, Henry
Kimberly, John
Klein, Calvin
Knight, Philip
Knox, Rose
Knudsen, William
Kohler, Walter
Kraft, James
Land, Edwin
Lannom, George, Jr.
Lauder, Estée
Lauren, Ralph
Lear, William
Lilly, Eli
Love, James
Lowell, Francis
Manville, Charles
Mars, Forrest
Martin, Glenn
Maytag, Frederick
McConnell, David
McCormick, Cyrus
McDonnell, James
McKnight, William
McNamara, Robert
Mead, George
Moody, Paul
Moore, Gordon
Morton, Joy
Mott, Charles
Nash, Charles
Noble, Edward
Norris, William
Northrop, John
Noyce, Robert
Oliver, Henry
Olsen, Kenneth
Otis, Elisha
Packard, David
Park, James
Parker, George
Patterson, John
Paulucci, Jeno
Perdue, Frank
Pillsbury, Charles
Post, Charles
Procter, William
Queeny, Edgar
Queeny, John
Revson, Charles
Reynolds, Richard J.

Reynolds, Richard S.
Rockwell, Willard
Rosenthal, William
Rubinstein, Helena
Schumacher, Ferdinand
Schwab, Charles
Scott, Edward
Simplot, Jack
Singer, Isaac
Slater, Samuel
Sloan, Alfred
Smith, Roger
Spalding, Albert
Spreckels, Claus
Steinway, Henry
Stern, Leonard
Stiegel, Henry
Strauss, Levi
Studebaker, Clement
Totino, Rose
Underwood, John
Vanderbilt, Gloria
von FŸrstenberg, Diane
Wachner, Linda
Wallace, Dwane
Wang, An
Watson, Thomas
Wilson, Joseph
Woodruff, Robert
Wrigley, Philip
Wrigley, William

Market Surveyor

Nielsen, A. C.

Meat Packers

Armour, Philip
Cudahy, Michael
Hormel, George
Hormel, Jay
Mayer, Oscar
Swift, Gustavus

Merchants

Alexander, Mary
Ash, Mary Kay
Astor, John Jacob
Bayard, William
Burpee, Washington Atlee
Cabot, George
Carter, Edward
Corning, Erastus

Cunningham, Harry
DeLuca, Fred
DeVos, Richard
Duer, William
Faneuil, Peter
Field, Cyrus
Field, Marshall
Fisher, Donald
Forten, James
Gimbel, Bernard
Gimbel, Isaac
Hancock, John
Hartford, George
Hartford, John
Hopkins, Johns
Hudson, Joseph
Huizenga, Wayne
Inman, Samuel
Kresge, Sebastian
Kress, Samuel
Kroc, Ray
Kroger, Bernard
Laurens, Henry
Lazarus, Charles
Low, Isaac
Macy, Rowland
Manigault, Pierre
Marcus, Bernard
Marcus, Stanley
Monaghan, Thomas
Morris, Robert
Palmer, Potter
Peabody, Joseph
Penney, James Cash
Pepperell, William
Phelps, Anson
Preston, Andrew
Rosenwald, Julius
Sage, Henry
Saunders, Clarence
Sears, Richard
Strauss, Levi
Tandy, Charles
Taylor, Moses
Thomas, Dave
Thompson, Jere
Thompson, Joe, Jr.
Thompson, John
Van Andel, Jay
Van Cortlandt, Oloff
Van Cortlandt, Stephanus
Vernon, Lillian

Walgreen, Charles
Walker, Sarah
Walton, Sam
Wanamaker, John
Ward, Aaron
Woolworth, Frank

Mining Executives

Daly, Marcus
Dodge, William
Guggenheim, Daniel
Hanna, Marcus

Newspaper Owners

Neuharth, Al
Scripps, Edward

Oil and Gas Executive

Pew, Joseph

Oil Industrialists

Davis, Marvin
Getty, J. Paul
Hammer, Armand
Hughes, Howard
Kerr, Robert
Phillips, Frank
Rockefeller, John D.
Rockefeller, William
Swearingen, John

Packer

Morris, Edward

Planters

Fitzhugh, William
Laurens, Henry

Printers

Franklin, Benjamin
Knapp, Joseph F.

Producers

Gordy, Berry
Lucas, George
Marbury, Elisabeth

Publishers

Annenberg, Moses
Annenberg, Walter
Ballantine, Ian
Chandler, Harry

DeBow, James
Doubleday, Frank
Dow, Clarence
Forbes, Malcolm
Gannett, Frank
Graham, Katharine
Graves, Earl
Guccione, Robert
Harper, James
Hearst, William Randolph
Hefner, Hugh
Knapp, Joseph P.
Knight, Jack
Leslie, Miriam
Luce, Henry
McCormick, Robert
McGovern, Pat
Nast, Condé
Newhouse, S. I.
Ochs, Adolph
Otis, Harrison Gray
Pulitzer, Joseph
Schiff, Dorothy
Wallace, Dewitt
Wenner, Jann

Railroad Executives
Dillon, Sidney
Flagler, Henry
Harriman, Edward
Hill, James J.

Huntington, Henry
Mellen, Charles
Pullman, George
Scott, Thomas Alexander
Spencer, Henry
Spencer, Samuel
Stanford, Leland
Strong, William
Vanderbilt, Cornelius

Real Estate Developers
Astor, John Jacob
Crow, Trammel
DeBartolo, Edward
Flagler, Henry
Palmer, Potter
Trump, Donald
Zeckendorf, William

Restaurant Executives
Johnson, Howard
Marriott, J. Willard
Sanders, Harland

Shipping Executives
Casey, Jim
Luckenbach, Edgar
Peabody, Joseph
Smith, Fred

Tax Preparation Entrepreneur
Bloch, Henry

Tobacco Executives
Carr, Julian
Hill, George

Transportation Executives
Hanna, Marcus
Huntington, Henry
Stevens, John
Wickham, Carl

Truck and Trailer Rental Entrepreneur
Shoen, Leonard

Utilities Investor
Insull, Samuel

Waste Manager
Huizenga, Wayne

Wine Makers
Gallo, Ernest
Gallo, Julio

Index

Note: Bold type page numbers after names refer to the entry devoted to that person.